41 American Colonies, 1707-1763. Doyle (J. A.). The Colonies under the House of Hanover. Folding map. 8vo, orig. cloth, uncut, pp. 629, index, Lond., 1907. 3.50
** Fine copy, in dust jacket. A valuable and important work, with chapters on Administrative Development, Ethnology of the Colonies, Colonization of Georgia, Conquest of Canada, Indian Campaigns, Economic & Social Life.

THE
ENGLISH IN AMERICA

THE COLONIES
UNDER THE HOUSE OF HANOVER

THE COLONIES

UNDER

THE HOUSE OF HANOVER

BY

J. A. DOYLE, M.A.

FELLOW OF ALL SOULS' COLLEGE, OXFORD

AUTHOR OF 'VIRGINIA, MARYLAND AND THE CAROLINAS'
'THE PURITAN COLONIES' ETC.

LONGMANS, GREEN, AND CO.
39 PATERNOSTER ROW, LONDON
NEW YORK, BOMBAY, AND CALCUTTA
1907

CONTENTS.

CHAPTER I.

THE GENERAL CONDITION OF THE COLONIES AT THE ACCESSION OF THE HOUSE OF HANOVER.

CHAPTER II.

ADMINISTRATIVE DEVELOPEMENT.

CHAPTER III.

ECONOMICAL PROGRESS.

CHAPTER IV.

RELIGION IN THE COLONIES.

CHAPTER V.

LITERARY AND INTELLECTUAL DEVELOPEMENT OF THE COLONIES.

CHAPTER VI.

THE COLONISTS AND THE INFERIOR RACES.

CHAPTER VII.

THE ETHNOLOGY OF THE COLONIES.

CHAPTER VIII.

THE COLONIZATION OF GEORGIA.

CHAPTER IX.

THE CONQUEST OF CANADA.

Errata.

Page 78, seventh line from foot, *for* Susquehanna *read* Susquehannah.
Page 79, line 20, dele *and*.
Page 98, line 4 from foot, after 'Rhode Island' insert 'and the Proprietary colonies.'
Page 113, line 10, *for* 1730 *read* 1727.
Page 184, note 1, *for* Spangenberg *read* Spandenberg.
Page 197, first line, *for* 1730 *read* 1710.
Page 217, line 25, *for* Sewell *read* Sewall.
Page 256, line 6, *for* fourth *read* fifth; and line 11, *for* fifth *read* sixth.
Page 286, note, dele last two lines.
Page 297, lines 15, 23, 26, and 27, *for* Kiemer *read* Keimer.
Page 331, second line from foot, *for* shareholders *read* slaveholders.
Page 411, note, *for* Turnbull *read* Trumbull, and *for* Martyr *read* Martyn.
Page 412, marginal note, *for* constraint *read* contrast.

THE COLONIES
UNDER THE HOUSE OF HANOVER.

CHAPTER I.

THE GENERAL CONDITION OF THE COLONIES AT THE ACCESSION OF THE HOUSE OF HANOVER.

Characteristics of the new epoch.[1]

As was said at the end of the work which precedes this, the accession of George I. forms a convenient landmark in colonial history. The more closely one studies history the more fully is the conviction borne in on one that all divisions into epochs and the like have in their nature something arbitrary. Communities do not undergo sudden changes any more than individuals do. As soon as minute inquiry begins, vestiges of the past, anticipations of the future, meet one at every turn. Yet with the community, as with the individual, the predominance of certain leading characteristics at successive stages of growth gives enough distinctness to serve as a basis for a convenient, though not a scientific, arrangement of facts. Speaking roughly, we may say that for the whole body of English-speaking colonies on the Atlantic the end of the seven-

[1] The material for this chapter is so scattered that it is impossible to give a comprehensive summary of it. As will be seen, I have relied largely on the various collections of printed records. On its own subject Mr. Weeden's *Economical and Social History of New England* is a most valuable guide.

91

teenth century was the point at which the era of formation ended and the era of fruition and repose began.

Those colonies, which had been invested with forms representing the views and wishes of individual thinkers,[1] in the main had worked themselves free from the limitations of their origin, and had, in true English fashion, shaped for themselves conditions not without compromise, at times illogical and defiant of system, yet in practical conformity with the needs of the community. Each colony had been, half through conscious imitation, half through instinct, putting on the recognised political forms of the parent country, each had in the process been acquiring a vague and imperfect sense of sisterhood.

Hostility to France creates the need for colonial unity.

There was another change which had its root in the Revolution of 1688, but which only made its full force felt as the eighteenth century advanced. Hostility between England and France had become a fixed and abiding condition in the political situation. The danger no longer lay in isolated bands of marauding savages, in the pay of some exceptionally enterprising French Governor. More and more, as the eighteenth century advanced, did it become clear that it was a case of internecine strife, that the inevitable necessity for expansion made it impossible for England and France to co-exist in North America as equal Powers. And thus, avoid it as they would, the problem of combined resistance was forced upon the colonists. It is hardly too much to say that the need under which every colonial Governor lay, for calling forth and organizing the resources of his colony for common defence, gave to colonial administration its one thread of unity.

The creation of these two conditions— similarity of political machinery, unity of political purpose—brings with it a marked change in the character of colonial

[1] *E.g.* Maryland and Pennsylvania.

history. During the seventeenth century the main interest lies in the internal history of each colony, the influence in all cases of industrial conditions, in most cases of religion—in one case, that of New York, of race—in developing special modes of life and types of character. Such men as Williams, Winthrop and Penn not only interest us as offering problems in character, they concern us both as creating and embodying the tendencies of the communities to which they belonged. But in the eighteenth century the main interest is not internal but external. External pressure, exercised by the mother country, becomes the main factor in colonial history, and is met in some cases by persistent and unintelligent resistance, in other cases by co-operation, occasionally strenuous, more often carefully qualified and fenced in by conditions.

Unity arising out of administrative conditions.

The result is an entire and important change in our point of view. Henceforth we can regard the colonies as an organic whole forming part of one administrative system. It is true that this view needs much modification when we apply it in practice. The unity which the attitude of the mother country was forcing upon the colonies was but inchoate, and had but a potential existence. It was a unity imperfectly perceived and little desired by the colonies themselves. Pre-existent conditions of diversity are still perpetually asserting themselves. These diversities not only affect the internal life of each colony. They also affect the administrative relations of the mother country to her American dependencies. In some matters we can deal with the colonies collectively or at least in groups. But when we come to administrative disputes we still have to keep the separate threads of colonial history distinct. The political history of the colonies may be largely dealt with as made up of successive administrative episodes, most of them conflicts, with a common origin of principle, between the representatives of local interests and the central authority.

Those conflicts turned largely on material issues. It may be well, therefore, at the outset to have before one a clear view of the external framework in which the life of the colonies was set. Let us picture to ourselves the successive scenes which would have come before a traveller who in or about 1720 was making his way from the northern extremity of Maine to the further boundary of South Carolina.

Material condition of the colonies.

Along the coast of Maine he would be constantly confronted with the traces of Indian devastation in the remains of empty houses. At Pemaquid and Penobscot he would find garrisoned forts, but nothing in the nature of town or village. The chief visible sign of industry or of civil occupation were the saw-mills along the various streams. At Scarboro', Biddeford and Berwick the traveller would find something like real townships, each with a church. At Wells, York and Kittery he would also find villages, but with only precarious and intermittent provision for worship.[1]

Maine.

In crossing the border which separated Maine from New Hampshire there would be at once revealed a great change alike in natural conditions and social life. From a wilderness of rock and pine-wood, the traveller would pass into a fertile, well-watered country, yielding corn and cattle beyond the wants of its own sparse population. At Portsmouth he would for the first time see a real town, where prosperous merchants lived in spacious houses and gave 'splendid treats' to their guests.[2]

New Hampshire.

[1] Sullivan's *History of Maine*.

[2] Weeden (p. 540) quotes this from a manuscript in the possession of the American Antiquarian Society. It is written by Robert Hale, of Massachusetts, and describes his visit to Portsmouth in 1731.

The peculiar formation of the country had indeed a somewhat cramping effect on its trade. New Hampshire has a wedge-shaped territory with its narrow end on the Atlantic, and thus the sea-board was small in proportion to the whole province. For most of the inland districts Boston was more accessible than Portsmouth, and thus the cattle and corn exported were for the most part transported overland through Massachusetts. The timber trade, however, with a little addition of fishing and cattle rearing, was enough to give full employment to the merchant shipping of the colony. New Hampshire vessels plied a circular trade, carrying timber, fish, fish oil, and cattle to the British West Indies, and then carrying a cargo of sugar, either to England or to the southern colonies, and in the latter case taking back corn, rice, and pork to be sold in Newfoundland and Nova Scotia.[1] Ship-building, too, was a staple industry. Vessels built in New Hampshire dockyards were loaded with timber and sent to England, where ship and cargo both were sold. The anxiety of the settlers to sell their ship timber in foreign markets, especially in Spain, and the determination of British officials to secure it for the royal navy, was, as we shall hereafter see, a frequent source of dispute.[2] Over this otherwise prosperous community there always hung one dark cloud. The inhabitants of every inland farmstead might at any moment find themselves suddenly awakened by the Indian war-whoop.[3] The diary of Timothy Walker, the minister of Concord, brings into full relief this tragic aspect of colonial life.[4] Three recurrent topics occupy nearly the whole of its pages.

[1] Weeden, p. 766.

[2] Palfrey, vol. iv. p. 352.

[3] The journal of John Pike, published in the collection of the New Hampshire Historical Society, vol. iii., is almost wholly a record of Indian outrages and alarm.

[4] This diary is published in the ninth volume of the New Hampshire Collection.

He records his every-day ministerial duties and his agricultural work, the felling and hauling of timber, the fencing of fields and the killing of cattle. There are interspersed such entries as 'Richard Blanchard scalped'; 'Benj. Blanchard of Canterbury was scalped by Indians'; 'Bishop captured by the Indians. John Bradley and als were killed by the Indians and the like.'[1]

Massachusetts.

The traveller could pass from New Hampshire into Massachusetts either by a ferry at the mouth of the Piscataqua or by one of various bridle-roads crossing the river by fords further inland.[2] In the externals of life, or the character of the houses and the tillage, no marked difference would strike the traveller in his passage from New Hampshire to Massachusetts. Yet evidence would soon be forthcoming to show that he had passed into a region where life was more progressive, more luxurious and better organized. From bridle-tracks, just passable for a waggon and team of oxen, he could come to roads probably as good as those which he would have found in the more backward parts of England. Once across the Charles River, which as yet had to be crossed by a ford or a ferry-boat, he might meet a rough wheel carriage, the property of a prosperous Boston merchant.[3]

Outward appearance of Boston.

At Boston itself he would be at once brought face to face with a life of great and increasing material prosperity, and of vigorous though still somewhat narrow intellectual activity.

In few towns has the hand of man wrought so complete a transformation in outward appearance. It is hardly too much to say that the two special features

[1] I am at a loss to know what 'als' stands for.

[2] Drake, in his *History of Boston*, says that there was no bridge over the Charles River before 1720.

[3] Sewell records in his diary for January 1699 that he took his family for an excursion in a coach. In 1728 a carriage was let out for hire. Weeden, p. 508.

which would have impressed a visitor upon his first view of the town in 1700 are now gone. The town was then approached by a neck narrow enough to be closed by a horse-gate and a foot-gate. This peninsular character was gradually destroyed, first by the throwing out of wharves at right angles to the neck, then more completely by the filling in of the intermediate spaces. This was done by taking away soil from the higher ground and thus greatly lessening the hilly character and the originally bold outline of the town itself. The ground occupied by the buildings was a promontory some two miles in length and about half a mile in width. In shape it conformed to the windings of the shore and the rise and fall of the ground. Lengthwise it was intersected by one main street, crossed at right angles by four shorter ones. Of the houses, a few of the best were of stone, some, about one in four, of brick, the majority of wood, with either stone or brick chimneys. The one building which dominated the town and served as a visible centre was the town-hall, a two-story brick building, open and arcaded below.[1] It replaced a building, similar in plan, which just a few of the original settlers had lived long enough to see and which was destroyed by fire in 1711.[2] There was as yet no public market. That came into existence in 1733.[3] The restrictions on trade which accompanied it show that it was designed not only as a convenience for buyers and sellers, but also as giving the community more effective control over the doings of individuals. All goods, save a few of the smaller necessaries of life, must be bought in the market, not in private houses.

[1] This was burnt in 1747 (Holmes's *Annals*, vol. ii. p. 176). Holmes describes it as a spacious and handsome edifice, but otherwise we have no account of it.

[2] For a description of this building see Dunton, p. 68. Sewell records the burning of it October 2, 1711.

[3] For the market see the Town Records.

In the true spirit of mediæval economy, no person might 'engross' goods in the market with a view to retailing them.

The proposal for a market was considered in a town meeting of over eight hundred, and only carried by twenty-five votes. We may reasonably suppose this opposition was due not to indifference to a scheme so evidently convenient in itself, but to dislike of the restraint on private dealing.

The market was to be held in three separate places. This was probably intended to suit the convenience of different parts of the town, and also necessitated by the difficulty of finding any site at once central and spacious enough.

The peninsular position of the town had not as yet brought with it any inconvenient compression. In some parts, indeed, houses were crowded together, as they can scarcely fail to be in a seaport town with a stirring business, where certain situations have obvious advantages. But the town was well furnished with lungs. The open common, where in the days of Winthrop and Dudley the town cattle had grazed, was now a lounge for a leisurely class with tastes and habits undreamt of a century earlier.[1] Gardens and orchards adjoining the town, and breaking the line of its outer buildings, give an air of space and freedom which Boston retained till late into the nineteenth century[2] through years of increasing prosperity.

Social life of Boston.

That men, not walls, make a city is specially true of the life of a young community, strenuous, fast-growing and self-conscious. Of the life of those who occupied the houses of Boston it is not difficult to form a distinct and fairly complete picture. That life was

[1] 'The gallants a little before sunset walk with their marmalade Madams as we do in Moorfields.' Dunton, p. 69; cf. Winsor's *Boston*, vol. i. p. 452.

[2] Dunton, p. 68.

limited enough to be capable of survey and description; it was definite, and to the eye of an outside observer peculiar enough to be impressive. The interests of the colonists themselves were not so diffused, nor their progress so much a matter of custom and routine as to prevent them from observing, and recording with eagerness and often self-complacency, the rapid development of their social and industrial life. Thus travels, journals, letters, biographies, as well as formal records, furnish us with abundant material wherewith to reconstruct that New England life of the eighteenth century of which Boston was the commercial and intellectual centre.

That life differed widely from what it replaced. New England at the outset was a section of English life cut out from the main body, narrow and intense in itself, made yet narrower and more intense by separation and transplantation. The indwelling spirit which gave to it peculiar force became of necessity spent. It must never be forgotten that English Puritanism was in a measure the product of those very influences which it formally repudiated. The exuberant life of the English Renaissance made itself felt even in those who outwardly denounced it. Winthrop and Bradford and their fellows were in some sort the offspring and heirs of Shakespeare and Spenser and Bacon, though they might ignore the kinship and repudiate the debt. In the atmosphere of colonial life those guiding lights grew dim. In the more serious branches of thought New England had to rely on home-made culture. The creeds and the habits of thought bequeathed to her by her founders had not elasticity enough to keep up their contact with the changing life of the mother country. Nor was that life itself one from which they could draw much strengthening or spiritualizing influence. From the Revolution till the opening of the duel with

Napoleon, the greatness of England was unconscious and inarticulate. Her professed thinkers and moralists touched but the fringe of life. She was really sustained by the memory of a great past, and by lofty aims definitely embodying themselves in act. Her teachers were Pitt and Wolfe and Clive. Those influences could not make themselves felt beyond the Atlantic. British rulers made no effort to give the colonists an interest in a life of which they themselves seldom saw the real meaning and greatness.

In another important point New England thought was affected by the change which had come over the mind, not only of England but of Europe. The early New Englander was in his own eyes one of a garrison holding a citadel, in which were treasured up those theological dogmas and those moral principles on which rested every hope for the regeneration of mankind. By the beginning of the eighteenth century Calvinism and the moral code which Calvinism brought with it are no longer in the eyes of its enemies a seriously disruptive and destroying force, nor in the eyes of their supporters the one saving power. There was no longer any need to keep the armour ready and the loins girt; the battle was over: one might rather say that to the descendants and representatives of the combatants the very existence of the battle was a dim and unreal tradition.

There were no doubt below the surface influences which kept alive a vigorous national spirit, and which owed much to those who had founded New England. But we cannot doubt that if one of those founders had returned to earth, gifted with no more than ordinary human powers of foresight, he would have seen in the Boston of 1720 a cemetery of dead ideals.

Politics apart, the life of Boston in the eighteenth century was a decorous, intelligent, rather commonplace reproduction of the life of an English country town. It impressed observers, as its memory charms a later generation, chiefly through the contrasts offered by a rather conventional life of wealth, comfort and decorous luxury set with picturesque quaintness amid the surroundings of a newly discovered and imperfectly explored country. If the spiritual and mental life of Boston lacked depth and originality, there were at least abundant proofs of intellectual activity and of the diffusion of literary interests and scholarly tastes. Booksellers' shops were numerous. But their shelves were filled not with the patriotic chronicles and controversial pamphlets which made up the literature of New England in the days of Winthrop and Dudley, but with such a collection of literature as might have been supplied in an English country town by a bookseller catering for sober Nonconformist customers, with a slight dash of mundane interest and fashionable tastes. Diffusion of knowledge and of literary interest had superseded productive originality and depth and extent of study.[1]

On every side the observer would see about him the marks of stirring commerce, the fruits of accumulated wealth, and the visible activity whereby that wealth was in process of creation. Hardly a week-day would pass without a merchant vessel clearing from the harbour of Boston,[2] hardly a week in which three new-built vessels were not launched from some port on the Massachusetts sea-board.[3]

That the seafaring trade of Massachusetts should increase continuously and rapidly was a natural result not only of economical, but also of social conditions.

[1] The Inventory of Michael Perry, a leading bookseller in Boston in 1700, is published as an appendix to Dunton's letters.

[2] In 1714 the clearances from Boston were estimated at four hundred and fifteen. Board of Trade Report, N. Y. Documents, vol. v. p. 618.

[3] *Ib.* p. 598. Both these authorities are quoted by Mr. Weeden.

The business of money-making had few serious rivals. None of the learned professions offered great prizes. Literature and the study of theology no longer held out any strong temptations to the ambitious. There were few distractions, few vents for superfluous wealth. There was no scope for the patronage of art or letters. The community had not yet passed into that rather artificial state when field sports have changed from a needful toil into a pastime, involving elaborate preparation and costly accessories. We read indeed of deer parks and a close time for deer in Connecticut,[1] but it is probable that those who owned them thought chiefly of the value of the flesh as food and of the skins as merchandise.

The costliness and scarcity of labour dammed up this and other methods of unproductive expenditure. Orchards were plentiful,[2] but the taste for horticulture and for ornamental forestry, so strong in Elizabethan England, disappears. We hear nothing of the flower-garden as one of the embellishments of life.

The town records of Boston reveal occasional attempts, almost always unsuccessful, to introduce some of the lighter diversions of life. In 1712 a conjuror who had given an entertainment without leave was forbidden to repeat his performance.[3] Three years later the Selectmen instruct the Representatives to procure an Act prohibiting stage plays as likely to corrupt youth. They also report to the magistrates two persons who had kept a dancing school and a music school.[4] Twenty years later dancing was allowed to slide in by being coupled with such useful attainments as reading, writing, cyphering, and the use of the needle.[5]

[1] Conn. Rec. 1730, p. 268; 1744, p. 68.

[2] 'They run mightily into orchardry.' MS. quoted in the *Memorial History of Boston*, vol. i. p. 465.

[3] Proceedings of Selectmen, 1701–15, p. 172. [4] *Ib.* pp. 236, 239.

[5] *Ib.* 1716–31, p. 276.

Two years later another teacher was allowed to extend this curriculum by the somewhat frivolous addition of painting on glass.[1] But an exhibition of rope-dancing was prohibited as 'likely to promote idleness and great mispence of time.'[2] The would-be performer repeated his petition, and rather oddly tried to better his case by including tumbling and posturing with swords. If he hoped by the latter addition to appeal to any memories of Standish or Underhill, he failed.[3] The only trace we find of any tendency towards athletic sports is a prohibition by the town meeting, more than once repeated, of football in the streets of Boston.[4] This at least shows that there were some who wished to play football. Whether they gratified that wish in some more suitable place does not appear. A notice issued by the Selectmen in 1726, summoning a meeting of townsmen to put down gaming in the streets, suggests a certain relaxation of morals.[5]

An 'Assembly' was introduced somewhere about 1730. But we read that the ladies who attended it were looked on as 'none of the nicest in respect of their reputation.' Yet the paucity of diversions did not exempt the wives of Boston merchants from the attacks of provincial Steeles and Addisons. We read that they 'visit, drink tea, and indulge every little piece of gentility to the height of the mode, and neglect the affairs of their families with as good a grace as the finest ladies in London.'[6]

The Sabbatarianism of earlier days was still operative, since in 1727 we find an order of the town meeting for the purpose of checking the disturbance

1 Proceedings of Selectmen, 1736–42, p. 71.

2 *Ib.* 1715–36, p. 259.

3 *Ib.* p. 260.

4 Town Records, 1677, p. 115; 1701, p. 12.

5 Records of Selectmen, 1726, p. 152.

6 Manuscript quoted in Winsor's *Boston*, vol. i. p. 452.

caused on Sunday by horses and carts crossing the creek. To this end the gates are to be shut on the evening preceding and following the Lord's Day, and only opened when necessary.[1] We may also take this as evidence of what is shown otherwise, the increase of communication between the capital of the colony and the outlying districts. This is confirmed by a resolution of the Selectmen in 1738, which aimed at suppressing, or at least controlling, Sunday trade in corn, apples, and the like, between Boston and Roxbury. The constables are to appoint a watch of eight to prevent unnecessary travelling and loitering.[2]

Sabbatarianism in Boston.

In a community where the enjoyments of life were thus curtailed and hemmed in, the wealthy Boston merchant soon exhausted his possibilities of extravagant or even luxurious expenditure. He could build a fine house. He could choose furniture made of costly foreign woods. He could cover his sideboard with valuable silver plate. He could import an English coach and horses. He and his family could dress expensively in imported stuffs. But the opportunities of recurrent expenditure would be few, checked, as was said before, by the cost of labour and also by the spirit of Puritanism. But while enough of that survived to discourage ostentatious living, good cheer was not costly, thanks to the resources of the country and to the facility for smuggling in French and Spanish wines.

Economical developement of New England.

There was but little too of that automatic trade, as one may call it, which asks from the capitalist merely the conception of a general plan and intermittent supervision. In a country where intelligent labour is scarce, the man who would in England be a

[1] Town Records, Dec. 27, 1727, p. 213.
[2] Minutes of Selectmen, Aug. 10, 1738, p. 128.

hard-working, fully trusted, and moderately paid subordinate, will be in business on his own account. Nor did the trade of New England admit of the application of large masses of capital to some one branch of production or distribution. There was no one staple export, ship timber excepted, of sufficient importance to form by itself a large business. Thus the Boston merchant found himself catering for many wants, drawing his commodities from many and different quarters, depending on a trade strangely complicated in proportion to its actual amount. A New England vessel would leave port with a cargo of corn, pipe-staves and tar. Some of these she would dispose of in Newfoundland, taking in exchange salt fish. Then she would touch at several West India islands in succession, getting rid of her own goods, and taking on board molasses to be used for distilling rum. Possibly she would touch at Edenton and take on board a lading of North Carolina tar.[1]

Beside such voyages as this and the direct trade with the mother country, there was a trade, partly illicit, with France, Spain, and the Canaries. The extent to which the law was broken is a question which more fitly belongs to a later portion of our subject.

Thus the qualities needed in the New England merchant were in some sort those of a retail dealer on a large scale. He had to understand the quality of many commodities, the needs of many customers, and the fluctuations of many markets. This co-operated with the conditions of colonial life to beget and keep alive that versatility of power which has been so marked a characteristic of the American Englishman.

There were other effects. Trade fortunes, such as they were, were built up slowly and visibly, not achieved at a stroke through the colossal and unseen

[1] Mr. Weeden (p. 584) gives an excellent account of such a voyage based on recorded legal proceedings.

efforts of great speculation. Accumulated capital was something which all men saw and could understand, not a mysterious and possibly maleficent power.

Moreover, though the old religious fervour of Puritanism had well nigh burnt itself out, that strong sense of civic unity, in which New England, in all things else so un-Hellenic, had a touch of the old Greek spirit, had scarcely abated. Thus with most of the paths of luxury blocked, with but little temptation to that vanity which finds expression in the foundation of a family, the New England merchant easily fell into a course which has been among the most precious and honourable traditions of his country. The building in 1740 by Peter Faneuil, the chief merchant of Boston, of the public hall which bore his name, and which figured in so many stirring scenes of civic life, is only the most conspicuous of many recognitions of such public service as an undefined but manifest duty.[1]

Expenditure on public purposes.

Another like instance is the establishment in 1735 of a workhouse, not by a rate but by public subscription. One hundred and twenty-two names appear in the list of contributors, in sums ranging from five pounds to a hundred.[2]

This workhouse was to supplement an earlier almshouse. In the records of the town meetings for 1712 we find a committee reporting that the workhouse which was intended for the deserving poor was long used for sturdy beggars, for whom a house of correction was better suited, and in the following year an order was made that the overseers of the poor should receive no one in the almshouse unless he was a legitimate object of charity.[3]

It is clear that during the first half of the eighteenth

[1] Winsor's *Boston*, vol. i. pp. 263, 463.

[2] Boston Records, 1729–42, p. 180.

[3] *Ib.* 1700, &c., pp. 101, 967.

century there was a real danger, lest the rapid material and intellectual progress of Boston should create a gulf between the urban life of the capital and the rural life of the rest of the community. The records more than once disclose a sense of jealousy and antagonism. In 1733 some of the adjacent towns ask to be set off as a separate county.[1] Their plea was based chiefly on considerations of convenience in legal procedure. It is 'hindersome' to come to Boston, and the law business of the country districts is so special that the city courts are ill fitted to deal with it. A committee of the town meeting was appointed to consider the question, and reported strongly against separation, mainly on the ground that it involved unnecessary and costly increase of legal machinery.

Relations between town and country.

Two years later the question was again opened, this time not by the outlying districts, but by certain Boston merchants.[2] Just as the countryman objected to his case being tried in a city court, so they objected to their cases being brought into a country court, ignorant of 'charter partys and other affairs of trade.' A committee was again appointed to deal with the question and again it reported against change.

To the arguments urged before, they added that 'the Assemblies of the courts at Boston give men decent opportunities for friendly society, and unite us more in our affections.' The argument as to the relative competence of different tribunals is disposed of by the plea that it is impossible to prevent litigants from choosing their own venue.

Boston did not escape those inconveniences with which a wealthy capital is almost always threatened by the comparatively poor country districts. We find in the town records complaints of the incursion of poor

[1] Boston Town Records, 1739–42, p. 50. [2] *Ib.* 1739–42, p. 116.

people who contributed nothing to the prosperity of the town, and caused an increase in the expenditure on police and other public charges.[1] We are apt to think that old-established communities with their complex and artificial life have a monopoly of the problems of pauperism and settlement. Massachusetts at the outset of the eighteenth century did not escape such difficulties. In this, too, we see a noteworthy instance of the manner in which the secular side of life was in New England overlying the religious. Admission to the community was still cautiously and jealously guarded. But, as formerly the new-comer had to give guarantees for religious orthodoxy and moral correctness, so now he had to satisfy the town government that he would not, at some later time, become chargeable to the public. That this was no mere formality is shown by the repeated orders for exclusion. Thus we find orders of the Selectmen excluding a lame maid and a man with one hand, while a shipmaster who has brought four convicts from Bristol is ordered not to land them, but to transport them to Piscataqua.[2]

An entry in the Connecticut Records for 1729 curiously illustrates the change from a religious to a secular qualification. A new-comer might be admitted to a township on any one of three conditions. He must own either (1) a freehold of eighty pounds value, or (2) be rated at forty pounds on the common list, or (3) be in full communion with the Church.

The tendency which would naturally have existed for Boston to overwhelm the life of the country districts was kept in check by a provision which has had an important effect, both for good and evil, in American politics down to the present time. No man might sit

[1] Boston Town Records, 1729-42, p. 119.

[2] Proceedings of Selectmen, 1701-15, pp. 13, 61, 178; 1716-36, pp. 15, 86; 1736-55, p. 212.

in the Assembly as the representative of any town other than that in which he lived. This system is denounced by a Governor of Massachusetts as 'filling the Assembly with persons of small fortunes and mean education.'[1] Yet we may well believe that this was more than counterbalanced in two ways. The urban and commercial life of Boston was not suffered to enjoy an undue predominance. Even more important was it that the outlying rural districts should be kept in real and direct contact with the life of the capital. There was no sharp and definite line of separation in tastes, thought, and habit between the townsman and the countryman. The sense of a common civic life and the familiarity with political organization which enables that sense to translate itself into action were the common possessions of the whole state, and the weapons to which, in the crisis of her fortunes, she mainly owed her victory.

The town meeting.

It is no paradox to say that the supremacy of Boston, which in one way endangered the corporate life of the community as a whole, in another way informed and developed it. Through a mere process of gradual and unconscious growth the town meeting of Boston acquired powers going far beyond the limits of municipal business as commonly recognised. Its strength was partly due to the fact that it suffered none of its powers to escape it by delegation. Either directly, or through the Selectmen acting as an executive committee, closely controlled and elected for short periods, the town meeting kept entirely in its own hands the control of such special questions as poor laws and education. Thus it was never confronted with departments virtually and practically independent. Such a system may often have

[1] Shute's Memorial, in which these views are expressed, is among the Colonial Papers.

militated against efficiency, and even more against expedition in public business; it could only have been possible where civic spirit was deeply rooted and the sense of public responsibility strong. But it fashioned an instrument, as we shall see again and again, singularly versatile in its capacities and wholly fearless in its assumption of new duties. Nor was it possible, in a community so homogeneous as Massachusetts yet was, that the use of these functions should be limited to the sphere to which they technically belonged. The town meeting of Boston became a power in the political life of the whole colony.

It is always difficult to say when a system which has grown up unconsciously and informally can be looked upon as having reached maturity. But we should probably not err in taking as a landmark the proceedings of 1728. In that year we find the town meeting of Boston presenting an address to the Representatives of the town in the Assembly, instructing them to oppose the vote of a permanent salary to the Governor. That proceeding was repeated in the following year, and is from that time on a definite feature in the political life of the colony.

With the exception of Boston the visitor to Massachusetts would find no place bearing the visible imprint of active urban life. Dunton described Dorchester and Roxbury as 'beautified with fair orchards and gardens, with plenty of corn land and store of cattle.' They were in fact collections of farmsteads, probably in outward appearance not unlike the large villages of southern Germany. A system of individual holdings was fast superseding that communal form of agriculture which had prevailed in the early days of New England. It is significant that when the township of Chester in New Hampshire was founded in 1720 it was organized on the system of communal land

The smaller town of Massachusetts.

tenure, but that seventeen years later this was superseded, and a division made into individual holdings.[1] So, too, we find it enacted in Connecticut that five-sixths of the proprietors of a common field might carry out any improvement that seemed good to them, subject to an appeal by the minority to the County Court.[2] Communal land tenure was well adapted for settlers applying themselves to the task of reclaiming the wilderness, and living in the midst of hardships and dangers only to be faced by mutual help; it was sure to fail as soon as any possibility of skilled husbandry showed itself.

To one imbued with the traditions of the Old World the farming of New England seemed deplorably slovenly and wasteful. When the fertility of the soil was exhausted no attempt was made to restore it by manuring, but fresh land was brought under tillage. Large roughly constructed fences of dead wood at once wasted ground and timber. Critics who blamed these practices forgot the special conditions of a country where land was cheap and plentiful, labour dear and scarce. Trim fences of hedge-row timber and the high cultivation which brings with it permanent improvement are out of place in a country where men are constantly emigrating, and farms are constantly changing their boundaries.

Agriculture.

Our traveller would make his southward journey under very different conditions from those which had obtained half a century earlier. Among Lovelace's administrative improvements was the establishment of an official as 'post rider,' travelling between Boston and New York. The messenger, however, only carried letters and did nothing

Journey from Boston to the south.

[1] N. Hampshire Historical Collections, vol. vii. p. 351.

[2] Connecticut Records, 1726 50, p. 239.

to help passenger traffic.[1] But as early as 1721 another rider, seemingly as a private venture, went from Boston to Newport carrying goods, and escorting travellers, whom he also provided with horses.[2] A bridge at Pawtuxet reached by a highway from Boston connected Massachusetts with the continental portion of Rhode Island. We need not draw on imagination in order to reconstruct the journey of a traveller from Boston to New York. We have the fully recorded experiences of one Mrs. Knight, a quick-witted and observant Boston schoolmistress, affecting a fastidiousness which nevertheless did not prevent her from heartily enjoying the humorous side of her hardships and misadventures.[3] Lack of safe bridges and of decent inns are her chief complaints. At one place she can get nothing to drink but milk sweetened with molasses, at another no supper but pork and cabbage, the remnants of the day's dinner. The physical consequences of these meals are described in a detailed fashion which rather reminds one of Smollett. At a tavern in Rhode Island annoyance of a different kind awaits the traveller. She is kept awake half the night by the wranglings of certain rustic philologers, who on the other side of a thin partition are disputing as to the meaning and derivation of the name Narragansett.

It is clear that we must discount Mrs. Knight's experiences, just as we must discount Captain Burt's account of the life of the Highlands. She was, like Burt, a Cockney, to whom every deviation from the ordinary routine of convention and comfort was a symptom of barbarism. A fastidious traveller used to London habits would probably have expostulated in much the same strain if he had found himself in some remote part of Cardiganshire in 1800.

[1] *Middle Colonies*, p. 172. [2] Weeden, p. 510.
[3] Mrs. Knight's journals, not published till 1825.

It is noteworthy, too, that Mrs. Knight throughout writes not as a New Englander but as a Bostonian. The outward material differences which severed Boston from the rural districts of New England were fully visible to her; that underlying unity, real though now obscure, which bound together the colonies of Puritan origin counted for little or nothing.

Though in accepting Mrs. Knight's picture we must make some allowance for the rather crude colouring of a provincial satirist and for the fastidiousness of a provincial fine lady, yet it is clear from other evidence that the whole life of Rhode Island alike, visible and spiritual, was rougher, poorer, and less completely organized than that of Massachusetts. The palmy days of Newport as a commercial seaport were at hand, but had hardly begun. Between 1713 and 1741 the number of vessels owned by residents in the town increased from twenty-nine to a hundred and twenty.[1] But in 1708 her business lay more in building ships than in manning and sailing them herself.[2] As the century advanced, the distilling of rum became an important business in Newport,[3] and the excellence of the pasture land of the colony enabled it to supply Boston with better cheese than could be made in Massachusetts.[4]

Rhode Island.

In Rhode Island, as in Massachusetts, an attempt was made to foster the production of linen. In 1722 one William Borden was promised by the legislature a

[1] These are the figures given in the reports of Governor Cranston and Governor Ward, referred to by Mr. Arnold, vol. ii. p. 35. The reports are to be found *in extenso* in the Rhode Island Records, vol. iv. pp. 55–60, pp. 8, 14.

[2] See a report in the Rhode Island Records, vol. iv. pp. 53–60. This states that of ninety-seven vessels built in eight years, sixty-eight had been sold out of the colony. Probably many went to Boston.

[3] The opposition to the Molasses Act, to which I shall revert, came mainly from Newport.

[4] Weeden, p. 582.

bounty for every bolt of hemp that he should spin 'equal to good Holland Duck.'[1] Apparently the encouragement did not have the desired effect, and in 1728 an advance of five hundred pounds was made to Borden to be held for three years without interest to assist him in his business.[2] In 1728 this loan was increased to three thousand pounds to be held for ten years, on the specific condition of making a hundred and fifty bolts of duck every year. There is nothing to show that this attempt to create an industry by state patronage had any success.[3]

But neither in extent nor in diversity could the trade of Rhode Island be compared with that of Massachusetts. She had no merchants of the stamp of Amory or Faneuil. Her trade was tainted by evil suspicions, not only of smuggling, but of connivance with pirates, a charge never brought against Boston even by enemies. Massachusetts might be seditious, but she was never anarchical. In Rhode Island, as in New Jersey, disaffection readily found expression in riot.

A low standard of political morality is further indicated by an Act passed in 1715, and re-enacted in 1738, against fraudulent voting. Any one voting twice was subject to a fine of five pounds, and in case of non-payment might be imprisoned or flogged.[4]

In facility of internal communication Rhode Island lagged behind Massachusetts. The main road which pierced the colony from north to south, and which carried all the land traffic between Boston and New York, crossed three bridges in Rhode Island, but it was not till 1711 that their maintenance was made a public charge.[5] Three years later a second road connecting Providence with some of the inland towns was

[1] R. I. Records, vol. iv. p. 317. [2] *Ib.* p. 363. [3] *Ib.* p. 407.
[4] *Ib.* pp. 196, 268. [5] *Ib.* p. 118.

recognised as a public highway.[1] The island of Aquednek was in the seventeenth century connected with the mainland only by two ferries. Tradition, unconfirmed by any specific record, makes the construction of a bridge date from 1712.[2]

In Connecticut the traveller would find himself among surroundings closely resembling those which he had left in Massachusetts. She had no port indeed such as Boston, and her whole shipping in 1730 did not exceed forty-two sail. But the deficiency in harbours was compensated for by the superiority of the soil to that of Massachusetts. Thus the Connecticut farmer was able to sell cattle to Boston, horses to the West Indies, and mules to Virginia. The colony also exported timber to the West Indies, bringing back in return sugar, rum, molasses and provisions. There was also a small exportation of turpentine, and to Boston, Rhode Island and New York, with a corresponding importation of European goods. Direct trade with the Old World she had seemingly none.[3]

Connecticut.

One may infer from Mrs. Knight's rather scanty description of Connecticut that the material condition of the colony was much what that of Massachusetts had been some forty years earlier. There are no bridges, and the rivers have to be forded. The people are 'grave and serious, very plain in their apparel.' In Fairfield the traveller finds a considerable town filled, they say, with wealthy people, with good buildings and a spacious meeting-house. But it is clear that a wide gap severed it from the opulence and dignity of Boston.

Yet, perhaps because Connecticut had no capital

[1] R. I. Records, vol. iv. p. 180. [2] Weeden, p. 510.

[3] See Governor Talcolt's report on the trade of Connecticut. Connecticut Records, 1728–35, p. 580. This is confirmed by another report drawn up by a committee of the Assembly, and sent to the Board of Trade in 1749. Conn. Records, 1744–50, p. 594. Cf. Fisher, *Men and Manners*.

which, measured by a colonial standard, might be called wealthy, luxurious and intellectual, the life of the colony as a whole had more extended and diffused vigour. Questions of theology and of Church government were disputed with an energy and strenuousness which was almost extinct in the older Puritan colony. Yale College was in its endowments and the studies which it professed a worthy rival to Harvard. Such failure as it met with was due not to any lack of zeal or activity, but to conflicting demands which were in themselves evidence of a keen and wide-spread desire for learning.

Moral and intellectual life of Connecticut.

In all its details the social and industrial life of Connecticut can have differed but little from that of Massachusetts. In both the cost of labour and the cheapness of land, rather than the restrictive policy of the British Government, checked manufactures. All commodities that called for skilled and well-organized labour could be imported more cheaply than they could be made. All the four New England colonies produced iron, but, owing to defect either in the material or in the processes of extraction and working, the wrought iron was of inferior quality. All that used in ship-building had to be imported from England, while at times enough of the coarser kind was produced to allow of exportation.[1] The working up of the iron, first by machinery into rods and then by hand into nails, was one of the few forms of manufacture which throve. The latter process needed no technical skill or special appliances. The farmer could spend the long winter evenings in making the nails which he needed for his rough carpentry. No cutlery seems to have been made in New England, and even scythes were imported.[2]

Industrial condition of Connecticut.

[1] See the authorities given in Weeden, p. 497.

[2] See the Report of Committee to the Board of Trade, referred to on last page.

Connecticut over and above iron produced copper, and in 1707 a company was formed for working copper mines in that colony.[1] But before the middle of the century the business had been given up as unprofitable.[2]

Attempts at textile manufacture in New England.

Towards the end of the seventeenth century it might have seemed as if New England would develop into a country of textile manufacture, making at least all the stuffs which were needed to clothe her own inhabitants. The farmers' hemp and flax were spun into linen by their wives and daughters, and their wool was made into clothes and bedding by professional weavers.[3] In 1708 an accurate and intelligent observer could report that three-quarters of the clothes worn by the settlers was home-made.[4] Forty years later things had changed, and two-thirds of the cloth worn by the settlers was imported from England.[5] There was no doubt a settled dread among those responsible for the colonial policy of Great Britain lest the colonies should break in on her monopoly of woollen manufacture. That found utterance in an order of the King in Council in 1699 prohibiting all exportation of woollen goods from the colonies.[6] But the very fact that this order, in itself of doubtful constitutional validity, was allowed to pass without any recorded protest or challenge shows that it inflicted no particular hardship, and that the British Government might very safely have trusted to the natural working of economic causes. The colonists were not withheld by any external restraint from pro-

[1] Weeden, p. 498.

[2] The Committee's Report.

[3] Mr. Weeden (pp. 389–92) adduces a mass of evidence proving the existence of the professional weaver.

[4] Caleb Heathcote's report in N. York Col. Documents, vol. i. p. 486.

[5] Governor Belcher's report to the Board of Trade.

[6] The order is in the New York Documents, vol. v. p. 149.

ducing up to the full limit of their own consumption. That they did not do so was due to a variety of causes. The improvement in roads enabled the inland districts to send corn into Boston to feed an increasing population or to be exported, and thus land which had been sheep pasture was coming under the plough. The increase of shipping and of foreign trade gave the settlers readier access to the English market, and the growth of comfort and of luxurious tastes made men dissatisfied with the coarse fabrics which were all that the colony could produce. Attempts were made in all the New England colonies to develop home manufacture. In 1719 a body of emigrants from Londonderry settled on the southern border of New Hampshire and introduced the Irish methods of spinning, but the industry does not seem to have extended.[1] Somewhat later a spinning school was established in Boston, but in a few years it was given up.[2] Connecticut, like Rhode Island, made unsuccessful attempts by means of bounties and monopolies to encourage the production of linen and duck.[3] An attempt was also made in Connecticut to encourage the growth of silk by a system of bounties. An Act for that purpose was passed in 1734, to be in force for ten years. As no attempt was made to renew it, and as we hear nothing of any successful results, we may assume that it was a failure.[4]

Population of New England.

That completeness of organization which marked the New England colonies from their outset makes their statistics of population fairly trustworthy, and we shall probably not be far wrong if we estimate the whole number of English-speaking inhabi-

[1] Belknap's *History of New Hampshire* (ed. 1813), vol. ii. pp. 30, 92.

[2] Boston Town Records, 1720, p. 141. *Memorial History of Boston*, vol. ii. p. 511.

[3] Conn. Records, 1726–30, pp. 495, 502.

[4] *Ib.* 1726–50, p. 495.

tants from the Kennebec to the frontier of New York, in 1720, at about a hundred and ten thousand, with a slave population slightly over four thousand. Of this white population Massachusetts had rather more than half, and Connecticut about a fifth. From New Hampshire we have no definite return, but it is probable that the populations of that colony and Rhode Island were about equal.[1]

Our traveller might either pursue his course along the mainland, or turn aside and take the ferry which would land him on Long Island. In the latter case he would see nothing to remind him that he was on what had once been alien territory. He would find himself among a group of townships with English names, inhabited by men of English name and descent, each like a New England town with a church, Independent in name, yet so far accepting a federal system, that an intelligent and ordinarily accurate observer would describe them as Presbyterian. The industry and the social life were those which the settlers had brought with them from their earlier homes in Connecticut.

Long Island.

As was said above, there is an inevitable tendency in history to accentuate too sharply the lines of division whether they be chronological or geographical, and to ignore those intermediate types which bridge over the apparent gulf between the most characteristic and conspicuous forms. We are apt to divide the American colonies sharply into Northern and Southern, the one group with free labour, varied industry, and expansive commerce, with urban life, intense, vigorous and fully organized, with a society which never wholly lost sight of the ideals of a somewhat ascetic culture ; the other relying for its productive labour on the slave-gang, monotonous therefore and

The middle colonies.

[1] For the details on which this estimate is based see Appendix.

unprogressive in its industry, pleasure-loving, with nothing in its social or political life to quicken or maintain the sense of civic unity. We are apt to forget that the tracts which were the homes of these two opposed systems were separated by what might be called an intermediate zone, with natural conditions and a social system in which we can find points of likeness to each of the types of life which flanked it on either side. In the valleys of the Hudson and the Delaware, and in the lands between, our traveller would not wholly lose sight of the small rural township and the group of yeomen farmers, with which he had become familiar in New England. But he would also find, not indeed the elaborately organized slave-gang of the Southern colonies, but slave labour employed on a large scale by comparatively wealthy landowners.

Mixture of nationalities in New York.

The first noteworthy point, however, which would strike the traveller crossing from Long Island to Manhattan would be that he had suddenly passed into a society un-English in origin and largely un-English in character. In some cases the original Dutch place-name had given way to an English one. This was sometimes a translation: Zandt Hoek, Vlacht Bos and Helle Gat spontaneously change into Sandy Hook, Flat Bush and Hell Gate. In the transformation of Beeren's Island into Barren Island, Deutel Bay into Turtle Bay, and Conyers Island into Coney Island, we see the result of a merely accidental likeness. English was the official language, as French is to-day in Brittany. But we may safely assume that only a small portion of the citizens spoke English with full familiarity, or used it in their own domestic circle. It is clear too, from more than one passage in the Records and the political literature of the time, that Dutch and English were still looked on as opposed nationalities with conflicting interests. Thus in 1705 we find it made a matter of reproach to Bellomont that he favoured the Dutch at the expense of his own countrymen.[1] By 1750 English had become the dominant language in the city of New York, but Dutch still held its own in the outlying districts.[2]

English, however, had to compete not only with the speech of the original Dutch founders of the colony. Successive strata of Swedish, German, Walloon and Huguenot migration could be traced in the every-day talk of the streets. In the markets, traders from the Levant might be heard doing their business in Jewish or Armenian. Dutch, English and French Huguenots had their own places of worship, while the German Lutherans borrowed the Dutch church, and there held service in their own tongue. Moreover, the well-to-do inhabitants of French and Irish extraction were numerous enough for each to have their own club.[3]

In Massachusetts the alien immigrant was an object of suspicion, and as far as might be of restraint. In New York the legislature did everything to encourage him by simplifying the process of naturalization.[4] The witness who has just been quoted, himself of French blood, assures us that 'the French have all the privileges that can be—they are of the Council and of the Parliament, and are in all other employments.'[5]

The city itself in 1710 numbered some six thousand inhabitants. The town had not yet put on that aspect of precise and geometrical symmetry which at a later

[1] Cornbury to Hedges, N. Y. Docs. vol. iv. p. 1151.

[2] Tuckerman, p. 185.

[3] Diary of Peter Fontaine, 1716, p. 297. This forms part of the *Memoirs of a Huguenot Family*, by Ann Maury, published in 1853 and re-edited in 1872.

[4] It was enacted in 1715 that all persons who take the necessary oaths shall at once become naturalized subjects. Acts of Assembly, p. 124.

[5] John Fontaine, as above.

day it borrowed from Philadelphia. Yet the Broad Way, the main thoroughfare of the country bisecting the town lengthwise, gave a certain definiteness and cohesion of form. There was also as at Boston the look of spaciousness given by an abundance of unoccupied ground, and houses surrounded by orchards and gardens. The construction of the houses, mainly of brick, gave a look of permanence and solidity, and protected the town against those fires which so often devastated the timber-built streets of Boston. In 1701 Bellomont could describe New York as the 'growingest' town in America, and could substantiate the claim by the fact that since his arrival in 1698 there had been no less than a hundred 'fair houses' built.[1]

Aspect of New York city.

The amount of trade may be best gauged by the fact that in 1729 two hundred and twenty-two merchants' vessels sailed from New York harbour.[2] It is estimated that by 1737 fifty-three vessels, averaging sixty tons freight, were owned by inhabitants of New York, and that twelve years later the tonnage was doubled and the number of vessels trebled. Corn, furs collected by trade with trappers and Indians in the Hudson valley, fish, and a little tobacco were the exports. Horses too were sent to the West Indies.[3] As in Boston the ships brought back European luxuries: wine, spirits, furniture, all the articles of clothing worn by the richer classes.[4] In time of war privateers came on freighted with the contents of French and Spanish prizes, and as in Rhode Island there was no rigid line of demarcation between privateer and pirate.

Commerce of New York.

The outward and visible symbols of wealth were more conspicuous in New York than in Boston. The

[1] N. Y. Docs. vol. iv. p. 820. [2] Kalm, vol. i. p. 258.
[3] This is stated in the *Memorial History*, vol. v. p. 228.
[4] N. Y. Docs. vol. v. p. 551; vol. vi. p. 29.

rich wore costlier clothes and gave better dinners; there was more of pomp shown in equipment and attendants.[1] On the other hand an educated Bostonian would have assuredly complained of a lack of the more refined side of life. While Boston had in 1720 its five printing presses, New York had but one.[2]

Habits of life.

In one important feature of material well-being New York was apparently no better off than the poorer colonies of Connecticut and Rhode Island. A traveller from Virginia at the beginning of the eighteenth century declares that the roads of New York were so bad that there were not two coaches in the whole colony. What is, perhaps, more surprising, he dwells on the goodness of the roads in his own colony.[3]

In one respect New York differed from all the other colonies. It was the only one in which the system of letting agricultural land was a normal feature. In 1724 it was thought necessary to pass an Act to prevent certain abuses arising from the relation of landlord and tenant.[4] The words of the Act show that the system was one of *métayer* tenancy. The lessor supplied stock and necessaries, which remained his property, and had to be restored to him at the expiration of the tenancy. Fraudulent tenants, however, sold the stock. In this they were assisted by a lawless population of backwoodsmen living in Ulster and Orange Counties, and able at any time to take shelter in the woods or mountains. To prevent this, power was given to justices in those counties to apprehend anyone who could not give proof of his ability to maintain himself. Another malpractice mentioned in the Act was the sale

[1] For the luxury of New York, see a report of travels in 1712, by Grafenried, published in the North Carolina Records, vol. i. p. 972.

[2] Thomas's *History of Printing*, vol. i. pp. 89–109, 294.

[3] John Fontaine's *Journal*, pp. 265, 297.

[4] Acts of Assembly, p. 295.

of timber off their holdings to ships' captains, who connived at what was at once a fraud on the landlord and a breach of the Navigation Acts.

Rural life in the colony.

An English observer would probably have found in the urban life of New York a somewhat monotonous round of coarse enjoyments. On the other hand, if he had extended his tour through the pine-woods and the undulating meadows which fringe the valley of the Hudson, he would have found a type of life un-English in origin, yet more in consonance with English tastes and traditions than he would have found in any other part of the colonies. A likeness to the life of rural England has often been attributed to the Southern slave plantations. In reality a far closer likeness might be found among the landed gentry of New York. Many of them had houses in New York town, and were thus in regular contact with a diversified and vigorous form of life. In England in the eighteenth century a wealthy landed family would have a house in the county town, where the winter was spent. So it was in New York. The head of an old Dutch family, a Schuyler or a Van Rensselaer, was at once a squire and a merchant. His winter was spent amid the gaieties of New York, his summer on his landed estate, where he was not only a farmer on a large scale, but often a fur trader and a timber merchant. Those who lived thus had become by repeated intermarriages a definite and exclusive caste. If we may believe Hunter, the colony suffered from the accumulation of land in a few hands. 'Single men possess tracts of twenty or thirty miles square which they keep in their own hands, in the hope of planting them with tenants of their own, which is never to be expected in a country where the property may be had at easy rates.'[1]

Slavery existed, and in the city the slave population

[1] N. Y. Docs. vol. v. p. 180.

was, as we have seen, regarded as a constant element of danger.[1] But in the country districts slavery seems to have been free from all specially harsh or repulsive features. There was no organized slave-gang under the control of an overseer. Rather, the slave had his place as a recognized member of a large patriarchal family, directly controlled by the head.[2]

We also hear from an acute if somewhat optimistic witness of the pleasant social intercourse and the plenteous but frugal hospitality which prevailed among the landowners at Albany; the easy and informal intercourse of the young men and women at picnics and fishing parties.[3] In none of the colonies did the Englishman, whose military or official duty had brought him there, find himself in so home-like an atmosphere. In New England he was alienated by the traditions of Puritanism. The Southern planter was sometimes an exceedingly strenuous and slightly contentious person, with a taste for legal and political speculation; sometimes he was a Squire Western. But in New York an average middle-class Englishman found himself among companions whose tastes, habits, and ideas were pretty sure to be in conformity with his own.

Village communities.

The city merchant and the large landholder might be the most conspicuous figures in the life of New York, but they did not make up between them the whole life of the colony. Over and above the half-Anglicized villages of Long Island there were, along the valley of the Hudson, small rural communities grouped together for purposes of defence and of common tillage. Such were Schenectady and Esopus, consisting, the former of some thirty houses, the latter

[1] *Middle Colonies*, p. 359.

[2] Mrs. Grant of Laggan. *Memoir of an American Lady*, vol. i. ch. vii.

[3] *Ib.* ch. x.

of nearly double that number, each surrounded by a palisade and standing in the middle of a tract of rich corn land.[1]

It would be absurd to liken these little communities, with nothing more in the way of local self-government than a few simple bye-laws and limited police powers, to the New England townships, with their ecclesiastical autonomy and their trained and disciplined town meetings. Yet we may believe that the New York villages did something to check centralization, and keep alive a sense of citizenship in the rural population.

Albany.

Thrust forward into the wilderness as an outpost, severed for nearly half a year from the community by impassable ice, guarded too at all times against peril from the north-west by an impenetrable wilderness, stood Albany, grown in population, but retaining the compactness and dignity of Dutch days. Cut off during the winter from all external influences, brought during the rest of the year into constant intercourse with savages and with hunters and woodmen, almost as wild and brutal as the savage, exposed to the demoralizing influences of the Indian trade, it is no matter for wonder if the population of Albany were in the eyes of their fellow-colonists, and even more of their New England neighbours, a set of lawless barbarians. They were even charged with driving a thriving trade with the Indians in the spoils taken from New England farm-houses, and the English attributed to a convict origin what was far more probably due to the temptations and the demoralization of circumstance.[2] It was indeed unfortunate that such suspicions should have attached themselves to what was virtually a garrison entrusted with the main key of British interests in America. Modern changes have left but few visible traces of the Albany of the eighteenth century. But in

[1] The Labadists, pp 315, 324.

[2] Kalm, vol. ii. pp. 262–6.

the smaller towns along the Hudson a few houses survive from that time which help us in the task of imaginary reconstruction. A good specimen of such is to be seen in the Manor House at Yonkers, the home of the Philipse family. It is a solid, square-shaped building; a portion of it of one story in brick, the rest of two stories in stone. The picturesque irregularity produced by the difference of elevation is increased by eaves, with one porch at the front and another at the side, while a projecting wooden string-course runs round the building. This last named feature is to be found in other New York houses of that date. Another such house, but strengthened by massive walls, with loopholes for musketry, is that once occupied by the Van Cortlandt family, and placed at the junction of the Croton with the Hudson, some forty miles above New York.[1] The ordinary New York farm-house was a much less pretentious structure, built, as a traveller of a somewhat later day tells us, of bricks dried in the sun, not in a kiln, and in some cases covered outside with boards.[2]

There are scenes which seem to be fittingly marked out by nature as the battle-ground of great principles and interests. The voyager up the Hudson in the days which we are considering, as his vessel passed by heights far statelier than those of the Rhine or the Danube, and valleys where rock and wood and water recall all that is loveliest in the Highlands of Scotland or Bavaria, might well have felt that he was looking on a scene fitted by nature, as it was destined by history, to influence the fate of great European Powers. The existence of the Hudson, carrying as it were a narrow isthmus of commercial civilization into the

Importance of the Hudson.

[1] I have seen the Philipse house at Yonkers, but unfortunately not the Van Cortlandt house. It is described in an interesting article in the American *Magazine of History*, vol. xv.

[2] Kalm, vol. ii. p. 285.

heart of the wilderness and linking the western waterways, with all their wealth of furs and timber, and their waste pasture and fertile corn land yet untilled, to the Atlantic seaboard, was the one supreme influence which bound up the fortunes of Northern America with those of the Old World.

A ferry boat southward to Staten Island and another thence to Elizabethtown furnished the usual transit from New York to the south.[1] In New Jersey and in Pennsylvania the visitor would find himself confronted with a type of life as cosmopolitan as that of New York. Yet it differed. In New York the main substance of the population was Dutch; the English element was only one, though the most important one, of later accretions. But in New Jersey and Pennsylvania the situation was more than reversed. The British were the dominant and, save for the slight and evanescent influence of the Swedes, the original population. One must say British, not English, for as we have seen both Scotland and Wales had at an early stage contributed their share to the population. The name of Perth Amboy was a living witness to the former influence, such places as Newtown, Radnor, and others before-mentioned to the latter.

New Jersey.

The social and industrial developement of New Jersey was largely determined by the fact that the whole coast between Sandy Hook and Cape May did not possess a single harbour. Thus the spread of population was of necessity restricted on the north to Raritan Bay and the right bank of the Hudson, on the south to the left bank of the Delaware. A track through forest and wilderness connected Perth Amboy with the settlements opposite to Philadelphia.

It inevitably followed that the commercial develope-

[1] A map dating from 1732, published in the *Memorial History* (vol. v. p. 254), shows the two ferries.

ment of New Jersey was stifled by the two great cities which flanked it on its borders, New York and Philadelphia.

Thus New Jersey was of necessity nothing more than a self-supporting agricultural community. As far as outward appearance went, a traveller would probably have seen a general likeness to New England, not confined to those settlements which actually took their origin thence. The country, indeed, was better wooded and more fertile. But the farmsteads stood in the same fashion, grouped together for purposes of worship, and in those early days at least for self-defence. The houses were mainly of wood, surrounded by orchards. Holdings were small and slave labour virtually unknown. For in a temperate climate, with a soil suited to mixed husbandry, and with no facilities either for producing or exporting any one staple product, the slave can have no chance of competing with the free labourer. Yet while New Jersey had no town with any pretensions to rival Boston, New York, or Philadelphia, Burlington seems to have presented somewhat the same attractive appearance which marks it at the present day. A traveller, quoted before, writing in 1712, describes it as 'a very nice borough built in the Dutch fashion.'[1]

Rural life.

The traveller crossing the Delaware into Pennsylvania would find no change in the outward aspect of rural life and industry. But in Philadelphia he would find a city with less indeed of dignity and less of historical character imprinted on its features, yet hardly inferior in the charm of its natural surroundings to Boston or New York, and endowed with a spaciousness, and even more with a regularity of aspect, to which they could lay no claim. The growth of

Philadelphia.

[1] Grafenried in N. Car. Records, vol. i. p. 965. I do not know what German word is translated by 'nice.'

trade and of luxury has left as few details of domestic architecture in Philadelphia as in New York. Yet fragments may still be found here and there, showing that something of external picturesqueness was obtained by carved barge boards and lintels.

Population of the middle colonies.

We shall probably be not far wrong if we estimate the population of New York in 1715 at thirty thousand, that of New Jersey at rather more than two-thirds of that number, while we may assign to Pennsylvania and Delaware two or three thousand more than to New Jersey. Of this whole number about eight per cent. were negroes.

General character of the Southern colonies.

Once let the traveller cross the boundary separating Penn's colony and the Territories from Maryland, and he would find himself confronted with a wholly new type of social and industrial life, differing as widely from all that he had seen before as though it had been separated in time or in distance by centuries and by thousands of miles. In one respect and in one only would Maryland remind him of what he had left behind. There, as in New York, he would find what an early Massachusetts writer calls 'polypiety' in full force—Anglicans, Roman Catholics, Presbyterians, Quakers, representing separate waves of immigration, all claiming and practically enjoying religious equality.

In every other respect there is entire change. Agricultural villages have vanished. Towns exist, but urban life is a comparatively unimportant element in the life of the community. Instead we have the mansion with its straggling appendages for the housing of a wastefully large establishment, and the wood cabins of servile labourers dotted round, as in the mediæval manor, though not, as these, destined under favouring conditions to grow into an urban community. We have no longer the yeoman farmer, wringing out of the soil his subsistence, and under favourable conditions a margin for accumulation by continuous toil and frugal living. Instead of that we should see the labour of the slave-gang working under an overseer, a labour so wasteful in its methods as to be possible only where there is an abundance of fertile soil. If a fortune is made it is not by devising new productive processes, nor in any great measure by personal industry and frugality, but by skill and good judgement in land speculation and in the organization of labour. In some instances the planter not only grew tobacco but made it the subject of speculative purchases. When capital increased it was not applied, as at New York or Boston, to the devising fresh modes of investment or the importation of fashionable luxuries from England, but either productively to the purchase of more land, or unproductively to the extension of a rough, bounteous hospitality, or to the improvement of the racing stud or the pack of hounds.[1]

Differences between the life of the South and that of rural England.

It is customary to liken the plantation of the South to that of rural England. A visitor fresh from that life would probably have been far more struck with the differences than with the likeness. The English village is a society, the plantation in Maryland or Virginia was a factory. There might be a superficial resemblance of tastes and habits. But there is not much of the essence of English life left if we cut off the free labourer at one end, the peer and the county member at the other. There was in the Southern colonies an aristocracy in a certain sense of the word; that is, there was a class in which land and the social dignity given by the possession of land were hereditary, a class with abundance of leisure,

[1] There were exceptions to this. Mead (*Old Churches, &c., of Virginia*) mentions as an instance of gross extravagance the importation of bricks from England for building (vol. i. p. 331). No doubt George Warrington was not the only young planter who imported books and fiddles.

with a certain prescriptive claim to political influence, and with a standard of manners, education, and intelligence which was at least far above that of the rest of the community. But they were not, save quite remotely and indirectly, what the corresponding class in England are, a link between their own district and the wider political and social life of the outer world.

Want of towns.

The peculiarities which marked off Maryland and Virginia were largely, though not wholly, due to physical causes. The formation of the coast, wholly unlike that of the Northern colonies, had a large influence. Combined with the fertility of the soil and the unfitness of the climate for free labour, it produced a special type of life and industry. Wide tidal rivers indented the coast deeply, converting the inhabited sea-board into something like an archipelago. Every planter could have his own wharf and landing-stage. Without ready access to a tidal river, a tobacco plantation was valueless, and thus the inhabited land was almost confined to the river banks. The occupants of opposite sides of the same river were neighbours; the tracts between the streams were barriers of forest, only to be penetrated, nor that easily, by horsemen. The only definite administrative areas were the parish with its church and the county with its court-house, and such was the size of each that a settler might find himself living fifty miles from his centre of religious or of civil life. Laws were passed from time to time, Cohabitation Acts as they were called, attempting to bring the settlers together in towns by special exemption from public dues, and even by immunity from liability for debt. But nothing came of this. Where, as we have just seen, every planter had his own private wharf, the need for seaports was not felt. The towns of the Northern coast, with their population of merchants, seafaring folk and craftsmen, had no place in the social and industrial economy of the South. Inland towns were even less needed, where every estate was a little self-supporting community, producing the necessaries of life, with a staff of workmen sufficient for the rough handicrafts which supplied the wants of life. For it is a sure economical law that where slave labour is the dominant system there cannot grow up alongside it any effective system of free labour. The atmosphere engendered by the one is both morally and economically fatal to the other. Not only does manual labour connote degradation, but the slave-holder inevitably becomes unfitted to be an employer of free workmen. Regularity, monotony, lack of technical skill become the recognised condition of labour. The production and distribution of the slave's food and clothing, the construction of his house, can be organized with a simplicity and directness, with a disregard to his individual wishes which are impossible with a free labourer. The lack of a medium of exchange is, one may almost say, the leading economic part in the history of the Southern colonies. Tobacco sufficed for their simple and limited commerce; it would never have so sufficed if a wage fund had been needed.

Such towns as there were—Annapolis in Maryland, Williamsburg in Virginia—were in no sense centres of economical or intellectual activity. They owed their continued existence to the exigencies of official life, and served as centres to which the wealthy classes resorted for assize balls, race meetings and assemblies.

Norfolk indeed was a seaport, with shipping and carrying trade. Yet this was really one of those seeming exceptions which prove the rule. For Norfolk depended for its exports not on the products of Virginia, but on those of North Carolina, a colony which possessed neither a good harbour nor tidal rivers.[1]

[1] Byrd, *The Dividing Line*, p. 28.

In no case did a town either in Maryland or Virginia contribute anything to the political or intellectual life.

In both colonies we see that not uncommon phenomenon, a community forced by economical influences into a method of life which its members protest against and deplore. There is among the Colonial Papers for 1697 a remarkable report drawn up by three influential and well-informed Virginians, and addressed to William Popple, then Secretary to the Board of Trade. The authors were Blair, Commissary to the Bishop of London—by far the most energetic and able official of the Church of England who had taken any part in colonial affairs—Hartwell and Chilton. The document is entitled 'An Account of the Government and Present State of Virginia,' and is divided into twelve heads.

'If,' they say, 'we ask for well-built houses, and convenient ports and markets, for plenty of ships and seamen, for improved trade and manufactures, for well-educated children, industrious and thriving people, and a happy government in Church and State, we find the poorest, miserablest and worst country in America. The bringing of the people to the improvements of inhabitation must be wrought against their will by the Royal Prerogative, not by expecting the concurrence of the general Assembly, the major part of whose members have never seen a town nor a well-improved country in their lives, and cannot imagine the benefits of them.' There is no market for any product except tobacco, and, owing to the want of a convenient medium of currency and the distance between plantations, tradesmen are few, dear and insufficient. Even when attempts have been made by the Assembly to erect towns they have been frustrated. Everyone wants the town near his own house, and the majority of the Burgesses have never seen a town, and have no notion of any but a country life.

Thirteen years later Spotswood confirmed this in a report which described the straggling method of life, planters living fifty miles away from the court-house of their own county.[1]

Again in 1705 we find an able and energetic Presbyterian minister, Francis Mackemie, writing a pamphlet entitled 'A Persuasive to Towns and Plantations,' urging the inhabitants of Maryland and Virginia to form towns, and pointing out with great force the drawbacks of the system under which they lived. There is no productive industry worked by free labour; the colony only exports raw material, for all manufactured commodities the settlers are wholly dependent on imports. There are no open markets: all business is done at taverns, where there is far more room for fraud. Drink, too, is given free at such places, a custom which 'has propagated drunkenness as much as anything in the plantations.'

Mackemie's pamphlet.[2]

According to Mackemie there were at one time numerous small holdings in one portion of the colony, Prince George County. But they had been swallowed up under the action of that inexorable economic law whereby the small holder, unless protected by some exceptionably favourable conditions, has to give place to the large landowner.

That economic and industrial solitude in which the planters of Maryland and Virginia lived did not bring with it social isolation. The planter, with few resources at home, vigorous, active, devoted to outdoor life and to the saddle, and to sports which involved social life as a necessary condition, journeyed through the forest with his saddle-bags to the distant mansion, where he was a welcome guest. His mental atmosphere might be somewhat gross: it was not stagnant. And his mental activity almost always ran

Social life.

[1] Letters, vol. i. p. 37. [2] *Virginia Magazine of History*, vol. iv.

into one groove. The relations between the representative of the Crown and the settlers usually brought with them enough tension to keep alive political interest, and those interests had no rival. The mental energy which in the Northern colonies was distributed between trade, literature and religion, was in the South all concentrated in public life. Moreover, the young Southerner did not find himself at once launched in a party system, where he was provided with a set of opinions ready manufactured for him. Throughout the eighteenth century, during the colonial period, we shall find repeated proof that the Southern planter was often more than a mere 'practical' politician; that he was a political thinker, and that the way was being prepared for the generation under whom Virginia became 'the Mother of Presidents.'

Differences between Maryland and Virginia.

Beneath the general pervading likeness which has just been sketched, a careful observer would have discovered underlying points of real difference, social and economical, between Maryland and Virginia. In Virginia the slave system was omnipresent and omnipotent; in Maryland it was checked and modified by various and counteracting influences. To begin with, Maryland had a population far more mixed in creed and in social antecedents. Virginia was for a while faintly leavened by Puritan immigrants from New England, but some passed on to South Carolina, the rest became absorbed and constituted a definitely separate element in the population. But in Maryland it was otherwise. Sectaries naturally would expect to fare better under the often-challenged and feebly administered control of a Roman Catholic proprietor, than in a colony directly dependent on the Crown and therefore directly connected with the Church of England. As a consequence, Independents and Quakers surpassed, if not in numbers, at least in political activity and influence, those Roman Catholics for whom Cecilius Calvert had designed his colony as a refuge.[1]

The class of emigrants thus attracted were for the most part industrious men of moderate means. Moreover, the difference in latitude between Maryland and Virginia, though not great, was yet enough to give the Northern colony a distinct advantage as a home for the white labourer. Thus in Maryland we find landed estates as a rule smaller than in Virginia, and at the same time we find more varied production and more free labour.

An enactment passed by the legislature of Maryland in 1716 is not without significance. It ordered that all persons holding innkeepers' licences should provide a fixed number of bedrooms and a fixed amount of stabling.[2] Clearly the object was to check mere tippling houses, and we can hardly suppose such a provision needed unless there was a lower or middle class not too scattered to haunt such places.

At the same time we find the legislature of Virginia repeatedly passing Acts against gaming, supplemented by one against cock-fighting and racing.[3] All that we know of the social life of Virginia makes it certain that such enactments were little more than a dead letter. But none the less do they presuppose a good deal of social intercourse.

Both colonies had begun with the same industrial system, with white labourers bound for a period of servitude, and in both the white servant was gradually superseded by the negro.

Slavery in the two colonies.

It is easy to see how such a change was made

[1] There is not as far as I know any means of ascertaining the number, actual or proportionate, of the various religious denominations. I infer that matters were as I have described from the general course of affairs.

[2] Acts of Maryland. Collected in 1729.

[3] Heming, vol. iv. p. 214; vol. v. p. 102; vol. vi. p. 148.

inevitable by economic conditions. The negro more easily took his place as an instrument in a mechanical system of labour organized on a large scale. The mixed slave-gang must always have presented difficulties. The negro would look with jealousy on the man who had before him a prospect of freedom. On the other hand the master had stronger motives for considering the physical well-being of the labourer in whom he had a permanent interest, and thus the indented servant would often have to put up with worse treatment than befell his black fellow-labourer. Moreover, the white servant, unlike the negro, might at any time escape into another colony, and be merged in the population without hope of identification or recovery.

Political as well as economical considerations helped on the change. The convict, often a Roman Catholic and a Jacobite, was a natural object of suspicion in a community where French invasion was becoming more and more a real danger. The substitution of the black for the white, and of negro slavery for the semi-servile labour of convicts and indented servants, went on alike in Maryland and in Virginia. But in the former colony the process was much slower. Even by the middle of the eighteenth century there was an annual import of convicts into Maryland, estimated at six hundred a year.[1] On the other hand we find a Secretary for Virginia at the beginning of the century reporting that the duty on the importation of white servants was too insignificant a source of revenue to be worth reckoning.[2]

Economically there can be no doubt that the larger estates and the exclusive employment of black labour were in favour of Virginia. Not only was the negro a more efficient instrument for the monotonous and

[1] *Maryland Gazette*, quoted by Mereness, p. 133.

[2] Jennings to Board of Trade, November 27, 1708.

unskilled labour needed in the production of a single commodity, but the system of large holdings lessened proportionately the cost of supervision and transport. Moreover, it was found wholly impossible to maintain the quality of the tobacco in either colony without a complete system of government inspection, and such a system was far more easily carried out when the production was in the hands of a few large proprietors, not of many small ones. By the beginning of the eighteenth century the superiority of Virginia to Maryland tobacco was fully recognised, and remained uncontested.

Relative merits of the economic condition of the two colonies.

Yet, as often is the case, the system which was economically worse brought compensating advantages in its train. The condition of industrial life in Maryland provided the colony with a class intermediate between the large landholder and the manual labourer, and the advantage of that was felt when the day came for extension into regions where the economic life of the community could no longer be maintained by the labour of the slave-gang and the commerce of the tide-way.

The population of Maryland at the time which we are considering may be put down as about thirty-five thousand, of whom about a third were negroes. Virginia could number some sixty thousand white, and forty thousand black inhabitants.

Population of the two colonies.

To the ordinary Englishman, perhaps even more to the New Englander with his urban associations, his inheritance of rigid corporate discipline, his acute and well-trained if somewhat narrow intellect, the rough, illiterate, outdoor life of Virginia

Colonel William Byrd.[1]

[1] I have already spoken of Byrd, *English in America*, p. 465. Since I wrote that, Byrd's writings have been collected and published, with an introductory Memoir, by Mr. J. S. Bassett (New York, 1902).

would have seemed to have in it a distinct element of barbarism. The wealthy Virginia planter when he crossed the border which separated his own colony from North Carolina felt that he had passed from civilization to savagery. Such a record we have in the diary of travel left by one of the most brilliant and highly cultivated Virginians of the eighteenth century, Colonel William Byrd, of Westover. The man and his writings are well worth our attention. He describes vigorously and picturesquely, though it may not always be quite fairly, the life of the neighbouring colony. He illustrates the habits, tastes and ideas of his own. Like many other young Virginians of the upper class, Byrd was sent to England for education. He entered as a student at the Middle Temple, and was called to the bar in 1696. At the age of twenty-two he returned to Virginia. Five years later he was appointed agent to the colony, with instructions to petition against the action of Nicholson, the Lieutenant-Governor, who was endeavouring to force the Assembly into contributing towards the defence of the New York frontier. That was an isolated incident in a prolonged strife between the colonists on the one hand, the Crown and its representatives on the other. Byrd's agency met with no success. But his visit threw him into the best literary and scientific society in London, and obtained for him the friendship of Boyle and the membership of the Royal Society.

In tastes and habits Byrd represented the life of the Virginia planter at its best. The combination of practical activity with cultured leisure, of keen interest in public life and even anxiety for its prizes, with a philosophical indifference to its vicissitudes, stands first among those qualities by which an aristocracy can justify its existence. All those qualities we find in Byrd. He was a Councillor and was never indifferent to the attraction of a well-paid post in the public service. Yet he was always prepared to risk his fortunes by a patriotic, if not always a well-judged, opposition to anything like arbitrary action on the part of the Governor. On the other hand, he could detach himself from the prejudices of his class and of the atmosphere in which he lived sufficiently to see and prophesy the moral and economic evils of slavery, and to press on the British Government the expediency of checking the slave trade.

He has also the instinctive extravagance and speculative optimism of the Virginia planter. Possessed of an ample fortune, he entangles himself, at least for a time, in difficulties by purchases of land which may enrich his family in some future generation.

There is yet another side to Byrd's character, without which he could have hardly been a type of his class. With all his high mental training and value for outward graces and refinement, there is in him a certain touch of boisterous indecency. In his record of every-day incidents there is at times an ingenuousness of self-revelation which faintly reminds one of Pepys. Not indeed that he ever startles us with confessions such as those of the Diarist. Byrd has at worst only to plead guilty to slight peccadilloes of thought or word. But we see something of the same temper, that of the kindly, self-complacent, sensuous observer.

The visit to the mines.

One of the most interesting and, autobiographically, one of the most attractive of Byrd's writings is his account of a visit to the iron mines in the western part of the colony in 1732. He is keenly interested in all the details of the business, and reports them all faithfully. He hears how the unfortunate producer has his profits shorn away by the shipper, the middleman, and the British iron producer. The ships carry the iron as ballast, and yet make a charge for freight which comes to more than six per cent. on the selling price. The middleman contrives to add on charges which make up, together with freight and custom, nearly twenty-five per cent. Finally the English competitor contrives, contrary to fact, to create an unfounded belief in the inferiority of colonial iron. On the last point it is not impossible that Byrd's colonial patriotism may have misled him; the other grievances are what we are accustomed to hear from those who have not the energy or the intelligence to emancipate themselves from a costly and cumbrous system of distribution. The most interesting part of the tour is the description of the visit to the iron-works which were long carried on by that sanguine, strenuous, versatile man, the ex-governor, Colonel Spotswood. Byrd had been among Spotswood's most resolute public opponents, and the cheerful good-fellowship which evidently marked the visit does no small credit to both men. Byrd indeed lets us see once or twice that he regarded Spotswood as a man with a somewhat keen eye to his own interest. But his hospitality and the divers little incidents which make up the domestic life of the house—the tame deer who smashes a large pier-glass, the lapdog who is sentenced first to death, and then to banishment for an indiscretion similar to that of Launce's Crab—all these things are told, with no elaboration or cumbrous attempts at humour, but in the pleasant, unaffected style of the eighteenth century essayist. Spotswood had been Governor of Jamaica, and his account of the relations between Spain and England in the West Indies is of real historical value. The smelting processes, as they appear to a shrewd observer with an interest in natural science, are described intelligently and untechnically as they might have been told by Evelyn.

Three years before his visit to the mines Byrd had

been appointed as one of three Virginian Commissioners, to act with a like number from North Carolina, in drawing the dividing line between the two colonies. At every turn Byrd is met by some instance of the sloth, the grossness, the discomfort which he saw about him. Some allowance no doubt we must make for a professed wit. But we must remember that Byrd was not, like Captain Burt or Mrs. Knight, a Cockney trained to regard the small luxuries of urban life as the essentials of civilization. He was a hardy, adventurous sportsman, with no dislike to roughing it. The inevitable privations of a journey through the backwoods he treats cheerfully and humorously. Fifty years later he would have shared the hardships of Boone and his companions contentedly. The stupid and indolent neglect of natural resources, the absence of even the redeeming virtues of barbarism, these are the things which stir his contempt. Among savages the women do all the hard work, that the men may have time to hunt and to fight. Here the women drudge in the fields, while the men sit in profitless idleness. The settlers do not take the trouble to rear cattle; swine which need hardly any tending are the chief stock kept, and the symptoms of scurvy produced by an unvaried diet of pork are hideously visible everywhere. The neglected spiritual condition of the people is shown by the fact that the chaplain who accompanies the Commissioners is everywhere pressed into the service to celebrate baptisms.

Byrd's account of North Carolina.

Byrd's testimony on this subject is confirmed by a letter addressed by the Virginian Commissioners to their colleagues from the neighbouring colony. 'Because we understand there are many Gentiles on the frontier who have never had opportunity of being baptized we shall have a chaplain with us to make them Christians; for this purpose we intend

Squalor and heathenism of North Carolina.

to rest in our camp every Sunday, that there may be leisure for so good a work, and whoever in that neighbourhood is desirous of novelty may come and hear a sermon. Of this you may please to give public notice, that the charitable intention of this government may meet with the happier success.' [1]

Even more emphatic is the testimony of a Church of England clergyman, John Urmston. He describes the people as living like beasts without any of the ordinances of religion. Their education had been in the 'famous colleges of Bridewell or Newgate.' Wives are sold and many live in open adultery. It is only just to say that Urmston appears to have been a somewhat querulous egotist, given to violent denunciation of his surroundings.[2]

We have, however, further confirmatory evidence in the report sent to Lord Wilmington in 1737 by Gabriel Johnstone, Governor of North Carolina.[3] He describes the people as 'living in a beastly sort of plenty, and devoting all the rest of their time to calumny, lying, and the vilest treachery and cheating. Imagine,' he says, 'the lowest scum and rabble of Change Alley transplanted into a rich and fruitful country.'

A single witness may be prejudiced and there may be exaggeration throughout. But after all such deductions there is a consensus of evidence pointing to a sordid and semi-barbarous form of life. In such a community no questions are asked about a man's antecedents, and as a consequence the colony became an

[1] N. Con. Records, vol. ii. p. 735. We need not have much hesitation in attributing this letter to Byrd.

[2] These statements are made in a letter from Urmston to the Secretary of the S.P.G., July 7, 1711. It is published in the N. Car. Records, vol. i. p. 763.

[3] This letter is printed in the Eleventh Report of the Historical Manuscripts Commission.

Alsatia for debtors and runaway servants.[1] The prevalent contempt for restraints is shown by an incident told us by Byrd, when a magistrate who had sentenced a man to the stocks for drunkenness was himself placed there and narrowly escaped a whipping.[2]

The boundary question, Byrd tells us, excited great interest, since the frontier settlers much preferred to belong to North Carolina, where criminal law was a nullity, and where neither private debts nor public dues were enforced, rather than to be under the more regularly administered government of Virginia.

That tendency was no doubt in part due to the Act passed in 1677 almost at the outset of the colony. This provided that no colonist might, during the first few years of his residence, be sued for any debt incurred beyond the colony.[3] In 1715 another Act was passed providing that if a man owed money both within and without the colony, his creditors within should have a prior claim.[4] It is hard to say whether such enactments were more likely to prejudice the morality or the commerce of the community.

Want of towns and of trade.

The capital of the colony, Edenton, as described by Byrd, was of a piece with the rest. It was bounded by a swamp swarming with mosquitoes. It numbered some fifty small houses, and a brick chimney was reported a piece of luxurious extravagance. The Court House 'had much the air of a common tobacco house,' and there was no place of worship of any denomination. The insignificance of Wilmington is negatively proved by the absence of any

[1] This is confirmed by Spotswood's letter to Dartmouth, July 23, 1711, vol. i. p. 105. See also a very full and important document entitled, 'Copy of a representation of the Lords Commissioners for Trade and Plantations to the King upon the state of his Majesty's Colonies and Plantations on the coast of North America,' Sept. 8, 1721. It is printed in the N. Y. Docs. vol. v. p. 591.

[2] *Dividing Line*, p. 47.

[3] Chalmers, p. 525.

[4] N. Car. Records, vol. iv. p. 844.

reference to it in the records till well on in the eighteenth century, and that as late as 1750 it had no custom house.[1] Even as late as 1756 a Governor could report that he had no official residence, and that there was not even a public office for the custody of documents. Each official kept his papers at his own private house, and after his death they were often lost.[2]

The production of marketable tobacco could hardly be looked on as a high form of skilled industry. Yet even this was beyond the reach of the North Carolina planter. The system of government inspection, not always carried out completely or effectively in Virginia, was not so much as attempted in North Carolina. So bad was the tobacco that in 1726 the legislature of Virginia passed an Act prohibiting the importation of it into that colony, lest it should be mixed with Virginia tobacco for exportation, and so discredit the whole colonial staple.[3]

The jealous watchfulness with which English officials sought to guard against any possibility of colonial manufactures is illustrated by the action of Fitzwilliam, the Surveyor of Customs for North Carolina. He protested against the action of the Virginia legislature, on the ground that the North Carolina planters being cut off from growing tobacco would take to manufacturing their own clothes.[4]

The one productive industry which was carried on with some success was the manufacture of pitch and tar. This might have been a valuable export if the colony had possessed more and better harbours, or if the colonists had done their best to develope and utilize

[1] N. Car. Records, vol. v., Preface.

[2] *Ib.* p. 594. For the inconvenience caused by the absence of an official capital see Governor Johnstone's Report, Records, vol. iv. p. 385.

[3] Hening, vol. iv. p. 195.

[4] N. Car. Records, vol. ii. p. 684.

those harbours which they did possess. As it was, a few small vessels from New England brought clothing and iron, and took away pork, even pitch and tar. Beyond that the colony had no external trade.[1]

In one important respect North Carolina differed from the other colonies south of Delaware Bay. The limitations of her economical life almost excluded slavery. While in Virginia and South Carolina the black population was a majority, in North Carolina the whites numbered in 1720 about eight thousand, the negroes only five hundred.[2]

One passage in the report of Byrd and his colleagues is interesting as showing that in one matter they forecast the future of North Carolina more correctly than the Representatives of that colony. When the party reached a point fifty miles west of any existing settlement the North Carolina Commissioners said that a further survey was needless. No settlement was likely to be made so far at least for a very long time. The line could then be drawn as occasion arose. The real reason, Byrd says, was they had wasted their supplies and were running short of provisions. The Virginia Commissioners protested. Their instructions were to go as far as the mountains. They added the prophetic words: 'If we reflect on the richness of the soil in these parts and the convenience for stock, we may foretell without the power of divination that there will be many settlements higher than these gentlemen went in less than ten years, or perhaps half that time.'[3]

One deduction must probably be made from Byrd's account. There seems little doubt that the northern portion of the colony into which his business led him was more backward than the south. Towards the

[1] Report of Boone and Barwell on the state of Carolina, N. Car. Records, vol. ii. p. 394. [2] *Ib.*

[3] The report is in the second volume of the N. Car. Records.

South Carolina frontier he would have found a more thrifty and less squalid population.[1]

Physical conditions of North Carolina.

Yet in truth the whole colony laboured under conditions which forbade any high degree of natural prosperity. The climate was unfit for white labour, the resources of the soil were not such as to allow of the slave-gang to be worked profitably. One has but to look at the coast of North Carolina, with its alternations of morass and pine-barren, its stagnant rivers, divided from one another by tracks of swamp, nourishing only a profitless and moribund-looking vegetation, with everything to oppress and stupefy the imagination as much as to impair the physical nature of man, and one at once comprehends the hopelessness of human life and human toil in such a home. Not till expansion westward had opened to her settlers wholesome and fertile tracts, and till new forms of locomotion had given her a share in the general prosperity of the young republic, could North Carolina be free from the sordid bondage which nature had laid upon her.

South Carolina.

Passing into South Carolina the traveller would find himself at once confronted with forms of social life and industry different from anything that he had yet encountered. In Maryland and Virginia we meet with negro slavery. But it is slavery adapted to methods of life not wholly unlike those of rural England. In South Carolina that likeness entirely disappears. As in the other slave colonies, mixed husbandry is unknown; the place of tobacco as the one staple product is taken by rice and at a later date indigo, produced by the monotonous labour of the

[1] In 1734 Governor Johnstone, while reporting, as we shall see, very unfavourably on the colony as a whole, says that the inhabitants of the southern part are 'a very sober and industrious sort of people.' Records, vol. v. p. 5.

slave-gang. But in the organization of that labour there are two important points of difference. The climate wholly excluded the indented white servant. The same causes too, aided by other natural influences, made the planter an absentee, and vested the practical control of the estates in an overseer. Virginia and Maryland, with pleasant stretches of riverside meadows and penetrable woods, offered to the landholder an attractive imitation of those English surroundings among which his ancestors had lived. In South Carolina river was separated from river by belts of noisome swamp, covered with ungraceful trees, or by broad expanses of flat soil, fertile indeed, but without a single charm of vegetation and with no attractions for the sportsman. Such a country offered no temptations to the resident landowner. Consequently, he left his estate under the control of an overseer, and sought refuge among the sea breezes and the comparatively healthy and pleasant surroundings of Charlestown.

In Virginia and Maryland, as we have seen, the abundance of navigable rivers prevented the establishment of any important seaport. In South Carolina, on the other hand, the impossibility of finding landing stages along the rivers forced the whole commerce of the colony to concentrate itself at Charlestown. Thus there came into existence a type of life different indeed in many of its features from that of the sea-board cities in New England or the Middle States, but as purely urban, as concentrated and as exclusive. As in Boston we have an oligarchy of religion and in New York of wealth, so in Charlestown we have an oligarchy of colour. In the life of the Charlestown planter of the eighteenth century, surrounded by those luxuries which slave labour, a thriving trade, and a warm climate placed at his disposal, bound by no tie of sentiment or interest towards those on whose industry he subsisted, we see the foundations of that oligarchy, at once sensual and intellectual, indolent yet strenuous, steeped in self-indulgence yet capable of sublime sacrifice, in which at a later date Southern slavery found its stronghold.

The commercial prosperity of South Carolina is sufficiently shown by the fact that the number of ships sailing from Charlestown increased from a hundred and fourteen in 1714 to two hundred and forty-eight in 1735. Yet there was but little in the outward aspect of Charlestown suggestive of wealth or luxury. The grandeur of the natural harbour and the semi-tropical vegetation which adorned its gardens and pleasure-grounds must always have given Charlestown something of splendour. But the houses were small and mainly built of wood, while the lack of grass plots and of pavements even now produces to our English eyes a singular look of crudeness, and almost squalor.

It was a peculiarity of Charlestown that there was a large class of semi-residents as they might be called. Many of the chief houses were in the hands of English merchants who divided their lives between the colony and the mother country. The colony suffered, we are told, by a system which placed a large part of the commercial resources of the colony in the hands of those who had but little experience of its needs, no abiding interest in its well-being.[1]

The best estimate—and the best is but conjectural—puts the population of South Carolina in 1710 at about twenty-one thousand, of whom twelve thousand were negroes or Indian slaves.[2] One effect of

[1] Memorial from he agent for Carolina (apparently for both colonies), July 18, 1715, in the North Carolina Records, vol. ii. p. 196.

[2] Report of Board of Trade, Sept. 8, 1721, in the same volume, p. 418.

the natural and industrial condition, both of North and South Carolina, was to isolate the inland portions of those colonies alike from one another, and from the settlements on the sea-board. Inland communication was almost impossible, and the inhabitants of the towns on the coast, whether of Wilmington or Charlestown, were more closely connected with the sea-board towns of other colonies than they were with the inland portions of their own.

Population of the colonies as a whole.

It has been already said that the estimates given of the population in the various colonies are but conjectural and imperfect. But we shall probably be safe in saying that in 1710 the total white population was between two hundred and fifty thousand and three hundred thousand, and was nearer to the higher than the lower figure, while the total number of slaves was about a quarter that of the white inhabitants.[1]

Lack of any sense of unity among the colonists.

Such were the elements out of which the future republic had to be built. A mere summary such as that just given is at least enough to show the difficulties which stood in the way of unison. It is assuredly not too much to say that for the colonists, the sense of a common nationality was non-existent. In moments of sentiment or for some rhetorical purpose the colonist might speak of himself as an Englishman. He was prepared to be called, and in some measure dealt with as, a British subject. He was also a New Englander or a Virginian, as the case might be. He never felt the slightest necessity for coining some intermediate term applicable to the whole body of settlers.

Moreover, though the colonist did after a fashion think of himself as a British subject, that was rather a vague sentiment than a practical working influence.

[1] See Appendix I.

It varied much in different colonies. It was probably stronger in Virginia and in South Carolina than anywhere else. There, far more than in the other colonies, the ruling class depended for the amenities, and even in some measure for the necessaries, of life on intercourse with the mother country. As we have seen, there were at Charlestown a class of merchants who divided their residence between the two continents. The same was to some extent the case in New York.

Again, whatever might be the political constitution of the Southern colonies, the system of the plantation and the slave-gang had imbued them, North Carolina alone excepted, with the temperament and convictions of aristocracies. That temperament and those convictions also dominated the mother country, at least as looked at from without, and it is an almost unfailing political law that aristocracies are more closely bound together by common political connexion than communities of any other form.

The New Englander or the Pennsylvanian, so far as he was bound to the mother country at all, was only bound to it by unity of speech, rendered incomplete by the presence of many alien elements or by a vague and traditional sentiment. He might claim a share in that great intellectual and literary heritage which past generations of Englishmen had bequeathed to their successors. In the existing political life of England he had no share. When he came in contact with it, it usually irritated and repelled him.

Yet that repulsion did little or nothing as yet to draw the colonies together, or to lead them to substitute any other conception of nationality for that which was being slowly undermined by political and economic influences.

The New England colonies had indeed enough

identity in origin, opinions and method of life to regard themselves as a single and united factor in the body politic. The old federation of the four colonies had achieved but little from an administrative point of view. But it had done something to bear witness to the need of union and to remind men of such a possibility. The colonies of Puritan origin formed in a certain sense an organic whole, with Rhode Island as a basely born Ishmael living outside the fold of the covenant.

Community of origin and of early traditions did something, too, to bind together those colonies which had once been Dutch territory. But the conception of a union of all the English speaking provinces along the Atlantic sea-board had no place as a matter of sentiment, hardly any as a question of policy. The New Englander or Virginian owned a double allegiance. He was a citizen of his own province and also of the British Empire. No intermediate conception of a corporate American nationality ever, so far as we can judge, presented itself to his mind.

There was, indeed, one class of men outside the colonists themselves to whom the necessity for colonial union was constantly present. There is hardly a single British official of any intelligence or independence of view from the Revolution of 1688 till the conquest of Canada who does not see the necessity for some measure not it may be of complete union, but of consolidation. Some such proposals have already come before us, others belong to a later stage of our subject.

Unhappily in the one instance where a scheme of colonial union was put into practice, the manner in which it was tried and the associations with which it was connected were such as not merely to ensure failure, but to prejudice all future attempts in the same direction. The crude attempt of James II. to unite all the Northern colonies into a single province under a Governor, well intentioned indeed, but wholly unfitted alike by character and antecedents for such administrative responsibility, made the very thought of colonial union stink in the nostrils of patriotic New Englanders. It is grossly unfair to treat that, as it often has been treated, as a conspicuous act of tyranny either in the ruler who devised the scheme or the servant who executed it. Dongan, a man undoubtedly wise and liberal-minded in his colonial policy, had always been in favour of consolidation. He had advocated the resumption of New Jersey and Delaware, and the annexation of Connecticut and Rhode Island. And as the policy of James in its underlying principle, if not in its details, was approved by the wisest of his colonial advisers, so was it also virtually condoned by those who succeeded to his responsibilities. In the State Papers for April 1689 are two entries showing this. One is an order from the King in Council that Lord Shrewsbury consult those most interested in New York, New England and New Jersey, and then recommend a Governor and Lieutenant-Governor. The other is a general approval of this line of policy by the Lords of Trade. It is significant that they give as a reason for their recommendation that it will 'enable the colonies not only to defend themselves, but to take the offensive.' The foreign policy of William and the policy of uncompromising hostility to France were henceforth to be the key-note of the colonial as well as the European policy of Great Britain.

As the eighteenth century advanced, that hostility became more and more firmly woven into the national policy. French encroachment in America, with its accompaniments of Indian raids and frontier massacres, became by degrees more systematic and threatening. The discovery and settlement of Louisiana gave a wholly new character to that encroachment. The British settlements might find themselves hemmed in as it were by a solid wall, and debarred from all possibility of extension westward.

Under such circumstances it was but natural that the need for some effective organization, whereby all the resources of the colonies could be turned to account for common defence, should have forced itself with increasing conviction on English officials. Various projects pointing in that direction have been described in an earlier volume. One of the most interesting documents bearing on this question is a pamphlet published in London in 1720, but written by a colonist, and entitled 'Some Considerations on the Consequence of settling Colonies on the Mississippi, from a gentleman of America to his friend in London.' The writer sees that the great danger to be guarded against is the possession of the Mississippi by France. The fur trade must be retained and developed not only for its own sake, but as the best means of securing the Indian alliance. So, too, the Five Nations must be protected against French encroachment.

The writer adds one remark which puts the question of salaries in a light somewhat different from that in which it is presented by the colonists themselves. The absence of fixed salaries led, the writer contends, to official extortion.

Projects for resistance to French encroachment no doubt carried with them as a necessary consequence a policy of union between the colonies. But it was a far cry from a general demand for defensive action to a scheme of union, and further still to such a scheme furnished with all the details needed for putting it practically in force. Nor, as far as existing records show, was there any British official with enough courage and originality to face a problem to

Obstacles to union.

which the conditions of colonial life presented so many and such weighty obstacles. The hindrances on the side of the colonists were both moral and material. The colonies in which civic feeling was strongest, and which could, therefore, contribute most to any collective scheme of defence, were just those very ones which were most fenced off from their neighbours by a spirit of vigorous local patriotism. The New Englander and the Virginian stood out as the best representatives of colonial intelligence and energy, while at the same time they, of all the colonists, would be slowest to merge their special position in a common nationality.

Want of communication.

Over and above that there were the difficulties begotten by widely differing modes of life and industry, and not overcome by any effective methods of communication. The difficulties of transit have been already incidentally touched upon. Epistolary communication between the Northern and Southern extremities of the colonial dominion hardly existed. In 1692 one Thomas Neal obtained from Government a patent for furnishing the colonies with a postal service.[1] Neal appointed Andrew Hamilton, Governor of New Jersey, as his Deputy. He adopted the sound policy of having departmental systems under the control of the different colonial administrators. A post office was thus established at Boston in 1693, communicating with Portsmouth to the North, Virginia to the South. The post, however, between Boston and New York only plied once a week in the summer, and half as often in the winter. A letter would, at times, take six weeks more in making its way from New York to Virginia. Of any regular communication between the Carolinas and their northern neighbours we hear nothing. It is hardly rash to say that the Virginia

[1] A full account of these postal arrangements with references to the original authorities is given by Mr. Palfrey, vol. iv. pp. 328, &c.

planter and the Charlestown merchant felt themselves in closer contact with Bristol and London than with Boston or New York.

Living-stone's scheme of three provinces.

Among the many suggestions as to colonial union put forward by English officials, one, and one only, really grapples with the main difficulty to be overcome, the wide dissimilarity of interests and conditions which kept the colonies apart. In 1701 Livingstone, in a memorial already noticed, suggested that the colonies should be formed into three provinces.[1] Such an arrangement would have conformed not only to the physical conditions of the colonies, but also, in a great measure, to their origin and to their political and religious views. To bring the Puritan of New England, the Quaker of Pennsylvania, the planter of the South, all under one comprehensive government might indeed seem a hopeless task. But if an English statesman had been found with enough insight and constructive power to take up Livingstone's scheme and persevere with it there might have come into existence three provinces, each homogeneous in itself. The scheme might even have served as a basis for a more complete union, for a system analogous to that of India with its three presidencies. And even if it had never reached that stage it would have done much to lighten the problems of administration and military defence.

Boundary disputes.

One influence there was which forced the colonies into contact with one another, but which made far more for alienation than for union. There was hardly one colony which was not in some measure entangled with its neighbours on questions of boundary. This was largely due to the recklessness with which the Crown had made its early grants of land and to errors arising from slovenly and ignorant

[1] N. Y. Docs. vol. iv. p. 870.

surveying. The trouble was enhanced by the unsystematic fashion in which the colonies had come into existence. The mere fact that two colonies were next-door neighbours did not carry with it any sort of guarantee for homogeneity of character or community of interest and sentiment.

Moreover the trouble was enhanced by this, that the absence of exact boundaries made effective control impossible just in those very places where it was most needed. One is often tempted, in reading the colonial records, to wonder at the heat and pertinacity with which the various governments did battle for unremunerative strips of territory in the backwoods. The real fact is that the jurisdiction of such tracts often became a question on which the peace and safety of the community depended. The men who pushed their way out westward into those regions whose boundaries were uncertain were just the very men who, alike from their temper and their surroundings, needed the restraints of law. The danger was that they would play off one jurisdiction against another, using the doubts about their boundary as a pretext for disclaiming the authority of tax collectors, sheriffs' officers, and the like.

There was yet another danger. The occupants of the frontier were often traders dealing with the Indians. If the relations between the colony as a whole and the natives on the frontier were to be peaceful and secure, it was absolutely necessary that the borderers should be amenable to legal control. Over and over again a single act of lawlessness going unpunished involved a whole colony in the dangers of devastation and massacre. Moreover, the spectacle of such disputes made it difficult to impress on the Indians the belief that the various English settlements really belonged to one common nationality.

In the case of the Northern colonies, with their common origin and modes of life, their settled habits and respect for law, and their disinclination to extend westward, such disputes were comparatively unimportant. In 1713 a difficulty arose about the boundary between Connecticut and Massachusetts. A compromise was arrived at. Four townships within the recognised limits of Connecticut were to belong for administrative purposes to Massachusetts. In 1747 the inhabitants of these townships became dissatisfied with the compromise and wished to be transferred to Connecticut. The legislature of Connecticut proposed to refer the matter to a joint commission. Massachusetts preferred to refer the matter to the Home Government, who decided in favour of Connecticut.[1] The reckless fashion in which the British Crown had from the early years of the seventeenth century parcelled out its American territory was responsible for much confusion and many disputes. In 1720 a boundary dispute arose between Connecticut and Rhode Island, and was referred to the Board of Trade. Their decision, or rather one should say their opinion, was embodied in a full and careful report. The claim of Rhode Island was valid under their charter, but was inconsistent with the charter of Connecticut which was of earlier date. It was probable that Charles II. had intended the later document to override the earlier one. But there was no specific declaration to that effect, and in the absence of any such the charter of Connecticut must hold good. However, as the question only concerned jurisdiction and not private property, there was an obvious and easy way out of the difficulty. Let both colonies surrender their charters and allow themselves to be

Dispute between Massachusetts and Connecticut.

[1] For these disputes see Connecticut Records, 1728–50, p. 339; Trumbull, vol. ii. p. 295.

annexed to New Hampshire. It would be difficult to find a stronger instance of that ineptitude in grasping and interpreting colonial opinion which far more than any spirit of deliberate harshness, of selfishness or of arbitrary temper was the fatal flaw in the British administration of the American colonies.[1]

James II.'s land grants.

We have already seen that the dispute between Virginia and North Carolina was settled by Byrd and his colleagues in a wholly amicable manner. Other disputes there were between New York and New Jersey and between the two Carolinas. But none of them had any marked effect on the condition or history of either colony, and their details have ceased to have anything more than an antiquarian interest. One dispute, however, was at once so embittered and prolonged that it needs special notice. We have already seen how Baltimore disputed the claims of the Dutch colonists, and how he dealt with the unhappy Swedes at the Hoarkill. Whatever hostility he may have felt towards them was sure to be increased by the transfer of the Delaware territory to Penn. If he resented the presence of the few scattered settlements, the remnants of Swedish and Dutch occupation, much more would he resent the occupation of the territory by an enterprising Proprietor with wide-reaching projects of colonization, and with views at once so peculiar and so definite as to suggest a perpetual possibility of friction.

Not much if at all earlier than June 1680 Penn petitioned for a grant of territory north of Maryland. So watchful were Baltimore's agents in England, and so well informed on all that concerned his territorial interest, that on June 23 we find them petitioning that Penn's grant should be carefully bounded so as not to encroach on Maryland, and that for the common good

[1] The report is in the R. I. Records, vol. iv. p. 307

the sale of arms and ammunition to the Indians be forbidden to the grantee.[1]

The difficulties which arose between Penn and Baltimore were no doubt in a large measure due to that unfortunate vagueness which characterized the original grant of Maryland. The northern boundary of the province granted to Cecilius Calvert was thus described. The territory was to extend northward 'into that part of the bay of Delaware on the north which lieth under the fortieth degree of north latitude from the aequinoctial where New England is terminated.' Its northern boundary was to run from Delaware Bay in a right line.[2]

Boundary dispute.

That might signify a line either parallel to the equator or parallel to the coast. That, however, is immaterial to the present issue. What was not immaterial was the unhappy insertion of the words 'where New England is terminated.' No grant could be so interpreted as to make the fortieth degree of latitude the southern boundary of New England. Yet there is no doubt that the existence of those words in the grant influenced Baltimore in advancing the untenable claim which he made against New Netherlands. And there can be equally little doubt that the very fact of his having thus abandoned sure ground prejudiced that portion of his case which was really good. For it is very certain that Penn's original grant did encroach, though but slightly, on the territory to which Baltimore had a legal claim.

That was a theoretical rather than a practical grievance. The supplementary grant, which gave Penn a tract of land on the south-west side of Delaware Bay extending to Cape Henlopen, was undoubtedly an encroachment on the boundary of Maryland as defined by the original grant to the first Lord Baltimore.

[1] Col. State Papers, 1680, 1404.

[2] *English in America*, p. 372.

That was not all. It blocked a considerable portion of Baltimore's province from direct access to the sea, and it gave him an eastern frontier in every way less advantageous: instead of an open arm of the sea, a tract occupied by settlers, possibly unfriendly and nowise under his control.

There seemed at the outset to be a prospect of an immediate and pacific settlement between Penn and Baltimore. In August 1681 Markham, who it will be remembered was then acting as Deputy-Governor, went by Penn's instructions to Maryland, furnished with two letters to Baltimore, one from the King, the other from Penn. Markham, however, fell ill, and nothing resulted from his visit. A meeting was arranged for the spring of 1682. At that time, however, the plant cutting riots were going forward in Virginia.[1] Baltimore feared that these might extend to his own colony, and therefore thought it best to remain on the banks of the Potomac. Markham too, according to Baltimore's report, evaded the meeting. Baltimore, however, sent commissioners who satisfied themselves that the latitude of Newcastle was thirty-nine degrees forty odd minutes, and that it therefore fell within the original grant of Maryland. Markham seems to have been positively determined to avoid an interview, and when at last Baltimore pursued him and brought him to bay at Uplands, he seemed equally determined not to commit himself to any declaration or admission.[2]

Penn's negotiations with Baltimore.

[1] We have very full reports of the interviews between Penn and Baltimore, and of their negotiations generally, written by each of the principals. We have also a report of their first interview taken down in shorthand by the clerk to the Maryland Assembly. Penn, however, in his statement denies the correctness of this report. Baltimore also described the record of his two interviews with Penn in a letter to Blathwayt. All these are printed in full in the Colonial State Papers, 1681-5, 847, 849, 1117, 1179.

[2] *English in America*, p. 346.

At length, in December 1682, Penn visited Maryland and conferred with Baltimore. Penn appears, even on his adversary's showing, to have been candid in his declaration of what he wanted. If Baltimore's interpretation of his grant held good, Penn's supplementary territory, as we may call it, would be left without a seaport, and his grant would be so far rendered valueless. As he himself expressed it in a private conversation, 'The King had given him a considerable tract of land to the backward of Lord Baltimore; he knew that such land was worthless to him without an inlet, and he begged Lord Baltimore to be so good and kind as to give him a back door for the improvement thereof; adding that what would be but a hundredth of Lord Baltimore's interest would be many more hundredths of his own.'

There was a widely characteristic difference between the attitude of each disputant. Baltimore held doggedly to the strong point of his own case. His original grant made his northern boundary the fortieth degree of latitude, and that was final. Penn urged one plea after another, mixing up law, equity and compromise. First he urged the authority. One cannot wonder if Baltimore resented a claim thus urged. The letter ignored Baltimore's patent, and authoritatively declared a new boundary. Baltimore might reasonably contend that the King's mere wish expressed in a letter could not annul a right conferred by a patent.

Penn then took up a sounder position. He virtually admitted that a correct scientific interpretation of the fortieth degree of latitude would bring Newcastle within the limits of Baltimore's grant. But that literal interpretation would also have the effect of excluding Watkin's Point, which had always been conventionally accepted as the southern extremity of Maryland. It was clear, so Penn contended, that the original grant to the first Lord Baltimore was meant to give him a sea-board of two degrees—that is to say, of one hundred and twenty miles. He had been allowed to place his southern boundary beyond the correct latitude scientifically ascertained. He had no right to take advantage of that error, and by claiming a scientifically ascertained boundary on the north, to extend his grant by twenty miles. According to Penn, the advisers of the Crown were misled by an inaccurate map, which placed Cape Henlopen twenty miles further south than it really was. Their intention was that Penn's grant should reach as far as the point erroneously designated Cape Henlopen. Baltimore interpreted it as only extending to the real Cape Henlopen, and thereby curtailed it of twenty miles.

Thus, under the grant to Penn as it was originally designed by the King and his advisers, Newcastle would have been ten miles north of the southern boundary assigned to Penn. In reality it was ten miles south of it.

This tallied with a statement made at a later day by Penn's agent, Logan.[1]

The attitude of the two claimants was characteristically different. Baltimore held strongly to the letter of his grant. Penn was indifferent to the legal aspect of the question, if only he could secure the practical end at which he aimed. He was ready to buy the territory in question from Baltimore, and thus acknowledge his legal right. Baltimore was deaf to all suggestions of compromise.

Finally Penn endeavoured to persuade Baltimore that the intended encroachment was a blessing in disguise. 'The ships that come yearly to Maryland for tobacco would have the bringing of both our people and merchandise, because they could afford it cheaper; whereby

[1] Pennsylvania Archives, vol. vii. p. 44.

Maryland would for one age or two be the mart of trade.' There is a touch of disingenuousness in this appeal. Penn's subsequent policy showed that he was determined as far as might be to keep the trade of Pennsylvania independent of other colonies. Yet we may fairly think that his inconsistency was no more than that of an inexact thinker, who could only see clearly that special aspect of a case with which he was at the time being concerned.

The net was spread in vain. Baltimore expressed a civil hope that Penn would change his attitude, and they parted. In the following year Baltimore took practical measures for resisting the threatened encroachment. In May 1683 he issued a proclamation on the subject of the acquisition of land. The existing system, it declared, enabled certain persons to monopolize large tracts, and was injurious alike to the bulk of the inhabitants and to the Proprietor. Henceforth every person taking up land was to pay a hundred pounds of tobacco for the purchase and two shillings a year rent, unless it were on the sea-board side or near the Hoarkill, in which case the price and the quit-rent were to be lessened by half.[1] This was plainly an attempt to direct the stream of emigration into the debateable land.

Baltimore attempts to exercise authority on the debateable land.

Next year a small armed party under the leadership of that disreputable firebrand George Talbot[2] attempted to terrify some of Penn's colonists into accepting Baltimore's supremacy and paying him rent. They do not, however, seem to have proceeded to actual violence.

In November 1685 the Board of Trade reported on

[1] Col. State Papers, 1683, 1069, 1070. The proclamation does not specify in detail the nature of the existing system.

[2] See *English in America*, p. 423.

the case. A new ground for deciding in Penn's favour was now introduced. 'The land intended to be granted by Lord Baltimore's patent was only land uncultivated and inhabited by savages, whereas the land in question was settled by Christians before Lord Baltimore's patent.' Technically that statement was true. There was, as we have seen, a Dutch settlement at Swanendael in 1631. But after its destruction by the savages in 1632 no attempt was made to restore it. Baltimore's patent dated from June 1632, and then, as the news of the destruction of Swanendael reached Holland in the previous May, it is very certain that at the time of the grant to Baltimore the land was unoccupied. Nor was it absolutely correct to say that Baltimore's grant was limited to land 'uncultivated and inhabited only by savages.' Those words did occur in the preamble setting forth Baltimore's wishes and purpose. But they do not occur as an actual limitation to the grant.

Decision of the Board of Trade.

Moreover the attack on Baltimore's rights was a double-edged weapon. If Dutch occupation barred Baltimore's rights, it equally barred those rights which the Crown granted to the Duke of York.

The practical solution arrived at was not a compromise but a simple reaffirmation of the grant to Penn. The King, acting on the report of the Board of Trade, ordered 'that to avoid further difference the tract of land between the river and bay of Delaware and the Eastern sea on one side and Chesapeake Bay on the other be divided into two equal parts by a line from the latitude of Cape Henlopen to the fortieth degree of Northern latitude, and that one half towards Delaware Bay and the Eastern sea be adjudged to belong to the King and the other to Lord Baltimore.' [1]

Setting aside however both the equity of the settle-

[1] Col. State Papers, 1685–8, 456.

ment and the correctness of the geographical data on which it rested, it is difficult to imagine a more unsatisfactory or incomplete solution. The territory in question was a long, narrow strip of land lying between two deeply indented sea-boards. How could a line be drawn which should with any precision divide such a tract into two equal parts?

For the remainder of the century Penn and Baltimore were too fully occupied with the protection of their own endangered interests to have any leisure for fighting. The first evidence of any renewal of the conflict was in 1707. In the August of that year the Sheriff of Cecil County, Maryland, ejected certain Welsh settlers who claimed to be within the territory and jurisdiction of Pennsylvania. The Sheriff of Newcastle thereupon arrested the offending official, and his action was approved by the Governor and Council of Pennsylvania. At first the Governor of Maryland appears to have disavowed the action of his subordinate. But within a few days news reached Newcastle that he had mustered the militia of Cecil County to support the Sheriff. There our knowledge of the matter abruptly ends. In all likelihood the Governor and Assembly of Pennsylvania were too fully occupied with their own internal disputes to be able to make any effective resistance to the encroachments of their neighbours.

Conflict in 1707.

For more than ten years we hear no more of the dispute. There is, however, evidence of commercial jealousy between the two colonies in an Act passed by the Assembly of Maryland in 1715 to prohibit the importation of tobacco, grain, and horses from Pennsylvania.[1] This must have excluded the Pennsylvania farmer from a profitable market, and deprived the Marylanders of a valuable source of supply. The

[1] Acts of Maryland, p. 343.

conditions of industry in Pennsylvania were far more suited for corn-growing than those of Maryland. It is clear too that horse-breeding was an important industry in Pennsylvania, since an Act was passed in 1723 appointing a public inspector to seize all horses 'under-sized or out of comely proportion,' running in the public pastures.[1]

In 1718 some dispute seems to have arisen which rendered a conference between the authorities of the two colonies necessary.[2] Keith with one Councillor from Pennsylvania met Hart, the Governor of Maryland, with three members of his Council. That the dispute turned on a question of jurisdiction seems clear; it is also clear that the arrangement of 1685 had never been put in force by the actual drawing of a boundary line. For it was agreed between the two Governors that till such boundary was drawn settlers on the debateable land should consider themselves within the jurisdiction of that colony to which they had previously belonged. Such an arrangement was a mere imperfect stop-gap. The most troublesome cases would be those of squatters, coming it might be no one knew whence, and determined as far as might be to evade all authority.

Dispute revived in 1722.

In 1722 the dispute revived. Certain Marylanders, authorized by Lord Baltimore, were surveying for copper mines on the Susquehanna. As they bore arms their proceedings had alarmed the natives, and there was a possibility of trouble with them. At the same time a party from Cecil County, also armed, had arrested two Pennsylvanian magistrates. Keith therefore wrote to Calvert, the Governor of Maryland, complaining of those 'who justly bear

[1] Laws of Pennsylvania (p. 301). So in the travels of the Quaker Cheeseman, we read of a company of wild horses in Pennsylvania.

[2] My account of this and the following disputes is taken from the Pennsylvania Records, vol. iii.

the title of land pirates,' and announcing that he 'was resolved to put it out of their power to embroil us by their ridiculous projects.' What intended action, if any, was described by those words does not appear.

In the November of that year Keith addressed the Pennsylvania Assembly on the subject. He recapitulated the dispute with Maryland, and he pointed out that the cheap rate at which Baltimore had been selling land in the debated district raised a presumption that he distrusted his own title. The question, he said, was one on which neither party to the dispute could have an impartial and independent opinion, and it ought to be referred to some independent arbitrator. Nothing could better illustrate the necessity for some central authority, a body such as the present Colonial Department with executive powers of its own, which the Board of Trade and Plantations had not, and also better equipped with special information than that body was.

Next year Keith received from Charles Calvert and the Governor of Maryland a letter stating that Baltimore had instructed him to draw a boundary line, taking the fortieth degree of latitude. In reply Keith sent a letter received four years before from the Board of Trade,[1] with the accompanying comment, 'There is nothing therein which will direct or countenance you to discover the boundaries of Maryland by astronomical rules and uncertain observations.' The matter, Keith says, could best be settled by a conference. Calvert in reply declined the conference, and declared that he should hold to his instructions.

In 1733 one Thomas Cresop, claiming to be under the jurisdiction of Maryland, settled on the debateable land. He was the father of that Michael Cresop whose lawless violence brought about one of the most hideous tragedies in colonial history. The son apparently

[1] This letter does not appear to be extant.

came by his character by legitimate inheritance. By various acts of violence Cresop embroiled himself with the local officials appointed by the Pennsylvanian Government. They seem in their turn to have exceeded their legal powers. A recriminatory correspondence followed between Lord Baltimore and Patrick Gordon, the Governor of Pennsylvania. The latter was conciliatory, the former certainly violent in his tone, and, if we may believe Gordon, reckless in his statement of facts. In one case Baltimore complains of an act of civil war, while Gordon explains that the alleged outrage was nothing more than an ordinary boxing match.[1] Two Commissioners from Pennsylvania reported to the Assembly on the question, but this led to nothing.[2] A surveyor from Maryland, one Ramsay, was arrested for acts of violence done in the execution of his business;[3] the Sheriff of Lancaster County in Pennsylvania in attempting to execute a writ was beaten, to the endangering of his life.[4]

In the following year a fresh element of confusion was introduced by the appearance in the disputed territory of a body of settlers having no integral connexion or community of interest with either of the two colonies in question. A body of German emigrants settled in the debateable land. It is not easy to unravel, from the conflicting statements made, the real position of these settlers. Apparently however they originally settled under the belief that they were within the territory of Pennsylvania. Then as the result of pressure put upon them by Cresop they acknowledged the jurisdiction of Maryland. But afterwards, either because they believed that they had been misled by Cresop or, as Ogle suggests, in order to escape from taxes imposed by the Government of Maryland, they

[1] Pennsylvania Records, vol. iii. pp. 467–95.

[2] *Ib.* p. 547. [3] *Ib.* p. 591. [4] *Ib.* p. 612.

disclaimed the jurisdiction of that colony. Thereupon Ogle granted the land in question to a party of his own settlers, undoubtedly with the purpose of evicting the Germans, while at the same time he offered a reward for the arrest of two citizens of Pennsylvania. Even if the Maryland claim was well founded, it is impossible not to condemn a proceeding which would have turned the unhappy Germans out into the wilderness, homeless at the beginning of winter.[1]

The government of Pennsylvania at once met force with force, and arrested two of the principal Marylanders concerned. An incident followed which recalls some tale of violence and outrage from the Scotch Border. A warrant for murder was issued against Cresop. He with six followers barricaded his house, and fired on the party who came with the warrant. The house was set on fire. In the confusion which followed one of the besieged party was shot by his own side. A second escaped by the chimney; a third, against whom there was a warrant out for rape, was captured. Finally Cresop himself surrendered. Ogle thereupon wrote to the government of Pennsylvania demanding Cresop's release, and complaining of 'the horrid cruelty' of 'those monsters of men' who had acted for Pennsylvania.

Ogle's attitude could hardly fail to beget a continuance of hostilities, and in the following November a party of sixteen Marylanders broke into the house of the gaoler in Lancaster County, seized his keys and released certain prisoners. This outrage did call forth a reproof from Ogle, but it was not accompanied by any practical attempt either at punishment or redress.

Now at last the Home Government stepped in. Before the perpetration of the outrage just described

[1] Pennsylvania Records, vol. iv. pp. 100–1, 251, *passim*.

the Board of Trade had issued an order that both sides were to keep the peace, and that no more grants were to be made in the disputed territory. In the following May this was followed up by an order from the King in Council, drawing a provisional line between the two colonies which was to be observed, pending a final settlement based on an exact survey. The danger of hostilities was averted, but the question of boundary remained unsettled until after the revolution.[1]

Incidents such as have been just described enable one to understand how great were the hindrances to effective colonial co-operation. The real subject for wonder is not that those difficulties should have operated so long as they did, but that at length a motive could be found strong enough to bring about union in defiance of such obstacles.

Meanwhile an agreement had been made in February 1723 between the representatives of Penn—that is to say his widow and the mortgagees of his estate—on the one side, and Baltimore on the other, that till a settlement had been arranged the existing rights of private landholders should be respected, and no land taken up in the debateable territory.

Agreement in 1723.

This as we have just seen only succeeded so far as to bring about a temporary suspension of hostilities. It did nothing towards effecting a definite settlement.

The dispute between Pennsylvania and Maryland was the most conspicuous instance of the evil done by James II.'s dealings with his territory. But we may doubt whether it was really the worst result. By breaking up his territory into wholly separate provinces the Proprietor of New York sacrificed the best chance, or rather the one chance, of colonial union. The New England colonies were so

Effect of James II.'s policy.

[1] Pennsylvania Records, vol. iv. pp. 254, 298.

strongly imbued by their antecedents, by political and religious sentiment, with the spirit of civic unity among themselves and isolation from the external world, that nothing but some overwhelming necessity appealing to their self-concentrated patriotism could force them to accept any system of colonial union. As isolation was forced on the North colonies by their historical past, so, too, was it forced on the Southern by the physical obstacles to communication. Moreover, in the Northern and the Southern group of colonies alike, the line of continuity was broken by the presence of an element wholly different in character, and, as its neighbours would have deemed, greatly inferior. The heretical origin and antecedents of Rhode Island, the wide religious toleration, the somewhat lax commercial morality, the absence of literary and intellectual life, were as distasteful to the orthodox, law-abiding, well-read Bostonian, as the squalid barbarism of North Carolina was to the Virginia planter or the Charlestown merchant. But if James II.'s territorial rights had been used with wisdom, and his schemes supported by the personal influence which he enjoyed, there might have come into existence, between the southern boundary of Connecticut and the northern of Maryland, a province homogeneous in industry and, therefore, in its method of life, and a stronghold of British authority; ultimately, it may be, capable of serving as the nucleus for a wider unity.

Not merely had James failed to lay the foundation of union, he had introduced active elements of disunion.

On the one hand homogeneity of economical conditions made unity possible, yet on the other hand when once the attempt to impose political unity failed, that homogeneity became in itself an influence making for discord. The sections of what might have been a united province were, by the very similarity of their commerce, driven into rivalry. The colonial documents in the State Paper Office and the records of New York, New Jersey and Pennsylvania tell us of continuous attempts to construct commercial legislation which should either help or hinder the formation of a monopoly favourable to some individual colony. We have seen how in 1679 a dispute arose as to the Duke of York's right still to exercise certain fiscal control over the territories which he had granted away.[1] Eight years later we find the Proprietors of New Jersey protesting to the King against the attempts of the Governor and Assembly of New York to control the trade of their colony by imposing duties.[2]

It is not easy to understand the precise nature of this complaint, since at the time there was no Assembly of New York in existence. But the rest of the document is sufficient as an illustration of the point now before us. 'All colonies,' the Proprietors say, 'must be put on an equal footing, otherwise trade will leave one set of colonies and flow to another.'

Perhaps the only instance of any administrative intelligence shown by Cornbury is when he wrote that traders were leaving New York for places where duties were lower, and that one uniform system of revenue was needed for the whole body of colonies.[3]

Two documents in the State Papers for 1697 illustrate the evils resulting from the absence of any actual control over trade.[4] Penn complains that when goods intended for Pennsylvania are exported in ships which touch at any of the Maryland ports, they have to pay a ten per cent. duty to that colony. As is often the case with Penn, the details are not very clearly set forth. Whether the goods were landed in Maryland and then

[1] Col. State Papers, 1679, 1123.
[2] *Ib.* 1687.
[3] N. Y. Docs. vol. v. p. 55.
[4] Col. Papers, 1696–7, 987, 1358.

forwarded by land or in coasting vessels, or whether the ship carried a joint freight, and landed part of it in Maryland and part afterwards in Pennsylvania, does not appear. All that is clear is that when a ship carried tobacco from Maryland the imports to that colony did not suffice for a return freight, and that the difference was made up by goods for the Pennsylvania market. These goods were, Penn states, delivered in Pennsylvania unopened. Nothing could be more unsatisfactory than a system which enabled one colony to levy duties on the trade of another.

In the same year we find the Proprietors of East New Jersey complaining of the conduct of the revenue officers at New York, in endeavouring to make all vessels bound for New Jersey touch at New York and pay duty there.

We have already seen how a legal adviser of the Crown had, in 1693, put forward the doctrine that the Crown might so far override the special provisions in colonial charters as to appoint Governors.[1] Trevor's opinion only professed to deal with Connecticut and New Jersey.

But to threaten those two colonies was to threaten Rhode Island, Maryland, and the Carolinas, and to take a view of proprietary rights which had never been even suggested before. Charters might be revoked for special cause; to hold that they were, as grants of political power, null and void was to introduce an entirely new principle into colonial administration.

Logically there was nothing in Trevor's opinion to exasperate the men of New Jersey against New York. But in such matters sentiment is at least as strong as logic. Resentment was sure to be as strong against the colony for whose benefit, as it would seem, New Jersey was being sacrificed, as against the power which

[1] *Middle Colonies*, p. 295.

arbitrarily exacted that sacrifice. Nor can we wonder if the colonists looked with distaste on schemes of union, and were backward in co-operation, when they were taught by English officials that union was synonymous with loss of liberty.

Commercial disputes between Virginia and the Carolinas.

Difficulties due to intercolonial trade jealousy were not confined to the middle colonies. In September 1711 we find Spotswood complaining that traders from Virginia passing through South Carolina are subject to duties imposed by the Assembly of the latter colony.[1] We have seen Fitzwilliam, the Surveyor of Customs for North Carolina, complaining that the Assembly of Virginia had prohibited the importation of tobacco from North Carolina,[2] and by this prohibition were possibly driving the North Carolina settlers to manufacture. The action of Virginia was defended by the Governor, William Gooch, on the plea that the system for inspection of tobacco was nullified if North Carolina was allowed to import. He meets Fitzwilliam's argument as to the danger of the colonists manufacturing by pointing out that North Carolina had other commodities to export, whereas if the Virginia tobacco trade failed the inhabitants of that colony would be left resourceless and have to manufacture.[3] In spite of Gooch's defence of the Act it was vetoed on the recommendation of the Lords of Trade.

Difference of currency.

Another hindrance to intercolonial trade was found in the differences of currency which obtained. Theoretically indeed the British currency was the medium of exchange everywhere. Practically it was superseded in the South by tobacco, in the North either by that curious system of barter under which

[1] Spotswood's Letters, vol. i. p. 112.

[2] *V.s.* p. 84.

[3] N. Car. Records, vol. ii. p. 773.

commodities were made currency at a rate arbitrarily determined,[1] or else as we shall see in paper, depreciated in different degrees in the various colonies. Intercolonial trade might exist in defiance of such conditions; it could hardly thrive.

More serious still, especially in the eyes of English administrators, was the military weakness which resulted from the lack of colonial unity. It may be argued that the failure of the expedition against Canada in 1689 was due not so much to the difficulties which necessarily beset a confederated force, as to the personal failings of Leisler. But the records of the colonies are full of lessons as to the weakness created by colonial disunion. Here again the policy of James introduced disunion into that very quarter where union was of the greatest importance. The valley of the Hudson and the other lines of communication between the Ohio and the Atlantic were the points where the English colonies had most to dread from a civilized enemy. If such an attack were supported by a force acting from the sea, France might be established in a central position where she would be a source of danger to the whole group of colonies.

Military dangers of disunion.

Fletcher's one redeeming virtue as a colonial official was his energy and promptitude in military matters. In March 1694 he reported to the Secretary of State, Lord Nottingham, that his demands for help were ignored by Connecticut, and that from Pennsylvania he could get nothing but good wishes. Phipps, the Governor of Massachusetts, is, Fletcher says, 'a machine moved by every fanatical finger, the contempt of wise men and the sport of fools.'[2]

Two years later Fletcher reports that the Assembly of Rhode Island have raised troops and voted a sum for

[1] *Puritan Colonies*, vol. ii. p. 44.
[2] Col. State Papers, 1693, 178.

the payment of them. But they are so long raising it that the troops get tired of waiting and disperse.[1]

In 1708 we find an entry in the Pennsylvania Records which illustrates the difficulties arising from a want of organized control. Evans, the Governor of Pennsylvania, called the attention of the Assembly to the undefended condition of the coast. A discussion then arose as to the supreme naval authority on the adjoining waters. Evans held that it was vested in Seymour, the Governor of Maryland. The Assembly contended that it belonged to Cornbury.[2]

In 1711 North Carolina was invaded by the Tuscarora Indians. For two years the colony suffered all

Virginia and North Carolina.[3]

the horrors of an Indian warfare. Had the two neighbouring colonies, Virginia and South Carolina, been under some central authority there can be no doubt that joint action taken with vigour might at once have crushed the enemy. As it was, when Spotswood proposed that help should be given he met with no support from either the Council or the Assembly. They felt that the settlers of North Carolina had brought their misfortunes on themselves by their own misconduct and by encroachments on the Indian territory. The Governor of North Carolina could not give any guarantee that he would be able to find rations for the Virginian contingent.

Spotswood did not think a whit better of the North Carolina settlers than the Assembly did. But he saw that the real question to be considered was not the deserts of North Carolina, but the security of the English colonies as a whole. After much difficulty he induced the Assembly to vote three hundred men and a thousand pounds, together with a supply of cloth, for

[1] Col. State Papers, 1696, 522. [2] Pennsylvania Records, vol. ii. p. 144.

[3] For all this see Spotswood's Letters, vol. i., and the North Carolina Records, vol. ii.

the deported fugitives from North Carolina. He himself fully admits that his policy of co-operation was hampered by the factious and short-sighted action of North Carolina. 'That country,' he writes, 'is so miserably distracted that they are not like to do anything for their own defence, their later Assembly having in a manner resolved to sacrifice their country to the rage of the heathen, because they could not introduce into the government the persons most obnoxious for fomenting the late rebellion and civil war there.' And even at the very time that he was urging the Assembly with such measure of success as we have seen to come to the help of their neighbours, he is in his despatches complaining that the people of North Carolina 'have drawn misery on themselves' by continued disorders and general licentiousness, and by encroachments on Indian territory, and he is denouncing 'the stupidity and dissensions' of their government.

Colonial supineness and intercolonial discord were not the only difficulties with which Spotswood had to contend. Quakerism has played a conspicuous, and at times an honourable, part in the drama of American colonization. But there were many times when those responsible for the safety of the colonies must have wished that no Quaker had ever set foot on American soil. If we may believe Spotswood, the Quakers in North Carolina 'broached doctrines so monstrous as their brethren in England never avowed. They refused to work at the fortifications, and declared that if the French came as invaders they would be forced to supply them with food. They were, Spotswood thinks, hardened in their resistance by the action of their brethren in England, who kept a common fund to bear the legal expenses of any of the society who might be prosecuted for such conduct. Yet so lightly and inconsistently did these Carolina Quakers hold their doctrines, that they had only a few years before borne part in an armed rebellion.

The dissatisfaction of the Virginians with their neighbours was not allayed by the termination of the war. We find the Assembly making it matter of complaint that the Governor of North Carolina had concluded an independent peace with the Indians without inserting any stipulation for the security of Virginia.

Conversely three years later the North Carolina settlers fell out with the Saraw Indians. The Secretary of that colony wrote to the Assembly of Virginia requesting them not to supply the Saraws with arms. The Virginian Assembly replied that their colony was in alliance with the Saraws, and that in their opinion the blame of the quarrel lay with North Carolina.

South Carolina had also sent a contingent, not of her own colonists, but composed of seven or eight hundred Indian allies, with apparently a small auxiliary force of white soldiers.[1] The uselessness of the savage as an ally for any sustained operation is a lesson written large on almost every page of colonial history. After an initial success, five hundred of the Indians dispersed, and thereupon the government of South Carolina made an independent peace with the enemy, without making any stipulation for the security of Virginia.

Two years later South Carolina was invaded by the Yamassees. North Carolina had but little to lose. Such a semi-barbarous community could quickly reconstitute itself even after something like extirpation. It was very different with a wealthy commercial colony, such as South Carolina. The destruction of such a province would, as Spotswood pointed out, do

[1] The Records say 701 Indians, and make no mention of a white contingent. Glen also in Records says 800 Indians and fifty whites. N. Car. Records, vol. i. pp. 839, 954.

much to liberate the savage from that consciousness of inferiority which was our best safeguard. There was also the very real danger that while the colonists were defending their inland possessions, Charlestown and Port Royal might fall a prey to France or Spain.[1]

Everything tends to show that the general standard of intelligence and public spirit was far higher in North than in South Carolina. Yet to help South Carolina was almost as difficult as it had been to help her northern neighbour. At the first alarm Spotswood sent a hundred and sixty muskets with ammunition, followed soon after by a contingent of a hundred and eighteen men. The Virginians subsequently averred that this assistance had been granted on the following conditions: The men were to receive twenty-two and sixpence a month in Virginian currency and their uniform. South Carolina was to send slaves to take the place of the men who were in service. Moreover, the Virginian troops were to be commanded by their own officers.[2] If we are to believe one witness, these conditions were only asked for by the Virginian government, and not approved by that of South Carolina.[3] Be that as it may, it seems certain that the South Carolina government tried to compound for all its obligations by a lump payment per man of four pounds in South Carolina paper-money, a sum only equal, as Spotswood tells us, to one pound in Virginian currency. The result was that no volunteers could be had for service in South Carolina. It was not merely on the

[1] Spotswood to Secretary Stanhope, Letters, vol. ii. p. 121.

[2] The conditions are stated in a memorial drawn up by some Virginian traders, and printed in the N. Carolina Records, vol. ii. p. 201. The statement, with the exception of that about the officering of the Virginian troops, is confirmed by Spotswood in a despatch to the Lords of Trade, Letters, vol. ii. p. 238.

[3] This is stated in a document unsigned, but seemingly put forward by some responsible person. N. Car. Records, vol. ii. p. 253.

occasion of some special emergency or in actual time of war that the evil effects of disunion were felt. They ran through all the relations and dealings of the colonists with the savages. The latter saw the contrast between the definite and uniform policy which guided the action of the French colonists and the wavering attitude and internal dissensions of the English. Spotswood, more than any other English administrator, seems to have been alive to this danger. At the very outset of the Tuscarora war we find him complaining that the natives see each colony acting for itself, and cannot understand that all belong to one nation.

Again, in 1717, he complains that the Senecas, in spite of being in formal alliance with New York, have been raiding on the Virginian frontier. They must be made to understand that their engagements with New York bind them to the whole body of English colonies.[1]

In 1720 he writes to the President of the Council of New York. His letter recapitulates the old grievances and sets forth new ones. In 1719 the Mohawks attacked the Indian allies of Virginia and carried off fifteen prisoners. The party halted at Conestago in Pennsylvania. John Cartledge, a justice in Pennsylvania, finding that the prisoners were 'Virginians born,' intercedes and sues for their release. The Mohawks refuse this contemptuously. They have, they say, 'made a clear path to pass and repass to and from the southward. They have removed all obstacles out of the way, and they expect to have free recourse for their people among all the English plantations while they are making war.'

This is not the only instance of Mohawk arrogance. Spotswood himself made overtures to one of the chiefs, which were 'haughtily refused.'

The truth is, he points out, that New York in its

[1] Letters, vol. ii. p. 252.

anxiety to stand well with the Five Nations, has been over-submissive. 'The burden of your Indian song, that Albany must be the only place of their treating with the Indians and their allies, is a concession which lessens the English in the eyes of both the pagan and Christian world.'

Finally, Spotswood recalls that sombre Virginia tradition, Bacon's rebellion, and all the calamities which then followed from a lack of firmness in dealing with the savages.[1]

Inter-colonial difficulties about piracy.

The lack of any organized methods of action also did much to hinder the effectual suppression of those kindred evils, piracy and smuggling. Here, again, we are dependent for detailed information on Spotswood.[2] Early in 1719 the noted pirate Teach, or as Spotswood calls him Thatch, lost his ship and was left off the coast of South Carolina with four sloops. His crew mostly dispersed, some going to Pennsylvania, others joining a well-known pirate, once a reputable planter in South Carolina, Major Steed Bonnet. Teach was left with one sloop, with which he pretended to have taken up the calling of a peaceful trader. Spotswood manned two sloops with officers and crews borrowed from King's ships. They attacked the pirates and captured the sloop, killing Teach and seven of his men.

The South Carolinians, not satisfied at being rid of a public pest, complained that they had not been allowed a share in the enterprise, and that the vessel was taken to Virginia to be condemned and sold. Spotswood's attitude was conciliatory. He explained that secrecy was necessary, and that the risk was less for Virginia than for South Carolina, since the latter colony was more exposed to reprisals from the pirates.

[1] The letter is in the Pennsylvania Records, vol. iii. p. 83; cf. Proud, vol. ii. p. 132.

[2] Letters, vol. ii. pp. 273, 305.

The goods will sell better in Virginia than in South Carolina, and they shall not be disposed of till any claims that the inhabitants of South Carolina may make have been considered.[1]

The men of South Carolina had at least the decency to abstain from any display of sympathy with Teach, and only complained that they were not allowed a share in his destruction. But, if we may believe Spotswood, the pirate had an active friend in the Governor of North Carolina. In spite of Teach's well-known reputation, the Governor had allowed him to retain plundered goods on the plea that they were salvage from a wreck, and there were others in the colony who denounced Teach's captors as the murderers of an honest man.[2]

Schemes for colonial union.

As we have already seen, during the latter years of the seventeenth century colonial union was in modern language 'in the air.' The need for it is urged by more than one colonial official, and definite suggestions are made for partial consolidation on the same lines as James II.'s creation of a province under Andros. But the first definite and comprehensive scheme of colonial union was put forward by Penn. In February 1698 he submitted to the British Government the details of his proposal.[3] The very first provision shows how widely Penn differed on one essential question from most of his co-religionists. It also shows a characteristic tendency to use terms which were incapable of precise definition. Two delegates from each colony, men 'qualified for sense, sobriety and substance,' were to meet once a year or oftener in time of war, every two years in time of peace. A Commissioner appointed by the King was to preside, and was also to be Commander-in-Chief. New York was

[1] Letters, vol. ii. p. 274. [2] *Ib.* p. 318.

[3] Colonial State Papers, 1698, 694.

suggested as a convenient meeting place. The Congress was to settle all judicial questions in which two or more colonies are involved, and to deal with questions of intercolonial commerce and common defence.

The dissimilarity of interests and conditions was perhaps not the most serious obstacle to any scheme of union. Every such scheme carried with it as an almost inevitable condition some strengthening of the control exercised by the Home Government. Not till union presented itself in a form which made it the enemy, instead of the ally, of British supremacy would it be acceptable to the colonists.

Improved communication between the colonies.

In the meantime something was being done to overcome the merely physical and mechanical hindrances to union. We have seen how, during his short and unhappy tenure of office, Lovelace had established postal communication between New York and Boston. In 1692 this was extended, and a patent granted for a general postal service between Philadelphia and Piscataqua.[1] In 1710 Parliament passed an Act determining the rates of postage to be paid in the colonies.

The service seems to have fallen into good hands and to have been efficiently administered, with the result that by 1715 there was one service from Philadelphia to Portsmouth. The time occupied varied, as in such a country was but natural, in summer and in winter; in the former a letter took a week to travel from New York to Boston, in winter double that time. We are not told how long was needed for the further journey at each end.[2]

In 1712 a clumsy attempt was made to introduce

[1] Letter from Hamilton to the Postmaster-General, Col. Papers, Jan. 24, 1722.

[2] Note to Herman Moll's Map, May 1715. Quoted by Mr. Palfrey, vol. iv. p. 330.

a postal service into Maryland. The duty of transmitting letters was intrusted to the various county sheriffs.[1]

In 1718 the Postmaster-General for the colonies endeavoured to extend the existing communication by post from Williamsburg to Philadelphia. The Assembly of Virginia, then in a disaffected mood and hungry for a fight with government, protested on the ground that the post-office brought in a surplus revenue over and above its expenses.[2] It is singular that it should have been left to Virginia to take up this line while the objection had escaped the ever watchful patriots of Massachusetts. Probably the explanation is to be found in the fact that the postal service was a far greater boon to the Boston merchant than to the Virginian trader.

The agitation, however, appears to have subsided, and at least as early as 1732 the colonies from Virginia to New Hampshire were linked together by a postal service.[3]

The difficulties of communication, perhaps even more the habits and temper of the settlers, prevented any extension of the system to or through North Carolina, and thus South Carolina stood detached, resembling in that, as in other respects, the West Indian Islands rather than the colonies on the mainland.

The value of the postal service was not limited to the delivery of letters. It was easily combined with, even if it did not formally include, a system of providing horses and escorts for travellers. It also brought as a natural consequence the developement of roads.

[1] Laws of Maryland. Mr. Mereness makes no mention of this. As a rule it is ill gleaning after that most diligent inquirer.

[2] Spotswood's Letters, vol. ii. p. 280.

N. York Gazette, July 8, 1732. Quoted in Mr. Whitehead's edition of the N. Jersey Archives, vol. xi. p. 289.

We cannot say that these increased facilities for communication did much to create a sense of colonial unity. The utmost we can say is that, when the time came that a sentiment of nationality was aroused, the mechanical hindrances which might have neutralized it were in part at least swept away.

CHAPTER II.

ADMINISTRATIVE DEVELOPEMENT.

General character of the subject.

THE student of colonial history during the seventeenth century is mainly concerned with the construction and growth of political machinery within the various colonial areas. By the end of the century that process was practically finished. In each colony the constitution of the legislative and of the executive bodies respectively might be considered as settled and complete. The interest of the history turns not on the composition of those bodies, but on the limitation or extension of their powers, on the adjustment whether by conflict or compromise of the relations between the various members of the body politic in each colony. This is further complicated by the addition of a new factor. With the accession of the House of Hanover, Parliament by an undefined but real process acquired powers and functions to which it had before been a stranger. This brings with it a change, important though informal and indefinite, in the position of the colonial legislatures. Hitherto the Governor and the Council had been, save in the self-governed colonies of Connecticut and Rhode Island, the representatives of the Crown,[1] and in no way connected with or dependent on any other external power. Parliament had no part in either the appointment or the control of

[1] There was one exception to this. In Massachusetts the Council was originally nominated by the Crown, but afterwards elected by the General Court. See *New England*, vol. ii. p. 375.

the colonial Governor. The instructions which he had to carry out were given him by the Crown, acting with the advice of the Privy Council and of a special body of Commissioners, the Board of Trade and Plantations. The only manner in which Parliamentary authority touched the colonies was through the very broad and general restriction imposed by the Acts of Navigation. But as the eighteenth century advances the relations between the colonies and Parliament become more intimate and more complex. This is due to two causes. Under the first and second Hanoverian Kings the nominal authority of the Crown becomes more and more the virtual authority of a cabinet dependent for its continued existence on the House of Commons, and continuously amenable to that body. The line which had hitherto separated, not in theory merely but in practice, the administrative action of the Crown from that of Parliament becomes vague and indefinite. In the instructions given by the Crown to Belcher in 1720 there is a most significant clause. He is to warn the colonists that in the case of misbehaviour their conduct will be brought under the notice of Parliament.[1]

In 1716 Northey, then Attorney-General, gave an important opinion on the relations of the colonies to Parliament. In a Crown colony a temporary Act might be vetoed by an instruction to the Governor; but in the case of proprietary colonies such veto must be made by Act of Parliament. This attributed to Parliament authority over the colonies which, alike in kind and extent, went wholly beyond anything that had been claimed for it in the seventeenth century.[2]

Again, concurrently with this change, a change took place in the relations of the colonies to the mother

[1] The instructions are given in Winsor's *Memorial History of Boston*, vol. i. p. 58.

[2] N. Car. Records, vol. ii. p. 136.

country. Their trade becomes so complex and is so important a factor in the general well-being of the empire that it imperatively demands regulation and control. And as from a commercial, so too from a military, point of view the colonies are no longer disconnected items. In 1660 the conception of America as the battle-field of the Old-World Powers, striving for empire, had not, so far as we can judge, crossed the mind of a single Englishman. By 1720 it was a commonplace among politicians and pamphleteers. Thus the problems of colonial administration were inevitably forced upon a Parliament which was unhappily furnished neither with the machinery, the knowledge, nor the principles needed for the task.

One consequence of this is that for the student of American constitutional history the area of observation, if one may use the expression, changes. Massachusetts still maintains its importance by its continuous and organized resistance to the authority of the Crown. Connecticut and Rhode Island, so full of interest in the seventeenth century, fall into the background. On the other hand the middle provinces, commanding as they did the gateway to Canada, and offering beyond any other of the colonies a vulnerable point for the attacks of the French and their Indian allies, become of the first importance. The relations, mainly relations of hostility, between the colonies and the Home Government during the eighteenth century turn chiefly on two sets of issues, and may be divided into two groups. The one set arise out of detached questions of policy, mostly of military policy. For the most part they resemble one another, and turn on the unwillingness of the colonies to bear their share in any connected scheme of military action. But they can scarcely be regarded as continuous, and can be best dealt with incidentally as they come before us. The second group, and constitutionally by far the more important of the two, turn on permanent questions of principle, on the persistent determination of both parties —the Home Government on the one side, the colonial Assembly on the other—to deal with certain regularly recurring questions either by interpreting enactments and precedents in their own favour, or, where no enactment or applicable precedent could be found, by creating such.

The subjects of dispute fall under certain well-defined heads. But before dealing with them it will be well to do again shortly and comprehensively what has been already done implicitly and in detail, to review the composition and attitude of the conflicting forces.

Distribution of political forces.

In each colony, setting aside the Proprietary colonies and also those abnormal cases which have just been mentioned, the interests of the Crown were secured by the right to nominate a Governor and a Council. The Council had three distinct sets of functions. It formed an upper chamber, and as such its consent was necessary to all legislation. It was the supreme judicial court, and it advised the Governor on executive questions. Pennsylvania and Maryland differed in that there the Governor and Council were nominated by the Proprietor. Moreover in Pennsylvania the Council was merely an administrative body with no legislative status.

The absence of any permanent guiding principle in the adjustment of power between the Governor and the Council was a fruitful source of dispute in more than one colony.

Such a dispute was natural enough in Massachusetts where the members of the Council were, as we have seen, not the nominees of the Crown but the representatives of the people. It may seem singular that it should have extended to those colonies where the Council and the Governor were both appointed by the Crown. But the temper in which political power is exercised does not depend solely on the source from which it proceeds. In 1729 Governor Cosby, of New York, in spite of the decision of the law officers in the case of Massachusetts, claimed the right to sit and vote when the Council was acting as a legislative chamber. Cosby was arbitrary and unpopular. The Council, headed by Lewis Morris, resisted his claim and were supported by the Board of Trade.[1] Inasmuch as New York and New Jersey were then and often afterwards placed under one Governor, this victory of the Council in the one colony brought about a like result in the other.

Similar disputes arose in North and South Carolina. In North Carolina the Council prevailed. In South Carolina a compromise was arrived at, and the Governor was allowed to be present at the meetings of the Council, but neither to join in discussion nor to vote.[2]

This series of disputes is a good illustration of the weakness of the colonial system in the eighteenth century. Its main defect was not that the control exercised by the Home Government was lax, but that, such as it was, it had no definiteness and no uniformity. This was largely due to the manner in which the authority was scattered among bodies with no common principle of action. The King and Council both vetoed the Acts of the colonial legislatures, and also issued instructions to Governors, which in many cases were practically enactments binding on the colonists. The every-day details of administration were controlled by the Board of Trade. The action of the King in Council and that of the Board of Trade were, on the whole, likely to be in harmony. But, as we have just seen in questions affecting the trade of the colonies, it was impossible to exclude the action of Parliament. At the same time there was no machinery through which

[1] N. Y. Docs. vol. v. p. 975.

[2] Authorities quoted in Greene's *The Provincial Governor*, p. 42.

Parliament could be kept informed of the special conditions of colonial life and the needs and sentiments of the colonies. It was an equally serious defect that there was nothing to ensure any harmony of action or any uniformity of system among those various controlling powers. This defect meets us at every turn during the whole of the eighteenth century, and goes far to account for the tragedy with which the colonial history of that period ends. What was needed was a permanent colonial department, through which and in concert with which both Crown and Parliament should act in all colonial questions. Especially would such a department have been valuable in connexion with the endless disputes between Governors and Assemblies on questions of fees, salaries, and tenure of subordinate offices. As it was, such questions were determined to some extent on general principles and according to precedent, but far more in conformity with the judgement of individuals and according to the pertinacity shown by the conflicting parties.

One result of a permanent department would have been to call into existence a class of colonial officials with definite principles and traditions, and with abundant facilities for exchanging ideas and experiences. As it was, a Governor more often than not went out as it were into an unexplored territory, profiting nothing by what his predecessors had done or failed to do, learning no useful lesson from past victories or defeats.

Need of a colonial department.

It would have been not a less important function of a special colonial department to furnish both the advisers of the Crown and the Houses of Parliament with the special information which they needed on colonial questions. That want was inadequately and unsatisfactorily supplied by the system of colonial agents, a system which steadily developed during the eighteenth century.

The colonial agent.[1]

The earliest form of agency was usually of the nature of a commission appointed to approach the Home Government on some special question. We have seen how important a part the agency of Massachusetts played in the disputes over the charter towards the end of the seventeenth century. Gradually, as legislative and administrative interference became more frequent and more continuous, the importance of the agency increased. The agent was not always an inhabitant of the colony for which he acted. In some instances he was an English merchant, a *proxenos* as one may call him. In such cases it is evident that he would have to rely not so much on his familiarity with the wants and conditions of the colony as on his knowledge of English politics and his capacity for influencing leading politicians. The lack of an agent or the incompetence of an agent appointed might seriously prejudice a colony. Thus, when the subsidy was granted to the Southern colonies as remuneration for their sufferings and expenditure in the war against Canada, North Carolina was at a disadvantage because she had no agent.[2] This was due to the action of Governor Dobbs, who asserted his own right to appoint the agent for the colony, and, when the Assembly refused to admit it, vetoed their nomination. This is not the only instance to be found in the colonial records of disputes arising out of the claim to appoint an agent. In 1748 we find Clinton, the Governor of New York, protesting against the appointment of an agent in which the Governor and Council had not been consulted, and petitioning the Board of Trade that the man so appointed should not

[1] The history of the colonial agency is well treated in an article in the *Political Quarterly* for March 1901. There are also some pertinent remarks on the subject in Mr. Saunders's Introduction to the sixth volume of the North Carolina Records.

[2] Records of North Carolina, vol. v. p. 477.

be allowed to present any memorial or petition without Clinton's approval.[1]

It would be hard to find a stronger instance of the unintelligent and unsystematic fashion in which colonial administrators approached political problems. The Governor was in regular communication with the authorities in England. To supply him with an advocate who should speak with the authority of a colonial representative was on the face of it an absurdity. There was far more reason in the claim often made by the colonial Assemblies to nominate the agent as their own special spokesman, for it is obvious that if the agent were appointed by the Governor, the Assembly and their constituents had no channel through which to communicate with the Home Government. Yet undoubtedly the most effective and satisfactory arrangement would have been one which vested the appointment jointly in all the parties interested, and which thus gave to his position something of a quasi-judicial character, and in some measure guaranteed impartiality.

Apart from questions arising out of some special and individual circumstances, we may classify the subjects of dispute between the colonies and the mother country during the eighteenth century under three heads:

Various subjects of dispute.

1. Official fees and salaries.

2. The right of the colonial Assemblies to issue paper money.

3. The restrictions imposed by the British Government on the commerce and the productive industry of the colonies.

If we accepted the traditional view of this subject we should probably regard this order as representing the exact reverse of the real importance of the respective

[1] N. Y. Documents, vol. vi. p. 420.

issues. But a careful study of records will show that the restraints on production, even if unwise in themselves, only enforced and confirmed a system which had its rise in the economic conditions of colonial life. On the other points just named the attitude of the Home Government, and perhaps even more of the colonial officials, was felt to be a real grievance. The demands made from the colonists, the restrictions imposed on them, were often in perfect conformity with equity and reason. It can seldom be said that the method of enforcement was sympathetic, conciliatory, or even intelligent.

These are faults whose appointed Nemesis cannot fail. The revolt of the colonies undoubtedly had for its immediate occasion a developement of British fiscal policy, in theory a mere extension of the existing system, but in fact so violent that it could not but be regarded as a revolution. But the temper of mind, the habits of thought and action which made successful resistance possible had their origin mainly in the other causes which have been specified. The disputes over salaries and over paper money had kept alive an abiding spirit of bitterness and vindictiveness between the colonists and those set in authority over them, and had furnished the former with continuous training in the arts of political conflict.

It will probably be the best method of treating the administrative history of the colonies during the eighteenth century to take the above-named causes of dispute in order, and to deal with them as we find them displaying themselves in the various fields of action.

I. FEES AND SALARIES.

This subject admits to some extent of being subdivided into two heads. In several instances the colonial Governors put forward a claim to fix the fees which had to be paid in connexion with certain official transactions, such as the formal transfer of land. The question of salaries was a much more serious one. Economical restrictions apart, almost the only fixed principle to which the British administration of the colonies held with real persistence was the determination that neither Governors nor judges in the colonies should be dependent for their payment on the good-will of colonial Assemblies, but that a fixed salary should be voted once for all, and should not be revocable.

Two questions involved.

These two subjects of dispute were so far alike that they both turned on the right of the colonial Assemblies to keep the power of the purse in their own hands, and on the right of the colonists to be taxed only by their own Representatives. But though the theoretical principle involved in both disputes might be the same, they differed widely in their practical importance. The determination to make the whole of the executive and the judiciary dependent for their support on the good-will of the Assembly went in practice far nearer to a claim of administrative independence than the attempt to transfer from the Governor to the Assembly the regulation of official fees. There is, moreover, this important difference. The dispute over the fees was fought out between the popular Representatives and the Governor without the intervention of the English authorities. The battle over the salaries of the Governor and judges involved the Assembly of Massachusetts in a bitter and prolonged conflict with the Crown and its advisers.

Fees in Maryland.

The colony in which the question of fees first gave rise to dispute was Maryland. There in 1689 the House of Representatives had formally claimed the right to determine the amount of official fees. That claim was resisted by the Governor and Council. A compromise was arrived at; fees were not to be altered without the consent of the House of Burgesses; they were to have a veto, but no independent control over the fees.

In spite of this the Burgesses originated more than one motion for the reduction of fees, but in no case could they obtain the concurrence of the Upper House.[1]

Like every question of finance in Maryland and Virginia, that of fees was complicated by the want of a proper medium of exchange. The recognised currency, tobacco, was of varying quality, and its value varied with abundance or sparseness of crop. As a consequence a claim for a change in fees might always be fortified by an argument based on altered value.

A somewhat similar process took place in North Carolina. The Assembly did not claim the right to fix fees. But they did claim the right to declare the value at which silver should be accepted in payment of fees, and to permit payment to be made in paper depreciated to one third of its nominal value. In forbidding this the Governor and Council were, so it was usually contended, claiming the right to fix fees. In the course of the dispute the Assembly used ominous words. 'Whereas by the Royal Charter granted by King Charles the Second to the Lords Proprietors of Carolina it is granted that the inhabitants of the Province shall have, possess, and enjoy all Liberties, Franchises, and Privileges as are held, possessed, and enjoyed in the kingdom of England.' They go on to say it is the undoubted right and privilege of the people of England that they shall not be taxed or made liable to pay any sum

Fees in North Carolina.[2]

[1] Proceedings and Acts of Assembly. Journals of Upper House, referred to by Mr. Mereness. Stainer's *Restoration of the Proprietors of Maryland*, p. 298.

[2] N. Car. Records, vol. iii. pp. 262, 271, 297.

or sums of money or fees other than such as are by law established. Apparently Burrington's resistance was so far effectual that the Assembly failed to carry any formal vote embodying their views. But an expression of opinion is not necessarily a *brutum fulmen* because it is not adopted. Declarations such as those made by the Assembly helped to hold up that constitutional claim to which the colonists clung in their contest with the mother country.

Dispute about the Governor's salary in Massachusetts.[1]

The disputes in Maryland and North Carolina might be looked on as an isolated skirmish, illustrating the watchfulness of the Assembly over the financial rights of their constituents, and suggesting rather than actually asserting a claim to fiscal independence. Far wider reaching in the principles involved and in its methods was the struggle over official salaries in Massachusetts.

The battle began with the appointment of Colonel Shute as Governor in 1716. The conclusion of peace with France had left a large number of unemployed soldiers, with claims on the Crown, and a colonial governorship was an easy and obvious form of recognition. Such was Hunter in New York and Spotswood in Virginia. Shute may not have had the exceptional tact and conciliatory temper of Hunter, nor the strenuous energy and public spirit of Spotswood. But he appears to have been a painstaking, conscientious, and clear-headed official. Unfortunately his lot was cast among a community which could be understood and controlled only by a man of exceptional perception, experience, and strength of will. Throughout the eighteenth

[1] In 1729, the Lower House of Assembly in Massachusetts instructed the members for Boston to prepare a full report of all the proceedings in connexion with the Governor's salary. This was published as a pamphlet in the same year. A copy of it is in the British Museum. I have relied on this for my account of the dispute, with occasional help from Hutchinson and Chalmers.

century the representative of royalty was to the politicians of New England a man to be suspected, thwarted, and outwitted, and we shall find over and over again men who in other colonies would have had creditable careers failing when brought face to face with those persistent and often unscrupulous masters of political strategy who guided the councils of Massachusetts.

In one way the appointment of Shute might have been supposed to be specially acceptable to the people of Massachusetts. He was a Dissenter. His brother, afterwards Lord Barrington, was a member of Parliament and an influential man among the Nonconformists. Their mother was a daugher of Joseph Caryl, a leading minister among the Independents.[1] If this in any measure influenced the advisers of the Crown in making the appointment, they deserve credit for more sympathy with the special needs and wishes of the colonists than has often been attributed to them.

There were other matters beside the question of salary which begot and kept alive a spirit of hostility between Shute and the colonists. He was instructed to enforce certain unpopular, though perfectly reasonable and necessary, restraints on the wasteful cutting of ship timber on unoccupied lands by private individuals.[2] The Assembly on the other hand showed their resentment of Shute's policy by refusing to vote money, as was usual, for the public celebration of the King's birthday, accession, or coronation, and, which was far more serious, by withholding the small grant which was necessary to enable the Governor to keep the neighbouring Indians in good humour.[3]

Another matter of dispute was the right of the Assembly to elect its own Speaker independent of the Governor. In 1720 Elisha Cooke, a leading member of the popular party, was chosen Speaker. Cooke had

[1] Hutchinson, vol. ii. p. 215. [2] *Ib.* p. 230. [3] *Ib.* pp. 238–9.

been prominent among those who had encroached on waste ground and destroyed the timber claimed by the Crown. Possibly for this reason Shute vetoed the appointment. The Assembly protested. Shute however obtained an opinion from the Attorney-General confirming his action. The Assembly then chose another Speaker, and reported their proceeding to the Governor, who approved. He was then told by the Assembly that they had reported the appointment to him not for approval, but only for information.

Shute's right to veto the Assembly's choice of Councillors could not be contested. But it was rendered of very little effect, since whenever it was exercised the Councillor in question was chosen a member of the Assembly. Three 'negative' Councillors, as Shute somewhat oddly calls them, sat for Boston, and it was a common maxim that a negative Councillor makes a good Representative.[1] The explanation which Shute himself gives of the temper and methods of his opponents does not give one a high idea of his power of clear thought. 'Owing to the requirement the men must reside in the town for which they sit. Thus, the greatest part of them are of small fortunes and mean education, men of the best sense and circumstances generally residing in or near Boston. . . . Were it not for this Act the Assembly would undoubtedly consist of men of much better sense, temper, and fortunes than they (*sic*) do at present.'

Yet Shute then goes on to say that 'the inhabitants of Boston are too much disposed to a levelling spirit, too apt to be mutineers and disorderly, and to support the House of Representatives in any steps they take towards encroaching on the prerogatives of the Crown.'

[1] All this is set forth in a Memorial from Shute sent to the King soon after his arrival. It is published in Perry's *Collections relating to the American Colonial Church. Massachusetts*, p. 121; cf. Hutchinson, vol. ii. p. 235.

Boston is the centre of disaffection, and yet the Assembly is to be made less disaffected by a change which would strengthen the influence of Boston.

Despairing of a peaceful settlement Shute obtained leave of absence, and, coming to England, laid his grievance about a salary before the Privy Council. The form of the proceedings which followed will illustrate the cumbrousness of the existing colonial system. The matter was referred to a commitee of the Privy Council, and by them passed on to the Board of Trade and Plantations. They reported that the Assembly of Massachusetts should be advised to pay the salary, and the Secretary of State drafted an order to that effect. But the death of the King, bringing with it an entire change of State officials, wiped out all that had been done, and left the Assembly practically masters of the field. That well illustrates one main advantage which the popular Representative enjoyed in any contest with authority. Governors and their subordinate officials came and went, and nothing kept alive any permanence or continuity in their policy. Their local experience was short; their local interest evanescent. On the other hand, the Assembly was an undying body with a continuous policy, not distracted by cross-purposes or variations of personal character, ever on the scene of conflict, and following every incident of the strife with unsleeping watchfulness.

Appointment of Burnet.

Shute, intelligent and well-intentioned though he was, and a Nonconformist to boot, was probably not a man of exactly the type to commend himself to the citizens of Massachusetts. His successor, William Burnet, might be supposed to start with antecedents which would give him a strong claim on the good-will of New Englanders. His father was one of the most conspicuous of Whig and latitudinarian Churchmen. The son had theological interests which would recommend him to the New Englanders. He had written a book on the Interpretation of Prophecy, designed to show that Daniel foretold the political events of the sixteenth century. Burnet had also attested his loyalty to Protestantism by a controversial letter designed to reclaim one who, having in infancy been taken prisoner by the French Canadians, had been brought up in the tenets of Rome. Nor was Burnet without colonial experience, as he had held from 1720 to 1730 the governorships of New York and New Jersey. His introduction to official life was characteristic of the eighteenth century, and of the methods adopted in selecting men for posts of responsibility in the colonies. He was Controller of the Customs in London. Being a heavy loser by the South Sea Bubble and having a large family he wished for a more lucrative post. Accordingly he arranged with Hunter, who was probably anxious to return to England, for an exchange of offices, and the exchange was approved by the advisers of the Crown. After holding the governorship of New York for eight years, Burnet was transferred to Massachusetts. We read that Burnet was received into his new province 'with a splendour and magnificence never known in these parts of the world.'[1] A train of carriages met him at Roxbury and escorted him to Boston. A member of the house of Mather welcomed him in couplets of astounding pomposity and inanity. It is startling to find this descendant of the great Puritan house disporting himself amid the polytheistic conventions of Augustan literature:

> 'What the tall cedar shows to different woods
> Is Burnet's comely stature 'mongst the gods.'

The public is confidently assured that the Governor's

[1] Taken from a contemporary authority by Drake, *History of Boston*, p. 581.

greatness in this world is to be made complete by glory in the next:

'Then may the widening soul, arrayed in light,
Thro' flaming squadrons wing its spacious flight,
Where, 'midst the immortal gods' superior states,
Your crown all gilt with dazzling glory waits.'

It was soon made clear that the courtesy with which the citizens of Massachusetts received their new Governor was not intended to carry with it any abatement of their claim to fiscal independence. Burnet at once told the Assembly that his instructions required him to secure the grant of a fixed salary. The amount was specified; it was to be a thousand pounds yearly. The omission to comply with this would be regarded as 'a manifest mark of undutiful behaviour,' and would require the special consideration of Parliament.[1]

The Assembly refuses to grant a fixed salary.

Burnet added a comment of his own. As the King had through the Civil List a fixed grant from Parliament, so ought his representative to have one from the Assembly. Otherwise the dignity of the Governor would suffer, and with it that of the other branches of the legislature. We may be sure that every member of the Assembly felt that this mysterious advantage which the Assembly were to derive from the reflected dignity of the Governor would be a very poor equivalent for the substantial power given by the control of the purse.

The Assembly, however, showed their personal good-will to Burnet by voting not an annual salary, but a grant of seventeen hundred pounds. There can be very little doubt that this was intended as an appeal to Burnet's personal cupidity. If so, however, the move failed. Burnet in his reply pointed out that the system of temporary grants

Attempts to buy off Burnet's opposition.

[1] Mr. Palfrey (vol. iv. p. 500) gives the text of the instruction and of Burnet's comment.

made the Governor dependent on the Assembly, and that it had been used in previous years to extract from his predecessors their consent to laws.[1]

Symptoms now showed themselves of a certain disunion among Burnet's opponents. The Council advocated the granting of a fixed sum for a term to be named by the Assembly. The House of Representatives refused to make such concession, and issued a manifesto to their constituents setting forth and justifying their attitude from the beginning of the dispute.

Burnet replied by first hinting at and then openly threatening a suspension of the colonial charter, and reminded the colonists that six years earlier, during the dispute with Shute, Carteret had warned the agent for Massachusetts that this might befall his clients. It is an odd illustration of the mutability of political combinations to find the son of Gilbert Burnet appealing to Carteret as his ally in an attack on popular liberty.

Again the Assembly strove to buy over Burnet, and, Balak-like, increased their previous offer by a supplementary vote of sixteen hundred pounds. The Governor answered plainly that he had no intention of being bribed into transferring the King's displeasure from the Assembly to himself. At the same time he met his opponents with a counter-appeal to self-interest. The Assembly had in the previous year voted the issue of sixty thousand pounds in paper money. That vote would be ineffective unless approved by the King. His approval would probably be given if the interest of the money so raised was appropriated to the Governor's salary.

The only effect of the suggestion was to obtain an emphatic declaration from the Assembly that in no shape or manner would they consent to vote a fixed salary. Simultaneously we find what is perhaps the first

[1] Hutchinson, vol. ii. pp. 333-4.

recorded application of a power already mentioned and destined to have great influence in the struggles of the future. On September 30, 1728, a Boston town meeting considered all that had been said in the Assembly for and against the grant of a fixed salary, and then voted, *nemine contradicente*, that no such grant should be made either in perpetuity or even for a limited time.[1]

The Assembly supported by the Boston town meeting.

The Assembly thus supported stood firm. Burnet thereupon transferred the session of the Assembly from Boston to Salem, hoping, as he explained to the Board of Trade, to withdraw the members from the influence of the seditious town, and also to punish Boston by withdrawing from it the commercial advantages which necessarily followed the meeting of the Assembly.

Burnet transfers the Assembly to Salem.

The Assembly so far accepted the situation as to meet at Salem. But they protested that there was no precedent which gave the Governor such a right of transfer. As a matter of fact the question belonged to that class of which many might be found where there had been an assertion of right on each side, and nothing in the nature of a conclusive decision. In 1721 an outbreak of small-pox had made it desirable to transfer the session of the Assembly to Cambridge. The Governor intervened, declaring that the right to make such adjournment was vested in him. The change was a measure of which he approved, but it must be carried through in proper form, and by a petition to him. The Assembly maintained that the place of meeting was determined by law, and could only be changed by joint action of the Governor and the two houses of Assembly. This was met by an emphatic declaration of the law officers of the Crown that the right of adjournment either in time or place

[1] Boston Records, 1700–1728, p. 226.

was in the Governor alone. The situation was one which we shall often meet with again, where each party, the representatives of the colony and the Home Government, set up conflicting claims, while the matter was complicated by the fact that one of the litigants, as we may call them, also claimed a certain superior authority, and thereby a right of interpretation.

Appointment of an agency.

The next step of the Representatives was to draft a memorial to the King setting forth the objections to a fixed salary, and to retain the services of an agent in London to advocate their case, with a stipend of a hundred a year. The Council who had hitherto taken no part in the contest now intervened, and refused to sanction the payment on the ground that they had not been made parties either to the drafting of the memorial to the King or the appointment of the agent, Francis Wells. This opposition was withdrawn when Andrew Belcher was associated with Wells in the agency. Belcher had been formerly a member of the Council, had stood high in the good graces of Shute, and had actually been displaced from the Council at the last election by the votes of the party opposed to the Governor. He was now, as events soon showed, fully reconciled to those who had been his opponents, but apparently the Council did not recognise the completeness of his conversion, and accepted his appointment as a concession.

Proceedings in England.

The address to the King was referred to the Board of Trade, and the parties concerned were heard by counsel. The Attorney- and Solicitor-General appeared for Burnet. The Board after hearing both sides decided in favour of the Governor's claim, and a report to that effect was transmitted to the Privy Council. That body after further consideration declared that the grant of a fixed salary was necessary if the colony was to be maintained in dependence on Great

Britain, and above all if the Act of Navigation was to be enforced. Finally they recommended that the whole matter should be laid before Parliament.[1]

Against this the counsel for the Assembly, Sayer and Fazakerly, argued that the charter of Massachusetts gave the colonists the exclusive right of raising money for the support of government. The action of the Privy Council was an affirmation of the principle that Parliament was entitled to intervene in colonial affairs not only when such intervention was a necessary consequence of legislative action, but also for administrative purposes. On the other hand, all that was essential in the doctrines of Samuel Adams and his followers was inherent in the contention now set up on behalf of the Assembly. The parallel is complete if it be true, as is alleged, that the Duke of Newcastle, in whose department as Secretary of State the colonies lay, while maintaining the abstract right of the Crown, abandoned it in practice by instructing Burnet to withdraw or modify his demands.[2] The Governor, on the other hand, sorely straitened for means by the action of the Assembly, was actually calling for military force.[3] Nor was there now any more than in the later dispute among the colonists themselves and their friends a unanimity of purpose. Jeremiah Dummer, who had before acted as agent for the colony, and who had written a defence of the colonial charters when they were threatened with extinction, now warned the colonists that the matter would be taken up by Parliament, and that in that case resistance would be useless.[4]

Anticipation of the Stamp Act dispute.

The Council might be regarded as representing the more moderate and pacific section of the colonial party,

[1] Journal of Board of Trade, quoted by Mr. Palfrey, vol. iv. p. 519.

[2] Chalmers, vol. ii. p. 219, quoted by Palfrey.

[3] Register of Privy Council, also quoted by Palfrey.

[4] The letter is in the possession of the Massachusetts Historical Society. Mr. Barry quotes it textually. *History of Massachusetts*, vol. ii. p. 127, *n.*

and their character was largely determined by the Governor's veto on elections of Councillors. They, as we have seen, refused to commit themselves to supporting the action of the Representatives. They protested against the statement in the address to the Crown that the Council had concurred in refusing a salary to the Governor, nor would they approve of the vote of payment to the two agents. On this latter point the Representatives accepted their defeat, and the sum demanded, three hundred pounds, was raised by voluntary contribution, with a vague promise of repayment by the House of Representatives. That body not improbably saw that such an expression of confidence and approval from without would do more for the cause than could be gained by persistent opposition to the Council.

Dispute about the appointment of Attorney-General.

In May 1729 a new Assembly was elected. Belcher having made his peace with the electorate was re-elected to the Council, but was excluded by the Governor's veto. The breach between the two branches of the legislature was at once revealed and confirmed by a dispute as to the right of nominating the Attorney-General. This again was one of those open questions on which there were conflicting precedents, and no definite and overruling decision.

In the early days of the charter the appointment had been made by the Governor. The Assembly had taken advantage of an interregnum during which authority was in the hands of the Lieutenant-Governor to effect an encroachment, and to secure and retain the appointment, a right which they exercised annually.

During Shute's governorship the Council had made an ineffectual attempt to reclaim the right for themselves in conjunction with the Governor. That claim was now again made on behalf of the executive by a clause in Burnet's instructions. The Representatives yielded the point. The Council, however, did not in practice press their victory, and Dudley who already held the office was re-elected.[1]

The Assembly made another attempt to shake Burnet's determination by a grant of six thousand pounds. It is not unlikely that this was designed to propitiate those whose opposition could not make them unmindful of the Governor's attractive qualities, while the more extreme men might be reconciled by the reflection that the vote involved no abandonment of principle, and was certain to be refused. Burnet, taking the same line as before, reproved the Assembly for their attempt to seduce one of the King's servants from his duty.

Death of Burnet.

On the very same day Burnet's coach was upset at Boston ferry. He was thrown into the water, and the drenching brought on a fever which proved fatal in a week.[2] The Assembly was able to force upon him in his death the benefits which he had refused in his life, and he was interred at a public cost of over a thousand pounds.[3] Now, as later, a certain generous forbearance, occasionally though intermittently shown towards individuals, born perhaps of calculated self-restraint rather than impulse, was to be found mixed with that spirit of factious tenacity in which the patriots of Massachusetts fought their battle.

Belcher appointed Governor.

The British Government by their choice of Burnet's successor threw away every chance of success in the struggle on which they had entered. *Hoc Ithacus velit.* Had the opponents of Burnet been granted the right of electing the next Governor they could hardly have used it more judiciously than by choosing Belcher. To buy off an agitator by turning

[1] For this dispute see Hutchinson, vol. ii. p. 358.

[2] *Ib.* p. 364.

[3] Hutchinson (vol. ii. p. 366) says the Assembly ordered a very honourable funeral. Palfrey (vol. iv. p. 527) states the precise sum (1,097*l.* 11*s.* 3*d.*) on the authority of the Massachusetts Records.

him into a placeman may at times be a successful stroke of policy. But it is seldom that the apostate can be effectively placed in the front of the battle. Men of forceful will and unflinching purpose have when so placed achieved but imperfect success. Belcher's character was not of the stuff from which Straffords and Cliffords are made. His repute was already tainted by one act of apostasy, and a second could not but be fatal. Henceforth he must be content to stand not as a politician with convictions, but as a mere advocate, a political *condottiere* fighting for the cause for which he was retained.

Belcher's instructions.

His instructions on the subject of a salary were explicit, and were communicated to the Assembly on his arrival. The Assembly were told that they were endeavouring by this and other 'unwarrantable practices to weaken, if not cast off, the obedience they owe to the Crown and the dependence which all colonies ought to have on their mother country.' The sands were running out: if they did not avail themselves of this, the last opportunity of repentance offered them, their conduct would be brought before Parliament.[1]

Continuance of the dispute.

Neither then nor at any later period during Belcher's term of office did the Representatives show the slightest sign of yielding. The battle was in the main a repetition of that fought between the Assembly and Burnet, save that Belcher, as might have been expected, showed less persistence and less dignity than his predecessor. The Council urged a compromise. Let a fixed salary be granted during Belcher's tenure of office. The Representatives however stood firm.[2]

As before, the town meeting of Boston stepped in to lend its weight and authority to the support of the

[1] Hutchinson, vol. ii. p. 372. [2] *Ib.* p. 373.

brought themselves into further conflict with the Governor by refusing to admit the right of the Council to make any amendments in money bills.[1] Hunter's usual attitude was, as we have already seen, one of suavity and conciliation. In 1715 he succeeded in obtaining a Revenue Act from the Assembly by allowing them to include in it a provision for the payment of members. In 1720 Hunter was succeeded by Burnet, and in that year the Act was renewed for five years. This compromise seems to have been accepted by both sides and to have remained in force till 1742.[2] Then on the appointment of Clinton as Governor, the Assembly took up the policy of Massachusetts, and refused to make a grant for a longer period than one year. As in Massachusetts, the pertinacity of the popular representatives carried the day. In 1755 the Board of Trade, in their instructions to the Governor of New York, authorised him if he thought it advisable to forgo the demand for a fixed salary.

II. THE DISPUTE OVER PAPER MONEY.[3]

The battle over the Governor's salary did much to define and intensify the sense of independence in Massachusetts. But there its influence ended. So slight was the community of thought and feeling, so scanty the exchange of information between the colonies, that we may be sure that only a small minority elsewhere would know or understand what was done at

[1] Smith, p. 173; N. Y. Docs. vol. v. p. 348.

[2] N. Y. Docs. vol. vi. p. 432. It is not quite easy to see how quinquennial votes beginning in 1720 could have ended in 1742. The year is named in a report on the subject drawn up by Shirley at the request of Governor Clinton. Probably the vote was regarded as personal, and lapsed if the governorship was vacated within the specified time.

[3] H. Phillips's *Historical Account of the Paper Currency of the American Colonies* is a valuable authority on the subject.

Boston. We can see, too, from contemporary references that the New Englander did not habitually so bear himself us to win much good-will in neighbouring colonies.[1] He was reputed pushing, grasping and litigious. The defence of the charter privileges of Massachusetts was not likely to awaken sympathy outside that colony: the time had not yet come when an appeal to 'natural rights' could be effective. But the determination of the British Government to restrain the colonial Assemblies in their issue of paper money at once opened a question in which every colony was interested, which appealed in some measure to almost every class, on which men without any far-sighted or comprehensive political views could form a decided opinion.

The causes which led the various colonial governments to a reckless issue of paper money are not far to seek. There was no hoarded supply of the precious metals, because there was no class living on its accumulations, and because the wage-earners played an insignificant part in the social and industrial life of the colonies. Hence such makeshifts as the adoption of tobacco as the medium of currency in the Southern States, and payment in commodities taken at a fixed rate as practised in New England. As soon as military operations had to be provided for these devices failed, and it became incumbent on the colonial legislatures to arrange means for the purchase of stores and the payment of soldiers.

Lack of specie.

Moreover, young and expansive communities will always be reckless in mortgaging their future, nor is it an unreasonable view that a future generation should pay a full share towards those advantages which are being won for it by its predecessors.

[1] See, for example, Mrs. Grant's description of the New Englanders who emigrated into New York. *Memoirs of an American Lady* (ed. 1901), vol. ii. p. 137.

Nevertheless the matter was one in which the Home Government was bound to exercise a watchful discretion. It is needless to dwell on the obvious and normal evils which accrue from a reckless issue of paper money: temporary inflation of trade, followed by collapse and want of confidence, the destruction of credit by the reckless abuse of it. But, over and above these, there were special dangers involved, dangers not merely to the prosperity and safety of individual colonies, but to the whole colonial fabric of the empire. Reckless issues of paper money would leave the colonies without any current medium for intercolonial trade, and so introduce hindrance to imperial unity and complications in intercolonial relations. Worse still, it would prejudice any common scheme of colonial defence in two ways. It would make all payments for military purposes fluctuating, and thereby kill that credit which is an essential necessity. It would also make any uniform system of military finance for the whole body of colonies impossible.

Evils of paper money.

These considerations absolutely forbade the Home Government to leave the question to the uncontrolled discretion of the various colonial legislatures. There were three obvious forms which interference might take.

Three methods of restraint by the Home Government.

1. The Crown might at its discretion veto bills for the issue of paper money.

2. It might embody its wishes in the instructions issued to each Governor on his entry into office.

3. It might issue a comprehensive order of restraint applying to the whole body of colonies.

In other words, it might deal with individual cases, with individual colonies, or with the whole body of colonies. All these courses were adopted successively, the last when the other two seemed fruitless.

The best method of dealing with the question will

be to take the cases of the different colonies successively, dealing in order with the colonies where the executive was under the direct control of the Crown, the proprietary colonies, and the two colonies, Connecticut and Rhode Island, whose charters placed them in a position of *quasi* independence.

In New Hampshire the matter played an unimportant part, and so far as it went took an abnormal course.

Paper money in New Hampshire.[1]

Elsewhere, as we shall see, the demand for paper money was a popular cry, urged by the elected delegates and checked or controlled by the representatives of the Crown. But in New Hampshire in 1717, after the Assembly as a whole had agreed to issue bills to the amount of ten thousand pounds, the Council proposed to enlarge the issue to fifteen thousand. This was resisted by the Representatives. Shute, who combined the government of New Hampshire with that of Massachusetts, supported the Council, but without success. He therefore dissolved the Assembly, and the newly elected House of Representatives complied with the Council. This dissension was not improbably due to the fact that in New Hampshire the Lower House of the Assembly represented and mainly belonged to the class of small farmers for whom the extension of commercial credit had no special attraction, while on the other hand the Council represented the mercantile interest.

The next House of Representatives was more compliant and consented to an issue of ten thousand pounds. But it is clear that paper money never lay on New Hampshire as the incubus that it proved elsewhere.

In Massachusetts it was otherwise. There the trading class had sufficient numbers, influence and organization largely to determine the policy of the

[1] Belknap, vol. ii. pp. 19, 20.

colony as a whole. The issue of paper money, not indeed by the State, but with its approval, began in 1686. In that year Joseph Dudley, then President of that short-lived government which followed the overthrow of the charter, acting in conjunction with his Council, gave authority to John Blackwall, of Boston, and others to issue bills on security of real and personal estate as imperishable merchandise.[1] This was followed in 1690 by an issue of bills of credit by the government of Massachusetts to the amount of seven thousand pounds.[2] The main plea put forward for this was the necessity for meeting the expenses of the unsuccessful expedition against Canada.

Issue of bills of credit in Massachusetts.

The newly issued paper currency at once showed a tendency to fall, which was only checked in part by the public-spirited conduct of Phipps, who by redeeming a large number of bills became himself the chief State creditor, partly by the action of the Assembly in granting favourable terms to those who employed the bills for public payment, thus making them for all practical purposes convertible.[3] This check, however, was practically abandoned in 1703. In that year the demand for payment of taxes was postponed till 1706, and this method of evading redemption was continued and extended, till by 1711 the period of postponement had reached six years.[4] It might have been thought that such a frank declaration of insolvency would have opened men's eyes to the evils of the system.

Difficulties which resulted.

The embarrassment in which the treasury was thus involved was far from completing the calamitous state of affairs, In 1712 the government, frankly abandoning all attempt at redemption, enacted that their bills of credit should be legal tender in all

[1] Records quoted in Felt's *Currency of Massachusetts*, p. 46.
[2] *Ib.* p. 49. [3] Hutchinson, vol. i. p. 402. [4] Felt, p. 63.

cases where there was no special stipulation in writing to the contrary.[1] As might have been foreseen Gresham's law acted: specie fled before the steady influx of paper money. Trade seemed well nigh paralyzed by the lack of specie and by the impossibility of making contracts, when the medium of payment was being continuously and rapidly depreciated. Government had to lighten the distress which its own action had created by allowing public dues to be paid in commodities, and thus taking on itself the risks and inconveniences of a fluctuating trade.[2] It seemed as though society was returning to the primitive conditions of barter.

Further issue of paper money.

It was certain that a community such as Massachusetts, conscious of increasing productive resources of the essential elements for prosperity, would clutch at every device, however essentially worthless or even dangerous, for surmounting what she must have regarded, not altogether unjustly, as a mere mechanical hindrance to progress. The delusive belief in the value of a paper currency has enslaved minds of wider experience and more exact economical training than were to be found in the New England of that day. So far the government of the colony had only attempted to meet its own financial needs by the issue of bills of credit. In 1714 it took a further step and issued notes to the amount of fifty thousand pounds, to carry five per cent. interest, payable by the government to the recipient, and to be redeemed and extinguished at the rate of one-fifth in each year.[3] There is nothing to show precisely what equivalent the treasury was prepared to take for its notes, but we cannot doubt

[1] Felt, p. 64.

[2] *Ib.* p. 53. He gives an instance of the practice and of the inconvenience which ensued.

[3] Hutchinson, vol. ii. p. 208.

from the general conditions that prevailed that the greater part of these notes were issued on loan, largely we may suppose on personal security.

Action of Governor Shute.

An intelligent observer suddenly brought face to face with this state of things, not familiarized with it by watching its successive stages of growth, could not but be horror-struck at such a spectacle of universal insolvency. The case might well seem one of those where a Governor, free from any bondage to colonial interests and backed by the authority of the Home Government, might profitably intervene. In 1716, almost immediately after Shute's arrival, the Assembly proposed a fresh issue of a hundred thousand pounds of paper money, the redemption to be spread over ten years. Shute was not unnaturally aghast at the proposal to flood the market with more paper money in the face of the existing depreciation, and he besought the Assembly to take measures to reduce 'the intolerable discount' on their bills. The fact that the Governor's own salary was, as he complained, paid in a currency depreciated to fifty per cent. of its nominal value doubtless brought home to him the evils of the existing system.[1] Yet it would seem as if Shute vetoed the bill for the issue of more paper money not so much on its own demerits as from a resolve to use that veto as a weapon in other administrative conflicts. The Assembly had neglected to provide for the proper inspection of the naval stores which the colonists exported, or to take proper steps for checking the waste of ship timber, and they had set at nought most cherished principles of British administration by proposing to lay a duty of one per cent. on goods imported from the mother country.[2] Unless, Shute told them, they complied on all these points with the wishes of the

[1] Hutchinson, vol. ii. pp. 217–8.

[2] *Ib.* pp. 226–31; cf. Palfrey, vol. iv. p. 405.

Home Government he could not consent to the proposed loan.

Deplorable state of the public finances.

By 1720 the want of an effective currency had reached such a point that it was necessary to make an official list of commodities which might be taken in payment of public dues. Meat, fish, butter, cheese, grain, leather and wax were all in the list.[1] The confusion was in all likelihood made worse by an order issued by the Town Council of Boston that their treasurer should accept bills of credit of Connecticut, Rhode Island and New Hampshire 'provided they were fit to pass from man to man.'[2] Nevertheless, the legislators of Massachusetts were firmly convinced that the trouble was due not to the inherent worthlessness of the paper issued, but to the insufficient quantity of it. As for depreciation, that might be checked by an Act prohibiting anyone to exchange paper for bullion except at a fixed rate.[3] Accordingly in 1721 fifty thousand pounds more was issued.[4] The total disappearance of specie was the inevitable result. The situation cannot be better described than in the words of Thomas Hutchinson, one of the few among the public men of Massachusetts who throughout perceived and withstood the reckless financial policy of his fellow colonists. 'As soon as the silver and gold were gone, and the bills were the sole instrument of commerce, pounds, shillings and pence were altogether ideal, for no possible reason could be assigned why a bill of twenty shillings should bear a certain proportion to any one quantity of silver more than another: sums in bills were drawing into the treasury from time to time by the taxes, or payment of the loans, but then other sums were continually issuing out, and all the bills were paid

[1] Records of Boston Selectmen, 1721, p. 92; cf. Felt, p. 76.

[2] Boston Town Records, 1719, p. 143.

[3] Felt, p. 77.

[4] *Ib.*

and received without any distinction either in public or private payments, so that, for near forty years together, the currency was in much the same state as if a hundred pounds sterling had been stamped in pieces of leather or paper of various denominations, and declared to be the money of the government, without any other sanction than this, that, when there should be taxes to pay, the treasury would receive this sort of money, and that every creditor should be obliged to receive it from his debtor. Can it be supposed that such a medium could retain its value? In 1702, six shillings and eightpence was equal to an ounce of silver. In 1749, fifty shillings was judged equal to an ounce of silver. I saw a five-shilling bill which had been issued in 1690 and was remaining in 1749, and was then equal to eightpence only in lawful money, and so retained but about one-eighth of its original value. Such was the delusion, that not only the bills of the Massachusetts government passed as money, but they received the bills of the government of Connecticut, New Hampshire and Rhode Island also as a currency. The Massachusetts bills passed also in those governments.'[1] Shute was unable wholly to resist the popular demand, and in 1721 he consented to a further issue of fifty thousand pounds.

Action of Belcher.

The issue of paper money continued to be a subject of dispute during the governorships of Burnet and Belcher, and both were supported by the Council in their opposition to the Lower House. Yet it is to be noticed that their opposition was not based on an abstract objection to paper money. The concurrence of the Governor and Council was refused because the Representatives would not agree to the conditions proposed as to the control of the money when raised.

[1] Hutchinson, vol. i. p. 402, *n.*

It is clear, however, that Belcher was fully alive to the commercial evils of the existing state of affairs. He called the attention of the Home Government to the deplorable depreciation of the public currency, sixteen shillings in their paper being not worth five in specie. The matter was made worse by the issue of bills by private persons or companies. These were expected to help the deficiency of currency. Instead they accelerated the general depreciation.[1]

He is thankful that the Assembly are kept from ruining all the estates in the province by issuing out floods of these pernicious bills.[2]

Belcher's views might be sound; when however it came to action, he made no attempt to give effect to them. On the contrary, we find him in his despatches to Lord Wilmington making a complete surrender, and supporting the application of the Council or Assembly to be allowed to make a further issue of sixty thousand pounds of paper money.[3] The belief of the colonists in the timidity and flexibility of English officials did not a little to strengthen them in the coming struggle, and few did more to teach and confirm that belief than Belcher.

Belcher's warnings when thus contradicted by his action were not likely to carry much weight. So far were the citizens of Massachusetts from accepting them, that in 1740 a scheme was floated for erecting a land bank. Shareholders were to give security in land or otherwise, or were to pay interest, three per cent. annually, in manufactured goods. As raw produce was excluded, it is not unlikely that the encouragement of colonial manufactures was among the motives operating on those who advocated the scheme.

Scheme for a land bank.[4]

[1] Colonial State Papers, November 1735.

[2] Hist. MSS. Commission Report xi. App. part iv. p. 2875.

[3] *Ib.* p. 281.

[4] Hutchinson gives a full and clear account of this, vol. ii. pp. 393–6.

The shareholders were to receive notes, which would be accepted by the company itself as legal tender, and which were to be redeemed not in specie, but in currency at the expiration of twenty years. The scheme was simply one of those recurrent quack projects for embodying credit as floating capital, without the security of immediate redemption, if required, in some medium of fixed value.

Belcher's instructions had showed that the Home Government was by this time alive to the dangers in which the colony had entangled itself. The date of redemption for the outstanding bills was 1741. The instructions provided that if there was any further issue of paper money it should be made redeemable also by that date. The Assembly made more than one attempt to legislate in defiance of that limitation, but were at once confronted with Belcher's veto.

By this time, however, the issue of paper money in the various colonies had reached a pitch at which the evil could not be effectively met by isolated instructions to individual Governors. But, before considering the more comprehensive measures adopted, it will be well to trace the progress of the trouble in other colonies.

Paper money in New Jersey.

In New Jersey the first issue of paper money appears to have been made in 1709, to the amount of three thousand pounds, to meet the expenses of the expedition against Canada.[1] That the colony suffered from lack of specie is shown by the fact that in 1720 jewellery was accepted in payment of public dues.[2] In 1724 Burnet, then Governor of New York and New Jersey, reports to the Board of Trade that the latter colony was entering on dangerous financial courses by a public loan of forty thousand pounds. He contrasts this with the cautious policy of the Government of New York, who though they had issued

[1] New Jersey Archives, vol. ii. p. 372. [2] Phillips, p. 62.

paper money were making full provision for its redemption. Their notes were issued to individuals on the security of land or plate, and such loans were to be paid off in instalments.[1] Burnet's warning was so far effective that in 1727 the Board of Trade issued an instruction to his successor, Montgomerie, to the effect that no Act for issuing paper money should take effect till it is approved by the Crown.[2]

This restriction however was apparently disregarded or evaded, since by 1740 no less than sixty thousand pounds' worth of paper money was in circulation.[3]

Lewis Morris, who was Governor in 1740, was, as was said before, a man of definite mind and strong will, and, supported by his Council, he made strenuous attempts to restrain the further issue of paper money. In 1742 he reports to the Board of Trade that he has been offered five hundred pounds if he will assent to a bill for raising forty thousand pounds.[4] At a later day, after Morris's death, the Assembly averred that the refusal was made because the bill did not take the form of a permanent increase of salary.[5] In 1730 the Assembly had made a futile attempt to escape the inevitable consequences of their own action by enacting that no one should make any charge for exchanging New Jersey paper money for that of any other colony.[6] It seems hardly credible that any legislative body should not have seen that this could at once be evaded by a slight alteration in the rate of exchange. The incident illustrates both the difficulties which the issue of paper money necessarily introduced into the trade between the various colonies, and the hopeless confusion of thought of the colonial legislatures on the subject.

1 New Jersey Archives, vol. v. p. 86. 2 *Ib.* vol. iii. p. 173.
3 Phillips, p. 69; cf. N. J. Archives, vol. vi. p. 52.
4 N. J. Archives, vol. xi. p. 305.
5 *Ib.* vol. xvi. p. 100.
6 *Ib.* vol. iii. p. 265; L. Morris's Papers, p. 154

A bitter dispute followed in which the question of paper money was mixed up with other administrative questions, which will more fitly come before us later. The Council concurred in the Governor's veto and gave reasons for their action. Paper money was necessarily subject to fluctuation; the demand for it when once started was sure to increase; it formed a tax which did not fall on the rich. It is not easy to see the force of this last argument, but the use of it rather suggests that the Assembly was acting in the interests of the wealthy classes.[1] The Assembly had also pleaded that the money to be raised was needed to build public offices and a house for the Governor. The Council met this by pointing out that there was no clause in the bill to secure such an appropriation.

Morris supplemented this by a speech addressed to the Assembly, in which he laid down doctrines which might well alarm the colonists. It might be, he admitted, that the right to issue paper money was given to the Assembly in the charter, directly or by implication. But such a grant was revocable. If any such right had been granted in the most express terms a British Parliament can abolish any constitution in the Plantations that they deem inconvenient or disadvantageous to the trade of the nation, or otherwise, without being said to encroach, all encroachments being in their own nature said to be illegal, which cannot be said of an Act of a British Parliament without indecency.[2] It may safely be said that up to that time the annals of British colonial administration can show no claim on behalf of Parliament approaching that in the unqualified directness of its assertion or in its far-reaching consequences.

It was not to be expected that the Assembly should sit down quietly under such a claim. Their reply in

[1] N. Jersey Archives, vol. xv. p. 387. [2] *Ib.* p. 397.

every respect anticipates the language and sentiments heard a quarter of a century later. There are vague professions of loyalty, but along with them are the ominous words, 'we are a nation famed for its liberty.' . . . 'The acting by our own judgement is such a valuable part of our liberty contained in our constitution . . . that we hope it will always be promoted and protected by you.'

They plainly tell Morris that their conception of the public good differs from his, and they are willing to leave it to public opinion to say which is right. In short things have reached a deadlock, of which the constitution as it stands offers no solution.[1]

Absence of paper money in New York and Virginia.

New York seems to have escaped the evils of paper money by traditional adherence to a sound system of finance.[2] So also did Virginia by its peculiar conditions. A modern writer who has made a careful study of the financial history of that colony has put forward the view that the absence of paper money in Virginia shows that the colony was well supplied with specie.[3] It was more probably due to the fact that in tobacco the colony possessed a medium of currency capable of easy expansion. The use of tobacco as currency, inconvenient as it was in many ways, at least averted the evil of paper money. The tobacco plantation in a sort played the part of a gold or silver mine. The Virginian planter had only to diminish his staple export and he was supplied with additional material for barter. We should probably find, if it were possible to have exact statistics, that as prices of commodities in Virginia rose or fell, so her export of tobacco contracted or expanded. Fluctuations of price no doubt there were, but they were less sudden

[1] N. Jersey Archives, vol. xv. pp. 410, &c.

[2] For this subject see Smith, p. 279.

[3] Ripley, *Financial History of Virginia*, p. 147.

and less violent than those caused by a large issue of paper.

It is true that promissory notes on the security of tobacco in the public warehouses were issued by individuals,[1] but this was merely anticipating the sale of an available commodity with a definite marketable value, and differed entirely from the wholesale issue of government paper. It is claimed for Virginia that there was no public issue of paper money till special pressure was put upon the resources of the colony by the war for the conquest of Canada.[2]

In the despatch above mentioned we find Burnet singling out Maryland and North Carolina as special offenders. There can be little doubt that this was specially directed against North Carolina. The law passed by the legislature of that colony dealing with debts contracted outside their own bounds had tended to fill the province with the thriftless and the dishonest, and to engender an atmosphere of laxity and improvidence.[3] In 1716, before the colony had passed under the authority of the Crown, paper money to the amount of twenty-four thousand pounds was issued, and an Act passed making commodities for certain purposes legal tender.

Paper money in North Carolina.

This was met with remonstrances both from the Governor and the Proprietors. The former complained that it was impossible to fix official fees. The latter protested against having to receive their quit-rents in depreciated paper. The Assembly with audacity, to which perhaps a harsher name might be given, replied that anyone who refused to accept the colonial paper at par was lessening the credit of the bills, and 'committing a great breach of the Act for their currency.'[4]

[1] Ripley, p. 147.

[2] Phillips, p. 193.

[3] *V.s.* p. 55.

[4] N. Car. Records, vol. ii. pp. 235, 243; vol. iii. p. 177.

Moreover, the question of paper money was inextricably mixed up with the other administrative questions, that of fees and salaries. We have already seen how this acted in New Jersey. So, too, it was in North Carolina. There, in 1731, a dispute arose between the Governor and the Assembly which was complicated and intensified by the absence of a fixed currency, and the consequent responsibility of deciding on a scale which should not give rise to dispute and evasion.[1]

In South Carolina, on the other hand, we meet with no trace of financial difficulties. There, as in Virginia, we have a simple form of life, with one uniform and on the whole increasingly productive industry. When each plantation is practically a self-supporting community, and when the external trade is a simple one, flowing in certain fixed channels and dealing with a limited and specified number of staple commodities, the lack of a medium of currency does not make itself acutely felt.

In Maryland and Pennsylvania the matter was complicated by the introduction of a special factor, the authority of the Proprietor, with important financial rights and somewhat vaguely defined legislative and administrative powers. In Maryland, as in Virginia, the economic condition of the country soon led to the acceptance of tobacco as a medium of currency. There was, however, as we have seen, a difference between the industrial condition of Virginia and that of Maryland. In the former colony tobacco was the one staple product. In the latter there was a growing tendency to divert industry into other channels. We may be certain that socially this was a gain. But the lack of a circulating medium was beyond doubt a hindrance to the prosperity of the colony. In 1729 we find a Governor complaining that 'where the staple

In Maryland.

[1] N. Car. Records, vol. iii. p. 266.

of a country . . . yields no return of money to circulate in such a country, the want of such circulation must leave it almost inanimate; it is like a dead palsie on the public.'[1]

Nevertheless, it is not unlikely that the colony might have scrambled on, grumbling at the fluctuations of tobacco yet making no attempts to seek a remedy, if it had not been for the financial pressure caused by the necessity for paying the Proprietors' dues in some fairly stable medium.

In 1732 the legislature resorted to an issue of paper money to the amount of ninety thousand pounds. Adequate provision, however, was made for the redemption by a sinking fund, to be raised by a duty on tobacco, and the bills at one time fell to half of their nominal value.[2] But the introduction in 1747 of an effective system of inspection so bettered the tobacco trade as to render the work of redemption easy, and to save the colony from the curse of a depreciated paper currency.[3]

In none of the colonies was the question a more acute one or attended with more disturbance than in Pennsylvania. The use of paper money appears to have begun in 1723 with an issue of seven thousand five hundred pounds. The report in which this fact is communicated to the Home Government is a remarkable document. It is signed by the Governor Keith. It states that Pennsylvania had special claims to indulgence, since of all the colonies it was the only one which had observed Queen Anne's proclamation, confirmed by Act of Parliament, determining the value of foreign coins in the plantations. Owing to the disobedience of the other colonies, Spanish coins are useless for intercolonial trade. One

In Pennsylvania.

[1] Colonial Papers, quoted by Mereness, p. 126.

[2] Mereness, p. 126.

[3] *Ib.* p. 127.

certainly would have thought that Pennsylvania paper would be equally so. The framers of the report also admit that the issue of paper, and the consequent depreciation in the value of money, will be a hardship to individuals. This, however, they say is outweighed by the public and general gain. As early as that the Board of Trade were alive to the dangers of such a system of finance. In acknowledging the receipt of the Act they warn the Assembly that the issue of paper money has been attended with evil effects in other colonies, especially in North Carolina. Out of tenderness for the holders of bills they will not disallow the measure. But there must be no further issue and there must be speedy redemption.[1] The warning had but little effect. Three years later a bill was introduced for the issue of fifty thousand pounds, such bills to bear interest at four per cent. The Governor, Gordon—a man lacking in force of character and power to resist popular demands—offered some feeble opposition, and so far succeeded that the sum was reduced to thirty thousand pounds, and the credit of the bills somewhat strengthened by the interest being raised to five per cent. He also endeavoured to get the period of redemption reduced from sixteen years to twelve, but without success.[2] There are references to popular disturbances and disaffection, and it seems likely, though not certain, that these were due to the action of the Governor and Council in endeavouring to withstand the financial policy of the Representatives.[3]

Two years later a bill was introduced for continuing in circulation notes which had been ordered to be redeemed and destroyed. Here the Governor again protested and again yielded.[4]

Gordon's successor, Thomas, was a capable and a

[1] Pennsylvania Records, vol. iii. p. 261.
[2] *Ib.* pp. 352–4.
[3] *Ib.* p. 360.
[4] *Ib.* p. 393.

clear-headed man, who did his best to hold the scales even in all disputes between the Proprietor and the colonists. But prevention is easier than cure, and the action of Gordon had given such an impetus to an unsound system of finance as to render effective resistance impossible.

Thomas was not wholly opposed to the issue of paper money. But he pointed out that it should be made legal tender only in the case of internal trade, that debts to English subjects elsewhere and the Proprietors' quit-rents should be paid in, or at least at the rate of, sterling coin.[1]

The latter limitation would have deprived the issue of paper money of that which was to the colonists one of its main attractions. The Assembly replied to the Governor with something like a frank avowal of insolvency. The Proprietors, they said, must choose whether to receive their dues in depreciated paper or to forgo them altogether. They will be moreover indirectly compensated, since the restoration of the currency will enable them to sell vacant tracts of land which would otherwise be left on their hands. Moreover, to impose limits on the circulation of the paper will tend to discredit it. The Governor, in reply, asked the members of the Assembly whether any of them individually would care to take sixteen-pennyworth of colonial paper for an English shilling? The attempt to force all creditors to accept such payment would at once call out united resistance from English merchants.

By his resistance Thomas would seem in some measure to have stemmed the tide and stayed the further issue of paper. But, as we shall see, the evil broke out with renewed violence when demands for a universal system of colonial defence began to press on the colonists. And if something had been done to avert or

[1] For this dispute see Pennsylvania Records, vol. iv. pp. 320–5.

delay insolvency, a heavy price had to be paid. Self-interest of a purely personal kind no doubt prompted the action of many members of the Assembly. But we may be sure that many of the colonists were honestly convinced that the prosperity of the province was being sacrificed to the Proprietors and to the English merchants. The citizen of Pennsylvania was taught to regard both with aversion, and to include in that feeling those who stood for their interests, the Governor and the authorities at home.

Rhode Island, enterprising in trade, somewhat Alsatian in morals, and but remotely amenable to any external authority, outstripped all the other colonies in its reckless employment of a paper currency. There, as elsewhere, paper money was first used to meet the special needs of the war with Canada in 1690. The colony, however, was far from unanimous in its wish to make the system permanent. Specie *versus* paper became a test question in elections. In 1714 the 'hard money' party were in the ascendant, and an order was issued for the redemption of bills to the amount of two thousand pounds. Neglect to comply with this order led to the dismissal of one treasurer and the appointment of a successor. Ultimately only eleven hundred and odd pounds' worth of paper was redeemed.[1]

In Rhode Island.

The attempt to keep the colony within the path of sound finance was short-lived and ineffectual. In 1715 thirty thousand pounds' worth of paper money was issued.[2] Six years later this was followed by a further issue of forty thousand pounds. So rapidly did the process go on that by 1731 the public debt amounted to one hundred and twenty thousand pounds,[3] and the colonial paper was depreciated to the extent of sixty per cent. The 'hard money' party already mentioned

[1] Arnold, *Hist. of R. I.*, vol. ii. pp. 52–4.

[2] R. I. Records, vol. iv. p. 191.

[3] *Ib.* p. 295.

was neither defunct nor prepared to accept defeat. When in 1731 the Assembly proposed a further issue, a number of merchants remonstrated and the Governor, Jenckes, had the courage to face unpopularity and apply his veto.[1]

It is clear that the issue was that which usually underlies such disputes, the issue between the capitalist and the debtor who seeks to escape his liability by depreciating the currency. The Assembly denied the Governor's right to veto a measure, and the question was referred to the Attorney- and Solicitor-General, Yorke and Talbot. Their decision was based on a strict constitutional interpretation of the law, and had no reference to the administrative necessities of the case. They decided against the Governor's veto. He was, they held, a necessary constituent part of the Assembly, but when once the Assembly was in existence he had no separate power.[2]

A few years later Rhode Island had a Governor whose views on this subject were wholly in conformity with those of the community. We find Governor Ward sending home a report in which the praises of paper money are sung as enthusiastically as they ever were by any fanatic of the school of Attwood. 'If this colony be in any respect happy and flourishing it is paper money that has made it so.' The shower of manna had by this time mounted up to three hundred and forty thousand pounds, which Ward with perfect frankness admits was worth eighty-eight thousand and one pounds sterling.[3]

The authorities in England might be short-sighted and narrow-minded and negligent in many features of their colonial policy. But the one matter which they did watch with careful, if not always judicious,

[1] R. I. Records, vol. iv. p. 457. [2] *Ib.* p. 461.
[3] *Ib.* vol. v. pp. 8, &c.

vigilance was the trade of the colonies. And it needed no technical knowledge or special insight into commercial problems to see what sectional feeling and self-interest, in a great measure, concealed from the colonists, the injury done to colonial commerce by the inextricable confusion of currencies. The intermittent exercise of the royal veto hardly made matters better. For it was obviously inconvenient that a financial issue such as was involved should be held over pending the exchange of possibly long and almost certainly complicated communications between the colony and the authorities at home. The battle, too, was fought with unequal weapons. The Home Government could resist successfully only if their representatives in the colonies stood by them without flinching. It needed no little resolution on the part of a colonial Governor to bear up persistently against the continued and unanimous demands of those among whom he lived, on whose good-will he was dependent, in some instances for the actual means of living and in all for everything which was needed to make life pleasant, or even endurable.

Difficulties of the Home Government.

That Parliament should be led into intervention was almost inevitable. Even if it did not interfere by any direct administrative process, it could hardly avoid touching the question in the process of commercial legislation. The first enactment which in any way bore on the subject had, in all likelihood, an origin wholly unconnected with colonial finance. In 1719 a statute was passed which prohibited the formation of any commercial company publicly issuing stock to shareholders unless chartered by the Crown or authorized by Act of Parliament.[1] The statute, or at least this clause in it, was probably designed as a check on that reckless outburst of speculation which

Action of Parliament.

[1] 6 George I. c. 18.

hemp, grain, and tobacco to any country other than England.

An Act of 1663 introduced that practice on which the whole execution of the existing law depended. Either security must be given that the cargo would be landed in an English or Scotch port, or if it was destined for a port in any British colony duty must be paid at the time of loading.

The colonists endeavoured to interpret this as giving permission to land goods in a foreign port by the payment of a duty on loading. In 1696 this was met by an amending Act requiring that such payment should not supersede the necessity for giving security that the cargo would be landed in an English, Scotch or colonial port.

During the course of the eighteenth century the Navigation Act was made more stringent by the addition of various commodities to the list of those already specified. Rice, molasses, beaver and other furs, and copper ore were successively included; while in 1742 the provisions for securing that all vessels trading with the colonies should be British were made more stringent.

The Molasses Acts.

Undoubtedly the Act which if rigidly executed would have borne most hardly on the colonists was that passed in 1733, prohibiting the importation of molasses from the French islands into the English colonies. That cannot with fairness be cited as showing any wish on the part of the legislature to sacrifice the prosperity of the colonies to that of the mother country. It was an honest, though no doubt mistaken, attempt to benefit one particular group of English colonies by forcing the American rum distiller to obtain the molasses which he needed from the British West Indies. For years the rum distillery had been for New England a business of supreme importance.

Rhode Island, backward in other forms of industry, took the lead in this.[1]

Moreover, the French colonies dealt largely with New England for commodities not enumerated in the Navigation Acts, and thus anything which crippled their purchasing power was a distinct loss to the English colonists. To the French West Indies it was of the greatest importance to retain this trade. For the distilling of rum was prohibited to them as likely to interfere with the sale of French brandy, and thus if they were deprived of the New England market their molasses was a drug on their hands.

If the legislature of the eighteenth century added to the stringency of these regulations in some directions it relaxed them in others, and it also made amends for them by compensatory advantages. Drawbacks were granted on goods warehoused in England and then exported to the colonies, so that the colonial buyer actually got better terms than the British. This benefit was increased in 1704 by an extension of the time during which the goods might remain in warehouse. Two other Acts were passed in the reign of Queen Anne of special benefit to the colonies. One gave bounties on naval stores imported into England, and the other allowed Irish linen to be imported into America duty-free. There was also an important reservation in the original Act. Salt needed for fish curing might be imported into New England from any European port, and in 1727 this privilege was extended to Pennsylvania. Specially harsh in its operation was the Act of 1705, whereby rice, of which a large quantity was imported from South Carolina to Portugal, was made an enumerated commodity. The result was that the trade passed to the Italian rice-grower. In 1720 the Lords

[1] There is a consensus of opinion on this point, but I cannot find any exact statistics.

of Trade reported in favour of relaxing this so far as to allow rice to be carried to any port south of Cape Finisterre,[1] and in 1731 their recommendation became law.

There does not, however, seem to have been any intention to remedy a grievance under which North Carolina suffered. One of the few industries possible in that thriftless and resourceless colony was the exportation of pickled beef. For this Portuguese salt would have been far more serviceable than English. Yet the boon which, as we have just seen, was granted to New England and Pennsylvania was withheld from North Carolina.[2]

Smuggling in America.

To what extent these restrictions in trade were evaded and how far they were felt as a real grievance are questions to which it is hard to give a definite answer. Of the Act restraining the importation of molasses one may at once say that it was by the connivance of British officials and, as it would seem, with the tacit consent of the government rendered a dead letter. The general question of smuggling is more difficult to deal with. Beyond a doubt the reports of colonial officials teem with complaints on the subject. But it must be remembered that each colony had its own revenue laws and its own duties, imposed by the representatives of the colonists and administered by a separate set of officials. It is not easy to say how far the evasions complained of were evasions of local or of imperial regulations. Nor is it often that the complaints pass from generalities to definite facts. Certain specific statements, however, do stand out, and may, taken in conjunction, give us some clue to the real nature of the colonial contraband trade.

As early as 1663 we find the Council for Plantations

[1] Report of Lords of Trade in N. Car. Records, vol. ii. p. 499.

[2] Governor Dobbs's report in N. Car. Records, vol. v. p. 314.

reporting that, contrary to the Act of Navigation, tobacco was exported from New England, Long Island, Virginia and Maryland to the Dutch colonies, whereby the revenue lost ten thousand pounds yearly. Letters of caution on the subject were to be sent to the Governors of the various colonies concerned.[1]

In 1697 Nicholson, then Governor of Maryland, sent home a very full, though not altogether lucid, account of the contraband trade in that colony. It is clear that the kind of smuggling which he viewed with apprehension was the illicit exportation of tobacco. This was mainly carried on by two methods, by the use of forged certificates and by the connivance of the custom officials both in the colonies and the mother country.

Nicholson's report.[2]

The main check on which Nicholson relies is a more complete system of communication between the authorities in the colonies and those in England. The invoice of goods was transmitted by the same vessel which carried them. Nicholson proposes that after the invoice has been sworn to, it should be kept in triplicate, one copy to be retained by the Governor, one sent to the custom house in London, the third to the port where the vessel would unload.

The evil, Nicholson says, is partly due to the fact that the custom house officials in the colonies are allowed to trade on their own account, and do so largely, buying contraband goods and thus having an interest in allowing the law to be broken. They ought to be restricted to such purchases as were actually needful for the support of their families.

Nicholson also proposes that these two sets of

[1] Calendar of Col. Papers, 1663, 597. It is evident that the loss of revenue is merely a conjectural estimate. There could be no certainty that if the Dutch colonial market had been closed the tobacco would have been exported at all.

[2] Cal. Colonial Papers, March 27, 1697.

officials in the colonies, the naval or, as we should now call them, the preventive officers and the Commissioners of Customs, should be kept wholly distinct. At present both functions are often discharged by one man, who is thus practically irresponsible.

He also proposes that the officers of King's ships should insist on enforcing the revenue laws—an anticipation of the disastrous policy adopted by George Grenville.

In 1702 Penn, in his dispute with Quarry already mentioned,[1] took exception to the latter as judge of Admiralty cases and Commissioner of Customs, on the ground that he was the greatest merchant or trader in the colony. Quarry answered that he could not be a great trader if he would, as he could not compete with smugglers from the West Indies and Scotland.[2]

Spotswood, the Governor of Virginia, states in a letter to the Commissioner of Trade that it was customary to export tobacco to the French West Indies entered as beef and pork, or with the amount falsified in weighing.[3] We learn elsewhere that the cargo for which security had been given was often supplemented by boat-loads brought on board after the vessel had cleared out of port. This was a form of fraud to which the natural condition of Virginia with its paucity of seaports and abundance of landing-stages specially lent itself.

There is also a report from an English official, a description of a disturbance in Rhode Island in 1719 when Kay, the collector of customs, seized several hogsheads of smuggled claret. The mob rescued the wine, staved it, drank some and threw away the rest. No violence was done to Kay, but he was immediately subjected to what seems to have been a vexatious prosecution.[4]

[1] Middle Colonies, p. 537.
[2] Cal. State Papers, Pennsylvania, 559.
[3] Letters, vol. i. p. 9.
[4] R. I. Records, vol. iv. p. 258.

In 1721 we find the Governor of Massachusetts complaining to the Assembly of the illegal importation of French silks, and instructing them to make it a subject of inquiry.[1]

We also read in a pamphlet written not earlier than 1733 of a regular trade with ports in the South of France and Holland. Pitch, tar, ship timber, furs and skins are brought to Europe, and the ships return freighted with French wines and silks. Ships are specially built for and appropriated to the trade. American factors live in the European ports, European ones in America.[2]

In 1742 Bollan, the agent for Massachusetts, reported that there was an extensive illicit trade both in exports and imports with France, Holland, and Spain. 'The men concerned in this commerce are many,' Bollan says, 'some of them men of the greatest fortunes.' He adds, 'If effectual measures be not taken to stop this growing mischief, the British commerce to these plantations and their dependence will be in a great measure ere long lost, and the illicit traders, by their wealth and wiles, have got such power in those parts that laws and orders may have come too late to have a real effect.'[3]

Perhaps the most definite statement on the subject made by any British official is a report by Hardy, the Governor of New York, in 1757.[4] He says that tea, canvas, gunpowder, and arms for the Indians were imported as contraband. They 'render to his Majesty no duty in

[1] Boston Town Records, 1721, p. 156.

[2] This is stated in a broadsheet of which there is a copy in the British Museum. It is entitled *A Short View of the Smuggling Trade carried on by the British Northern Colonies*. It is undated, but there is a reference to an Act of 1733. Tobacco is not mentioned among the contraband exports. This, and the expression *Northern* Colonies, suggests that the writer is dealing with New England and the Middle Colonies only.

[3] Quoted by Chalmers, vol. ii. p. 141.

[4] N. Y. Docs. vol. vii. p. 271.

Europe, and almost totally discourage the importation of these commodities from Britain. In some cases duty is paid on a portion of the cargo. Vessels from Holland are the chief offenders.' Hardy has checked the practice in New York, but the result has been to drive the smugglers to Connecticut and Philadelphia. These statements are confirmed by another New York official, De Lancey.[1]

Owing to the system of drawbacks the amount to be gained by the direct importation of European goods would hardly, by itself, have been worth the risk involved. But to enlarge the tobacco market and break through the monopoly of the English buyer was undoubtedly a lucrative undertaking. And, under the conditions of colonial navigation, clandestine exportation almost of necessity brought clandestine importation as a needful consequence. If a vessel, British or American, ran a cargo of tobacco into Toulon, her best chance of escaping detection would be to make for an American port with a contraband cargo of French goods. Her appearance in an English port unloaded or with a French cargo would inevitably excite suspicion. To return to America empty would be out of the question. Thus it is at least probable that the illicit exportation of tobacco was really the pivot on which the contraband trade turned, though the other subsidiary features of it were those which came more conspicuously under the notice of English officials.

There was also no doubt a marked difference in this respect between the different groups of colonies. Neither the habits nor the resources of the Southern planter created much demand for luxuries from Europe, while every opportunity which offered of extending his sale of tobacco would be eagerly accepted. On the other hand the wealthy merchant at Boston, New York or

[1] N. Y. Docs. vol. vii. p. 273.

Philadelphia was a willing buyer of French silks and foreign wines, while rum distilleries, which played such an important part in the industry of New England, created a continuous demand for molasses from the French islands.

Such expressions of colonial opinion as come before us would not lead us to think that these restrictions, perfunctorily enforced and easily evaded, had any marked influence in the feeling of the colonists to the mother country. Yet some harm no doubt was done. British officials felt that they were being outwitted and defied; ill-temper and alienation followed. It is an unwholesome state of things when the law prescribes one course and the conventional and accepted morality of the community persists in another. The laxity of tone thus begotten showed itself, at times, in forms more serious than the smuggling of wines and tobacco. Connivance with piracy was undoubtedly a blot on the morals of Rhode Island and New York. In time of war the French settlers in Canada could rely on the English colonies for those supplies which were so inadequately furnished by their own resources. In 1751 a letter appeared in a London newspaper, signed 'Publicus,' setting forth very vigorously the erroneous policy of Great Britain in seeking to encourage the West India Islands at the expense of the American colonies. 'There is no comparison in the quantity of the English manufactures that are annually consumed in the Northern colonies and the Sugar Islands. Besides the West Indian trade is a perpetual destruction of seamen, whereas the Northern colony trade and the Fishing especially is a continual nursery for their increase, and it is, therefore, my humble opinion that an exclusive fishery alone would be of more benefit to the nation than all the Sugar Islands put together; for whatever nation has the greatest naval force will always command the trade.'

The writer points out that this view is borne out by the case of Spain, where the mere growth of a colonial empire has brought no corresponding increase of commerce.[1] Three years later we find Governor Dobbs, of North Carolina, endeavouring to impress on the Board of Trade the harm done to his own colony by the restrictions on commerce.[2] They might, if allowed, do a good trade with Madeira and the Azores, exchanging their own products for wines. So, too, they might trade with Ireland, importing rice and indigo and bringing back linen. They are prejudiced by not being allowed to bring salt from continental ports. This practically makes them dependent on British salt, which is unsuited to pickling, and thus what might be a valuable trade in pickled beef is made impossible. It is certainly not easy to see why a restriction which had been waived in the case of New England and Pennsylvania should have been retained in the other colonies.

Restrictions on productive industry.

The advocates of the colonies in their struggle with the mother country occasionally made capital out of the restrictions imposed on their productive industry, and they have not been without later imitators. The worst that can be said of such restrictions is that they were a possible cause of irritation, and, except perhaps in two cases, a wholly superfluous cause. There was little chance that a community where the abundance of fertile land and the paucity of population kept wages up to a high level could possibly compete in productive industry with the over-peopled countries of the Old World. We have seen how the attempts of the legislature in Massachusetts to

[1] Mr. Whitehead publishes this letter in his collection of New Jersey Documents, vol. xix. p. 139. The letter was originally published in a London paper, Sept. 1, 1751, and afterwards republished in the *Pennsylvania Gazette*, March 17, 1752. The name of the paper in which it originally appeared is not given.

[2] N. Car. Records, vol. v. p. 314.

foster textile manufactures failed. The attempts of Spotswood to establish iron-works in Virginia fared little better.

Yet there can be no doubt that the restrictive policy of the British Government did leave on the minds of the colonists a vague feeling that the mother country was willing to sacrifice the commercial prosperity of her children to her own. And, as was said above in two instances, this went beyond intent and did, to some extent, hinder or divert the forms which colonial industry was taking. The colonial hat-maker buying his beaver fur, without the cost of a voyage to England, and selling his manufactured goods without the cost of a voyage to America, was a dangerous rival to the English producer. Not only did the American hat-maker supply his fellow-colonists, but he ousted his English rival from the markets of Europe and the West Indies. We find the Hat-makers' Company in 1730 petitioning to be protected against this competition.[1] Two years later we find that energetic though not very wide-minded philanthropist, Thomas Coram, addressing a memorial on this subject to the Board of Trade.[2] The colonists are beginning to manufacture hats, shoes, and woollen goods. This may be checked now without exciting much opposition; let the system once establish itself and any restriction on it will be felt as a grievance. Coram points out that by the system of drawbacks on goods imported into England and re-imported to the colonies the colonial purchaser is unduly favoured as against the British purchaser, and the British manufacturer is deprived of an advantage which he would otherwise enjoy. He further states that the drawback on foreign cordage had been withdrawn expressly in compliance with a petition from the Rope-makers' Company. It evidently does not occur to Coram that

[1] New Jersey Archives, vol. iii. p. 301.

[2] *Ib.* p. 308.

this system of drawbacks was regarded by the colonists as no more than a legitimate equivalent for the restrictions laid on their productive industry and their export trade.

The American hatter had probably not much difficulty in turning his manual skill into some equally lucrative channel. In another department of industry there can be little doubt that the colonists had a real grievance. The great extent to which wood was used in building created a large and constant demand for iron nails. The process of converting rods into nails employed the New England farmer in the long winter evenings. In 1750 an Act was passed which put an end to this by prohibiting the erection and maintenance in the colonies of 'slitting mills' for converting bars of iron into thin rods.[1] The object of this was to insure that the raw material should be imported into England. The price of the New England farmer's nails was increased by a double voyage across the Atlantic, by the cost of manufacture, and the profits of two middlemen.

We also find the Board of Trade giving instructions to Hunter to take some steps to check the manufacture of woollen and linen stuffs in New York. They have been informed by Cornbury and Heathcote that it had increased to such an extent that two-thirds of those articles used in the colony were manufactured there.[2] Cornbury and Heathcote were not the men to give trustworthy evidence on a question which required careful and exact inquiry. We do not find any trace either of repressive measures by Hunter or of further complaints.

Growth of linen and woollen manufactures in New York.

Again we find the Council and Assembly of New Jersey petitioning the Governor to obtain a relaxation of the Act or Acts which prohibited the importation of iron into England. That the colo-

Iron in New Jersey.

[1] 23 George II. c. 29. [2] N. Y. Docs. vol. v. p. 413.

nists imagined this to be a grievance does not prove that under different conditions any iron would have been imported.

A country where the material resources were far in advance of the demands made upon them, and where industry has that elasticity which is begotten of education and energy, is not likely to suffer greatly even if ill-advised politicians should attempt either through selfishness or paternal benevolence to prescribe the direction which it should take. The worst that can be said of the industrial legislation of Parliament was that it presented the mother country as selfish in its purposes and not specially intelligent in its execution of them, and that it might at any moment furnish a colonial agitator with a plausible theme for complaint and denunciation. One grievance of the colonists arose out of the perfectly reasonable claim of the British Government to secure for the royal navy all ship-timber growing on unappropriated ground. Unfortunately, the claim was one which had to be enforced in sparsely populated and, therefore, somewhat lawless districts, such as New Hampshire,[1] and the annals of that colony show more than one disturbance arising out of the action of British officials in this matter.

On the other hand we find the Assembly of New Jersey in 1693 passing an Act forbidding the exportation of timber unless the master gave security to the amount of a hundred pounds that he could export it to Great Britain or the West Indies.[2] Yet this very compliance had in it an element of danger. For the claim of the local legislature to give additional force to an Act of Parliament by its approval seemed to carry with it a right to disapprove.

[1] N. Hants. Prov. Papers, vol. iv. pp. 874–5; vol. v. pp. 12, 20 cf. p. 122.

[2] Col. Papers, July 2, 1693.

It would not be fair to overlook the fact that the Home Government did at least in one instance endeavour unsolicited to be of assistance to colonial productive industry. In 1734 the Board of Trade inquired of the Proprietors of Pennsylvania what encouragement the trade of the colony specially needed in the production of naval stores and of other commodities which would not interfere with the trade and produce of Great Britain. The matter was laid before the Assembly, who recommended the encouragement of hematite and of pig and bar iron.[1]

So, too, we find Spotswood, in a despatch to the Board of Trade, regretting the over-production of tobacco, and suggesting that the colonists should be encouraged in the manufacture of pitch, tar, and hemp, for the use of the navy.[2]

Keith, too, both in the report already referred to[3] and in two letters written about the same time, deprecates any fear of the colonies becoming rivals to the mother country in manufactures.[4]

A good deal of rhetoric has been at various times expended on the selection of colonial governors during the eighteenth century. It is often said that a colonial governorship was a refuge for a broken-down courtier. Thus we find Lewis Morris, at the time when he was attacking Cosby, complaining of 'colonial Governors who do not come here to take the air, but generally to repair a shattered fortune or acquire an estate.'[5] That one department would have been strangely unlike everything else in eighteenth-century politics if there had not been venal appointments and discreditable jobs. But we may also confidently say that the administrative capacity in which the

Colonial Governors.

[1] Pennsylvania Records, vol. iii. p. 576.
[2] Letters, vol. i. p. 72.
[3] *V.s.* p. 140.
[4] N. Jersey Archives, vol. iii. p. 203.
[5] N. Y. Docs. vol. v. p. 882.

English race has never shown itself lacking did not wholly fail in this special province. The names of Craven, Hunter, Spotswood, Dinwiddie, Burnet, Shirley and Dobbs are an abundant answer to any charge of general incompetence or dishonesty.

What evil there was lay more in the system than in either the men who carried it out or those who selected them. The work of a colonial Governor was done wholly under the supervision and in some measure under the control of the Board of Trade. Yet that Board had no voice in his selection and no power to enforce their wishes by dismissal. Here, as everywhere, our colonial policy was ruined by the lack of a central department, with continuous traditions and a definite policy.

Position of the Governor.

Again the Governor, let his administrative ability and his integrity and public spirit be what they might, was constantly hampered by the vagueness and indefiniteness of the system with which he was dealing.

Appointment of judges.

A typical instance of a question on which no definite and general usage obtained was the appointment of the judiciary. In some cases the appointment was for life, in others the judge was removable by the Governor. The arguments for the latter course were that there was a paucity of capable men, and that by this system when one such could be found a vacancy could be made for him at once. Moreover, the fear of removal might check a tendency on the part of the judiciary to become the servants of the Assembly on whom they depended for their salary. Yet it is clear that these possible advantages brought the corresponding dangers of jobbery and intimidation on the part of the Governor A bitter and somewhat discreditable dispute, and one injurious to the credit of the British Government, arose in New York in 1733. Cosby endeavoured to bring a case in which he was personally interested before the Court of Chancery, in which he as Chancellor of the colony presided. Chief Justice Morris denied the Governor right of jurisdiction in the case, and for this was dismissed, as Cosby expressed it, to discourage Boston principles.[1] So, too, we find Cosby complaining in a despatch to the Duke of Newcastle that 'the example and spirit of the Boston people begins to spread abroad among these colonists in a most marvellous manner.'[2] The expressions are interesting as showing that then, as later, Boston was looked on as a focus of disaffection extending beyond its own borders.

Bradley's report.

Before we quit the relations of the colonists to those in authority over them, it may be well to single out a few specially illustrative incidents which have not come before us in the direct course of the story. We have already seen how definitely the party system had established itself in New York. During the reign of George II. the colony was seething with faction, and no Governor after Burnet was able to avoid becoming entangled in it. In 1729 we find Bradley, the Attorney-General to the colony, sending home to the Board of Trade a violent and alarmist despatch on the condition of the colony.[3] According to him, the Assembly use their financial powers to reward friends and punish enemies. His warnings of disaffection do not apply merely to New York. 'Other neighbouring provinces seem to show the same kind of spirit and a strong inclination to take the earliest opportunity of setting up for themselves.'

Bradley reminds the Board of all the danger and cost incurred through the supineness which allowed Bacon's rebellion to come to a head unheeded. The

[1] N. Y. Docs. vol. v. pp. 942–55. It is but fair to say that Cosby also charges Morris with drunkenness and malversation of justice.

[2] N. J. Archives, vol. v. p. 320.

[3] N. Y. Docs. vol. v. p. 901.

increase of population has made such a danger more serious than before. This is followed by words of warning which now sound strangely prophetic, and on which English statesmen would have done well to ponder. 'It may be thought impracticable at present for any of these provinces or places alone to attempt anything of that kind, yet if several of them should even at this time join in such a conspiracy (and could these Assemblies openly do more tho' they had actually so engaged ?), it would be extremely difficult and expensive, if not impracticable, at the distance, and in such a thicket of wood and trees as these countries are, to reduce them to their duty and obedience, in regard of their populousness at present, the skilfulness, strength, and activity of the people who are inured to hardships, can defend themselves in woods and behind trees, can live on roots and what the woods afford without bread, beer or spirits, or forage for horses, &c., and can travel in the woods without guides or the help of roads, few of which are yet made, which forces that have not been so used cannot possibly do. Besides the impracticableness of drawing the necessary carriages for an army in such woods as these, the difficulties of passing great lakes and rivers, the severities of summer's heat and winter's cold, the great perplexity from flies and vermin in the former and deep snows in the latter.

'While Assemblies dare act thus and seem to have it in their power to obtain what laws they please, how can his Majesty's interests be secure in so remote a country where people multiply so fast, a country of so vast extent, so considerable for its navigation and which takes off yearly so great a quantity of the woollen, iron, and other manufactures of Great Britain, besides the dependency which that valuable branch of the revenue arising from the Virginia tobacco seems to have on the security of the obedience of the people of these provinces and countys to his Majesty. Upon the whole would it not be advisable that no Assembly for the future should transact any affair in the house without the presence of a Commissioner on behalf of the Crown, as 'tis said is used in the General Assembly of Scotland, which Commissioners should therefore be rendered independent of the Assembly and entirely dependent on the Crown, and also that some effectual speedy course be taken to render all the officers of the Crown entirely independent on (*sic*) Assemblies?'

We seem to be reading a warning sent home by some official of the school of Hutchinson or Oliver. The parallel between the present and the future dispute is strengthened by a document of two years later. There Rip Van Dam, who is acting as President of the Council during an interregnum in the governorship, complains to the Board of Trade that the interests of New York are sacrificed to those of the British sugar islands by the prohibition of molasses from the French colonies, financial ruin will follow, and the only effective barrier against French invasion will be swept away.[1]

Colonel Cosby, who succeeded Montgomerie in 1732, had no colonial experience, and was wholly unfitted by character to deal with a state of things such as now existed in New York. Before he had been in office two years we find Van Dam formulating a long string of charges against him.[2]

He had in various ways ignored the Council and deprived them of their constitutional rights. He had not communicated his instructions to them. He had appointed and displaced judges, justices and sheriffs without consulting the Council. He had assumed the right, not given him by the constitution, of acting as President of the Council. He had packed Councils by summoning only those members whose views agreed

[1] N. Y. Docs. vol. v. p. 926.

[2] *Ib.* p. 975.

with his own. He had on his own responsibility established a Court of Equity, and thereby encroached on the rights of the Assembly. He had also been guilty of various isolated acts of maladministration, such as conniving at French contraband traders and falsifying his returns of soldiers.

According to Cosby, Van Dam was the mere tool of Morris and his ally, Alexander.[1] Yet a little while before we find Van Dam accusing Morris of bringing scandalous charges against him and one of his colleagues. Morris replies that the only charge he brought was ignorance of English, and that is well founded. 'All the world knows that they were never masters of the English tongue nor never will be, and if they understood the common discourse it is as much as they do.'[2]

In one instance, if we may believe Cosby, he had embroiled himself with the settlers by protecting the Indians against a gross attempt at fraud. The corporation of Albany had, he says, frightened the Mohawks into a belief that Montgomerie, when Governor, would take away their land. To save it they had best grant it in trust to the corporation. This was done, and the corporation then treated the trust deed as an absolute conveyance. Cosby obtained the deed and restored it to the Mohawks, who tore it to pieces.[3]

The most conspicuous incident in the conflict between Cosby and the popular party was the Zenger trial. John Peter Zenger had been brought to New York as a child by his mother, one of the refugees from the Palatinate. About 1726 he set himself up as a printer, and seven years later he started a

The Zenger trial.[4]

[1] N. Y. Docs. vol. vi. p. 9. [2] *Ib.* vol. v. p. 886.

[3] Cosby to Board of Trade, Dec. 15, 1737. N. Y. Docs. vol. v. p. 960.

[4] The best authority for the Zenger trial, though of necessity to some extent an *ex parte* one, is the report drawn up by Zenger himself and republished in London in 1750. Cosby in his despatches is significantly reserved about it.

newspaper, 'Zenger's Journal.' The paper was adopted as the organ of the party opposed to Cosby and his supporters, whom it attacked with ability and with considerable license of language. In 1734 Zenger's paper was brought under the notice of the Governor and Council. To those who have grown up in an atmosphere of free speech and almost unrestrained political criticism it will seem well nigh incredible that any government should have been so ill-advised as to make Zenger's utterances the subject of formal notice and official proceedings. The passage selected as matter for procedure was a conversation, probably imaginary, between a citizen of New Jersey and certain inhabitants of New York, one of whom was about to migrate to Pennsylvania. The New Jersey man, observing his New York friends to be full of complaints, tried to persuade them to migrate to his own colony. The answer was that they would be leaping out of the frying pan into the fire since both colonies had the same Governor, and the Assembly of New Jersey had shown what was to be expected from them. Thereupon the intending emigrant to Pennsylvania condoled with his fellow-citizens on the evils resulting from the action of men who were the tools of government, and expressed a hope that the Assembly would not be influenced by the private interests of individual members or by the smiles and powers of the Governor. The supposed accuser then enumerates Cosby's misdeeds. Judges have been arbitrarily displaced, trial by jury in some cases denied, and qualified voters disfranchised without reason.

The first stage in the conflict was that the Council ordered the offending papers to be burnt, and moreover commanded the Mayor and magistrates as the Court of Quarter sessions to be present at the burning. One member of that body protested on the ground that there was no precedent for such an order. The feeling of the

Court in the matter was sufficiently shown by their action. They refused to make any record of the proceedings in their minutes, nor would they allow one of their minor officials to carry out the sentence, and when the burning was performed by the sheriff they stayed away. These may only have been the proceedings of a majority, but if there was an adverse minority there is no sign of its taking any action.

Eleven days later the Council ordered that Zenger should be committed to prison, to be tried for publishing seditious libels tending to raise faction and tumults, to bring government into contempt, and to disturb the peace of the colony.

Thereupon Zenger was taken into custody and, if we may believe his own statement, refused the use of writing materials, and not allowed to communicate with anyone. His friends, however, obtained a writ of habeas corpus, and he was brought before the Chief Justice and committed for trial. Thereupon Zenger applied for bail, at the same time making affidavit that, excepting his printing apparatus and wearing apparel, he was not worth forty pounds. The Court, however, demanded personal security for four hundred pounds. It is difficult to suppose that, when popular feeling ran as high as it did, Zenger could not have got help for the required amount. Probably, however, he thought that it would serve his turn better to influence popular opinion by returning to prison, which he did.

The trial came on in the following April. Zenger's counsel, Alexander and Smith, at once raised an important constitutional point. They denied the competence of the Chief Justice De Lancey, and of Philipse who sat with him, on the ground that the commissions were made out to last not during good behaviour, but during the King's good pleasure. This plea if admitted would practically have nullified all legal proceedings in the colony. De Lancey, however, did not content himself with overruling the objection, but treated the action of Zenger's counsel as contempt of Court, and excluded them both by another order from further practice.

The result was the postponement of the trial till the following August. The cause of authority gained nothing by the silencing of Zenger's counsel. Their place was filled by Alexander Hamilton, of Philadelphia. He clearly saw that he was dealing, not with an ordinary criminal trial, but with a question which involved constitutional issues, and also gave scope for an appeal to popular passion.

Bradley, the Attorney-General, who prosecuted took his stand upon Zenger's criticism of the government already quoted. That he could adduce nothing stronger was the most complete proof that could be found of the folly and futility of the course adopted by Cosby and De Lancey.

The speech of Bradley as prosecutor was virtually a denial of all right of political criticism. He did not endeavour to prove that Zenger's charges against Cosby were untrue or even exaggerated. Nor did he take the ground that Zenger's utterances were dangerous as likely to lead to any breach of the peace. Zenger was in Bradley's words a man who notoriously scandalized the Governor and principal magistrates and officers of the government by charging them with depriving the people of their rights and liberties. Cosby was no more a Strafford than Zenger was a Hampden. But the logical conclusion to be drawn from Bradley's plea was—let a Governor be never so arbitrary, protest and comment were alike illegal.

It was no hard matter for Hamilton to meet such a plea. The whole essence of his argument came to this—that free criticism, free expression of public opinion on the conduct of those in authority was a necessary condition for the maintenance of liberty. He also pointed out with considerable dexterity that to criticize the unconstitutional proceedings of a colonial Governor is not merely consistent with loyalty to the Crown, but absolutely essential to the fulfilment of such loyalty, since only so can the delegated authority of the Crown be saved from abuse.

Hamilton's speech was decorated with appeals to the memory of the earlier and the later Brutus. Without such an eighteenth-century appeal on behalf of liberty it would have been incomplete. But there was no attempt to make rhetoric do the work of argument. And there was assuredly ample ground for Hamilton's claim that the question was 'not of small or private concern, not the cause of a poor printer, nor of New York alone,' but that it might 'affect every Freeman that lives under a British government on the main of America.'

De Lancey's summing up must have seemed to many who heard it the fullest admission and confirmation of those words. He quoted with approval a dictum of Chief Justice Holt: to say that corrupt officers are appointed to administer affairs is certainly a reflection on the government. If people should not be called to account for possessing the people with an ill opinion of the government, no government can subsist. For it is necessary for all government that the people should have a good opinion of it.'

The jury disregarding De Lancey's charge acquitted Zenger, and six weeks later the Town Council of New York presented Hamilton with the freedom of the city in a gold box.

The Zenger trial has more than a local or personal interest. It strikingly illustrates the change of political thought which was making itself felt both in the mother country and the British dependencies. It marked the era of transition when the right of free speech, which to an earlier generation had seemed a daring paradox, was understood and claimed, yet far from universally accepted.

New Jersey was not so steeped in faction as New York. Yet in both colonies we see a marked difference from the political life of New England. There the conflict with government was fought in a spirit which invests it, despite much that is factious and ungenerous, with a certain moral dignity. In New York and New Jersey the central conflict is at every step obscured and entangled amid petty sordid intrigues and personal squabbles.

In 1732 we find Morris informing the Duke of Newcastle, then Secretary of State, that 'the rendering governors and all other officers directly dependent on the people is the general inclination and endeavour of all the plantations in America, and nowhere pursued with more steadiness and less decency than in New Jersey; and were they indulged with a separate Governor before they had made proper provision for his support and that of the officers of the government he must be a man of very uncommon abilities who is capable of working them up to their duty.'[1]

A private letter from the same writer, at a somewhat later date, shows what was meant by 'less decency.' Morris there describes the Assembly 'scolding, giving the lye, threatening to spit in the face.'[2]

In a somewhat later letter to the Board of Trade, Morris charges Cosby with accepting a thousand pounds from the Assembly to use his private influence against the Molasses Act.[3]

One expression used by Morris, 'were they indulged with a separate Governor,' reminds us that the people

[1] N. J. Archives, vol. iii. p. 315. [2] *Ib.* vol. vi. p. 60.
[3] *Ib.* vol. iii. p. 349.

of New Jersey had a real grievance. The system of uniting them with New York under one Governor could not fail to bear hardly on the smaller and poorer colony.

The social attractions of New York made it almost certain that the Governor would usually reside there. Consequently he has none of that local knowledge of New Jersey which is needed for good administration, especially for making appointments. The Council also have to go frequently to New York; there is a delay in obtaining writs, and the salaries paid to officials in New Jersey are mainly spent in New York.[1]

Upon Cosby's death in 1736 the grievance was remedied. The province was then separated from New York, Lewis Morris was appointed Governor, and remained in office for the rest of his life. He died in 1746, and an interregnum of nearly a year followed.

Under the government of his successor the colony was thrown into a condition which, if we can believe some contemporary witnesses, bordered closely on anarchy. We have already seen what a tangle of confusion had been created by the successive sub-infeudations, as one may call them, which the soil of New Jersey had undergone. About 1745 a crop of territorial disputes sprung up, having their root in titles said to have been granted immediately after the conquest of New Netherlands. In 1664 Nicolls, acting on behalf of the Duke of York, had sold certain lands to John Bailey, Daniel Denton, and others, and under this grant the settlement of Elizabethtown had come into existence.[3] One condition of the grant was that

Territorial dispute.[2]

[1] In 1730 the Assembly of New Jersey petition for a separate Governor, and in 1731 a similar petition is made by the Council. The evils of the existing system are set forth in the petition of the Council, and also in a memorial drawn up by Partridge, the agent for New Jersey. N. J. Records, vol. iii. pp. 270, 296, 451.

[2] In my account of this I have relied on the New Jersey Archives.

[3] Brodhead, vol. ii. p. 64; cf. *Middle Colonies*, p. 368.

the recipients should 'do and perform such acts and things as shall be appointed by his Royal Highness the Duke of York and his deputies.' Obviously it might be a nice legal point how far the proprietary rights thus reserved by Nicolls had been transmitted to the various successive purchasers. No conflict or dispute, however, seems to have arisen till nearly a hundred years from the date of the original grant. It would seem, too, that the greater number of the freeholders at Elizabethtown had acknowledged the territorial rights of the Proprietors by obtaining grants from them. The existing documents bearing on the matter, though copious, do not tell us the precise form which the dispute took at the outset. In all likelihood the Proprietors proposed either to re-grant lands included, or said to be included, in Nicolls's grant, or else to exact dues from the present occupants. At all events in the summer of 1744 the freeholders of Elizabethtown thought it necessary to lay before the Privy Council a memorial claiming to be independent of the Proprietors of New Jersey under a grant made by Nicolls.[1] They also either now or at a later stage of the dispute put in evidence a document, dated 1666, by which Philip Carteret gave the grantees of Elizabethtown leave to purchase from the Indians 'what quantity of land they shall think convenient.'[2] This was at best a vague foundation on which to build a claim adverse to that of the Proprietors. The matter was referred to the Board of Trade, and both the applicants and the Proprietors expressed themselves willing to abide by their decision.

The next incident we hear of is, an encroachment in the autumn of 1745 by one Baldwin, who proceeded to cut trees on the lands of the Proprietors. For this he is imprisoned at Newark, and speedily liberated by

[1] N. J. Records, vol. vi. p. 205.

[2] *Ib.* vol. vii. p. 32.

a mob. Three of his supporters are committed for trial. One is at once rescued; the other two are put into prison, but again the gaol is broken and they escape. The disaffection spreads, and for the next five years the colony is almost in a state of anarchy and of what would be called in modern times agrarian war. Not only is the authority of the Proprietors defied, but those who hold lands under grants from them are evicted by force, and are in some cases subjected to brutal violence. Feeling became so acute that the rioters are even suspected of introducing a troop of Indians to assist them.

Gradually the rioters become definitely organized. They raise money for purposes of resistance, in some cases extorting it by force, and individuals not merely occupy the lands in dispute but grant leases of it.

A race element was in some measure present in the conflict, suggestive of later incidents in American history. A burlesque letter ascribed to one of the rioters, and written in that form of German-English with which modern humorists have made us familiar, is of little value as direct evidence, but shows that many of the rioters were German and talked German. There were also, we read, many Irish of the poorer sort among them.

The conflict, however, was mainly one between rich and poor. On the one side were the Council as the representatives of the Proprietors, and also as practically representing the wealthy merchants and larger landowners. They were led by two men of abundant energy and pugnacity, James Alexander and Robert Morris, the son of Lewis Morris. On the other side were the elected Representatives.

The Governor unhappily was not one qualified either to compose strife or to assert authority. The appointment vacated by Morris's death was granted to

Belcher. He brought with him from his previous governorship of Massachusetts the reputation of a trimmer and a time-server, at once unscrupulous and unskilful. It is clear that he had no intention of defying popular opinion on behalf of the Proprietors, or even on behalf of the authority of the Crown and of law. The situation is of a kind not unfamiliar to us in modern times. Belcher and the Assembly minimize the resistance to law, and would fain represent it as no more than a dispute between the Proprietors and private landholders, and arising out of territorial claims. On the other hand Morris and Alexander write home describing it as a war of class against class. The Proprietors are 'wigmen and gentlemen,' the Assembly are 'capmen and mobmen.'

In 1747 the Governor and the Assembly made what was from the point of view of the Council an absolute surrender to the rioters. A fine of ten pounds was imposed on all who had broken gaols and rescued prisoners. With that exception a complete indemnity is granted to the rioters provided they make good all damage done and undertake to keep the peace for three years. Thereupon twenty-three of the rioters submitted. The rest continued their course of disturbance. More gaols are broken open and timber is cut upon the lands in dispute. From mere rioting the disaffected pass to something like organized rebellion. They enter into engagements for mutual support and levy money for defence, in some instances by force.

The mutual relations of the Council and the Assembly now became more definitely hostile. The former urged the need of strong measures, and proposed that the Governor be furnished with money wherewith to raise troops. But when a preliminary resolution was proposed in the Assembly setting forth the need of effectual measures for quelling the riots, it was rejected by fifteen votes against three. Not content with that, the Assembly passed a resolution declaring that the demand of the Council reflected injuriously on them. This was met by the Council with a recriminating resolution.

At length the Council in despair memorialized the British Government. 'The Government,' so their words run, 'is weak, the rioters are powerful and strong, and property is held at the mercy and pleasure of a rebellious mob.' Arms and a man-of-war should be sent from England. Assistance should be obtained from New York, Pennsylvania, and Connecticut. One is lost in wonder at the ineptitude of a proposal which would have thus extended the area of strife.

The action of the Home Government was not such as to encourage their supporters. The Board of Trade drew up a lengthy and minute report, admirable as a summary of the past struggle, but practically valueless as far as any administrative instruction or suggestion went.[1] All that it did in that way was to invest Belcher with certain coercive powers, which his previous conduct made it very certain he would shrink from using effectually. We hear nothing of any penal measures, and it would seem as if the rioters were left, if not in undisturbed possession of what they had seized, at least unpunished. It should not be forgotten that only sixteen years separated the New Jersey rebellion from the passing of the Stamp Act.

Dis-affection in Penn-sylvania.

In no colony did discontent take so acute a form as it did in New Jersey, but both in Pennsylvania and North Carolina there were abundant symptoms of disaffection and alienation. In 1729 we find the Assembly of Pennsylvania protesting against the Governor and Council sitting as

[1] Printed in the New Jersey Archives, vol. vii. pp. 466, &c. My account is mainly based on this.

a Court of Chancery, on the ground that such a court nominated by arbitrary authority might become an instrument of tyranny.[1] It is clear that this contention if accepted would introduce a new and serious limitation on the authority of the Crown.

In 1740 the Assembly, pursuing the same policy, denied the Governor's right to a final veto on bills. He might criticize and point out objections, and no more.[2] In other words, like their successors in the Revolution, they made a claim which implied absolute sovereignty, though in all likehood it did not present itself in that light to those who urged it. Over and above this, every call for defensive measures in Pennsylvania whether against Indians or French was certain to be the signal for a protest and a dispute. But those matters belong to other branches of our subject.

In considering the disputes between authority and the popular party in Pennsylvania, one point must not be forgotten. The authority attacked was at least in name not that of the Crown, but of the Proprietors. The difference, however, is more apparent than real. The proprietary colonies were more and more becoming parts of a body administered on a comprehensive system under the Board of Trade. It was not easy for the colonial Assembly to defy the authority of the Proprietors without coming into conflict with that of the Crown. Moreover, the disputes which occupied colonial officials and colonial assemblies were important, not so much from the specific points at issue, as from their effect in calling into existence a spirit of watchful jealousy towards every exercise of authority which had its seat outside the limits of America. Every colonial official, however appointed, might in a certain sense be looked on as belonging to a hierarchy, acting under the authority of

[1] See Appendix i.

[2] Pennsylvania Records, vol. iv. p. 214.

the Crown, an authority to a share in which Parliament was now making somewhat undefined claims.

The composition and antecedents of North Carolina made it almost certain that if disaffection and anarchy existed anywhere they would be found there. The province, too, seems to have been singularly unfortunate in its Governors. Sir Richard Everard, appointed Governor by the Proprietors before their surrender, seems to have been a turbulent Jacobite. He is accused by the Council of violent language, of imposing arbitrary fees, and of wishing to make the death of George I. an occasion of public rejoicing.[1] A presumably impartial witness speaks of Everard's 'weakness and indiscretion,' whereby the colony was 'run into the utmost confusion and disorder' and 'the administration rendered contemptible and odious.'[2] Everard's own denial of these charges is so vague and general as to carry little conviction.[3]

Disaffection in North Carolina.

The Crown was hardly more happy than the Proprietors in its choice of a representative. The first royal Governor was George Burrington.[4] He had already held the office as Everard's predecessor, and was charged with describing the latter as 'a noodle and an ape—no more fit to be Governor than a hog in the woods.' Later on we shall meet with specimens of Burrington's invective which show that this charge was in no way improbable.

Burrington was soon at loggerheads with the Assembly. The impression left by the charges brought against

[1] Address of the Council of North Carolina to the King, Records, vol. viii. p. 2.

[2] Lowick, the Public Surveyor to the Colony, in a letter to the Board of Trade, Records, vol. viii. p. 1.

[3] *Ib.* p. 5.

[4] My account of Burrington's official career and of the disputes in which he was engaged are taken from the third volume of the North Carolina Records.

him, and also by his own copious and outspoken correspondence, is that he was not lacking in public spirit. As an administrator he was certainly energetic and, as it would seem, not without capacity. It is noteworthy, too, that no charge of personal corruption or immorality is brought against him. The nearest approach to such is a statement that he used a criminal charge as a means of exacting his full due from a private debtor. His main fault was his utter want of restraint in his public utterances. Men of the eighteenth century were used to strong language, nor was North Carolina a home of refinement. But even there some of Burrington's utterances must have been startling. Men were not used to hear a legislative Assembly told in a formal address that 'Bodies of men cannot blush, and that's your advantage. If Assemblies in this province proceed in the manner you have done with heat and partiality they will themselves give the greatest grievance and oppression to this country. Burgessing has been for some years a source of lies and cause of disturbances which has deterred good men from being candidates or entering the list of noise and of faction which every common observer knows.' He concludes with a more formal and definite complaint: 'Neither doth the King's instructions, that only freeholders should vote, find any weight in your elections.'[1]

We have seen how Burrington had spoken of his predecessor. In a speech to the Assembly we find him describing an official whom he disliked as 'a stupid, inconsiderate blockhead, a perfidious creature, a promise-breaker, a horrible bear, a most ungrateful wretch that has not one good quality in him.'[2] And in a despatch to the Board of Trade Burrington describes the same man and two other leading settlers as 'guilty of

[1] Burrington's address to the Assembly; Records, vol. iii. p. 610.
[2] *Ib.* p. 615.

wickedness, villainies, follies and madness,' and refers to their 'detestable mode of lying and inventing calumnies.'[1] It is also alleged that when Burrington saw persons walking with officials whom he disliked he would shout across the street warning them that they were in bad company.[2] It is clear that Burrington was one of those who believed that every opponent must be actuated by thoroughly corrupt motives, and who resented every constitutional restraint which in any way hindered what he personally believed to be for the public good.

Apart from mere bickerings arising out of hot temper and tactlessness, there were two definite administrative questions on which Burrington and the Assembly differed. One was the quarrel over fees already described. In a despatch sent home soon after that dispute Burrington states his opponents' case with a definiteness of which he is perhaps hardly conscious. 'It has been a policy of this subtle people of North Carolina never to raise any money but what is appropriated, and to pretend and insist that no public money can or ought to be paid but by a claim given to and allowed by the House of Burgesses.'[3]

Another financial dispute arose out of Burrington's claim as representative of the Crown to appoint the Treasurer of the colony. He defended it by the plea that in England Parliament raised money, the Crown administered it.[4] It might have been fairly answered that in practice Parliament had transferred to itself a share of those powers which in theory belonged to the Crown, and that the Ministers who controlled the public finances, though nominally the servants of the Crown, were in real truth the nominees of Parliament. The incident showed how dangerous it was to draw

[1] Records, vol. iii. p. 623.
[2] N. Car. Records, vol. iii. p. 356.
[3] *Ib.* p. 331.
[4] *Ib.* p. 484.

analogies from such a system as that of the British constitution, bristling with anomalies and in no way conforming to any precise theory.

In one instance Burrington seems to have been held back from a policy of conciliation by the somewhat pedantic attitude of those to whom he was responsible. He wished to settle his disputes with the Assembly by a personal conference with a committee of that body. The Board of Trade pointed out through their Secretary, Popple, that this would be unconstitutional. The Governor had his prescribed form of action through his veto, and having that he could not exercise any further control over the Assembly.[1]

Dispute about electoral districts.

Another dispute arose turning on the right to create new electoral districts. Was that right vested in the Governor or in the Assembly? The Assembly charged Burrington with creating constituencies so as to further his own views—in the political slang of a later day, with 'gerrymandering.'[2] The necessity for new constituencies equitably formed is supported by the general proposition of which we hear so much twenty years later. 'It will, we believe, be acknowledged the birthright of British subjects to be governed by no laws but those of their own making—that is, such as they have assented to.' Throughout these disputes we are reminded how the conditions of a new country, where established political arrangements had to be perpetually shifted and modified to adapt them to altered circumstances, begat a peculiar type of political ability, a lawyer-like ingenuity of interpretation and a subtle dexterity in taking advantage of technical points.

Burrington was no doubt acrimonious and hotheaded. But he had grounds for bitterness if we may believe his own statement, set forth in a petition to the

[1] N. Car. Records, vol. iii. p. 351.

[2] *Ib.* pp. 383, 449.

Board of Trade, that some of his enemies in the colony had attempted to murder him, and had, when molested, fled to Virginia.[1] We find him, too, after his retirement from the post of Governor, making rational and useful suggestions as to the commercial prosperity of the colony.[2] There was no attempt made, he points out, to utilize the natural harbours of the colony. Cattle are sent to Virginia overland, and negroes who might be imported direct are brought from South Carolina. Instead of aiming, as they ought, at developing a regular trade with the West Indies, the Assembly cripple it by their system of import duties.

It is worth noting that Burrington's successor Johnstone accuses him of supporting the popular agitation against the payment of quit-rents. It is of course possible that Burrington was willing to sacrifice the rights of the Crown in order to better his own position with the Assembly; but there was so little of the time-server or the diplomatist in his character that one is disposed to put a better interpretation on his conduct.

Disputes between the Assembly and Governor Johnstone.[3]

Two subjects of dispute disturbed the colony under the governorship of Johnstone. One was that of quit-rents, to which we have just referred. Like almost every financial dispute in the colonies the question was inextricably mixed up with that of currency, or one should perhaps rather say complicated by the lack of currency. The demand made by the landholders and supported by the Assembly was that quit-rents might be paid in commodities valued at arbitrary rates, much in advance of their real price in open market. They also asked that payment might be made at various stations in the colony instead of at one central office.

[1] N. Car. Records, vol. iv. p. 165.

[2] *Ib.* p. 169.

[3] For these, see N. Car. Records, vol. iv.

The difficulties of communication made this demand not unreasonable, but it could hardly be considered fair that the extra cost involved in collecting should all fall upon the Crown.

Though Johnstone's career was marked by more than one official dispute, yet he seems to have been personally conciliatory and popular, and always to have leant to a policy of compromise. He now assented to an Act which allowed the quit-rents to be paid at local stations, and in paper money taken not at its nominal value, but at a rate to be fixed by a committee, one half to be made up of the Governor, the Council, the Attorney-General, and the Receiver-General, the other half from the Assembly.[1]

This Act of compromise was, however, vetoed by the Crown, mainly on the ground that the provisions for fixing the value of the paper money to be received in payment gave no sufficient protection to the recipient.[2] At the same time we find McCulloch, the Agent for the colony, opposing the Act on widely different grounds. The Act provided that the additional cost of collection should not fall on the Crown, but be defrayed by a poll-tax. McCulloch points out that this will bear heavily on the poor man with a large family.[3]

The difficulty about collecting stations is a good illustration of the way in which the colony suffered from lack of means of communication. So, too, we find Johnstone complaining in his address to the Assembly of the inconvenience caused by the want of a fixed place for public business: 'It is impossible to finish any matter as it ought to be while we go on in this itinerant way. We have tried every town in the colony, and it is high time to settle somewhere.'[4]

Not only was business hindered, but it was scarcely

[1] N. Car. Records, vol. iv. p. 415.
[2] *Ib.* p. 425.
[3] *Ib.*
[4] *Ib.* p. 735.

possible to secure the effective representation of the whole colony. In 1746 we find Johnstone frankly admitting, in a despatch to the Board of Trade, that in order to carry the quit-rent bill he had held the Assembly at Wilmington, 'on purpose to keep at home the Northern members who are most numerous, and from whom the greatest opposition was expected.'[2]

The dispute between the two counties.[1]

Johnstone's manœuvre had far-reaching results of a kind probably widely different from anything which he had anticipated. The colony consisted of two counties, Albemarle and Bath, each divided into electoral districts called precincts. In the former county each precinct returned five members, in the latter only two. As Johnstone had expected, at the Assembly of 1746 the members of the Northern county, Albemarle, were for the most part absent. The majority most audaciously took advantage of this to carry an Act reducing the representation of the Northern precincts to two members apiece. At the next election the voters in Albemarle county ignored this. They appear, though this is a little obscure, to have pleaded that such a change could only be made constitutionally by an actual majority of the whole Assembly, and that this condition had not been fulfilled. They then proceeded to elect, as before, five members to each precinct. Thereupon the legislature as a whole declared the election null and void. The inhabitants of Albemarle county accepted the situation, and retaliated by refusing to pay taxes. The result was that one-half of the colony was thrown into a state of anarchy. The inhabitants of Albemarle refused not only to pay taxes but to acknowledge the validity of any law passed by

[1] N. Car. Records, vol. iv. pp. 1201 &c. Mr. Saunders gives a good account of this dispute in his introduction to the fourth volume of the Records.

[2] N. Car. Records, vol. iv. p. 504.

the Assembly. Robbery, we are told, and even murder, became common; gaols were broken up, and it was impossible to empannel juries.[1]

The inhabitants of Bath county soon became dissatisfied at having the whole maintenance of the colony thrown on their shoulders, and likewise refused to pay taxes.[2]

For eight years this state of anarchy seems to have continued. Then the Board of Trade took up the question and decided, after consulting the law officers of the Crown, that the precincts in Albemarle were entitled to five members each. The original Act reducing the number was, as those opposed to it held, unconstitutional and should have been vetoed by the Governor. At the same time, while upholding the view of those who declared that an absolute majority was needed for such a change, they condemned the condition as inconvenient, and recommended that it should be modified.[3] The report of the Board of Trade was adopted by the Crown, and embodied in instructions to Johnstone's successor, Arthur Dobbs, and the Albemarle precincts were once more allowed their five members.

The conflict between the two sections of the colony was closely mixed up with considerations of financial policy. The Northern section of the colony was largely dependent for its trade on Virginia. They had therefore a special interest in maintaining the value of the currency, and checking the profuse issue of paper money.[4] The Board of Trade in their report dealt with two other controversial points. They recommended

[1] This is stated in a report from the Moravian bishop, Spangenberg. N. C. Records, vol. iv. p. 1211. I have already referred to this report.

[2] N. C. Records, vol. iv. Preface.

[3] The Report of the Board of Trade is in the Records, vol. v. p. 81.

[4] This is stated in a memorial drawn up by the inhabitants of Albemarle, N. C. Records, vol. iv. p. 1204.

that the Crown should refuse to accept the depreciated colonial paper in payment of quit-rents except at its real as distinguished from its nominal value. Any hardship, however, which might result from this was modified by an opinion given some years before by the law officers of the Crown, ruling that the quit-rents might be paid in commodities to be taken at their market value.[1]

Another question dealt with in the report was that which had formed a subject of dispute in Burrington's time, the right of the Assembly to create fresh constituencies. This they had lately done by twelve separate Acts, each creating an electoral district. The Board of Trade reported that this ought to be done only by the Crown and not by the Assembly. The Crown therefore instructed Dobbs to veto the above-mentioned Acts. The colonists met this with a memorial pointing out that incorporation of constituencies by a charter from the Crown was undesirable, as making redistribution difficult, and depriving the electoral system of the needful elasticity. Dobbs accepted this view and a compromise was arrived at. The Assembly was to select constituencies and the Governor was then to incorporate them by charter.[2]

Dispute about electoral districts.

The action of those in authority, whether in England or in the colony itself, throughout these disputes may not have been free from errors. But it at least showed a real wish to understand and meet the wants of the colonists, and a patience in unravelling administrative difficulties which disposes of a good deal of vague talk about the selfishness and indifference of the English Government and its servants in their dealings with the colonies.

Before leaving the question of colonial administration

[1] N. C. Records, vol. iv. p. 239.
[2] *Ib.* vol. v. Preface, and p. 301.

it may not be amiss to consider four documents in which the views of responsible officials acquainted with the wants and views of the colonists are set forth in detail, and evidently with a full sense of responsibility.

Schemes of colonial administration.

In 1715 Secretary Stanhope presented to the Board of Trade a memorandum on the subject of colonial administration. There is nothing to show who was the author. Whoever he may have been his views are at once typical of the better and the weaker side of British colonial administration. As far as administrative details go he is a reformer. He complains of the insufficient care exercised in the choice of Governor.

Memorandum submitted by Stanhope to Board of Trade.[1]

'Governments,' the writer says, 'have been sometimes given as a reward for services done to the Crown, and with design that such persons shall thereby make their fortunes. But they are generally obtained by the favour of great men to some of their dependents or relatives, and they have sometimes been given to persons who were obliged to divide the profits of them with those by whose means they were procured, the qualification of such persons for government being seldom considered.' Under such conditions corruption was almost inevitable. Governors sell offices. They induce the Assemblies to raise money for public purposes, and then some portion of it sticks to their fingers.

The judicial system is that part of our colonial administration which the writer condemns most strongly. The courts are incompetent. This discourages trade, while at the same time it encourages factious and frivolous litigation, since even with a weak case a man feels that he has a chance of success. The nominal right of appeal to the Crown is really a nullity—at least

[1] This is in the New Jersey Archives, vol. iv. pp. 345, &c.

it can be made so if the Governor chooses. He can make a false declaration that the property at issue is not worth five hundred pounds, in which case it cannot be the subject of an appeal. He can hinder appellants from obtaining the necessary documents. Moreover, apart from the possible interference of the Governor, appellants have no power to force witnesses to attend in England and depose.

Again, the duties laid on a colonial Governor are too multiform to be effectively discharged by one man. He has to be at once Captain, General, Admiral, Chancellor and Chief Justice. Who is sufficient for these things?

The writer clearly sees that the true solution of the colonial problem lies in the creation of a colonial department. The Board of Trade ought to be strengthened by the presence of legal experts, commercial experts, and retired Governors, who had given proof of administrative capacity. In the duties of such a board there is plenty to satisfy ambition. 'As no part of the British dominions has been hitherto so little understood and so much neglected, so there is more room there than in any other part of the King's dominion for the gaining much honour to the administration of his government and much good to his subjects.'

Yet with all these enlightened and even generous views on colonial administration, the writer does not in the matter of colonial commerce in the least rise above the ordinary doctrines then current. He assumes without hesitation that the trade of the colonies is to be subordinated to the material welfare of the mother country, and he looks with suspicion on the increasing commerce of America as likely to injure that of the West India plantations.

In 1721 the Board of Trade presented to the

Crown a report dealing at great length with the whole question of colonial administration.[1] After a general statement of the resources of the colonies they go on to set forth 'considerations for securing, improving, and enlarging your Majesty's dominions in America.'

Views of the Board of Trade in 1721.

They are fully alive to the dangers of French aggression and to the necessity of retaining the friendship of the Indians. They clearly see that the weak point of our colonial system is its lack of centralization, and the absence of any one department in England on which responsibility can be clearly fixed. There should be a Governor-General for the whole body of colonies. 'The present method of despatching business relating to the plantations is liable to much delay and confusion, inasmuch as there is at present no less than three ways of proceeding therein: that is to say, by immediate application to your Majesty by one of your Secretaries of State—by petition to your Majesty in Council—and by representation to your Majesty from the Board, from whence it happens that no one office is thoroughly informed of all matters relating to the plantations, and sometimes orders are received by surprise disadvantageous to your Majesty's service, whereas if the business of the plantations were entirely confined to one office these inconveniences would be thereby avoided.'

Nor can it be fairly said that the commercial policy foreshadowed in this document was a narrow or selfish one. There is no desire to sacrifice the colonies to the mother country. Their productive industry is to be directed into such channels as shall be profitable to the whole empire.

The production of iron, flax, hemp, and ship-timber is to be specially encouraged, and the industry of the

[1] New York Documents, vol. vi. p. 591.

colonies is to be kept in such channels as not to compete with the mother country. But there is no trace of any morbid or exaggerated dread of such rivalry.

The commercial bond is to be one of mutual interest. The colonies consume more than one-sixth of the woollen manufactures exported from Great Britain, which is one chief staple and the main support of the landed interest. They buy linen, calico, silks and furniture. Some of these Great Britain produces, for all of them she is the carrier. The mother country draws a revenue from colonial tobacco; the mercantile trade with the colonies is a nursery for seamen. The colonies supply timber and naval stores. Thus there is ample room for a flourishing colonial trade, which shall not encroach on the productive industry of the mother country.

These documents, undesignedly and by significant silence, throw considerable light on a question which has been already discussed. The writers just quoted show thorough familiarity with the details of colonial administration, a keen interest in colonial industry, and a steady determination to make that industry subservient to the commercial prosperity of the mother country. Yet neither they nor other writers who are about to be quoted, and who deal with the same class of subjects, make the slightest reference to colonial smuggling. Can we believe that this would have been so if the contraband trade had been, as some would have us believe, continuous, extensive, and systematic? It must be remembered that colonial smuggling involved much more than the loss of revenue. It struck at the root of the principle on which British colonial policy was based, the commercial supremacy of the mother country, and it assisted the trade of continental rivals.

The memorial of the Board of Trade was signed by

four officials, none of them men of any special note. Five years later we find one of these four, Bladen, presenting to Lord Townshend on his own responsibility a long paper on the same subject.[1] This does not seem to have been intended by the writer exactly as a formal and official communication. In these days it would probably have appeared as a special communication in a newspaper, or as a magazine article. The views are more definite and detailed, and far more open to the charge of readiness to sacrifice the colonies to the mother country than those which we have just examined. Bladen starts with what we may regard as a *locus classicus*, in which his leading principle is set forth without any modification or reserve. 'Every Act of a dependent Provincial Government ought to terminate in the advantage of the mother State unto whom it owes its being and by whom it is protected in all its valuable privileges. Hence it follows that all advantageous projects or commercial gains in any colony which are truly prejudicial to and inconsistent with the interest of the mother State must be understood to be illegal and the practice of it unwarrantable, because they contradict the end for which the colony had a being, and are incompatible with the terms on which the people claim both protection and privilege.'

Bladen's proposals.

After this exordium Bladen sets forth in detail all the advantages which the mother country derives from the trade of the colonies. His arguments are little more than a repetition of those urged in the Board of Trade memorial, of which he was one of the signatories. Over and above the advantages there enumerated, he points out that if it were not for the colonial supply of timber and naval stores, Great Britain would be dependent on importation from the Baltic. Moreover the West Indian

[1] It is printed in the North Carolina Records, vol. ii. pp. 626 *et seq.*

sugar islands have to depend for their subsistence on corn imported from the North American colonies. Not a word is said of any corresponding benefit to the colonial producer.

From these principles and premises Bladen deduces certain administrative rules.

1. All goods for which there is a special demand in England must be transported to Britain before they go elsewhere.

2. Every commodity in the production of which the colonies have a monopoly and which is of value in Europe is to be similarly treated, in order to assist Great Britain in the balance of trade with other countries. In other words, the export trade of the colonies is to be so arranged that the whole benefit of it shall accrue to the British consumer and the British merchant.

So, too, the mother country is to enjoy an entire monopoly of the colonial import trade. All necessaries, such as woollen goods and linen, are to be purchased by the colonists from Great Britain or Ireland; all European goods are to come by way of British ports, and the colonial legislatures are to have no power of laying on import duties. 'Supposing these things done it will evidently follow that, the more extensive the trade of the colonies is, the greater will be the advantage to Great Britain.'

Bladen does not in the least shrink from the logical and thoroughgoing application of his own principles. He would leave the colonists without a shred of any legislative or administrative power which could hinder the policy which he has set forth. When one records the summary manner in which he deals with the supposed constitutional rights of the colonies, one is tempted to think that one has come upon a *reductio ad absurdum* of the British colonial system written by some precursor of Franklin. Bladen after a fashion follows his colleagues in desiring centralization. But it is to be a centralization imposed from without, in which the colonies themselves are to have no part. There is to be a comprehensive judicial system applicable to all the colonies, with a judiciary directly dependent on the Crown. A colonial militia is to be avoided as fraught with possible danger to the supremacy of the mother country. 'It may be questioned how far it would consist with good feeling to accustom all the able men in the colonies to be well exercised in arms.' Each colony therefore is to have a small garrison of regular troops. These could be at once concentrated, and used as a single force in case of invasion or rebellion.

The general policy is to be *divide et impera.* It is morally impossible that any dangerous union can be formed among them. 'The emulation that continually subsists between them in all matters of intercourse and traffic is ever productive of various jealousies and cares how to gain upon each other's conduct in government and trade, everyone thereby endeavouring to magnify their pretension to the favour of the Crown by becoming more useful than their neighbour to the interests of Great Britain.' One hardly knows whether to call the writer a hardened cynic or a deluded optimist. Few better instances could be found of the administrative incapacity of the so-called 'practical man,' for whom everything outside the most obvious and purely material aspects of human life has no place.

Bladen repeats the recommendation made by his colleagues five years earlier, of a central department to which all colonial officials should be responsible.

The document ends with a singular and ominous recommendation. 'All that has been said with respect to the improvement of the Plantations will it is supposed signify very little unless a sufficient revenue can be raised to support the needful expense, in order to which it is humbly submitted whether the duties of stamps upon parchments and paper in England may not with good reason be extended by Act of Parliament to all the American Plantations.'

It is a curious coincidence, though probably no more than a coincidence, that these recommendations should have been made to the father of that very politician whose crude and reckless adoption of a like policy did so much to bring about the revolt of the colonies. It is perhaps out of place to apply the term policy to the conduct of an irresponsible rhetorician such as Charles Townshend. But one may certainly say that the policy of Bladen was the same as that of Grenville, clearly stated and pressed to its logical conclusion.

Suggestions by Keith.[1]

Sir William Keith, Governor of Pennsylvania, was a man of no special ability or elevation of character, nor was there any exceptional value in his colonial experience. But for that very reason, because he fairly represents the average colonial official of his day, it is worth our while to consider a document in which he set forth for the instruction of his inferiors his conceptions of colonial policy. He, like Bladen, starts with the axiom that every act of a colonial government ought to aim at the advantage of the mother State. And from this he deduces the practical conclusion that no commercial enterprise can be permitted, however gainful to the colony, if it in any way conflicts with the interests of the mother country.

This view is then intelligently worked out in detail. As consumers the colonists are to be dependent upon England for such necessaries as they need to import, 'for all those articles which an ordinary taste for

[1] 'A short discourse on the present state of the Colonies.' New Jersey Archives, vol. iii. p. 215.

luxury and ability to pay for it demands.' Especially they are to take our woollen goods and thereby to enhance the value of land in England. As producers the function of the colonies is to supply England with naval stores and her West India Islands with grain.

To keep colonial industry and commerce within these channels is to be the work of legislation. That this may be so, the colonial legislatures must be treated merely as corporations, with a right to make by-laws, in no way interfering with the royal prerogative or with the legislative power of the mother State.

Keith did not, any more than the statesmen of the next generation, perceive how much danger was involved in a concurrent exercise of authority by the Crown and by Parliament.

Commercial jealousy will, in Keith's opinion, keep the colonies asunder, and prevent any such united action as can be injurious to British supremacy.

On two points Keith is at one with Bladen. He advocates what is practically a colonial department—as he expresses it, the appointment 'of particular officers in England only for the despatch of business belonging to the plantations.' As it is, there is no special department to which persons coming from the colonies on public business can apply. All colonial officials should be directly appointed by the Board of Trade and should be responsible to that body. We may fairly assume, though Keith does not make this clear, that his proposed body of colonial officials in England are also to be directly connected with the Board of Trade.

Clinton on a Stamp Act.

We have seen how the policy of a Stamp Act, a policy which we usually associate with all that was unwise and disastrous in colonial administration, commended itself to a man whose counsels were otherwise not lacking in sagacity. George Clinton, who became Governor of New York in 1742, was neither a successful administrator nor do his despatches show any sign of popular sympathies. Yet in this matter he showed insight which was denied to abler men. He tells the Board of Trade 'the people in North America are quite strangers to any duty but such as they raise themselves, and was such a scheim (*sic*) to take place without their knowledge it might form a dangerous consequence to his Majesty's interest.'[1] Not many are the political prophecies which have found a fulfilment so exact, so speedy, and so tragic.

[1] N. Y. Docs. vol. vi. p. 26.

unnecessary European goods are imported, yet they contribute nothing towards the support of the public charges, but for the most part thereof, are owned by merchants in London, and consigned to their own factors there, and no advantage reaped by them but by the ship-holders and a few tradesmen, whereas we apprehend this town is taxed as if the said goods were owned by their immediate possessors, but in truth all we get by them is the commission.' This would seem to mean that the goods were bought on credit, in which case no doubt the merchant had to pay taxes in proportion to his supposed capital and also interest on his capital. But this was the grievance of an individual, not of the community as a whole. Nor is it easy to reconcile the complaint of widespread distress with the extensive importation of foreign luxuries.

So, too, in 1750 we find the town meeting protesting against certain duties which the Assembly proposed to impose on tea and coffee, and dwelling on the poverty of the town as compared with the adjacent districts. Yet in the very same document they plead that a duty on carriages will fall with special severity on Boston.[1]

Between 1733 and 1742 we find no fewer than three sets of instructions issued by the town meeting to the Representatives of Boston and the Assembly, asking them to lay their grievances before that body.[2] In the last-named year a committee was appointed to consider the question. They report a falling off in trade in every direction. The West India Islands have taken to making rum on their own account instead of selling their molasses to New England distillers. Salem and Marblehead have become successful rivals in fishing, and probably as a consequence of these changes the ship-building trade has become almost extinct.

[1] Minutes of Selectmen, 1750, pp. 240–1.
[2] Boston Town Records, 1736, p. 145; 1738, p. 197; 1742, p. 313.

This diminution in resources was accompanied by an increase in public burdens. In spite of all precaution for excluding persons likely to be chargeable, the poor rate had risen from just on two thousand pounds a year to close upon five thousand pounds. At the same time the number of rateable inhabitants had in five years diminished by over four hundred.[1]

The highly organized civil life of New England always carried in itself certain socialistic tendencies, nor had the New Englander ever learnt by the practical teaching of distress and failure the difficulty, usually the futility, of attempts to override the working of economical causes. Nothing had occurred to shake his faith in the conception of the State as a beneficent autocrat. One of the complaints contained in the report was that the citizens of Boston now obtained their meat direct from the outlying country districts instead of through the Boston butchers, that the latter were being ruined, and that other trades such as tanning and shoe-making had suffered.

To remedy this the butchers of the town were to be formed into a guild, bound to supply meat at a price named by the Selectmen. At an acknowledged time of distress a monopoly was to be created which would enhance the cost of one of the chief necessaries of life.[2]

Other suggestions are made for economy, harmless indeed, but too insignificant to be likely to bear any fruit. The number of bells publicly rung was to be lessened. Bulls were no longer to be kept at public cost, but to be paid for by those who needed them. This may be taken incidentally as evidence for the change from communal to individual land-holding.

Free education was one of the burdens heavily felt. A suggestion was made that those who could afford to do so should voluntarily assess themselves for an

[1] Town Records, 1742, p. 12.

[2] *Ib.* 1745–6, pp. 84, 140.

educational rate. But no definite test of such ability was suggested, nor any method of distributing the burden.[1]

It is probable that Boston had a real and a remediable grievance. Everything seems to show that the prosperity, and therefore rateable value, of the smaller towns had increased while that of Boston had stood still. This clearly could have been met by a general readjustment of rates. It is not unlikely that this was hindered by the system which made it necessary that every member of the Assembly should be an inhabitant of the town for which he sat. This robbed Boston of that advantage in the way of indirect representation which the capital of the colony would otherwise have enjoyed. Another grievance, and probably a real one, was the inequitable operation of the press-gang system. The officers in charge of press-gangs usually procured their men from Boston. Thus the Boston merchants see their cargoes rotting for want of sailors to man their ships, and the town suffers from lack of the necessaries of life, while Connecticut, Rhode Island and New York are able to send out ships for the lucrative business of privateering.[2]

Yet it is not unlikely that the decadence in the prosperity of Boston was relative rather than positive. In 1748 five hundred and forty ships sailed from Boston, a state of things hardly consistent with the lamentations just quoted. But at the same time over a hundred and thirty sailed from Salem.[3] Probably, as is the wont of human nature, the trading classes were alarmed at seeing themselves overtaken in the race by hitherto unsuccessful rivals.

In Connecticut we find no trace of these economical troubles. On the other hand we find far less of luxury, more of the frugal simplicity of early Puritan days.

[1] Town Records, 1745–6, p. 197. [2] *Ib.* p. 84.

[3] Douglass, vol. i. p. 538.

Life in Rhode Island, too, was frugal, if we may apply that term to a scale of living which results from lack of culture rather than from self-restraint. Commercially the colony was prosperous, and by 1740 no fewer than a hundred and twenty ships were owned by residents in Rhode Island.[1]

The other New England colonies.

Probably the only two towns in which an observer whose memory could carry him from 1715 to 1745 would have observed any pronounced signs of increased opulence would have been New York and Charlestown. It is probable that in both cases the change would have been seen not so much in any increase either in the number or splendour of the buildings, as in a freer and more varied fashion of life. It is noteworthy that at the outset of the revolutionary war we find the delegates from Massachusetts when visiting New York greatly impressed with the luxury which they saw about them.[2] One would not infer from such scanty contemporary evidence as is accessible that at the beginning of the century a visitor from Boston would have noticed any such marked difference between the conditions of life which he saw and those with which he was familiar at home. Smith, the historian of New York, writing in the middle of the century, could describe the capital of the colony as 'one of the most social places on the continent,' with its weekly clubs for men and concerts and assemblies for both sexes.[3]

New York.

Such evidence as is available shows no marked increase in the shipping trade of New York during the first half of the eighteenth century. Furs and deer-skins brought down the Hudson from the western forests were among the chief exports. Besides, ships

[1] Gov. Ward's Report, R.I. Records, vol. v. p. 12.

[2] John Adams's Journal in his *Life and Works* (ed. 1850), vol. ii. pp. 349, 354.

[3] Smith, p. 271

plied to the West Indies freighted with corn, flour, meat, butter, and timber; some of these went direct to the West Indies, others touched at some New England port where the cargo was sold, and the proceeds invested in rum for the West India Islands.[1]

Save that the Delaware was not so effective a waterway for the Indian fur trade as the Hudson, the commerce of Philadelphia went on the same lines as that of New York. It, however, showed a greater and more uniform increase. In the ten years following 1735 the number of vessels sailing from Philadelphia had increased from two hundred and twelve to over three hundred, while the number of those visiting the port, which in 1735 was under two hundred, had reached two hundred and seventy-three. During the same period the value of goods imported had risen from under five thousand pounds to over seven, an increase entirely due to the growth of trade with the mother country.[2]

Economic and social condition of the Southern colonies.

The economical condition of the Southern colonies had been, as we shall see, modified, but its essential structure remained unchanged. Slave labour employed upon large estates, and applied to the production of a single staple commodity, still dominated every other form of industry. Something indeed of urban life had found its way into Maryland, and in a less degree into Virginia. Annapolis, as we learn from a casual reference in Whitefield's diary, had its fashionable society and its worldly diversions.[3] Baltimore, too, was incorporated as a township, but unlike Annapolis had no representation.[4]

In Virginia Hampton was the chief seaport, and is described as having a hundred poor houses.[5] Williamsburg was the Governor's place of residence. The

[1] Smith, p. 274.

[2] Kalm, vol. i. pp. 52–3.

[3] *Whitefield's Letters* (ed. 1772), vol. i. p. 135.

[4] Mereness, p. 418.

[5] John Fontaine's Journal in the *Memoirs of a Huguenot Family*, p. 272.

meeting of the Assembly, filling the same place socially as Assizes did in England, brought balls and entertainments in its train, and some of the wealthier planters had town houses as places of occasional resort. In spite of that a traveller, writing in 1745, describes it as a poor and ill-built town. Yorktown, if we are to believe him, had better houses, such as would not have disgraced the fashionable parts of London.[1]

In 1752 we find no fewer than seven townships incorporated by the legislators.[2] The proviso that in all such towns the chimneys should be of brick, not wood, suggests that these were at least intended to be actual towns in the modern sense, not merely rural townships incorporated for purposes of government. But if such was the intent, the action of the legislature had little more effect than had the laws for 'cohabitation' in the early days of Virginia.

The difficulty of communication in Virginia is illustrated by the various excuses given by sheriffs' officers for failing to serve writs. 'No road,' 'excess of weather,' 'because the defendant's horse was faster than mine,' 'because the defendant got into deep water out of my reach' are among the difficulties alleged. Such entries as by 'reason of an axe' or 'of a gun' throw light on another side of Virginian life.[3]

Towns in North Carolina.

The descriptions which we have of North Carolina show that by the middle of the century it had made but little progress from the condition described by Byrd. We read that two hundred and fifty ships sailed from Edenton every year, fifty of them belonging to inhabitants of the colony. Wilmington had seventy houses and Brunswick twenty, and each had a brick church. Yet although vessels could

[1] Itinerant observations in America, from the *London Magazine* of 1745, republished in the Georgia Hist. Soc. Coll. vol. iv.

[2] Hening, vol. vi. p. 356.

[3] *American Magazine of History*, vol. xii. p. 548.

reach Wilmington the trade there was not enough to require the establishment of a custom-house.[1]

As to the general condition of the colony we have the testimony of Burrington, of his successor Johnstone, and of the Moravian bishop Spandenberg, and a consensus of evidence proves that by the middle of the eighteenth century the moral and industrial state of the colony showed little advance on the state of things thirty years later.

Burrington complains that the settlers take no advantage of their natural harbours. Cattle are imported into Virginia overland when they might more easily and economically be carried by sea.[2]

Johnstone dwells more on the lack of schools and of religious ordinances than on the material shortcomings of the colony. He dwells on the illiteracy of the Assembly, and also on the brutality of settlers as shown by the fact that during two years four people have been killed in boxing matches.[3]

But by far the most condemnatory evidence is that of the Moravian bishop, Spandenberg. Owing to the dispute between the two sections of the colony, the older counties are in a state of absolute anarchy. No one will act as a juror, murder and robbery are common, gaols are broken up, and the country is patrolled by bands of horse thieves. A class of indolent and thriftless settlers have been attracted by the story that in North Carolina cattle could run out all through the winter without any special feeding. The majority of farmers acted on this opinion, and the result was stunted and valueless stock, and the total want of milk during the winter. Another result of this was that farmers were perpetually moving in search of fresh and better pasture. Men's habits of life became unsettled,

[1] N. Car. Records, vol. v. p. 158.
[2] *Ib.* vol. iv. pp. 226, 1318.
[3] *Ib.* p. 1211.

and newcomers, ignorant of the country, usually occupied the soil which their predecessors had neglected and abandoned.

Charlestown.

In Charlestown, on the other hand, urban life had steadily developed, on lines not wholly unlike those which we have just been observing in New York. In the Southern capital, however, trade was less varied and politics less absorbing, and there was more of that leisure which the climate tended so to foster. The trade of Charlestown was important enough to induce English merchants to set up branch houses there,[1] and thus an influence was at work counteracting that isolation which was elsewhere the characteristic of Southern life. Charlestown, like New York, could offer much the same social attractions as a prosperous provincial town in England. There were balls, assemblies and concerts. As early as 1735, or possibly earlier, Charlestown had a theatre, fourteen years before one was established elsewhere in the American colonies.[2] The turf developed much as it did in England during the same period. From an unsystematic amusement where a race-horse was trained by his owner's groom, and ridden by the owner himself or a private servant, it became a regular business in which colonial Pantons and Vernons found their place.[3]

Rice and indigo.

It was said above that the commercial developement of the colonies during the first half of the eighteenth century was brought about not so much by the discovery of new products and resources as by the extension of those already existing. To this, one exception must be made in the case of South Carolina. Before 1740 the commercial prosperity of the colony

[1] *V.s.* p. 60.

[2] Mr. McCrady gives a full account of the developement of the stage in South Carolina, based on contemporary newspapers, p. 526.

[3] Here again I rely on Mr. McCrady. He refers to a *History of the Turf in South Carolina.* I have not been able to meet with this book.

had almost wholly depended on the production and export of rice. That was as much the staple of South Carolina as tobacco was of Virginia. It is not unlikely that if the nature of the article had admitted it would have been used for currency. As it was, in 1723 a tax was levied which might be paid in rice. Taxpayers were allowed, subject to the approval of specially appointed commissioners, to draw orders for the delivery of a certain quantity of rice, and these orders were made legal tender in private transactions.[1] It is not expressly stated that the issue of these orders was limited to the amount of taxation imposed, nor is it easy to see how the commissioners could effectively impose such a restriction. This legalized form of barter does not seem to have been enduring, or to have had any extensive or lasting influence on the commerce of the colony.

That commerce was increased about 1740 by the introduction of a new commodity. The indigo plant had been for some time cultivated in the West Indies, where it was indigenous.[2] In 1741 or 1742 seeds were brought from Antigua and planted in South Carolina. The new crop throve, and in 1748 the South Carolina merchants succeeded in inducing Parliament to grant a bounty of sixpence a pound on indigo grown in the American colonies and imported direct to Britain.[3] The commodity was not enumerated, and consequently the Carolina indigo-grower had the full benefit of the continental as well as the British market. Indigo became a far more profitable crop than rice, and it is said that in the early days of its production many planters doubled their capital every three or four years.[4]

[1] Statutes of S. Carolina, quoted by Mr. McCrady, vol. ii. p. 13.

[2] Bryan Edwards's *Hist. of the W. Indies* (ed. 1793), vol. ii. p. 280.

[3] 21 George II. c. 30.

[4] McCrady, vol. vii. p. 269.

As in New York, the commerce of the colony did not depend merely on its own products, but was supplemented by an extensive trade with the Indians in beaver and deer skins.

We may form a fair notion of the trade and industry of South Carolina from a report sent home by Governor Glen at the end of 1748. The total value of a twelvemonth's exports was something over a million sterling. Of these rice formed more than a half, skins and furs a quarter, and indigo one tenth.[1]

In one respect South Carolina was in advance of its neighbours to the North. We are told that the colony was well supplied with causeways and bridges.[2] This is not difficult to understand. In Maryland and Virginia inland communication without anything more than rough tracks might be difficult and inconvenient, but it was possible. Among the swamps of South Carolina causeways were an absolute necessity. The skilled labour which it was thus necessary to bring into the colony would naturally be employed in bridgemaking. Yet we may be sure that it was only the creeks and tributaries, not the main streams, that were bridged over. In all the Southern colonies the chief lines of inward communication were parallel to the main rivers and at right angles to the coast. The writer to whom we have just referred tells us of the hospitality shown by the planters of South Carolina to travellers. Usually a negro was posted at the gate of a plantation to look out for passing travellers, and to conduct them to the planter's house, where board and even lodging was always forthcoming, while at the visitor's departure a guide was provided.

Roads in South Carolina.

Over and above the increase of wealth and con-

[1] Glen's Report is in Weston's Collection, pp. 65–99.

[2] De Brahm's Report in Weston's Documents connected with the History of South Carolina.

sequent developement of comfort and luxury another principle of social and industrial growth was at work in the South. The legislature of Maryland had never been blind to the evils of allowing the colony to depend upon a single product, or upon exclusively servile labour. In the seventeenth century Acts had been passed requiring every landholder to grow a small quantity of corn, and also encouraging the production of cereals by fixing a rate at which they might be taken in payment of public dues.[1] In the following century attempts were made by a system of bounties to encourage the growth of hemp.[2] In 1726 an Act was passed whereby immigrants from Wales were exempted from taxes for ten years on condition that they grew no tobacco.[3] Efforts in the same direction were made in Virginia.[4] These, however, did but little to modify the social and industrial life of the colony. Natural conditions proved too strong, and the tideway portions of Virginia and Maryland remained almost wholly tobacco-growing regions, cultivated by slave labour. But further inland new forces were at work. Maryland had more than its share in that wave of emigration from the Palatinate which had so large an influence on the social and industrial life of the colonies. Before the middle of the eighteenth century Maryland had in Frederic county, more than a hundred miles from the mouth of the Potomac and about forty miles from the head of Chesapeake Bay, a district peopled by yeomen farmers, living by the work of their hands. In 1745 a leading Marylander could write, 'You would be surprised to see how much the country is improved beyond the mountains, especially by the Germans.' As waggon roads took the place of mere bridle-paths

Extension westward.

[1] Mereness, p. 121. [2] *Ib.*

[3] Acts of Maryland, 1726.

[4] Hening, vol. iv. p. 225; vol. v. p. 357; vol. vi. pp. 137, 144.

through the forest the exportation of hempseed from these districts to the seaport towns became an important business. Ironworks, too, throve, and by 1749 there were no fewer than seventeen furnaces. It was no doubt due to this that in 1749 Maryland was able to export sixteen thousand pounds' worth of goods other than tobacco.[1]

A like process, though hardly on the same scale nor attended with the same economical results, went on in the western regions of Virginia. There was, however, one important difference between the process of westward expansion in Maryland and in Virginia. In Maryland it was wholly a continuous movement, a rolling westward of the existing population which had at first found its home entirely along the coast.

The Irish Presbyterians in Virginia.

In Virginia it was this to some extent. But it was also in a great measure caused by the influx of an element altogether new to the colony. About 1720 and in the years that followed there was a great wave of migration from Ireland into Pennsylvania. Of the emigrants some were oppressed and discontented Papists. Others were of that stubborn stock which carried into the north of Ireland many of the most marked attributes of the Lowland Scot, whether for good or evil, and in their new homes developed them in an intensified form. The success of the French arms at the outset of the great struggle for supremacy in the New World, and the persistent refusal of the prosperous settlers in the secure portions of Pennsylvania to take any effective measures of defence, made the situation of the Irish settlers intolerable. Some dispersed, withdrawing within the settled portions of the colony. Others, representing, we may be certain, what was most stubborn, persistent and enterprising among them, moved southward and sought

[1] All these facts are taken from Mereness, pp. 123–5.

were the most adventurous and tenacious, passed into South Carolina and formed settlements in what is now Lancaster county. The migration was fraught with fateful results, since among the citizens whom South Carolina thus received were the forefathers of John Calhoun and Andrew Jackson.

CHAPTER IV.

RELIGION IN THE COLONIES.[1]

Religion in New England during the seventeenth century.

ONE of the most notable and interesting features which distinguishes the colonial life of the eighteenth century from that of the seventeenth, is the wholly different part played by religious and ecclesiastical questions. During the seventeenth century in one section of the colonies these preponderate to the exclusion of all others, or it might be truer to say they invade and

[1] The material for the Ecclesiastical History of the Colonies during the first half of the eighteenth century is abundant and trustworthy. There is a remarkable change in its character. In dealing with the seventeenth century nearly all our information comes from New England and has to do with Nonconformity. In the eighteenth century we hear but little about the doings of Nonconformists in the colonies, a great deal about the action of the Episcopalian Church. Nonconformists no longer felt the same satisfaction in praising the fathers that begat them. On the other hand the Society for the Propagation of the Gospel in Foreign Parts, which came into existence in 1701, has preserved for posterity a mass of records illustrating the work done by the Anglican clergy in the colonies. The most important of these records are embodied in Bishop Perry's *Collections of Documents,* in five volumes, dealing respectively with Virginia, Pennsylvania, Massachusetts, Maryland, and Delaware. Bishop Perry also published a *History of the American Episcopal Church* in two volumes.

Other authorities of value are Hawks and Perry's *Documentary History of the Protestant Church in the United States,* and Hawks contributes to the *Ecclesiastical History of the United States.*

The following works are also of value as embodying, and in some cases textually reproducing, important original papers:—Bishop Meade's *Old Churches, Ministers, and Families of Virginia.* Foote's *Sketches of North Carolina* and *Sketches of Virginia.* These are exceedingly valuable as throwing light on that most interesting subject, the extension of Presbyterianism westward. Crosse's *The Anglican Episcopate and the American Colonies* is a most carefully constructed monograph, excellent

dominate every province of life. The New England township was essentially a congregation, and it is therefore no exaggeration to say that the history of New England is primarily the history of Churches, of the processes by which they were formed, extended and limited. Nor was the New England Church of the seventeenth century a body whose religious character was largely a matter of tradition or convention. The differences which marked off the Independent Churches of New England from other religious communities were matters of conviction, felt with intense strength, and extending their influence into every phase of life, alike individual and corporate.

In the colonies founded by Quaker influence, differences of creed and form made themselves felt, yet with nothing like the definiteness and intensity which they assumed in New England. For, as we have seen, Quakerism was to a great extent negative. Its essence largely consisted in denials and protests. The spiritual element, so strong in the founders of the sect, lacked that definiteness which can only be obtained by some embodiment of dogma and form; it became fluid, vague, and for many of its professed adherents unreal.

In the Middle Colonies.

It would hardly be an exaggeration to say that in the Southern colonies religion as a social and political force was during the seventeenth century non-existent, a state of things in no wise inconsistent with individual piety, with a reputable standard of morality for the whole community, and a decent

In the South.

in its use of authorities, which are always indicated and often reproduced. Anderson's *History of the Colonial Church,* based largely on the Records of the S.P.G., is also valuable.

Among the colonial historians of the eighteenth century, Trumbull stands almost alone in the fulness with which he treats ecclesiastical questions. For Whitefield's doings in America, his own letters and journals are the best authority.

attention to the formalities of worship by a large portion of it.

Change from the seventeenth to the eighteenth century.

In all these respects the eighteenth century brought with it a marked change. In New England ecclesiastical considerations were in two ways thrust into the background. In the first place material interests more and more made their influence felt. Furthermore the influence of the clergy was year by year waning and vanishing. That was no doubt largely due to the harshness and narrowness with which that influence had been exercised, and to a reaction against claims which outraged men's consciences and feelings, and which could only be upheld under peculiar and transitory conditions. It was due also to a relative change in the intellectual position of clergy and laity. The latter had advanced, the former had gone back. The New England minister of the seventeenth century was a learned man in a community trained to reverence learning, yet personally cut off from any large share of it by the exacting demands of a toilsome and restricted life. He was not unfrequently a graduate of one of the English universities, he had at all events associated with men trained in an atmosphere full of the direct influence of Milton and Robinson, of the indirect influence of Spenser and Hooker. His successor in the following century had been probably trained at Harvard; he found his exemplar of learning and of thought in the cumbrous erudition and in the shallow and commonplace teaching of such a pedant as Cotton Mather. Around him were men over whom questions of theology or ecclesiastical history wrought no such spell as they did over an earlier generation. Moreover, if the conditions of colonial life had lowered the standard of thought and learning among the clergy, they had raised that of the laity. A growing foreign commerce brought the New England trader into contact with wider and more varied aspects of life. The class of Englishman with which he was connected, and from which his ranks were not unfrequently recruited, was putting on, in a somewhat superficial fashion, the literary and æsthetic culture from which his ancestors had mostly stood aloof. On the one hand the intensity of feeling on theological and ecclesiastical matters was relaxed, while at the same time the barriers that marked off the clergy from the rest of the community were weakened.

Meanwhile in the Middle and Southern colonies ecclesiastical questions were forcing their way to the front. That very real revival of Church life which made itself felt in the reign of Queen Anne had its influence in the colonies. It acted not so much as an internal influence as in determining the attitude of Englishmen towards the dependencies. Gradually the feeling forced itself upon Churchmen that the existence of communities, nominally Anglican, yet inadequately supplied with clergy, wholly without effective control over those who did exist, and with no kind of systematic provision for ministration and teaching, was a scandal. Thus while in the Northern colonies religious and ecclesiastical questions, for an earlier generation so overwhelming in their importance, fall into the background, in the South, which had hitherto existed untouched by such influences, and even more in the Middle colonies, they assume something of definiteness and prominence.

Change in the relative positions of Massachusetts and Connecticut.

At the same time, within New England itself the centre of religious thought and ecclesiastical influence had shifted. During the seventeenth century Massachusetts overshadowed its neighbours in ecclesiastical and spiritual, as much as in civil matters. In the eighteenth, Connecticut becomes the centre of religious activity and movement. This was no doubt in part due to the change effected by the Massachusetts Charter of 1692, which removed all ecclesiastical restrictions on the franchise, and thereby destroyed the bond which had kept within the fold of the Church many on whom Puritanism as a religious force had no hold. It was also due to an essential difference in the moral and intellectual structure of the two colonies. The clergy of Connecticut had not, like the spiritual teachers of Massachusetts and their civil allies, alienated support by their stubborn and unrelenting adhesion to outworn forms of thought, and even more to conceptions of policy which outraged all decent and moderate-minded men. Judged by a Puritan standard Connecticut was tolerant even to laxity, and she found her reward in the wholesome and continuous growth of her spiritual life.

Yet at the same time there was an undercurrent at work running in a direction opposite to that which has been just noted. As Connecticut did not share in the spirit of bigotry which inspired the counsels of Massachusetts during the seventeenth century, so she remained untouched by the reaction of the next generation against that bigotry. Brattle's protest against the witchcraft delusion, Sewell's public acknowledgement of repentance for his share in that wretched tragedy, were the evidences of a spirit not limited, we may be sure, to individuals. By the middle of the eighteenth century Boston had learnt to look back with some abasement on such an incident as the execution of the Quakers.[1] Connecticut had no such errors calling for repentance.

[1] Hutchinson, who may be taken as a fair exponent of intelligent opinion in Massachusetts, writes, 'In the year 1656 began what has generally and not improperly been called the persecution of the Quakers.' 'May the time never come again when the government shall think that, by killing men for their religion, it is doing God good service.' *History of Massachusetts*, vol. i. pp. 196–205.

Moreover in Massachusetts the abrogation of the colonial charter had broken the main link which bound State and Church together. The presence of British officials and the increase of foreign commerce had brought influences to bear upon the parent colony which were unfelt by the daughter. In religious matters Connecticut was liberal in comparison with the Massachusetts of 1650, rigid in comparison with that of 1720. Of this change we shall meet with two marked instances, one connected with the teaching of Whitefield, the other with the educational history of the two colonies.

Foundation of Yale.

The circumstances attending the foundation of Yale College illustrate in a singular fashion the working of the two tendencies which have been mentioned, the tolerance of Connecticut and the reaction against that tolerance. In 1700 ten of the principal clergy of the colony took steps towards the foundation of a college in Connecticut. The first step taken was a contribution of books, amounting to forty folio volumes, by the ten co-founders. A petition for incorporation was then laid before the legislature, and it is worthy of notice that the purpose of the college as therein set forth was 'the upholding of the Protestant religion without any narrowing or sectarian qualification.' In 1701 the college was incorporated and endowed with an annual grant from the legislature, terminable at pleasure, of a hundred and twenty pounds in colonial currency, a sum equal to about sixty pounds in actual money. It was some years before the college found a settled home or arrived at a fixed constitution. The history of it, however, as an educational institution belongs rather to another portion of our subject. The feature with which we are at present specially concerned is that the eponymous benefactor to whom Yale College was indebted for a large share of its prosperity was a member of the Church of England. Thomas Yale was a Denbighshire squire who for conscience' sake made one of the first settlers in Newhaven. His son Elihu was sent to England for education, and became a conforming Churchman. He held office in India under the Company, and returned to England a wealthy man. His change of religious opinion had not alienated him from the place of his birth, and a share of the fruits of the pagoda tree, amounting to about four hundred pounds, found their way to the college as benefactions, while a further legacy of five hundred pounds only miscarried through some error or neglect on the part of his executors. The rulers of the college, with a liberal-minded indifference to what must have seemed to New Englanders Yale's apostasy, gave his name to the foundation which he had so largely aided.[1]

Yet though Yale College was in some measure a monument of the liberal and moderate temper of Connecticut, its early history served also to illustrate that process of reaction by which Massachusetts was becoming the home of theological freedom, Connecticut that of dogmatic orthodoxy. In spite of the Anglican associations connected with Yale College it is clear that many of the strictly orthodox Calvinists of Massachusetts sympathized with and supported the foundation of a society likely to be an effective rival to Harvard. Personal feeling, we may be sure, contributed to this. The exclusion of Increase Mather from the headship of Harvard not only called into the field the persistent and clamorous hostility of his son, but had no doubt alarmed many in whose eyes the ejected President represented the best traditions of New England orthodoxy and learning. Yet over and above this it is clear that the supposed laxity of the religious

[1] Trumbull, vol. ii. p. 28.

teaching at Harvard was an important element in the new movement.

Ecclesiastical changes in Connecticut.

Early in the eighteenth century the rulers of Connecticut modified the ecclesiastical constitution of the colony in a manner which, though not directly designed to further freedom of thought or worship, yet indirectly had that effect. Alike in Massachusetts and in Connecticut the strict theory of Independent congregations had broken down under the pressure of two external influences. In the first place that theory is incompatible with the recognition and control of religion by the civil government, and to abandon those would have involved conceptions of national life utterly repellent to the Puritan. So, too, the intensely strong sense of civic unity which pervaded New England life carried with it, as an almost inevitable consequence, the joint action of the various Churches meeting in synod. Such synodal meetings were only held, however, on special occasions, when there appeared to be need for ecclesiastical legislation or when some special administrative difficulty arose. But in Connecticut the synodal action of the whole body of Churches was supplemented by what one might call a subordinate form of federal union. Annual meetings of the clergy were held, not claiming any legislative authority, but exchanging opinions and passing resolutions upon questions of ecclesiastical practice. Over and above these annual meetings, associations were formed at different centres throughout the colony, some of which by voluntary agreement on the part of their members acquired quasi-legislative authority.[1]

The formation of such bodies almost of necessity carried with it the need for some effective central control. Diversities in ecclesiastical practice or in the

[1] Trumbull, vol. i. ch. xix. He is also my authority for what follows.

interpretation of formulæ which might exist without creating disturbances under the system of purely Congregational churches could not fail to have more serious consequences when the conflicting societies were changed from small isolated communities into bodies covering a wider area, and possessing a more representative character.

There were other influences at work which brought home to the Congregationalists of Connecticut the necessity for closing their ranks. In 1704 the Society for Propagating the Gospel in Foreign Parts sent a clergyman of the Church of England to Rye, in the colony of New York. Two years later he extended his operations into Connecticut, preaching at Stratford, and in spite of opposition from the Independent ministry, baptizing twenty-five persons, mostly adults. A second missionary journey was undertaken in the following year, including Fairfield as well as Stratford.

Episcopalians in Connecticut.

One cannot doubt that the success of this invasion brought home to the clergy of Connecticut the need for more complete union and more definite organization. In 1708 a synod, in which each county was represented by clerical and lay delegates, met at Saybrook, and drew up an ecclesiastical constitution in fifteen articles. The essential features of the new scheme were the division of the colony into districts, circuits as they were called. The whole body of elders in each church were to have jurisdiction in ecclesiastical cases within that circuit, and their decisions were to be enforced by excommunication. Furthermore there were to be annual meetings of the representatives of the whole body of churches, and any district association might refer a case to such a meeting. That right of appeal was not, however, extended to individual churches or members of churches.

The Saybrook platform.

Two features of this at once strike one. The meeting declared in general terms its acceptance of the confession of faith drawn up by the Boston synod in 1680; but beyond that there is no reference to dogma, nor is there any attempt to invoke the help of the civil power.

It soon became clear that Anglicanism was establishing itself as a real factor in the life of the colony. In 1722 a regular Episcopalian congregation was established at Stratford, numbering some hundred and fifty, of whom twenty were communicants. Simultaneously with this an event took place which must have stirred colonial feeling, as the Romeward movement of the nineteenth century stirred Oxford and the Church of England. Timothy Cutler, the minister of Stratford, had been in 1719 appointed head of Yale College. Three years later, without, as it would seem, any premonitory symptoms visible to ordinary observers, he and one of the college tutors named Brown declared their adhesion to the Church of England, and their intention of obtaining Episcopal orders, and were followed by two of the clergy, Johnson and Wetmore. By 1733 the Episcopalian church in Stratford included two hundred families, and we find an Anglican Churchman reporting to his co-religionists at home that there was scarcely a town in the colony where there were not a considerable number of professed members of his Church.[1]

Secession from Independency to Episcopacy.

The action of the people of Connecticut showed an honourable adhesion to those traditions of toleration which had marked the colony from the outset. The discussion which took place among the trustees of Yale is recorded.[2] Alarmed and disconcerted as they well might be, yet their action showed no extravagance or panic. Throughout the debate the question of

[1] Perry's *History of American Episcopal Church*, p. 298.
[2] Trumbull, vol. ii. p. 34.

Episcopacy against Presbyterianism is regarded as arguable. There is not a trace of that grotesque and bigoted horror of Anglicanism which revealed itself in the public utterances of leading men in Massachusetts a generation earlier. The dismissal of Cutler and Brown, the passing of a resolution disqualifying anyone of prelatical or Arminian opinions from holding office in the college was necessary if the college was in any way to express the views or to retain the confidence of the whole body of inhabitants.

Concurrent endowment adopted.

In 1727 the legislature granted to the Episcopalians what might be called concurrent endowment. An Act was passed which provided that any person living within reach of an Episcopalian church might allocate the payment levied from all citizens for the maintenance of the clergy to that particular church.[1]

It speaks but ill for the judgement and fairness of some of the Episcopalian party, that after this concession we find them still complaining of the hardship imposed on them in having to pay Church dues in districts where there was no Episcopalian church.[2] It does not seem to have struck them that the alleged hardship was identical with that inflicted in the mother country by the payment of Church rates on all those who stood outside the Establishment.

Narrow attitude of Episcopalians.

Nor was it difficult to foresee a result which, as a Churchman actually admits, took place. If in places where there was no Episcopalian church Churchmen were granted entire exemption from contribution to the support of public worship, it was certain that all those who were wholly indifferent to religion would avail themselves of the plea. Throughout we feel that there is a depressing narrowness in the views expressed by even the better sort of

[1] Connect. Records, 1727, p. 202. [2] Perry's *History*, p. 298.

colonial Episcopalians, and an inability to do justice to the good side of the national life around them. Johnson was undoubtedly a thoughtful and high-minded man, usually temperate in his utterances. His habitual toleration is illustrated by a letter to the Secretary of the Society for the Propagation of the Gospel, in which he excuses himself for attending the preaching of Whitefield and another Revivalist preacher, and in which he complains that he had been 'much faulted by some over-zealous people whose venomous spirit towards the Dissenters has very much hurt the Church.' It was, he says, imputed to him as a crime that he had sent his son to a Dissenting college, rather than leave him without education, and that he therefore allowed him occasionally and of necessity to attend a Nonconformist place of worship.[1] We can best judge of the temper of these Episcopalians who distrusted Johnson when we read a letter written by Johnson himself to the Bishop of London, in which he says that it would be 'much happier for the Church, especially unless we had a bishop, if the charters were taken away, and most people begin to think once they have got into such a wretched mobbish way of management that it would be best for the people themselves.'[2] We find him writing in a like strain, but more fully, to the Secretary for the Society of the Propagation of the Gospel.[3] He dwells in very general terms on the evil which the democratic government of Connecticut inflicted on the colony, and suggests that it would be a gain alike for the colony and the Church if the charter was revoked and a new one granted, giving the Crown a full right of veto on all legislation. Yet he can bring no specific charge against the Assembly except their reckless issue of paper money. Cutler, writing in a like

[1] Johnson's letter to the Sec. S.P.G., January 10, 1744. Hawks, p. 203.
[2] *Ib.* p. 126. [3] *Ib.* p. 271.

strain says, 'If the King punishes our obstinacy by vacating our charter I shall think it an eminent blessing of his illustrious reign.'[1] The men of Connecticut might fairly ask what Church of England clergymen had to do with the civil constitution of the colony, and whether they reckoned themselves better judges of its interests than the citizens themselves. They might feel, too, that Johnson's action was a poor return for a measure of toleration far in advance of any granted in the mother country either to Roman Catholics or to Protestant Dissenters.

This feeling could not but be intensified by the attitude of the Episcopalian clergy towards the Congregationalism which surrounded them. What that feeling was we can judge from their letters to their co-religionists in England. One complains that the leading men in New England 'try to possess the people with the absurd notion of their worship and discipline being an establishment here.'[2]

We feel throughout that the Episcopalians of New England and their allies in the mother country were quite unable to understand that they were face to face with something which differed wholly from English Nonconformity, with a truly National Church, which with all its faults (and from those faults the Church of Connecticut had largely disengaged itself) had identified itself with all that was strongest and most definite, and with much that was best, in the history and character of the community.

Episcopalians in Massachusetts.

In Massachusetts there seem to have been by 1713, in addition to the Episcopalian church at Boston, one at Newbury and another at Marblehead.[3] Ten years later a second Episcopalian church was built at Boston.[4]

[1] Perry, Massachusetts, p. 672. [2] *Ib.* p. 138.
[3] *Ib.* p. 147. [4] Winsor's *Memorial History of Boston*, vol. i. p. 225.

About this time two incidents served to create in the colony a feeling of bitterness, neither unnatural nor unjustifiable, against the Episcopal Church and its clergy. In 1725 the Congregational ministers of Massachusetts, acting it is said under the lead of Cotton Mather, proposed to hold a synod, and applied for permission to the Assembly. The fact of the application is a full illustration of the intimate connexion of Church and State in the colony, and of the full acceptance by the clergy of a certain measure of control by the civil power. In the absence of Shute the authority of the Governor was vested in the Lieutenant-Governor, Jeremiah Dummer, a man fully in sympathy with the dominant Church in Massachusetts, and it is not unlikely that this circumstance determined the time chosen for the movement. The Assembly did not give their decisive approval, but left the matter open till a future occasion.[1] Before the question came on again, Gibson, the Bishop of London, instigated we can hardly doubt by the Episcopal clergy in the colony, intervened and reported the matter to the law officers of the Crown. They ruled that the synod could not be held without the approval of the Crown, and that an application to the Assembly was a contempt of the Sovereign and should have been condemned by Dummer. He was now instructed by the Lords Justices to prohibit any further action in the matter, and to warn the clergy that persistence would be treated as a misdemeanour.[2]

Dummer was at this time in England doing all he could to avert an open breach between the colony and the Home Government. He succeeded in explaining away his own share in the offence on the plea that the matter when it came before the Assembly was only in an inchoate state, and not ripe for interference.

[1] Hutchinson, vol. ii. pp. 322–3. [2] *Ib.* The King was in Hanover.

He wrote home to those responsible for the proposal, urging them to abandon it, and using language which showed that he understood the actual as well as the avowed reasons for disapproval. The proceeding might form a dangerous precedent. 'It has also,' he wrote, 'been insinuated that the clergy would have come to some resolution to the prejudice of the Church of England if they had been permitted to convene.'[1]

Dummer's advice was taken and the synod was abandoned, but we cannot doubt that the action of the British Government left behind it a sense of soreness, nor can we see in it anything but a wanton and irritating interference with a right alike presumptive and natural. To suppose that Congregational Massachusetts could furnish Episcopal England with a precedent showed a total inability to comprehend the difference between the relations of Church and State in the two communities respectively. And even if the suspicions of a wish to deal harshly with the Episcopal Church were justified by facts, yet the authority of the Crown was amply sufficient to avert any attack when the need arose.

Soon after this the Episcopalians in Massachusetts advanced another claim which the dominant sect might not unfairly regard as an encroachment. The constitution of Harvard College made the President and fellows a corporation. A subsequent Act of the legislature vested certain authority in a Board of Overseers. These overseers were to be the Governor, the Lieutenant-Governor, the magistrates of the colony, and the 'teaching elders' of the existing Churches.

The Harvard dispute.[2]

[1] Dummer's letter is given by Hutchinson in a note.

[2] Quincy's *History of Harvard College*. He quotes in full (vol. ii. pp. 560–74) the memorials presented by Cutler and Myles, the reply of the overseers, and the rejoinder of the petitioners.

In 1720 one Harris, an Episcopalian clergyman, assistant to the rector of King's Chapel, Boston, was summoned to attend this board apparently in the capacity of a teaching elder, and did attend from time to time. It was also alleged that the rector himself, Myles, was so summoned, but on that point there seems some doubt. It is evident that the term 'teaching elder' could only be applied to a Church of England clergyman by a very liberal interpretation. In all likelihood the official whose duty it was to convene the overseers had in a somewhat lax fashion interpreted the term 'teaching elder' to apply to any minister of religion, and the fact that the Governor and Lieutenant-Governor were both Episcopalians may have helped to bring about the error.

In the case of Harris the claim may well have seemed too unimportant to be worth resisting. But the matter soon assumed a different aspect. We have seen how Timothy Cutler forfeited the presidency of Yale College by his conversion to Anglicanism. After his dismissal he went to England, received a doctor's degree both at Oxford and Cambridge, and then returning to America was established at Boston as the minister of an Episcopalian congregation. He and Myles, the incumbent of King's Chapel, now claimed to be admitted to the Board of Overseers as 'teaching elders,' and endeavoured to support their case by pleading the precedent of Harris's admission. We can judge of the feelings of the Governors of Harvard if we suppose an Anglican educational body, on which an obscure Romanist priest had through some lax interpretation of their constitution obtained a seat, suddenly confronted with a claim for admission made by Cardinal Manning. When the Vestry of King's Chapel authorized their churchwardens to support the memorial of Cutler and Myles pleading for admission, and if necessary to expend the funds of the church in furthering that demand, the adherents of Congregationalism might well suppose that they had to deal with the deliberate attempt of a hostile sect to capture the educational stronghold of the colony. The memorial urged that, as ministers to a recognised congregation, Cutler and Myles were 'teaching elders.' In a subsequent document they went further, and contended that the framers of the Act of 1642 actually had such an interpretation present to their minds!

The overseers had little difficulty in meeting the chief plea urged against them. The term 'teaching elder' was a technical one, with a definite and specific meaning which excluded a clergyman of the Church of England. They could further plead that the interests which Episcopalians might have in Harvard did not need to be specially safeguarded, since students of every denomination were admitted without any kind of test or qualification. It might have been answered that this was quite compatible with an unfair spirit of sectarianism in the choice of teachers and the arrangement of studies. A better defence might have been found in the fact that the Governor, Lieutenant-Governor, and the magistrates formed a large majority of the Court of Overseers. That insured at least that the religious and theological temper of the college would be in conformity with that of the colony as a whole. In the Governor the Episcopalians would in all likelihood have an influential ally, and it was certain that if they at any time became an important minority they would have among the magistrates a fair share of their own body to represent their views.

Cutler and Myles accepted their defeat. It was soon after this that the former wrote, in the hostile and vindictive strain already noticed, suggesting a repeal of the charter.

An alien clergy representing a minority are inevitably exposed to one of two charges. Either they are supine and therefore superfluous, or they are energetic and therefore guilty of proselytism. It is to the credit of the Episcopalian clergy in New England that they preferred the latter alternative. There is extant an interesting and characteristic document, dating from 1734, in which a number of Nonconformists in New England memorialize the Bishop of London.[1] They are, they say, orthodox Christians and do not need missionaries. The Anglican clergy show an unchristian spirit in denying the validity of Independent orders, and therefore of Independent ministrations. They teach 'that our churches are no churches of Christ, and that our people are to be looked upon as strangers to the commonwealth of Israel.' Here we may suspect that the views of the Episcopalians have been translated into the language of their opponents. Moreover, the memorialists complain that their rivals are making Church discipline impossible by receiving excommunicated persons. They end up with a perilous admission. If the Church of England can offer a better salary than the Congregational churches can, it will draw away promising young men from the ministry. Nothing could show more strongly how the intensity of conviction which marked the early days of New England had given place to lower and more commonplace motives.

In 1743 Shirley used his influence with the Assembly of Massachusetts to obtain for Episcopalians a concession similar to that which had already been granted in Connecticut. They were exempted from all payment for the stipends of Nonconformist ministers or the repairs of Nonconformist chapels.

Concession to Episcopalianism in Massachusetts.

Episcopacy in the American colonies, and especially

[1] Perry, Massachusetts, p. 299.

in New England, was destined to profit indirectly by the labours of men who had assuredly no wish to help such a cause.

Jonathan Edwards.

That spirit of earnest and convinced Calvinism which had imbued the early theology of New England with so much that was vigorous and so much that was repulsive had spent its force; it had lost its hold on men's minds partly through its own shortcomings, partly under the pressure of a life more varied in its interests and less strenuous in its purposes than that of the founders. These seemingly extinct methods of thought revived under the influence of one fully as uncompromising in his views as any of the early teachers of New England, but far better equipped with the learning and the ability needed for the task of controversy and exhortation. The Calvinism of Jonathan Edwards is an intellectual and literary phenomenon standing by itself, not only from the indisputable vigour of his intellect and his exceptional power of exposition, but also from the peculiar fashion in which his principles were acquired. The earlier New England thinkers and teachers were born in an atmosphere of Calvinism; familiarity blinded them to the more repulsive features of the doctrine; its formulæ were conventions rather than living realities. In Edwards there was nothing of this. His birth and bringing up were of the kind best fitted to quicken mental activity. He had full access to books, yet he lived among surroundings which saved him from the stifling and distracting influences of luxury or of worldly pursuits. Precocious as a child, he grew up a true scholar, valuing the treasures of the intellect for their own sake, not as stepping-stones to wealth or instruments of ambition. The ordinary scholarship of the New England teacher and divine tended rather to extensive learning than to precision and originality of thought. But for one in whom those qualities are inborn, an atmosphere of definite and somewhat pedantic study is a restraining but not paralyzing influence. Inheritance and tradition may have done something to predispose Edwards to Calvinism, but every line of his writings shows that he had reached his conclusions by a process of independent thought. The conditions which surrounded him favoured the reception of his teaching. It sounds like a paradox to say that it was acceptable to New England alike from its familiarity and its novelty. On the one hand we can hardly suppose that men, unless they had been bound by a sort of formal loyalty to the damnatory teaching of the early Puritan divines, could have accepted without horror such pictures as Edwards delights to draw of the Father and Creator of mankind, regarding His infirm and imperfectly constructed children with loathing and contempt, and consigning them to endless misery with unmoved complacency. On the other hand it was because Edwards's pictures of what was in store for the sinner had all the force and definiteness of independent conviction that they appealed to hearers who would have turned away with weary indifference from a mere commonplace reproduction of the teaching which had awed their fathers.

Whitefield in America.

The work done by Edwards was taken up and completed by one immeasurably his inferior in everything except the mechanical artifices of the pulpit. It is easy to expatiate upon Whitefield's intellectual shortcomings, as revealed by his own letters. He seems wholly without insight into character. Save for references to external conditions his letters might be shuffled in a bag and allotted, each to any of his correspondents, without any loss of congruity. Of insight into the real difficulties and complexities of life he shows no trace. His belief in the efficacy of preaching is like the belief of the pious

Thibetan in the efficacy of his praying machine. He records the number of sermons preached by him—sometimes seven in a day—as a sort of feat in apostolic athleticism, without any self-questioning as to the resources of the mine from which he was working. The mere mechanical and external evidences of so-called conversions are hailed with satisfaction without the slightest attempt to look under the surface, or to estimate the real depth of conviction and its probable durability. Can we wonder that the clergy of New England, men trained in a severe and self-restraining school of moral and intellectual discipline, felt no sympathy with one who could thus describe the effect of his own preaching, 'the people seem to be slain by scores; they are carried off and come into the house, like soldiers wounded on and carried off a field of battle—the Lord is much with me'?[1]

One is tempted to explain the apparent paradox of such qualities winning such success by generalities as to the potency of rhetoric over uneducated minds and morbidly weak natures. Unfortunately for this view, we are met by the fact that the people of New England were neither uneducated, unthinking, nor emotional. In considering such a community the hypothesis of widespread and contagious folly is not to be adopted till we have at least exhausted all other possibilities of solution. In the first place in estimating Whitefield's influence it must be remembered that, if Whitefield was conspicuously wanting in the qualities of the systematic thinker and the practical philanthropist, he was also conspicuously free from their defects. Though he undoubtedly lacked insight into individual character, he had no lack whatever of individual sympathy. Men were never to him items in a system. The expressions of affection in his letters are characteristically

[1] Letters, vol. i. p. 405. Edinburgh was the scene of this triumph.

crude and commonplace; the reader is wearied, almost nauseated, with the recurrence of 'dear Mr.' This and the indiscriminate bespattering of 'sweet.' But one sees that the feeling, though conventionally and even vulgarly expressed, is absolutely real.

Moreover the condition of Whitefield's work in America effectually saved him from certain attacks which in England might be made with some show of plausibility. Satirists of the baser sort delighted to picture Whitefield as a Tartuffe, a fluent mountebank deliberately putting on a mask of piety as an instrument for the gratification of evil appetites. Setting aside these grotesque libels, there was yet undoubtedly a feeling that the charm of aristocratic patronage had done something to turn Whitefield's head, and that the idolatry of a certain section of the fashionable world was welcomed and even sought by him. No such suspicions could hang around his American career. There men saw him, in an almost Franciscan spirit of self-denying devotion to duty, facing hardship and sickness that he might bear the message of salvation to perishing souls.

The difference, however, between Whitefield's position and work in England and in America lay not so much in his own position as in the temper and antecedents of his audience. In England his followers were mainly of two kinds. On the one side were superficial people in search of a new sensation, to whom the melodious voice and appropriate gestures were a pleasant change from the acting of Garrick or the singing of Monticelli. On the other side were men brutalized in sin to whom the elementary truths of salvation, set forth with fluent rhetoric, appealed with all the force of novelty. In America Whitefield was working a soil more truly fitted than either for the reception of spiritual truth, and therefore more likely to bear abiding fruit. In the first place we must remember that the life of New England, rich in a certain sense in intellectual activity, was starved on the æsthetic side. Poetry, fiction, the drama, art, hardly had a place in the life of the New Englander. Whitefield's preaching in a measure supplied the place of all these: it appealed to the emotions, which were denied any other nutriment. His sermons were to the people of Boston what such a picture as Orcagna's 'Judgement' was to the non-reading Italian. Besides, the Calvinism of Whitefield appealed to a deep-seated hereditary creed, overlaid, but not eradicated.

With Edwards the practical application of predestination was wholly subordinate to its logical truth; with Whitefield the appalling doctrines of Calvinism were simply the stock-in-trade of the Revivalist preacher. Whitefield's career as an itinerant preacher in America began with his first visit to Georgia in 1740. It included seven separate visits, covering in all a period of more than nine years, and it ended with his death in Massachusetts in 1770. In Georgia he was not content with the duties of a preacher and a philanthropist, but strove to pose as a social and political reformer. The results of that attempt belong to a later phase of our subject. In the Southern States Whitefield appears on the whole to have had but little effect. In South Carolina he entangled himself in a squabble with Alexander Garden, a man of piety and high character, who acted as commissary for the Bishop of London in that colony. Garden at first found favour with Whitefield, who describes 'the most Christian manner' in which he was 'received by the Bishop of London's commissary, the Rev. Mr. Garden, a good soldier of Jesus Christ.'[1] These friendly relations were but short-lived. Garden was justly incensed at the audacity with which Whitefield, himself nominally a clergyman in the Church of England, defied his authority, and claimed the right to

[1] For Whitefield's proceedings in South Carolina, see Appendix III

officiate when and where he pleased. Whitefield, too, excited indignation in South Carolina, as elsewhere, by his onslaughts on the memory of Archbishop Tillotson. According to Whitefield, Tillotson's writings might civilize, but not convert; his theology was built on so false a foundation that it proved that he was no Christian at heart, and had not so much as a head-knowledge of the true Gospel of Christ. He never once named regeneration. His faith was a bare historical one, and he 'knew no more of Christianity than Mahomet.' Finally Whitefield emphasized his condemnation of Tillotson by formally burning 'The Whole Duty of Man.'

Garden replied that the word regeneration only occurs twice in the Bible, and he quoted from Tillotson a passage which assuredly disposed of the allegation as to a bare historical faith.

A generation which has freed itself from personal and temporary prejudices can no doubt see in these utterances of Whitefield a certain element of truth, crudely and brutally expressed, a protest against the insufficient spirituality of the teaching of Tillotson and his school, a defect in no wise incompatible with that personal conviction of which Whitefield seemed to deny the existence. We cannot wonder at Garden or blame him if he only saw the outrage on the memory of one whom English Churchmen loved and revered, and the peril of adding disunion to the difficulties which already beset the colonial Church. Garden cited Whitefield before a court consisting of the commissary himself and four other clergymen. Whitefield was charged with using prayers other than those of the Church of England. Whitefield at once protested against the authority of the court, pleading (1) that it was doubtful whether the Bishop of London had jurisdiction in the colonies, (2) that in any case such jurisdiction needed to be defined by acts of the local assembly, (3) that as he himself had no fixed duty in South Carolina, but belonged to the colony of Georgia, he was not amenable to Garden's jurisdiction. He further added that in London he had preached in unconsecrated places without any reproof from the bishop.

It is not easy to see, if Whitefield's contention were accepted, what stood between the colonial Church and sheer anarchy. It was, however, thoroughly characteristic of Whitefield and his school not to look beyond the immediate practical results of each isolated case, to ignore the operation of precedent and the necessity of system.

After Whitefield had announced his intention to appeal and found security for doing so, the case proceeded. Whitefield was found guilty of having disregarded the forms of the Church of England and was suspended. The appeal came to nothing. The varied and distracting nature of Whitefield's vocations may have hindered him from following it up, or he may have felt that he had reached a point where the friendship or ill-will of English Churchmen and his own right to officiate as a clergyman of the Church of England mattered but little.

Over and above his own indiscretions in South Carolina Whitefield had to answer for the violence of a reckless partisan, one Hugh Bryan, who published a letter in a newspaper stating that 'the clergy of South Carolina broke their canons daily.' Whitefield made himself Bryan's accomplice by correcting his letter for the press, and for this both of them, as well as the publisher of the newspaper, were threatened with criminal proceedings. These, however, seem to have been abandoned.[1]

[1] Mr. McCrady (p. 239) states that he has been unable to find any trace of them.

There was room in North Carolina for genuine missionary work. How much might be done among that untaught and loose-living people by persistent and laborious ministrations was shown at a later date by the success of one of the most energetic and devoted of the colonial clergy, Clement Hall. But quiet underground work among squalid log-huts, far from the excitements and rewards of popular enthusiasm, would have had no charm for Whitefield. In Virginia he received kindly and sympathetic treatment from the Bishop of London's commissary, James Blair. There, as we shall see later on, Whitefield's missionary work was not without real value.

Nowhere, however, in the Southern colonies did Whitefield greatly excite general interest, or awake as elsewhere popular enthusiasm and contemptuous dislike. The truth was that the conditions of Southern life hardly lent themselves to such results as were sought for by Whitefield. In North Carolina he was face to face with dull unreceptive barbarism; elsewhere with a somewhat fastidious oligarchy, with a certain leaven of real culture and a stronger leaven of worldliness and the lusts of the flesh. In Whitefield's own language he found Maryland 'in a dead sleep.' He 'spoke home to some ladies concerning the vanity of their false politeness, but, alas! they are wedded to their quadrille and ombre.'[1] Moreover, it is impossible that the ruling classes in a community based on slavery should look without apprehension on teaching which has for its foundation the spiritual equality of all men in the sight of God, and which broke down the prescriptive barriers set up by reverence for authority.

It is also noteworthy that Whitefield's chief opponents in Maryland were not the members of the Episcopal Church, but the Presbyterian clergy, the seed of

[1] Letters, vol. i. p. 135.

the serpent, as Whitefield, in resentful impatience of temporary hindrance and forgetfulness of the need for definite permanent alliances, called them.

In the colonies of Quaker foundation Whitefield fared better. In 1739, the year of Whitefield's first visit to America, the Boston papers told their readers how he had preached at Philadelphia before a congregation of six thousand people 'in awful silence,' [1] and how both at Brunswick and Burlington crowds of unparalleled size, many in carriages and numbering at each place at least three thousand, had flocked to hear him preach.[2] The normal consequences of conversion, we are told, followed in due course. 'Our wild enthusiasts are incessantly gadding through the country and teaching the people to run mad, and when they do not fall down and beat their breasts and bellow, they tell them they are in a damned state and sentence them immediately to hell.' [3]

In the Middle Colonies.

Here, too, as in South Carolina, Whitefield excited disgust by his attacks on Tillotson. If we may trust the reports sent home by the Episcopalian clergy to the Society for the Propagation of the Gospel, he denounced the Anglican clergy as sorcerers and Simon Maguses, and 'made a great rent in all the congregations belonging to the Church of England.' [4] At the same time we are told that the Presbyterian congregations were equally annihilated by this new force, while even Whitefield's party was not united, since many of them had seceded under a rival enthusiast, a German count.[5]

In truth Whitefield's influence was upon the most

[1] *Boston Evening Post*, Nov. 26, 1739. Quoted in N. J. Archives, vol. xi. p. 534.

[2] *Boston Gazette*, Nov. 29, 1739; also Archives, vol. xi. p. 585. The mention of carriages throws an interesting light on the social condition of the two towns.

[3] Backhouse to Sec. S.P.G., in Perry's *Hist. Coll. Pennsylvania*, p. 217.

[4] *Ib.* p. 209.

[5] *Ib.* p. 235.

favourable view nothing but a moral force, acting on individuals; there is not a trace of any settled organic policy. The disturbing power of an explosion is determined by the amount of resistance with which it meets. When Whitefield found himself face to face with New England, definite in its theology and rigid in its ecclesiastical system, results followed which had no parallel in his earlier colonial experiences. Moreover, if the elements which opposed Whitefield were stronger in New England than elsewhere, so also were those which made for his cause. Elsewhere religious opinion was largely a matter of convention, there was no deep-seated conviction for such a teacher as Whitefield to build upon or to combat. But in New England, as we have seen, that Calvinism which was fast becoming a mere tradition had been reawakened into life by the teaching of Jonathan Edwards. The movement followed the normal law of developement. First comes the thinker, influencing men's minds and teaching the teacher. Then follows the rhetorician, popularizing the doctrines of his predecessor, investing them with sentiment and enlisting passion in their support.

In Massachusetts.

Whitefield's account of his experiences in Massachusetts is of no little interest as throwing light on the life and temper of the colony, on the combination of a restrained and tempered worldliness with a real, yet somewhat undemonstrative and unenthusiastic, spirit of religion. In Boston he is shocked at the outward symptoms of luxury, women commonly wearing jewels and patches, even the common people dressed up in the pride of life, and children brought to the font clothed as if, instead of renouncing the vanities of the world, they were about to be initiated into them. Yet there was no scoffing, and the temporal rulers united with the clergy in a respect for the externals of religion.[1]

[1] Whitefield's Journal.

In the earlier days of New England the intrusion of an unauthorized preacher of the Gospel, even if his views were in harmony with those of the majority, would have at once called forth resistance. But the time was past when the Puritan clergy could assume the privileges of an exclusive oligarchy. There can be little doubt from the evidence extant that Whitefield's reception in Massachusetts was at first almost wholly favourable, and that it was not till he had been discredited by the indiscretions and extravagances of his allies and followers, and especially by the results of his ministrations in Connecticut, that the minority hostile to him were able to assert themselves with any effect. In Edwards, Whitefield found not only a precursor but a willing and loyal ally.

It was, however, not in Massachusetts but in Connecticut that Whitefield found his most fruitful field of labour. This was no doubt in part due to the fact, already noticed, that those influences which in Massachusetts had alienated ordinary men from the Calvinistic creed, were absent in Connecticut, and that the Church had built up no such barriers between popular sympathy and the creed now preached by Whitefield. There is no reason to doubt the accuracy of the statements made by a sympathetic historian, himself a hearer of Whitefield, that 'Connecticut was more remarkably the seat of the work than any part of New England or of the American colonies,' and that 'in most of the towns and societies it was very general and powerful.'[1]

In Connecticut.

Yet the same writer tells us the movement 'was most violently opposed by ministers, by magistrates, by cruel and persecuting laws, by reprovals and mis-

[1] Trumbull, vol. ii. pp. 156, 160. Trumbull states that he himself, when a student at Yale, heard Whitefield preach. I have taken the greater part of what follows from him.

representation, and all the ways and means which its adversary could invent.'

In the very same passage he furnishes what must well be regarded as an ample explanation of such hostility. 'The glorious work of God which had effected such a wonderful reformation of manners throughout the country was marred and greatly injured by many imprudences and irregularities. Many lay exhorters sprang up among the people—and among some there appeared an inclination to follow impulses and a pretence to know the state of men's souls, who were converted and who were not.'

Two of Whitefield's adherents seem to have been more especially responsible for the discredit thus brought on his cause. One was Gilbert Tennant, a minister from New Jersey, who followed up Whitefield's work in Massachusetts. His methods may be inferred from his suggestive nickname of Hellfire Tennant.[1] Yet, it seems clear from contemporary accounts, and even more from his own writing, that he was not a mere windy ranter, but a man of real force and definiteness of mind. In a letter to a friend, one of his own party, written in 1741, in the very crisis of the excitement created by Whitefield, we find Tennant protesting against many of the worst features of the movement. To judge of men's internal condition, and to set up separate meetings because the clergy were supposed to be unregenerate, is 'enthusiastical, proud and schismatical.' Singing in the streets is 'enthusiastical foolery.' The 'pretence to immediate inspiration' and the 'following of immediate impulses' are an 'enthusiastical perilous *ignis fatuus*.' It is somewhat startling to find the term 'enthusiasm' thus used as one of condemnation by a member of that very party against whom it was so often brought as a charge.[2]

Gilbert Tennant.

[1] Perry, Pennsylvania, p. 209.

[2] N. J. Archives, vol. xii. p. 137.

Tennant may have been in a sense a fanatic; he may have been, and probably was, a man of one idea, and that idea the application of Calvinistic doctrine to the moral regeneration of mankind. But if he was a fanatic, he was clearly not a noisy nor an unthinking one. More discredit was brought on the cause by James Davenport, the minister of Southold, one of the settlements of English Independents on Long Island. He was the Fra Salvestro of his party, the chief instigator of those very practices which Tennant had the courage and the good sense to denounce. On one occasion he is said to have preached for nearly twenty-four hours at a stretch, and then to have fallen into a brain fever. He was a miracle-monger, promising to recover a sick woman by his prayers, and when she died, excusing his failure by the plea that death was the true recovery. He harried ministers with questions as to their spiritual condition, and approved of or condemned their ministrations according to the answer received.

James Davenport.[1]

Starting from Long Island, Davenport chose Connecticut for his scene of action. There he and his associates at once met with a summary check. He began his labours in July 1741, and in the following May the Assembly passed a law for the general purpose of protecting the established clergy against the intrusion of unauthorized preachers. Any minister invading another parish, unless by the request of the minister of that parish and the majority of his church, was to be punished by the deprivation of his stipend. The same punishment was to be inflicted on every individual member of any association

Repressive measures in Connecticut.

[1] Trumbull, whose attitude towards Whitefield and his followers is on the whole friendly, makes no attempt to conceal or extenuate Davenport's follies. Some of the specific charges may be false or exaggerated. There can be no doubt as to the general tenor of his teaching and practice.

of ministers who approved such a proceeding. Furthermore, every person committing such an offence was to be bound over in the sum of a hundred pounds not to repeat it, his bail to be forfeited by such repetition.[1]

In the following year further legislation was enacted to make these provisions more effective.[2] The result was, that the established ministry of Connecticut and their lay supporters became as odious to a large section of the community as the Church of England and its rulers in the previous century had been to the founders of New England. Men withheld their church dues and had their goods seized; those who refused to give security for compliance with the recent Act were sent to prison.

It was certain that the success or failure of the new movement in Connecticut would largely depend on its power of capturing the intellectual stronghold of the colony. The authorities there were not long in declaring themselves.

Attitude of the authorities at Yale College.[3]

In 1744 the church at Canterbury was vacant. The appointment was according to the Congregational system of the colony vested in a convocation or union of churches. They appointed one James Cogswell. He was unacceptable to the Whitefieldian section of his church, as we may call them. They being, it is said, a majority seceded, and held religious meetings in a private house where one Solomon Paine, a layman and a follower of Whitefield, prayed and exhorted. They furthermore refused to pay rates for the maintenance of Cogswell, and for this suffered distraint and in some instances imprisonment.

Among Paine's hearers were a family named Cleaveland, two of whom were students at Yale. They in the

[1] Connect. Records, 1742. [2] *Ib.* 1743, pp. 521, 570.

[3] For this dispute see Trumbull, vol. ii. pp. 179, &c.

vacation accompanied their parents to Paine's meeting-house. The statutes of Yale provided that no scholar should attend any religious meeting not established, or allowed by public authority or approved by the President, under penalty of a fine, confession, public admonition or expulsion. In conformity with this provision the two offenders were admonished, and warned that if they continued to justify themselves and refuse to make an acknowledgement they should be expelled. The elder of the Cleavelands thereupon stated that he did not know that he was transgressing the laws of God or the colony or the college, and therefore begged that 'his ignorance might be suffered to apologize for him.'

The President and the three tutors in whom the government of the students was vested did not think this sufficient. Declaring that 'to educate persons whose principles are directly subversive of the visible Church of Christ would be contrary to the original design of creating this society,' they inflicted the supreme penalty of expulsion.

Davenport excluded from the churches of Massachusetts.[1]

In Massachusetts as in Connecticut the action of Davenport called out a protest from those who had acquiesced, though it may be with ill-will and a bad grace, in the proceedings of Whitefield. The action, however, of the Massachusetts authorities was hesitating and half-hearted compared with that taken in Connecticut. The two colonies indeed seemed to have changed parts. Connecticut, once by comparison liberal and tolerant, was provoked into something not unlike persecution. Massachusetts met the invaders in a spirit which would have seemed to Dudley and Endicott one of sinful latitudinarianism.

[1] Mr. Palfrey, in his *History of New England*, 1728–65, gives a detailed account of the proceedings against Davenport in Massachusetts. He quotes the Records verbatim, but giving no reference for them.

Davenport began his campaign in Massachusetts by refusing to attend services at Charlestown on the ground that the minister was unconverted. Thereupon the ministers of the churches in Boston, who were just about to hold their monthly meeting, invited Davenport to attend and to confer with them. This he did, and the ministers then set forth their opinion of him and his proceedings in a singularly hesitating and compromising manifesto. They held him to be truly pious and an instrument for the saving of souls. At the same time they took exception to certain of his proceedings as breaches of established ecclesiastical order. The practical result was to encourage Davenport in his general line of action, but to necessitate certain changes in detail. The chapels of Boston were closed against him, and he was constrained to adopt the probably more effective method of open-air preaching. Resentment for what was withheld was stronger than gratitude for such concessions as he had obtained. He told his hearers that their ministers were unconverted, and were leading their flocks blindfold to hell. It was wholly in conformity with New England tradition to invoke the civil authority in such a crisis. For this very general expression of an unflattering opinion Davenport was put on his trial for libel. He received a humiliating acquittal on the ground that he could not be held accountable for his words.

The personal influence of Whitefield seems in some measure to have abated when the first impulse of novelty was spent. But it called into existence and for a while kept alive a definite school of religion. 'New Lights' was a name as well defined and as commonly recognised as 'Evangelicals' or 'Puseyites.' Men have sometimes written as though the condemnation of 'enthusiasm' was a special symptom of the torpor, often exaggerated, but

The 'New Lights' and their opponents.

no doubt in a measure real, which beset the Church of England in the eighteenth century. There were orthodox divines in the Independent Churches of New England who fell not a whit behind any Erastian bishop or canon in their denunciations. Such a one was Charles Chauncey, minister of the first church at Boston, a preacher and writer as contemptuously unsympathetic in his attitude towards the enthusiasts as Warburton or Lavington in the mother country, though, it is but just to add, a good deal more concise and argumentative.[1]

Whitefield and his followers hostile to learning.

Over and above the sense of disturbance created by the irregularities of Whitefield and his followers, they had wounded the better class of New England opinion in a sensitive place. Even in the days when for the New Englander religion dominated every other thought, when the theology of New England had been most rigid and her ecclesiastical system most exacting, there had never been any tendency to slight secular learning. Rather, one might say, the New Englander had clearly recognised the underlying falsity of the term secular learning, the unwholesomeness of any attempt to divorce the affairs of the mind from the affairs of the spirit. The clergy of New England might fairly claim according to their opportunities to be a learned clergy. The school to which Whitefield belonged, of which one may in some measure look upon him as the founder, is a school which has always inclined to rely upon impulse rather than upon reason, and to regard form and precedent with a contempt which has of necessity carried with it an indifference to history. It is not surprising to find a New England divine lamenting that one effect of the

[1] Mr. Palfrey in the book just mentioned, and Mr. Tyler in his *History of American Literature*, give numerous extracts from Chauncey, inveighing against the New Lights.

new movement had been materially to diminish the attendance at Harvard.[1]

It was but natural that men alarmed at the spectacle of a church thus rent and distracted, ill able as it seemed to check the in-flowing tide of fanaticism, should seek refuge in a community untouched by these new influences, and yet showing symptoms of real vitality and spiritual force. In 1742 we find Carr, an Episcopalian clergyman in Massachusetts, reporting to the Secretary to the Society for the Propagation of the Gospel that 'enthusiasm has been the means of reconciling many sober, considerate people to the communion of our Church,' and again stating 'that where the late spirit of enthusiasm has most abounded the Church has received the largest accession. Many of those deluded people, wearied in pursuit as their passion subsided, sought for rest in the bosom and communion of the Church.'[2]

Episcopacy profits by the movement

So, too, we find an Episcopalian clergyman in Massachusetts writing that, since Whitefield came into the colony, many 'who have before complained of the Church as Popery, wish for some of our good old bishops out of England.' Another writes that 'many have come into the Church on account of the feuds and discontents he has propagated among the Dissenters.' In like manner the churchwardens and vestrymen of Salem report to the Gospel Society that 'other friends to the Church wrote that the disturbances caused by Whitefield have "opened the eyes of some so as to see the beauty of our Church" and to "wish for some of our good old bishops out of England."'[3]

Again, a clergyman in Pennsylvania reports with satisfaction that Whitefield's teaching has almost broken

[1] *Boston Evening Post,* July 1749, quoted in N. J. Archives, vol. xii. p. 550.

[2] Documentary History, pp. 180, 201.

[3] Perry, Massachusetts, pp. 369, 388.

Presbyterianism to pieces, while the Episcopalian churches have lost but two or three.[1]

These are clerical witnesses, possibly prejudiced. But we find a layman, Sir Henry Frankland, also stating that the effect of Whitefield's teaching has been to dispose 'the soberer sort of Dissenters' to join the Church.[2]

Such exultations might have been checked by the reflection that a Church cannot live on negations, and that fear and reaction make but a poor foundation on which to build a faith. In the Episcopalian Church of New England there was no lack of piety or, measured by the colonial standard of that day, of learning. But the Church was an exotic, with no real organic connexion with the national life, rather taking an attitude which forced it into antagonism with that life.

Religion in New York.

We have already seen how by a process of administrative jugglery those interested in the government of New York had transformed a system intended to secure equality among all Protestant sects into one which gave supremacy to the Episcopal Church. By the middle of the eighteenth century an intelligent and well-informed writer could state that in his opinion the Episcopalians were not more than one-fifteenth of the whole population.[3] It is clear enough that there was an undercurrent of dissatisfaction at the claim to supremacy made on behalf of the Episcopal clergy. At the same time the whole situation was different from that in New England. There Episcopacy was alike checked and stimulated by the presence of a solid body of opposition. Massachusetts and Connecticut had each a national Church as truly as any community ever had. In New York the consciousness of unity and of an organic life was as much absent in spiritual as it was in secular

[1] Perry, Pennsylvania, p. 235.
[2] *Ib.* Massachusetts, p. 424.
[3] Smith, p. 281.

affairs. The cosmopolitanism of New York, its diversity of origin and speech, was fully reflected in the religious condition of the community. By the middle of the century there were in the city of New York two Episcopalian churches, two churches of Dutch and one of English Presbyterians, two of German Lutherans, one of French Huguenots, one of Baptists, one of Moravians, a Quaker meeting-house and a Jewish synagogue.[1] It is noteworthy that over and above the Church of England two of these bodies were in some measure dependent on societies in Europe. The Dutch Presbyterians acknowledged a certain supremacy in the mother Church of Amsterdam.[2] In 1730 the English Presbyterians, after various unsuccessful attempts to obtain a charter of incorporation, sought to secure their position by vesting the fee simple of their church and its grounds in certain officials of the Established Presbyterian Church of Scotland.[3] The Dutch Lutheran churches were allies rather than opponents of English Episcopalianism. There are but few signs of any spiritual vitality in the Episcopal Church of New York. But it had the advantage, and in such a community it was from the temporal point of view a very real advantage, of the continuous support of government and of the sympathy of most of the official class.

Talbot in New Jersey.

We have seen how the labours of Keith and Talbot had done something towards giving the Church of England a footing among the Presbyterians and Quakers of New Jersey. We have also seen how Hunter looked with but little favour on their efforts, and how Talbot's influence was impaired by his alleged sympathy with the Jacobite cause. The prejudice thus created was intensified by Talbot's later conduct. He saw more clearly, perhaps, than any of his

[1] Smith, pp. 251, &c. [2] *Ib.* [3] *Ib.*

contemporaries, and certainly expressed more forcibly, the necessity for colonial bishops and the helpless condition of the Anglican Church in America uncontrolled by any central authority. Unhappily his strong conviction of the necessity for colonial bishops, coupled with his Jacobite sympathies, led him to accept consecration as a bishop at the hands of the Non-jurors.[1]

The same step was taken by a man of far inferior stamp to Talbot. The career of Welton as a clergyman in England is only memorable for one incident. He expressed his opinion of the Whig Kennett, Dean and afterwards Bishop of Peterborough, by choosing him for the model of Judas in a fresco painted by Welton's instructions for his church at Whitechapel.[2] If we may believe a somewhat malevolent witness, Welton regarded this fresco with so much pride that he took a copy of it with him to America, together with an armament of guns and fishing tackle, valued at three hundred pounds.[3] Accompanied by this exceedingly unwise and discreditable ally, Talbot returned to New Jersey, and there at once justified Hunter's charges by refusing to take the oaths of allegiance or to pray for the reigning monarch. No course was open to the Society but at once to dismiss Talbot from their service. Welton, over whom they had no authority, was removed from the colony by a writ of the Privy Seal summoning him to England.[4]

Both in New Jersey and in Pennsylvania the Church of England had a serviceable ally in the Lutheran Church established by the Swedish immigrants. Through

[1] For the consecration of Talbot and Welton, Mr. Perceval (*Apology for Apostolic Succession*, 2nd ed. p. 247) quotes what seem to be authoritative documents.

[2] There is a very full account of this outrage in the Life of Kennett in the *Dictionary of National Biography*. Authorities are given.

[3] Letter from Urmston, Perry's *Collections*, Pennsylvania, p. 143.

[4] Hawks's *Protestant Episcopal Church in Maryland*, pp. 183–4.

the greater part of the eighteenth century the vitality of the Church was maintained by systematic communication with the mother Church in Sweden, and by a regular and continuous supply of ministers ordained. Their relations with the English Episcopalian Church were always those of inter-ecclesiastical comity. We read how about 1722 the vacant churches in Pennsylvania were served by two zealous Swedish clergymen who preached in English.[1] The Swedish buildings were put at the disposal of the English clergy, nor can we doubt that, as the Swedish language was gradually superseded, the members of the Lutheran churches were absorbed by English Episcopalianism.[2]

The Swedish Lutheran Church.

The records of the Episcopalian Church in New Jersey, Philadelphia, and Delaware are almost wholly derived from the reports of individual clergymen. So widely do those reports vary according to the temper of the man, and even according to conditions which changed from time to time, that it is no easy matter to arrive at any connected and consistent conclusion. Thus, in the very same year, we find two clergymen in Pennsylvania reporting, one that religion was never in a more flourishing condition, the other that he had found many of his flock ignorant of the very fundamentals of Christianity.[3] Six years later the more favourable of these two witnesses, Howie, admits that there are in the colony 'such a prodigious number of sectaries that the Church of England is like a small twig growing under the spreading boughs of a mighty tree.'[4] There is a like discrepancy in the reports sent home by Ross, an Episcopalian clergyman in Delaware. In 1729 he

State of the Episcopalian Church in New Jersey and Pennsylvania.

[1] Memorial, undated, but seemingly about 1722, from the clergy of Pennsylvania to the Secretary of the S.P.G. Perry's *Collections*, Pennsylvania, p. 122.

[2] *Ib.*

[3] *Ib.* pp. 188–9.

[4] *Ib.* p. 207.

reports that 'religion never appeared in the place in so shining and lively a state.' 'We are blessed with peace and mutual love, and communicants are both numerous and devout.'[1] Yet three years later he writes in a spirit of deep despondency: 'Our subscriptions are nullities,' and a magistrate speaking from the bench has denounced as idiots all who pay any regard to priests or churches.[2]

Clergy who have been accustomed to regard supremacy and State support as conditions inherent in the very nature of their Church are but ill-fitted to adapt themselves to an entirely different state of things, or to accept cheerfully and contentedly the position of a tolerated sect. Assuredly the constitution of Pennsylvania did not give the slightest countenance to the belief that the Church of England held any kind of supremacy. Yet we find an Episcopalian treating it as a grievance that Gordon, the Governor of the colony, granted licenses to celebrate marriages indifferently to Presbyterian and Anglican clergy.[3] That the Episcopalian Church did something for the cause of morality and spiritual enlightenment in the Middle colonies we cannot doubt. With equal certainty may we say that it never became an essential element in the national life.

The Church and the Welsh settlers.

In one quarter the Episcopalian Church in Pennsylvania threw away opportunities, precisely as the Church of England has done at home on a larger scale. An energetic minister named Hughes, presumably a Welshman, laboured among the settlers of that nation. He found hearers abundant and willing. But his work was crippled by lack of suitable buildings for worship and of devotional books in the Welsh language.[4]

[1] Perry's *Collections*, Delaware, p. 55. [2] *Ib.* p. 66. [3] *Ib.* p. 49.

[4] Letters from Hughes to the Secretary S.P.G. in 1734. Perry's *Collections*, Pennsylvania, pp. 138, 191.

Religious condition of Maryland and Virginia.

In the four Southern colonies the Church of England enjoyed a definite and specified supremacy, granted to it in Virginia by the original constitution, in the other colonies by legal enactmemt. In any estimate of the religious life of the colonies North Carolina may be at once set on one side. We have already seen how the settlers there took advantage of the chance presence of a Church of England clergyman to secure those religious ministrations for which the daily life of the colony made no provision. Something was done indeed by the Society for the Propagation of the Gospel. But it is clear that the presence of a few ill-paid missionaries, supporting themselves in that dismal and unwholesome country by the labour of their own hands, counted for little or nothing in the life of the community. In the other three colonies the Episcopalian Church might undoubtedly claim to be the dominant creed, more closely identified than any other with the spiritual life of the community. In Maryland there were Quakers, Presbyterians and Independents. Yet the predominance of Episcopacy is amply proved by the ease with which the law—or indeed we might say successive laws—endowing that form of religion was carried through the Assembly. That was no doubt in some measure due to the necessity which all Protestants felt for closing their ranks against a common enemy. As the danger of French invasion increased, as the British settlements extended westward, and drew nearer and nearer to those Indian tribes who were under the influence of French missionaries, so did the dread of Romanism become more and more a dominant motive with the English colonists. That motive was specially felt in Maryland, where the Church of Rome might reckon if not on the actual help of a Roman Catholic Proprietor, at least on the influence established by three generations of the Calvert family.

Thus in 1725 we find in Maryland clergymen complaining to the Bishop of London of the 'vast number of Jesuits who by their sophistry and cunning make proselytes daily throughout the whole government,' and who were 'advanced to such heights of assurance as to send public challenges, and to disperse their Popish books through all quarters of the country.'[1] Dread of the Scarlet Woman is apt to interfere with sobriety of judgement, and there was in all likelihood some exaggeration in that estimate. But fear is not less operative for being ill-founded, and we cannot doubt that the proximity of aggressive Romanism did much to reconcile the Protestant Dissenters of Maryland to the ascendancy of the Episcopalian Church. Their good will and confidence may have been weakened by the vagaries of one or two clergy with Jacobite and Non-juring leanings, but it was not materially impaired.

In Virginia the Episcopalian Church had no dangers to fear but those which resulted from her own shortcomings, and from the moral and spiritual inertness of the community. The administrative traditions of Maryland were far more favourable to the existence of Dissent than those of Virginia. Puritans and Quakers had met with a toleration from Roman Catholic Proprietors which had been denied to them by Anglican Governors, appointed by and dependent on the Crown. Moreover the social and industrial conditions of the country made in the same direction. In Maryland, as we have seen, the yeoman and the free artisan existed alongside of the planter. In Virginia *latifundia* based on servile labour were universal. There were no place in such a system for the compact, self-governing societies which were the life-blood of Protestant Dissent. The method of appointment for the clergy varied in the

[1] Perry's *Collections*, Maryland, p. 251.

two colonies, and by a singular and unhappy chance each had that system which would have been best fitted to the conditions of its neighbour. In Maryland the nomination of the clergy was by a law of the colony passed in 1702 vested in the Governor.[1] When however Charles, the fourth Lord Baltimore, conformed to the Church of England, he claimed the right of appointment.[2] The hanger-on of Frederick, Prince of Wales, was not very likely to exercise that power with much regard to the welfare of the Church, and it was more grossly abused by his notoriously profligate son, the fifth lord.[3] In Virginia, on the other hand, the choice of a minister had been practically though not formally transferred from the Governor to the vestry of the parish. It is easy to see how in a new country, where there was no central fund available for fresh endowments, and where the erection of a new ecclesiastical parish and the maintenance of a church was necessarily a matter of local effort, an arrangement whereby those who provided the funds should chose the minister would seem obviously equitable. Yet such a system was ill-fitted to a community with parishes of enormous size, where communication was difficult, and with little training in the principles or machinery of local self-government. On the other hand, there was, as we have seen, enough of labour and industrial life in Maryland for such a system to have worked with some chance of success.

Despite these differences the condition of the Church in each colony was sufficiently alike to be dealt with comprehensively in a single view. In both colonies the Church suffered from the absence of any central authority, bringing with it spiritual guidance and disciplinary control. Both were fortunate in that such

[1] Acts of Maryland; cf. Mereness, p. 439.
[2] Mereness, p. 450. [3] *Ib.*

limited and delegated authority as did exist was vested in men exceptionally fitted to wield it. Bray and Blair, the two commissaries to whom, in the closing years of the seventeenth century and the opening years of the eighteenth, the authority of the Bishop of London was delegated in Maryland and Virginia respectively, were men of high character, overflowing energy, and with a very adequate sense of the standard of learning, ability and conduct needed in the clergy. Unluckily when Bray and Blair were removed from the scene, there was no one to fill their place, and neither in Maryland nor Virginia was there that mechanism of Church government, nor that general feeling of loyalty and devotion to the Church, which enabled it to dispense with exceptional energy and devotion in individuals.

It is not difficult from the materials at our disposal to construct a fairly exact picture of the state of the Church and the clergy in Maryland and Virginia. Hostile critics and observers reporting from within are in one tale. Here and there were to be found men of industry and piety. But for the most part the clergy shared the somewhat gross tastes of their flocks, without sharing in those redeeming influences which made the Southern planter such a real power in the political life of the community. The planter might be a gambler, a cock-fighter and something of a sot. But he was the organizing and administering head of a little industrial community. The society in which he lived had the virtues of an oligarchy: self-respect, self-reliance, cohesion. The clergyman too often resembled him in his lower tastes, without being subjected to the redeeming influence of his worthier pursuits. We find one of Bray's successors reporting that it was necessary to prohibit marriages in private houses as a check on the drunkenness of the clergy.[1] We hear, too,

[1] Perry, Maryland, pp. 106–9.

of a Maryland clergyman whose relations with his flock were such that he had to go into the pulpit armed with a pistol.[1]

In Virginia we find a clergyman of the name of Lang who enjoyed the special favour of Blair, and who may therefore in all likelihood be regarded as a trustworthy witness, writing this of his brethren: 'The great cause of irreligion and ignorance is in the clergy, the sober part being slothful and negligent, and others so debauched that they are the foremost and most bent on all manner of vices. Drunkenness is the common vice.'[2]

And even when the clergymen were not actually vicious, they were for the most part wholly absorbed in secular business. In 1738 one of them complains to the Bishop of London that it gives him 'a great deal of uneasiness to see the greatest part of our brethren taken up in farming and in buying slaves, which in my humble opinion is unlawful for any Christian, and particularly for clergymen.'[3]

It is but fair, perhaps, to present that better side of the picture of which we have also evidence. The wife of a clergyman in Stafford county named Moncure has left a picture of the frugal, yet refined, life of herself and her husband, compact of plain living and high thinking, which might in its substance have come from the pen of Steele or Goldsmith. She tells how they had often to live by the produce of her husband's shooting or fishing, and how she used to accompany him in his woodland rambles. Yet he was no Parson Trulliber. His well-born neighbours would come over to spend the day at the parsonage, bringing their own victuals, and the one luxury of the house was a well-chosen library.

[1] Mereness, p. 457.

[2] Meade's *Old Churches of Virginia*, vol. i. p. 385.

[3] *Ib.* p. 456.

A consensus of evidence, however, forbids us accepting this as in any way typical.[1]

It was, too, with the religious as with the civil life of Virginia. Progress was made well nigh impossible by the lack of towns and the vast area over which the population was scattered. The parishes, Spotswood complains, were of such size that many of the inhabitants were wholly cut off from the ordinances of religion.[2]

In truth when we look at the conditions of the Church and clergy in the Southern colonies, how could we expect anything but failure? The inner vitality of a Church is maintained by the sense of a mission. Even if her ministers have no special work to do as evangelists, as the teachers of theological doctrine or the awakeners of spiritual life, yet the sense of a historical past and the inheritance of great traditions may keep alive responsibility. The springs within may flow sluggishly and grow stagnant, yet an environment of intellectual and moral activity may supply the needful stimulant. There have been periods in the history of the Church of England when the pulse of spiritual life has beaten faintly. That she has lived through such times has been mainly due to the latent and unacknowledged influence of a great past, and also to the fact that she has ever been in close, even if not always friendly, contact with the intellectual growth of a vigorous, progressive and sane people.

Mere machinery cannot keep a system in life and healthy activity. But it may preserve the external and protective shell, within which the organism lives dormant, yet with a possibility of revival. The discipline and the prizes of an established Church will at one time be fetters to her activity, at another they will tide her over a time of lethargy and depression.

Of all these conditions of successful activity not a

[1] Meade, vol. ii. p. 198.

[2] Letters, vol. i. pp. 37–9.

single one was fulfilled in the Episcopal Church of the Southern colonies. To make head, as an Episcopalian clergyman in New England was called on to do, against deeply rooted Calvinistic dogma, the continuous inheritance of nearly two centuries, was a stimulating task. His audiences might be hard to move, but once let him win their ear and they were sure to be alike receptive and retentive. In the Middle colonies the same conditions existed in some measure, and, as we have seen, Swedish Lutheranism did something to link Episcopalianism with the past by a real chain of sentiment. But in the South the Church had neither opposition nor sympathy to stimulate her. There was nothing in the life and duties of the clergy which appealed to ambition whether of the nobler or more worldly kind. The rector of a parish in Maryland or Virginia was burying himself in a sphere of scanty and monotonous duty, and excluding himself from all brilliant possibilities in the future.

Difficulties about stipend in Maryland.[1]

Moreover the economic condition of both colonies tended to make the position of the clergy difficult and to bring them into conflict with their flocks. In the Northern colonies the absence of any stable medium of currency would have made little difference to the relations between the Congregational clergy and their flocks. The maintenance of the Church was an obligation which the New Englander had no wish to evade or minimize. In the Southern colonies the obligation was felt to be that of debtor and creditor; any special condition which seemed to increase that obligation was regarded as an injustice; any legal device whereby formal compliance might be combined with practical evasion was looked on as justifiable, and welcomed.

In Maryland the clergy were maintained by a poll-

[1] For this dispute see Mereness, pp. 453-5.

tax of forty pounds of tobacco per head. It is clear that the soundness of such a system rested on the assumption that the value of tobacco in relation to other commodities, and especially to the necessities of life, remained fairly stable. As a matter of fact in Maryland that assumption was the very reverse of the truth. Much worthless tobacco was grown, and not unnaturally the worst of all was often appropriated to the payment of the clergy. In 1728 the legislature took measures for improving the quality of tobacco by restricting the number of plants. It seemed no more than a fair concession to the tax-payer that when his output was artificially limited, he should be indemnified by a compensating increase in its value. With this object the legislature reduced the poll-tax for the maintenance of the clergy to thirty pounds of tobacco. That measure, however, was vetoed by the Proprietor. A compromise was then arrived at. A law was passed limiting the number of tobacco plants which might be grown, but as a compensation to the tax-payer it was provided that one-fourth of the whole amount due to the clergy might be paid in grain, at a fixed rate.

This law, however, was only temporary in its provisions. At the end of two years it expired, with the result that the culture of tobacco relapsed into its former depressed condition. All restriction on the quality grown was removed, the market was glutted with an inferior article, and there was real danger that Maryland would be wholly ousted from the tobacco market by Virginia. On no class did this press more heavily than on the clergy. At the same time the fact that a large portion of the profit resulting from an increase in value would go into their pockets was a hindrance to any measure for improvement.

Thus the interests of the payer and the recipient

alike pointed towards restriction as the best course. A law was passed reimposing a limit on the number of plants which might be grown, and at the same time reducing the poll-tax for the maintenance of the clergy from forty pounds of tobacco to thirty pounds. A further provision was inserted permitting any person who did not grow tobacco to pay at the rate of three shillings and ninepence per head.

It is an interesting illustration of the industrial progress of the country and of the difference between Maryland and Virginia that in the former colony those who did not grow tobacco should have been numerous and important enough to be made the subject of special provisions. One slightly unsatisfactory result of this system was that it gave the clergy an interest in encouraging the growth of tobacco to the exclusion of other products, and this set them in opposition to the best industrial and economic interests of the colony. Thus we read of a clergyman actually making it a matter of reproach to his parishioners that out of sloth they grew other commodities instead of tobacco. On the whole, however, the compromise seems to have been accepted as satisfactory, and no further difficulty followed till, at a later day, the dispute between clergy and laity reappeared as an incident in the struggle between the colonists and the mother country.

In Virginia.

In Virginia as in Maryland the dues of the clergy were paid in tobacco. There the system brought about a fierce and fruitful dispute. That, however, has its place in a later chapter of American history. It is worth noticing that Spotswood foresaw and wished to guard against the troubles that might arise from the clergy being paid their dues in a commodity of fluctuating value. He suggested that every titheable person should pay forty pounds of tobacco. This should be sold by a public official. From the proceeds, eighty pounds in money should be allotted to each clergyman as his stipend. The rest of the proceeds should be applied to general Church purposes.[1]

This payment did not constitute the whole endowment of the clergy, since an Act passed in 1748 assigned to each a glebe of two hundred acres.[2]

We have seen from Byrd's evidence what was the spiritual condition of North Carolina. His account is confirmed by Spotswood, who in 1711 reported that there was but one clergyman in the whole colony.[3] As the century went on there were faint traces of improvement. Not, indeed, that there was anything like a settled clergy equal to the needs of the colony. In 1715 the colony was mapped out into nine parishes,[4] and one of the instructions to the first royal Governor, Burrington, was to see that every church had a minister, with a competent endowment and a glebe.[5] Those enactments, however, were virtually a dead letter. Such spiritual life as there was in the colony seems to have been due to two influences. Much good work was evidently done by the missionaries sent out by the Gospel Society. The fact that they were, as Burrington reports, so little approved by the colonists generally that they desired no more can hardly be taken as necessarily a condemnation. At least there is a consensus of opinion as to the good work done by Clement Hall, a native of the colony, who, having obtained ordination in England, returned in 1743, and thereafter laboured for twelve years with conspicuous success as a travelling gospeller, held for four more the incumbency of a parish, and then died, worn out with toil.[6]

State of religion in North Carolina.

1 Letters, vol. i. p. 128.
2 Hening, vol. vi. p. 89.
3 *Ib.* p. 135.
4 N. Car. Records, vol. ii. p. 207.
5 *Id.* vol. iii. p. 106.
6 Anderson, vol. iii. pp. 633–6.

Moreover the immigration of Quakers and Presbyterians brought in a type of life higher in religion, as in other matters, than that of the older settlements along the sea-board. In 1716 we find a foolish and uncharitable clergyman in North Carolina writing to the Gospel Society that unless able and sober missionaries are sent out, the colony [1] will be overrun with Quakerism and infidelity. Burrington saw the matter very differently. We may set it off against some of his indiscretions that, writing in 1732, he described the Quakers in the colony as 'considerable for their number and substance; the regularity of their lives, hospitality to strangers, and kind offices to new settlers inducing many to be of their persuasion.' [2]

But though these influences no doubt did something to drag the colony out of the slough of heathendom described by earlier writers, yet it is clear that the Church as an institution had but little hold on the colony. As late as 1757 we find Governor Dobbs complaining to the Assembly that in certain parishes the Act endowing the clergy is made a dead letter. A vestry is elected which either refuses to nominate an incumbent at all, or else bargains till it gets one at a low stipend. To prevent this he proposes that the Church rate shall be levied, not parish by parish, but on the province as a whole, and that out of this fund the clergy shall be paid and churches built where necessary. There is, however, no trace of the adoption of such a scheme.[3]

The Church in South Carolina.

In the annals of the Episcopal Church in America, South Carolina stands out as the one comparatively bright spot. Severed from the other colonies by an impenetrable wilderness, the colony had, as we have seen, developed a social and industrial life of her own. South Carolina had really

[1] Weeks's *Southern Quakers and Slavery*, p. 124.

[2] N. Car. Records, vol. iii. p. 429.

[3] *Ib.* vol. v. p. 870.

more in common with the West Indies than with the English settlements on the American mainland. In 1701 the colony only possessed two Episcopalian churches, one at Charlestown, the other at Goosecreek, some seventeen miles inland.[1] In 1706 the number of parishes was increased to ten,[2] and to twice as many by 1757.[3] The system of appointment was, as in Virginia, by popular vote. But the conditions of life in South Carolina divested such a system of many of its dangers. The population was far more concentrated, and therefore more amenable to public opinion. Charlestown furnished what was wholly lacking in Virginia, a real centre of educated thought. Moreover in South Carolina the election of the clergy was modified by the existence of commissioners appointed by the legislature of the colony with power of dismissal. Not only could they deprive in case of immorality, but even 'if there should arise such incurable prejudices, dissensions, animosities and implacable offences between the incumbent and his people, that reverence for and benefit by his ministry is to be utterly despaired of, though he is not guilty of more gross and scandalous crime.'[4]

In 1712 Governor Craven could write of the clergy of the colony, 'We may boast as learned a clergy as any in America, men unblemished in their lives and principles, who live up to the religion they profess—always indefatigable in their functions, visiting the sick, fearless of distempers and never neglecting their duty.'[5]

[1] McCrady, vol. i. pp. 183, 411.

[2] *Ib.* p. 416.

[3] *Ib.* vol. ii. p. 437.

[4] *Ib.* vol. i. p. 417. In all these cases Mr. McCrady quotes or refers to the statutes.

[5] Quoted by Mr. McCrady from the S. Car. Records. *Hist. of S. Car.* vol. i. p. 419. Mr. McCrady's history is published in a series of separate works, each with its own title. But as they are continuous I have ventured for simplicity's sake to refer to them as vols. i. and ii.

A touch of optimism may be suspected; yet among colonial administrators there were few more upright and independent than Craven, and the records of South Carolina are conspicuously free from clerical scandals and disputes.

This was not due to the absence of Nonconformists. Before 1690 a congregation was in existence composed of Independents and Scotch Presbyterians, with a leaven of French Huguenots, all worshipping together. The task of advancing the cause of Dissent fell into the hands of one who had been brought to the colony by a strange chance. In 1696 a ship touched at Charlestown bearing home the remnants of the Darien settlement. Among them was a Presbyterian clergyman, Alexander Stobo. He landed for the purpose of preaching in the Congregational church. During his stay on shore a storm got up and the vessel was dashed to pieces on the harbour bar. Stobo remained in the colony, became the minister of the Congregational church, and laboured with such energy that by 1710 five more churches had come into existence. This was accompanied or followed by the establishment of a presbytery.[1] This gained strength and expanded till the time came when it could effectively join hands with the Ulster Presbyterians, who about the middle of the century began to pour into the Western Highlands of South Carolina.

Stobo was accompanied ashore by his young daughter, who thus escaped shipwreck. That incident had an important influence on the history of the American republic, since from her is descended Theodore Roosevelt.[2]

There were also at Charlestown two congregations

[1] *Hist. of S. Car.* vol. i. p. 311; vol. ii. pp. 441–3. There does not seem to be any evidence as to the precise date of this.

[2] This descent is set forth in a paper in the *Scottish Historical Review*, vol. i. p. 416.

of French Huguenots. They appear to have become assimilated to their Anglican neighbours, while some of their members left their original fold and joined the nonconforming Protestants.[1]

Influence of Whitefield in Virginia.[2]

There seems to be evidence for the existence of Presbyterian congregations both in Virginia and Maryland before the expiration of the eighteenth century. But it was not till well in the eighteenth century that Presbyterianism had much influence on the life of either colony. Of all the Southern colonies Virginia was the only one where the preaching of Whitefield had taken any effective hold. Its influence there seems to have been more gradual and more wholesome than in the Northern colonies. It does not seem to have created any ecstatic outburst of devotional enthusiasm, but rather to have left behind it an influence which in time did something to quicken and strengthen the spiritual life of the community. The influx of Presbyterians from Scotland and Ulster into the Southern States is a matter which will come before us again. For the present it is enough to say that there was such a movement. The number of Congregational churches in the colony has been estimated by a careful investigator as having reached thirty by the year 1735. Nearly all of these were in the western district, and had therefore no connexion with the tide-water plantations in which the political and economic life of the community was centred. They seem, too, to have been isolated societies, with no kind of collective life or synodal organization. Among these congregations, one Samuel Morris, a disciple of Whitefield, began missionary work of a simple kind. He does not seem to

[1] Commissary Bull's Report.

[2] For my account of Nonconformity in Virginia I have depended on Foote. His account is based on original documents, many of which he quotes.

have had anything in common with firebrands, such as Davenport, and his work was limited to the reading of devotional books, amongst them Whitefield's sermons. The spirit extended and various associations sprung up at which such readings took place, not however accompanied, as far as can be learnt from their recorded proceedings, by any exposition or devotional exercise. But before long an impulse from without gave to the movement a scope beyond that originally aimed at. In 1743 a Presbyterian minister from Delaware, William Robinson, acting with the approval of his own church, visited Virginia and organized the meetings into regular Presbyterian churches, with a ministry and Confession of Faith.

One effect of this was at once to bring the Nonconformist congregations of Virginia into direct connexion with an authority outside the colony. In 1745 the Presbyterian synod at Newcastle, assuming a certain right of control over the scattered congregations of Western Virginia, sent one John Roan among them as a missionary. He, it is clear, had absorbed all that was most violent in the teaching of Whitefield. The Anglican clergy of Virginia probably fell far short of any high standard of moral or spiritual life. But a Christian preacher was not likely to commend himself to reasonable and moderate men by stating that the church was the house of the devil, to whom the clergy prayed, and that they and all their followers were on the road to hell. We cannot regard it as proof of a persecuting or even an illiberal temper that some of Roan's disciples were presented by a grand jury and fined. It is clear, too, that there was no wish on the part of the Governor, William Gooch, to stifle or silence Dissent. He had already granted a preacher's license to a Nonconformist minister of a very different stamp from Roan, Samuel Davies. His

Progress of Nonconformity in Virginia.

character and career, as revealed to us alike by his own writings and the testimony of others, show that a strenuous zeal for righteousness and a temper resolute almost to the point of pugnacity for the just rights of his own denomination were in nowise incompatible with a fair and judicial estimate of those who differed from him widely in speculative opinions.

Gooch might reasonably hold that Dissent among the obscure congregations of the West, without organization or internal alliances, was a very different thing from Presbyterianism in alliance with an impassioned crusade against Episcopacy, and carrying that crusade into those portions of the colony where hitherto Episcopacy had a secure foothold. There was another feature of the case which went far to justify the attitude of Gooch. The Presbyterian synod at Philadelphia, placing itself in opposition to that at Newcastle, assured Gooch that the Virginian Congregationalists were Separatists from their having been 'excluded for derisive and uncharitable doctrines and practices.' Some of them were fined, and a license to preach was refused to one of Davies's supporters, John Rodgers.

There was evidently no wish to silence Davies himself. He, however, had no intention of buying security for himself at the expense of his followers, and he put forward the contention that any minister had under the Toleration Act a legal right to such a license. The Council at first opposed this, claiming that the Governor and they themselves had discretion in this matter. Davies, however, stood firm. Gooch, though not a specially strong Governor, was a moderate and tolerant one, and his moderation was shared by Dawson, who as commissary for the Bishop of London exercised the supreme ecclesiastical authority in the colony. They were opposed by Peyton Randolph, the Attorney-General for Virginia. His opinion, however, was overruled by Dudley Ryder, who held the same office in the mother country, and the right of Nonconformists to preach within the colony was established. Davies lived to repay government by the courageous and inspiring counsel which he gave to the people of Virginia in an hour of sorrow and panic.

Davies's letter to Bishop of London.

That the dispute over the rights of Nonconformists was marked by a conspicuous and unusual absence of bitterness was largely due to the singularly tolerant and magnanimous temper of Davies. A letter which he wrote in 1752 to the Bishop of London strikes a note unhappily almost unique in the relations between Nonconformists and Episcopalians in America. It is throughout the work of a man consumed with zeal for righteousness, yet striving to the full to do justice to those who differed from him on questions of the method and form of government. His attitude throughout is, 'I do not say that Congregationalism is in the abstract better than Episcopalianism. I do say that in the present state of Virginia it is a more effective instrument of conversion.'

He had been denounced for preaching on week-days and thereby distracting people from labour. His reply is obvious but effective, and throws light on the social condition of Virginia: 'I wonder there is not an equal clamour raised about the modish ways of murdering time which are more likely to be remotely felt by the government and, which is worse, to ruin multitudes for ever. The religion of labour is held sacred among us, as the temporal circumstances of my people demonstrate; which are as flourishing as before their adherence to me, except that some of them have been somewhat injured by the fines and concomitant expenses imposed on them for worshipping God inoffensively in separate assemblies. But this hardship I will not aggravate, as

I believe it was not the effect of an oppressive spirit in the court, but of misinformation and the malignant officiousness of some private person.'

What follows is even more striking as showing how wholly Davies had divested himself of the spirit of partisan prejudice. He wishes to see Nonconformity strengthened, but he has not the least wish to see Episcopalianism weakened; they are in his eyes not rivals, but allies. 'I am satisfied,' he writes, 'that were there a pious bishop resident in America, it would have a happy tendency to reform the Church of England here and maintain her purity, and therefore upon a report spread in Virginia some time ago that one was appointed, I expressed my satisfaction in it, and my poor prayers shall concur to promote it.'

The sincerity of Davies is beyond question. But one may be permitted to doubt whether he was not going too far in imputing his own charitable and moderate temper to his co-religionists when he goes on to say, 'I know this is the sentiment of all my brethren in the synod of New York with whom I have conversed,' and it is very certain that he was out of touch with the opinion of the Northern colonies, when he went on to write, 'I am therefore extremely surprised at the information your lordship has received concerning the reception of this proposal in New England, and that they used all their influence to obstruct it. I never had the least intimation of this before, though some of the principal ministers there maintain very unreserved correspondence with me, and I have also the other usual methods of receiving intelligence from a country so near. If it be true I think with your lordship that it is hardly consistent with a spirit of toleration. But it is so unreasonable and so opposite to the sentiments of all the Dissenters whom I am acquainted with (and they are many both of the clergy and laity), that the informers must be persons of undoubted veracity before I could credit it.'

This letter was entrusted to Avory, a leading English Nonconformist, described by Davies in his journal as 'an amiable gentleman, very affable, of a soft ready address.' To him also Davies wrote a private letter, urging the importance of an American episcopate. Avory, however, told Davies that the proposal was intensely unpopular in New England, and took upon himself the responsibility of withholding Davies's letter to the Bishop. It is probably not uncharitable to suppose that the hostility to the episcopate represented opinion manufactured and organized by an official class, and that Davies was right in his belief that there was no strong element of popular feeling at the back. At all events, when the project for an episcopate is treated as an outrage on the feelings of American Nonconformists, it should not be forgotten that it commanded the full approval and sympathy of one of the best, wisest, and most courageous men to be found among their ranks.[1]

Lack of any central system of Anglican Church government.

The supineness of the British Government in their efforts to establish any effective system of control over the Episcopal churches in the American colonies has often been imputed for blame. Yet here as elsewhere failure was largely due to the lack of specific knowledge, to the absence of any machinery whereby the colonies might make their own wants known, and whereby the Home Government might be kept in touch with the divergent and often conflicting currents of colonial opinion.

There is no clear and definite documentary evidence as to the origin of that arrangement whereby the colonies were technically regarded as under the con-

[1] Davies's letter to the Bishop of London is given in full by Foote.

trol of the Bishop of London. The case cannot be stated better than in the words of a writer who has made the whole history of the American episcopate in colonial times the subject of a careful monograph.[1] He cites various documents, official and private, which assume rather than assert that the Bishop of London was in some fashion specially responsible for the state of the churches in the colonies, albeit none of them show either the origin of his authority or its precise limits. He then sums up the case thus: 'At the time of the Restoration the opinion was more or less prevalent that the charge of colonial ecclesiastical affairs belonged to the Bishop of London; and, according to the scattered instances related above, he seems even thus early to have taken some share in the administration of such matters. There was, however, no effort to place the jurisdiction on a legal footing and exercise it in anything like a systematic and efficacious manner until the accession of Bishop Compton.

Episcopal jurisdiction in the colonies.

'He, it is clear, started with the assumption that the episcopate of London invested him with some sort of spiritual jurisdiction over the colonies. In March 1676, when writing to a correspondent in the colonies, he used these words: 'The care of your churches with the rest of the plantations lies upon me as your diocesan.'[2] Not long after that we find the King in Council inserting a clause in the orders issued to Culpepper, Governor of Virginia, that no minister should be admitted to a benefice in any colony without a certificate from the Bishop of London.[3]

A little earlier the Board of Trade, probably at Compton's request, instituted an inquiry into the history and nature of the colonial jurisdiction of the Bishop of London.[4] As far as the existing evidence

[1] *The Anglican Episcopate and the American Colonies,* by A. L. Crosse.
[2] Crosse, p. 23. [3] *Ib.* p. 26. [4] *Ib.* p. 15, *n.* 3.

goes, this inquiry did not disclose any definite and formal proof of the alleged authority. Nevertheless the tradition served as a basis for a claim, and that claim was confirmed and extended by successive instructions, which might be interpreted either as creating such jurisdiction or as confirming a jurisdiction which in some form already existed.

Practically the result arrived at was that by the beginning of the seventeenth century the Episcopal Church in the American colonies was governed on a patchwork system, made up of the following elements:

1. The right of the Governor in certain colonies to induct ministers.

We have already seen how this right was acquired in New York. In Maryland it was conferred by an Act of the Assembly passed in 1700, and approved by the Crown.

2. The right of congregations to choose their own minister, as in Virginia and South Carolina.

3. The right of disciplinary control conferred on Governors from time to time by their instructions.

4. The rights above mentioned of the Bishop of London.

Alongside these various authorities was that of the Society for the Propagation of the Gospel, appointing and paying clergymen for work in the colonies. How far that Society was able to act in concert with the authorities in whom co-ordinate power was vested was mainly a question of individual character. One thing, however, at least is clear: there was perpetual danger of friction between all these co-ordinated forces. There was the further danger of a waste of energy and resources, and the probably more serious danger that any display of energy in one quarter might bring in its train some relaxation of effort in other quarters.

There was no wish on the part of Compton or of his successors during the first half of the eighteenth century to ignore the claims of the colonial Church. The only method by which an episcopal control could be exercised was by delegation to a commissary. That there was no lack of care in selection for that office is shown by the careers of such men as Blair, Bray and Garden. Yet it is clear that such a system was in many ways but a poor substitute for the authority of a resident bishop. It was admitted on all hands that the chief dangers to which the Episcopal Church in the colonies was exposed were lack of internal discipline and encroachment by the civil power. Both those evils were far more likely to be combated effectively by a single head able to claim co-ordinate authority with those whom the Church recognized as its fathers and rulers, than by a number of delegates only armed with that which was universally felt to be power of a lower type.

The commissarial system.

Moreover, there were two functions essential to the spiritual life of the Church—ordination and confirmation—which under the Anglican constitution could only be exercised direct by a bishop. It is difficult to overrate the paralyzing influence which the absence of any ordaining power resident in America inflicted on the colonial Church. It meant that no man could officiate in America as a minister of the Church of England unless he could afford time and money for a journey to England. It stood in the way of any systematic attempt at furnishing the clergy with a liberal education within the limits of the colonies. It converted the clergy into an alien caste, standing outside the organic life of the community.

Need of an episcopate.

The project of a colonial episcopate seems to have first taken definite shape at the beginning of the eighteenth century. In 1702 a letter was addressed by Talbot to the Gospel Society, stating that there were 'earnest addresses' from the colonies asking for a suffragan bishop. A similar statement was made to the Society by an earnest clergyman, Thoroughgood Moor,[1] and this was supported by a collective memorial from the clergy of New Jersey.

Attempts at the establishment of a colonial episcopate.

Satisfied with these opinions, the Society presented a memorial to the Queen, pointing out the need for a colonial episcopate.

In 1711, Sharp, Archbishop of York, Atterbury, then Prolocutor of the Lower House of Convocation, and other leading ecclesiastics discussed the question of establishing an episcopate in the colonies. The Bishop of London, however, either through accident or indifference took no part in the proceedings, and his colleagues not wishing to encroach on his diocesan functions let the scheme drop.[2]

In 1713 the Gospel Society returned to the charge and memorialized the Queen on the subject. Her answer was such as to raise their hopes.[3] They also had the sympathy and in some measure the practical help of the ablest man then administering the affairs of a British colony, Hunter. There seems no reason to think, as some have, that Swift's references to his own chances of a colonial bishopric were mere irony. His political connexion with Atterbury and his personal friendship with Hunter may well have suggested the scheme to him. The sense of failure and desertion which was never far from him may well have led him to fall back on such a hope in default of higher ambition. The post, too, which would remove him from the sphere of English politics was just that which a

[1] Moor's name suggests a Puritan origin. This may explain the fact that he was specially obnoxious to Cornbury.

[2] Newcome's *Life of Sharp*, vol. i. p. 352.

[3] Crosse, p. 101.

personal friend and political opponent, such as Hunter, might wish to see him fill. It is at least certain that early in 1709, when there seemed a chance of Hunter being Governor of Virginia,[1] Swift wrote twice to him referring to the prospect of his holding a bishopric in that colony, and that when Hunter was established at New York, he told Swift in a letter that he had bought a residence for a bishop and hoped to see him there some day.[2]

The ambitions of Swift and the hopes of the Society were overturned by the accession of the House of Hanover. The Society indeed at once memorialized the King on the subject, and even went so far as to present a cut-and-dried scheme for four colonial bishoprics.[3] It is possible that a more tentative and less confident application might have fared better. But in no case were George and his chief counsellors likely to look with favour on a scheme which had originally been brought forward by one of their chief political opponents, and likely to strengthen a Church from which they were receiving nothing more than sullen and half-hearted obedience.

Opposition to an episcopate in the colonies.

The rulers of the English Church during the eighteenth century may not have fully understood the needs of the colonies, but we cannot condemn them as wholly indifferent to the creation of a colonial episcopate. The real obstacles to the scheme were to be looked for in America itself rather than in England. In the Southern colonies there was indifference rather than active opposition. There was little desire for anything which could make ecclesiastical

[1] He was captured on his way by a French vessel, and was a prisoner in Paris when Swift wrote.

[2] Swift's letters of Jan. 12 and March 22, 1709, and Hunter's letter of March 1, 1713, Scott's edition of Swift's works, vol. xv. pp. 326, 337; vol. xvi. p. 21.

[3] Anderson, vol. iii. p. 164.

discipline prompter or more effective. In the North the opposition was of a wholly different kind. We can hardly wonder if the New Englanders, members of a community intensely alive to its own historical past, could not rid themselves of the idea that the re-introduction of episcopacy must bring with it some abridgement not only of their spiritual but of their temporal liberties. It is perfectly certain that no responsible British statesman, lay or clerical, ever dreamt of using an American episcopate as a weapon against the Congregational churches of Massachusetts. But it cannot be denied that the colonial advocates of such a scheme used language which justly laid them open to such suspicions. We have seen the kind of language which Johnson used about the civil rights of the colonists and the measures which he suggested for curtailing them. Johnson was a man of a more moderate and tolerant temper than the generality of his brethren, and we can hardly blame the people of New England if they saw underlying the scheme for an episcopate an insidious attack on their religious liberties. Moreover the action of the British Government and its servants in preventing the New England Churches from holding a synod could hardly fail to excite alarm and ill-will, and to awaken memories of past injustice.

Secker's sermon.[1]

That alarm might well be confirmed by a sermon preached by Secker as Bishop of Oxford in 1741, and published in 1766. He describes the condition of the colonies in the following language: 'No teacher was known; no religious assembly held; the sacrament of baptism not administered for twenty years together among many thousand people—such was the state of things in more of our colonies than one, and where it was a little better it was lamentably bad.' Secker seemingly imagined that the whole body of

[1] It is in a collection of Secker's sermons.

colonies were in a state closely resembling that of North Carolina, and must be redeemed from heathendom by the efforts of the Society for the Propagation of the Gospel. That Congregationalism in New England was a living force, pervading the national life, that the standard of morality and decency in Pennsylvania and New Jersey was to the full as high as that of the mother country, that the profligate luxury to be found at one extremity of London life, the squalid heathendom at the other, had no parallel in the colonies—these were unquestionable facts utterly ignored by Secker. That a fair-minded and conscientious man could put forward such a grotesque travesty of fact, that he could have done so without reflecting that he was inflicting a gross outrage on the feelings of a large number of British citizens, illustrates forcibly that appalling ignorance of colonial life and indifference to colonial feeling for which Great Britain was fated to pay so dearly.

Another argument used by the advocates of colonial episcopacy shows how far they were from understanding the real state of feeling in America. There was discontent and disaffection in New Jersey. There were also Jacobites in New Jersey. Therefore it was argued colonial discontent and Jacobitism are allies, and the existence of a sound Protestant episcopate is the remedy for the evil.[1] It is not a little strange that while the scheme for an American episcopate was thus exciting suspicion as dangerous to the liberties of the colonies, yet at the very same time the advocates of that scheme thought it necessary in approaching those in authority

[1] This is stated to be the policy of the English bishops in a letter written in 1749 by Paris, a leading man in New Jersey. N. J. Archives, vol. v. p. 238. At the same time the existence of a Jacobite party in New Jersey was no fiction. In 1722 Burnet had found it necessary to keep them in order by getting a special Act for administering oaths to suspected persons. *Ib.* vol. iii. p. 53.

not to be put to any charge in the matter, and that there was no intention of establishing bishoprics where as in New England forms of worship other than Episcopalian were adopted by the majority and recognised by the civil power.[1]

That, too, was the line taken by Sherlock in a report which he drafted in 1759 on the state of the Church in the colonies. He there strongly urged the need for colonial bishops, but expressly said that he should exempt New England and Pennsylvania from any such scheme.[2]

Meanwhile the only practical result of these schemes was to deprive the Episcopal Church of even that modified and imperfect discipline which it already possessed. Sherlock, as we have just seen, was a strong upholder of the view that the control of the Episcopal churches should be wholly withdrawn from the Bishop of London, and vested not in commissaries, but in a resident bishop or bishops. He possibly could not, far more probably would not, see that to carry out the first half of that change before it was certain that the second half would follow was to hand the colonial churches over to anarchy. Under his nominal rule that authority which had been exercised, imperfectly it is true, yet in some measure effectively and always beneficially, by Bray and Blair and Garden became a nullity. Such vitality as the Episcopal Church in the colonies retained was infused into her by the labours of the Society for the Propagation of the Gospel and by the efforts of individual clergymen reared in the stimulating atmosphere of the Northern colonies. The school of clergy of whom Samuel Johnson, already described, may fairly be regarded as the founder, never abated

Attitude of Sherlock.

[1] The Declaration is printed in Perry's *History of the American Episcopal Church*, p. 408.

[2] N. Y. Docs. vol. vii. pp. 360–9.

their zeal for the advancement of their own Church and their demands for an episcopacy. At a later day those demands, not always urged discreetly or with a due regard to surrounding circumstances, did much to embitter the relations between the mother country and the colonies.

CHAPTER V.

LITERARY AND INTELLECTUAL DEVELOPEMENT OF THE COLONIES.

As with the political, so with the intellectual and literary, history of the American colonies, there is a certain sense of decadence and impoverishment when we pass from the seventeenth to the eighteenth century. The impulses which swayed the colonies in their early days, which filled them with life and movement, were spent: the new impulses which were, at a later day, to supply the want as yet existed but in embryo: they had not put on definite shape nor formed for themselves articulate speech.

Change from the seventeenth to the eighteenth century.

It is true that in dealing with the seventeenth century we are hardly justified in speaking of colonial literature. One group of colonies, and one only, had anything which could be called literature. We may even go further and say that only in New England was to be found that self-consciousness, those impulses with imperative demand for articulate expression which form the springs that feed national literature. By the eighteenth century those springs were running thin and shallow. The New England chronicler, the New England theologian, was no longer stimulated by the conviction that he was one of a chosen and peculiar people. Thus we have no historians such as Winthrop and Bradford, no school of spiritual teachers such as that headed by Cotton and

New England.

Hooker, no controversial champion of unpopular doctrines with the bright vigour and freshness of Roger Williams. We have indeed, as was said before, one theologian of a high order.[1] But Jonathan Edwards is not typical and representative as the New England divines of the seventeenth century were. He is *primus* but not *primus inter pares*. There is no continuous hierarchy of thinkers to link him with popular feeling and opinion. New England literature was losing all originality, conforming more closely to contemporary English models, suffering under the chilly spell of borrowed and conventional 'Augustanism.'

It was indeed an unhappy chance for colonial literature that the connexion with the mother country was drawing closer just at the very time when that influence was least likely to be exercised with wholesome effect. The literature of a new country must be prepared to live upon the crude conceptions and peremptory emotions of an imperfectly developed life. It must have no strong craving for correctness, no uneasy dread of exaggeration and grandiosity. In other words it must be just what the canons of criticism accepted by England in the first half of the eighteenth century forbade it to be. Colonial writers, instinct with the passions and hopes of a new world, might have found congenial allies and sympathetic critics among the Elizabethans and their immediate successors. They would assuredly find none among the followers of Pope and the disciples of Addison. If a Walt Whitman had sprung up among the emancipated thinkers of Boston, or a Lindsay Gordon among the hard-riding squires of Virginia, the thought of the wits at Button's would have left him probably speechless, certainly without admirers.

Thus in the poetry of New England, in the writings

[1] See p. 231.

of Mather Byles, and the coterie of verse writers who glorified him, we see a formal and spiritless reproduction of Pope;[1] her essayists were little would-be Addisons, who drew their inspiration from the fashions and follies of Boston. Her historians, Hubbard, Niles, and Prince, are methodical, and more or less exact chroniclers. Hutchinson is something more. He is full of patriotism, at once convinced and rational; he is admirably lucid and a master of arrangement. But we never feel as we do in reading the works of Bradford and Winthrop, or the Wonder-working Providence, that

[1] Mather Byles was a Boston minister, in the pulpit an effective rhetorician. Mr. Tyler deals with him from that point of view, and is mercifully silent about his poetry. A specimen of the latter, his threnody over George I., is given by Mr. Hart in his *American History told by Contemporaries*, vol. iii. Extracts hardly do justice to it; the following passages, though notable, do not rise far above the average level.

'Shall unrelenting rocks forbear to bleed
While I proclaim the great Augustus dead?'

The physical results of the poet's sorrow are told with elaborate detail.

'Swift towards my heart unusual horror swims,
And strange convulsions seize my shivering limbs.

. . . .

The lingering remnant of my life's opprest,
And death-like damps bedew my lab'ring breast.'

The poet, however, finds consolation.

'Then wondrous Wales the sinking sceptre saves,
Then with her sparkling issue comes his queen,
Like night's fair empress with her starry train,
With cypress crowned, they gild the imperial seat,
And prop though weak with woe the tottering state.'

In 1744 there appeared a little volume composed by divers persons in glorification of Byles. He is likened in successive poems to Pope and Milton. The eulogy reaches its climax in a statement that the Muse

'triumphs to pronounce
The names of Byles, Pope, Homer all at once.'

I am indebted to Mr. Tyler's book for my knowledge of this volume. Byles, always a staunch supporter of government, may very well have been the author of the poem on Burnet's arrival, quoted at p. 113.

the live coal from the altar has now and again touched the writer's lips.

The New York writers.

It cannot be said that in the Middle colonies or the South there was anything like vigorous literary developement on definite lines. Yet there was a distinct advance on the work of the previous century. New York did produce at least two writers whose works deserve to live. William Smith's 'History of New York' is something more than a mere chronicle. It belongs to the same class of work as Hutchinson's history, though of distinctly inferior calibre. In the training and in the careers of the two men there were points of likeness. Each was a lawyer and attained high distinction in his profession; each was entangled in factious conflicts and emerged somewhat embittered each, when the crisis came, clave to the cause of the mother country, and died in exile. Yet there were wide differences between the two men. Hutchinson was a patriot as far as a man lacking in sympathy and imagination could be one. He firmly believed that he was carrying on the traditions of those who founded New England. Only it was not given to him to see that if the ideals and principles of the founders were to live, they must find expression in new forms. His bitterness towards opponents is no doubt accentuated by personal resentment, but it is mainly the outcome of public spirit, real, though it may be narrow and distorted. There is no touch of imaginative patriotism in Smith's work. He is a plain-spoken partisan, honest as far as honesty is consistent with the attitude of an advocate. To say this is little more than to say, in another form, that Hutchinson was a Bostonian, Smith a New Yorker. Each lived and moved in an atmosphere of faction. But in the faction of Massachusetts at its worst there were redeeming elements—patriotism, self-restraint, loyalty to an ideal, to great principles and inspiring traditions. The faction of New York was mainly due to her cosmopolitanism, to the poverty of her past, to her want of inspiring and restraining traditions, a want which left her political life a prey to personal intrigue and sordid materialism.

New York produced another writer who may be regarded as, in some measure, a pioneer of one movement in American literature. Penn's sympathetic mind had seen or imagined an element of romance in the contemporary life of the Red Indian, as it was presented to him. Cadwallader Colden, in his 'History of the Five Nations,' brought to bear something the same attitude of mind on the past history of the savage. His work is a picturesque, animated chronicle of the life of the Five Nations after their first introduction to Europeans, and especially of their dealings, mainly hostile, with the French. There is a touch of the saga spirit in Colden's work. He does not trouble himself with ethnological speculations as to the Indian's origin, or with moral and political speculations as to his destiny. He tells of the Indian's doings, bringing out with a good deal of dramatic skill those incidents which illustrate the Indian character as he wishes to present it. His picture may be a somewhat idealized one, but he at least gets a good deal nearer the truth than Penn does. Penn's imaginary savage is a peaceful, mirthful, companionable creature. Colden, while he is undoubtedly tender in his treatment of the Indian's failings, yet selects for praise those sterner virtues which really pertained at least to the Iroquois, whom he makes his special subject—concentration of purpose, stoicism in the endurance of pain, and contempt for death. The picturesque savage of American romance without doubt owed his origin, in a large measure, to Rousseau. But Colden had a share in his production.

Cadwallader Colden.

The Virginian writers.

In Virginia we have two writers who distinctly reflect the free, vigorous temper of the planter at his best—public-spirited, strenuous in prosecuting his own interests and those of the community, yet never losing a certain joyous irresponsibility. Byrd has already come before us. Robert Beverley, the author of a history of Virginia published in 1705, is a companion figure to Byrd. Throughout we feel that he writes as the educated man of affairs, not the student. He admits that what first led him to write was a wish to correct certain errors of Oldmixon and to clear away certain misconceptions prejudicial to Virginia. There were people in England, he tells us, who believed that in Virginia carts and ploughs were drawn by human beings, and that the effect of the climate was to turn white people black. The book is as much a description of the aspect and resources of the country as a history of its past. In its substance it reminds one of those glowing pictures of the resources and prospects of America put forth in the sixteenth and seventeenth centuries by advocates of colonization; but by its style it belongs wholly to its own age. Beverley expresses himself with easy and fluent alertness. He is occasionally epigrammatic, but the epigrams have their corners rounded as befits a contemporary of Addison.

A very different type of Virginian historian was the Rev. William Stith. His work has no colonial flavour about it. It might have been produced by a learned, leisurely and somewhat pompous English clergyman. The work is a torso conceived on so vast a scale that the writer never succeeded in carrying it as far as the twentieth year of the colony's existence. The writer is uncritical in his estimate of evidence, accepting, for example, without hesitation the romance which bore the name of John Smith.[1] Yet Stith's book is, unlike Beverley's, in modern language a work of research. He strives to get the best evidence, had access to the records of the Virginian Company, and thus during the many years when those records were lost to the world his book had a unique value. The style is rhetorical: at its best dignified and forcible; sometimes ponderous and over-elaborate, but always endowed with real definiteness and purpose, never sinking into mere windiness.

It was not to be expected that literature should find any place in the half-barbarized life of North Carolina. That South Carolina produced no writers may have been in some measure due to the fact that Charlestown, in which all the culture and leisure of the colony was centred, was in far closer contact than Virginia with the mother country. The colonist was not forced upon his own resources for culture. The life about him had not the same stimulating individuality and was not so inspiring a theme.

Thomas Godfrey.

Considering how large an output of what may be called realistic romance the mother country was responsible for during the eighteenth century, it is perhaps somewhat strange that the colonies should, in that department of letters, have been almost wholly unproductive. But colonial literature meant mainly the literature of Boston, and if there was little left of the underlying spirit of the founders, yet her conventional restraints of Puritanism were still strong. If established prejudice excluded the novel, even more did it exclude the drama. Yet the colonies could claim one author who deserves to be remembered and to be assigned a place among post-Elizabethan play-

[1] I say 'bore the name,' since John Smith's personal responsibility in the matter is open to question. See *The English in America*, Appendix E.

wrights.[1] Thomas Godfrey, a citizen of Pennsylvania, was born in 1736, and died in 1763. His father was a thrifty tradesman at Philadelphia, an acquaintance of Franklin, a man of some note as a student of natural science. Young Godfrey's taste for humane letters earned no sympathy from his family. At his death he left behind in manuscript a number of somewhat commonplace poems and a tragedy, of which the scene is laid at the Court of Parthia. Godfrey's play shows a sympathetic knowledge of the Elizabethan dramatists. There is an unmistakeable echo of Glendower in the lines:

> 'E'en such a night dreadful as this they say
> My teeming mother gave me to the world;
> Whence by those sages, who in knowledge rich,
> Can pry into futurity and tell
> What distant ages will produce of wonder,
> My days were deemed to be a hurricane.'

It was no small achievement for an imperfectly educated young colonist not only to have drawn from the Elizabethan spring, but to have absorbed what is best in it. Godfrey has some of the defects of Massinger: stiffness of diction, and a lack of spontaneity and impulse. But he also has Massinger's merits: his texture is woven close, and his hand is guided by scholarly self-restraint.

In the way of books the harvest from the American colonies during the period which we are surveying is but a scanty one. We should however greatly err if we supposed that the colonial intellect was stagnant and unprogressive. The diffusion rather than the creation of knowledge has been the characteristic of the American colonies ever since they put on

Colonial journalism.

[1] I am sorry to say that I can only speak of Godfrey at second-hand. I have been wholly unable despite much search and inquiry to find Godfrey's play. But Mr. Tyler (vol. ii. pp. 246–51) gives copious extracts from it, and these I think fully justify all that I have said. His poems I have seen.

the form of a republic, and that process had been at work for at least two generations before the era of republicanism. The eighteenth century saw journalism in the American colonies spring into existence, and become with astonishing rapidity a potent factor in national life. Yet more astonishing, if we look at the obstacles to be overcome, the difficulties of transit, the exacting claims of material needs and ambitions, was the rapid and almost universal extension of educational machinery.

It might have been foretold almost with certainty that American journalism would have its beginnings at Boston. In 1704 John Campbell, a bookseller in that town, who also held the office of postmaster, issued a weekly news-letter. The contents of the first number may be taken as fairly typical. It contained a few items of local news, shipping intelligence from Philadelphia and New York, the Queen's Speech to Parliament, and an extract from a London paper with information about the Old Pretender and his intrigues.

The Boston newspapers.[1]

The publication of the news-letter was followed in 1719 by the appearance of a second Boston paper, the Gazette, printed by Benjamin Franklin's brother James. The Gazette soon passed out of his hands, and he became the printer of a third paper which appeared in 1721, The New England Courant. The birth of the Courant marks an epoch in American journalism. It was not like its two predecessors primarily a journal of news and advertisement. It held a position more like that of a weekly paper in the present day, existing to give effect to certain political convictions and to ventilate current topics. The career of the Courant, extending over

Battle between the government and the Courant.

[1] For the following account of journalism in the colonies I have depended mainly on Isaiah Thomas's *History of Printing in America*.

only six years, was a striking illustration of the new spirit which was beginning to show itself in the politics of Massachusetts. Hitherto, whatever might be the attitude of the colony towards the Home Government, the underlying spirit which animated it was intensely conservative. Tradition and authority had laid a firm grasp on the colony. The representatives of the Crown might be opposed and their authority questioned, but there was always profound regard for the supremacy of those who were fighting a popular battle. Even the authority of the priesthood, an authority which had been abused to its own ultimate destruction, was being stealthily and half-consciously sapped, rather than openly threatened. The writers in the Courant shocked Boston respectability and reverence by the outspoken audacity of their youthful iconoclasm. Solemn opponents described them as 'the Free-thinkers'; for others they were 'the Hell-fire Club,' a levity of speech which would have shocked the generation of Winthrop almost as much as the utterances of the Courant itself. Increase Mather, writing in the Gazette, recalled the happy day 'when the civil government would have taken an effectual course to suppress such a cursed libel.' Unless this is done he fears 'that some awful judgement will come upon this land, and that the wrath of God will arise, and there will be no remedy.' It was a sound instinct which made Increase Mather discern in the growing influence of the press a force which would supersede and undermine the power of the pulpit. By a strange chance on one important issue Mather, in his controversy with the Courant, was on the side of progress. He, with a courage for which he deserves honour, was defying the prejudices of his clerical brethren, and advocating the newly introduced practice of inoculation. The Courant, we cannot doubt, out of personal hostility to Mather and in a mere spirit of faction, took the opposite line. If Mather could have emphasized that fact, and concentrated his attack on it, he would have done much to win the sympathy and respect of that very class to whom the Courant was appealing; the more enlightened and independent would have been with him. But, despite a single excursion towards enlightenment, the spell of New England conservatism and sacerdotalism was strong in Mather, and he had not learnt that a factious indifference to public interest was a worse crime than irreverence of speech and contempt for authority.

The civil government did not altogether deserve Mather's reproach of supineness, since they did put James Franklin in prison for four weeks.

A further proposal to gag the Courant, by requiring that its contents should be inspected before publication, was made by the Council, but rejected by the House of Representatives. Emboldened by this immunity, Franklin waxed more audacious in his attacks on authority, and in 1722, when the Council renewed their proposal in its general substance, leaving the details to a committee, it received the support of the Lower House. The committee, one of whom was that blameless representative of old-fashioned New England orthodoxy, Samuel Sewall, recommended that the secretary of the colony be *pro hac vice* constituted censor of the press, and that Franklin be not allowed to publish anything which had not been supervised by him. Franklin was also to give security for good behaviour. There could hardly be a stronger instance of the manner in which men, in their haste to punish or restrain some temporarily obnoxious opponent, will establish a precedent fatal to all the principles which they profess. It is not unlikely that the better judgement of those in power brought them round to this view. Franklin nominally transferred the control of the paper to his brother Benjamin. This somewhat transparent evasion was allowed to go unchallenged. The methods of the Courant lost the charm of novelty, the spirit which inspired them spent its force, and after six years of a stirring existence which we may be sure had a lasting effect on thought and sentiment, it disappeared.

Benjamin Franklin and the Courant.

There is no evidence of the exact part which Benjamin Franklin played in the production of the Courant. But the temper and the methods of it were so in accordance with his that we can hardly doubt that he had a large share, and that its pages were the training ground in which he first tested and strengthened his powers as a political controversialist. We can hardly err in identifying him with one phase of the battle. Two years before the Courant had come into existence a somewhat unmethodical and intermittently published broadsheet, ambitiously entitled 'The American Weekly Mercury,' appeared at Philadelphia. This paper vehemently took up the cause of James Franklin and the Courant. The Assembly of Massachusetts were 'oppressors and bigots who make religion only the engine of destruction to the people.' The article ended with a postscript. 'By private letters from Boston we are informed that the bakers there are under great apprehensions of being forbid baking any more bread unless they will submit it to the Secretary as Supervisor-General and Weigher of the Dough before it is baked into bread and offered for sale.' Surely there we can trace the hand of one who, at a later day, was unsurpassed among political controversialists in his use of homely parable.

Two obvious results followed from the establishment of the newspaper press in New England. The influence of the pulpit in determining and fashioning public opinion was already on the wane, and the existence of a rival power confirmed and accelerated the process. Moreover, though the outward form of the colonial government might approach to democracy, yet the life of Massachusetts was full of elements which made for oligarchy. The influence of the press did much to break this down. The Franklins were an advanced guard of skirmishers, clearing the ground for the onslaught of Samuel Adams and his well-organized democracy.

Influence of journalism on thought in New England.

Massachusetts did not long enjoy a monopoly of colonial journalism. In 1725 the New York Gazette appeared. It was a weekly broadsheet of apparently the same character as the first Boston newspaper. There, however, as in Massachusetts, journalism soon developed into an instrument of political warfare. That from the outset was the avowed purpose of the second New York paper, the Weekly Journal, published first in 1733. The story of Zenger's battle with constituted authority has been already told. The earlier paper, encouraged it may be by Zenger's success, took up the same line. In 1742 the management of the Gazette was changed; it appeared under the alternative titles of the New York Gazette and the Weekly Post Boy. Its somewhat reckless controversial temper twice involved the editor in trouble. In 1748 he published two forged letters reflecting on certain Philadelphian Quakers, and was forced to apologize. In 1756 an article appeared which incurred the displeasure of the Assembly. The two editors were arrested, and only released on begging pardon of the house and giving up the name of the writer. He and a missionary named Watkins, sent out by the Society for the Propagation of the Gospel, were taken into custody, brought before the Assembly and reprimanded.

In 1732 James Franklin transferred his printing press to Newport, and there started a weekly paper. But the soil was an unhopeful one in which to sow any literary seed, and the Rhode Island Gazette only lived through seven months of precarious existence.

Journalism in the other colonies.

Franklin's more famous brother fared better in his first venture outside Massachusetts. A paper, the American Weekly Mercury, was started in Philadelphia in 1721. It was an ordinary news-letter published somewhat irregularly. When in 1723 Benjamin Franklin betook him to Philadelphia, he at once devised a scheme for starting a rival newspaper to the Mercury. Accidentally the scheme became known to a printer named Kiemer. He at once anticipated Franklin and brought out a paper with the astounding title of 'The Universal Instructor in all Arts and Sciences, or the Pennsylvania Gazette.' The prospectus corresponded to the title. The happy subscribers were to 'possess the richest mine of knowledge (of the kind) ever before discovered, except in Europe.' Franklin, with characteristically acute strategy, determined to use the Mercury to drive Kiemer out of the field, and then to take up his enterprise in an improved form. He became himself a contributor to the Mercury, and in its columns cast ridicule on Kiemer's venture. Kiemer became bankrupt. Franklin bought his paper and dropped the more ambitious part of the title. As the Pennsylvania Gazette it throve under Franklin's editorship. In 1748 his various public vocations compelled him to resign the editorship and to become merely an occasional contributor. The paper, however, continued to prosper, and played a conspicuous part in the struggle with the mother country.

The conditions of the Southern colonies, with their lack of communication and of corporate life, were ill-suited to the success of journalism. Nevertheless all the Southern colonies, North Carolina excepted, witnessed some attempt at journalism during the first half of the eighteenth century. The first Maryland paper, published about 1728, has left indeed only vague traces,[1] and it was not till 1745 that the colony had a regularly published journal. In South Carolina the first attempt failed, and the South Carolina Gazette, started in 1732, only lived for seven months. It was, however, revived two years later, and lived out the century. Four years later Virginia followed in the same course, and by 1736 seven out of the original twelve colonies had their own newspapers.

The magazine in the colonies.

We have already seen how the journal passed at an early stage from a mere news-letter into an instrument of political controversy. That, however, was far from being the limit of its developement. The New England Journal, which first appeared in 1727, was, as an organ of news, meagre even for that day, and devoted itself mainly to literary and social topics. It took a part in the conflict which raged round the preaching of Whitefield, and Burnet is said to have been among its contributors.

In 1743 a monthly magazine, with fifty pages to a number, was published in Boston. Its character was adequately described by its title, 'the American Magazine and American Chronicle.' Its form and its general scheme were closely modelled on those of the London Magazine and the Gentleman's Magazine. Like them it was designed to be thoroughly catholic in its choice of subjects. It was to be a chronicle of leading events, an organ at once of political and literary criticism, and of moral instruction. The

[1] Thomas (vol. ii. p. 155) says that he has seen in the records of the vestry at Annapolis in 1728 an order that an advertisement should be inserted in the *Maryland Gazette*. He has also seen extracts from the paper dated August 1729.

literary resources of Boston were, however, unequal to the demands of such a production, and it only lasted a little more than three years.

There could hardly be a stronger illustration of the difference between the Boston of the seventeenth and that of the eighteenth century than the appearance, also in 1743, of a publication which bore the title of a Christian History, but which would in modern times be called an ecclesiastical or religious magazine. It was to publish letters from divers quarters, written by ministers and others, with details of such incidents connected with religion as had come under their notice. One cannot imagine the New England divines of the school of Cotton or Hooker giving to the world their experiences and reflections in such a slight and ephemeral form. The life of the Christian History was even shorter than that of the American Magazine, only extending over two years.

In 1741 Benjamin Franklin started a new venture in the form of a monthly publication entitled the 'General Magazine and Historical Chronicle for all the British Plantations in America;' its life however only lasted six months. A rival publication attempted simultaneously fared even worse and did not get beyond two numbers. A like venture started seventeen years later in New Jersey had no better success.[1]

Attempted magazines.

The failure of the magazine to establish itself in any of the colonies was perhaps due to the fact that the ground was already occupied by the Almanac, a form of publication which, if not peculiar to America, at least obtained a popularity and importance unknown elsewhere. It was in the eighteenth century the Spectator or Rambler of the colonial farmhouse. The Almanac, in its original

The Almanac.

[1] These unsuccessful attempts are all described by Thomas, vol. ii. pp. 129, 149.

and limited character a record and prophet of the weather, had come into existence in New England in 1639, and before the end of the century in Philadelphia and New York as well. But it was reserved for Nathaniel Ames, of Dedham in Massachusetts, the father of the revolutionary statesman Fisher Ames, to make the Almanac a real element in the literature of the country.[1] Ames was, like Franklin, a man of somewhat varied experiences and attainments, being at once a physician and a tavern-keeper. In 1725 he published an Almanac on the ordinary lines of record and weather prophecy, but superadding facetiæ of various merit in the ordinary affairs of life, prudential maxims and rules of health. As time went on and Ames's Almanac acquired a firmly established popularity, he grafted on to the original stock political information. His style has the same merits as Franklin's: it is direct and emphatic; never wasting its force on non-essentials. In 1728 James Franklin followed Ames's example and published a Rhode Island Almanac on similar lines, and five years later Benjamin Franklin appeared as the maxim-monger and practical counsellor, Poor Richard. That the reputation of his Almanac should have survived and superseded that of his predecessor's is perhaps mainly due to the distinction which the writer gained in other fields.

These Almanac writers are a factor to be reckoned with in estimating the intellectual life of the American colonies. They are at once popular in tone and in a sense philosophical in spirit. Their style is as simple and direct as Cobbett's, while, unlike Cobbett, they have a sense of self-restraint and proportion, and do not swerve off into irrelevance at the bidding of some personal impulse. They are philosophical in that they

[1] Mr. Tyler (vol. ii. pp. 122–30) gives a very full account of Ames's *Almanac.*

indicate, and also no doubt helped to create and foster, the tendency to apply critical thought and observation to every-day affairs. They are the literature of a people ever ready to frame for themselves new canons whether of social or industrial life, never inclined to look to tradition for its methods or its ideals of success.

Natural science in the colonies.

The conflict between humane letters and natural science, the study of man and the study of matter, was one which the seventeenth and eighteenth centuries never composed quite satisfactorily. Isolated writers there might be like Evelyn and Sir Thomas Browne who had a foot in each camp. But the dictum that the proper study of mankind is man, a dictum so copiously and pompously elaborated by Akenside, is really the dominant sentiment of those who in that age would have claimed to be the representatives of literature. Addison and, at a later day, Cowper could see little difference between the scientific student and the virtuoso. Yet despite such tendencies to treat natural science as the Cinderella of the literary family, one can hardly take up any diary or any record which illustrates the academical and literary life of the eighteenth century and not see at work a vigorous spirit of curiosity as to external phenomena. In that spirit the colonies, as might be expected, had their share. The conditions of life in a new country, bringing men into close contact with the phenomena of nature, were sure to cultivate that habit of observation which is not identical with scientific knowledge, but which is the foundation on which all scientific study must be based. John Bartram, a Philadelphian, was poor and self-taught. But he founded a botanical garden, corresponded with the chief European authorities in his own department, was elected a member of various scientific societies in the Old World, and won from Linnæus the praise of being the greatest natural botanist in the world.

John Clayton and John Mitchell, also both of Virginia, were likewise eminent botanists, the former a correspondent of Linnæus and a contributor to the 'Philosophical Transactions,' the latter a Fellow of the Royal Society.

Capacities such as Franklin's are not to be explained by any theory as to the conditions which created and developed them. But though their existence may be largely independent of external influences, yet such influences have a large share in determining the direction in which they are to be used. The colonies were eagerly bent on the subjugation of material nature and on the adjustment of political forces. It was altogether in harmony with the principles of their existence that he who was at once the greatest of their natural philosophers and of their political thinkers should have given his best powers to solving the practical problem of electricity, and to the detailed work of the political controversialist, the administrator, and the diplomatist.

As was said before, the eighteenth century was in the history of the American colonies a period not of individual creation, but of diffusion. New England already possessed an equipment both for higher and for primary education so complete in proportion to the needs and resources of the country that it hardly admitted of extension. Changed in many other features, in this matter New England kept the character imposed upon it by its founders. Harvard and Yale steadily held their ground as protecting influences against the tyranny of material life, nor do we find any tendency in the literature of New England to protest against the ascendancy of useless learning. The determination with which the colony had in its young and struggling days made an effective school system a first charge on its resources had its reward. Classes were bound together, and the community democratized by a common training. It was

Education in New England.

one of the most unhappy features in the attitude of the mother country to the colonies that this aspect of New England life was to the majority of Englishmen a sealed book. To educated Englishmen, men like the Adamses were incomprehensible, and Franklin was one of those exceptional portents, a self-made and self-taught man, who had raised himself wholly above his surroundings. It was not understood that the average Boston trader grew up in a mental atmosphere every whit as stimulating to the mind as that which surrounded the boyhood of an average member of Parliament, while at the same time no wide educational gulf severed the tradesman from the craftsman.

Harvard and Yale.[1]

This was due at least as much to the general respect and desire for learning as to the machinery for teaching provided by the community. Entries in the town records show that in Boston at least there was no abatement in the public care for elementary teaching. But well-equipped elementary schools will not of themselves make a learned community, nor even of necessity one which loves and reverences learning. What they may do, and did in New England, is to democratize education, to make it not a luxury for a class but a common necessity for all. That may mean the degradation of education into an instrument for the mere satisfaction of obvious and material wants. That danger, however, is not one from which a so-called aristocracy is necessarily exempt. If education in England to-day has escaped those dangers and remained 'liberal,' it is not so much from any reverent comprehension of high ideals in the

[1] For all that I have said about Harvard I have relied on Quincy's history of the college. He makes abundant use of original documents, many of which he publishes. We have two good authorities for the early history of Yale—Trumbull, himself a graduate there, and President Clap. Clap was head of Yale from 1740 till his death in 1765. *The History of Yale* was published in 1766.

class who benefit by it; rather because they inertly and unintelligently accept what has come down to them by a fortunate survival of tradition. New England also had widely diffused among its citizens a tradition of learning. We cannot indeed say that the education provided at Harvard and Yale rose to a high standard or can have satisfied far-reaching intellectual aspirations. Before the Revolution there were at Harvard but three professors: two, those of Divinity and of Mathematics, were founded by a munificent friend to the college, Thomas Hollis, in 1721 and in 1727 respectively. Neither Greek, Latin, Moral Philosophy, Metaphysics, nor any branch of History had a chair.

An exact and detailed account of the degree course in 1726 is extant. No classical authors are specified as objects of study except Cicero and Virgil. Rhetoric, Ethics, Geometry, Logic and Metaphysics, most of them studied in somewhat obsolete text-books, came into the range. Hebrew was taught, and the prescribed range of study therein was fuller and more exact than that of any other language. This was no doubt due to the fact that preparation for the ministry was one of the chief ends aimed at in the college.

Even more was this the case with Yale. In 1755 a chair of Divinity was established, and when Clap wrote in 1765 it was still the only one.[1]

In 1741 the number of students at Harvard was about a hundred,[2] at Yale about twenty less.[3] This, however, had risen by 1746, under the effective rule of President Clap, to a hundred and twenty.[4] The hold which Harvard had on the affections of Massachusetts citizens is shown by the fact that between 1700 and 1750 private benefactions reached upwards of five thousand five hundred pounds, contributed by thirty-

[1] Clap, pp. 67, 80.

[2] Whitefield's Journal.

[3] Trumbull, vol. ii. p. 305.

[4] *Ib.* p. 312; Clap, p. 54.

five donors, while during the same time it received grants from the Assembly to the amount of four thousand eight hundred pounds, to be applied in building a house for the President, followed in 1763 by a further sum to build a hostel for students.[1]

Private bounty such as that bestowed on Harvard was not to be expected in the poorer colony of Connecticut. The Assembly, however, dealt liberally with the college. At the outset they voted it a hundred a year, a sum which was doubled in 1735 and further increased later.[2] Conspicuous among the private benefactors of the college was Bishop Berkeley. He in his lifetime presented it with a farm of a hundred acres in Rhode Island for the maintenance of scholarships, and with a library of a thousand volumes valued at four hundred pounds.[3]

Influence of the New England colleges.

What Harvard and Yale really did for New England was to enable the citizens to become educated men without ceasing to be New Englanders. Elsewhere the colonist who wanted a liberal education had to seek it in England. He became tinged with a certain sense of being superior to colonial thoughts and ideals. The New Englander ran no such risk. Whatever pride of learning he might feel strengthened his sense of patriotism. The education which the New England colleges gave did nothing to separate the learned man from the ordinary citizen, since it was but the completion and continuation of that which all men, be their rank what it might, understood and desired.

There could hardly be a better illustration of the progress which liberality of thought had made in New England than is to be found in the diary of Ezra Stiles.[4] He graduated at Yale in 1746 and became President of

[1] These benefactions are all enumerated by Quincy in an Appendix, vol. ii. p. 526.

[2] Connecticut Records.

[3] Trumbull, vol. ii. pp. 301-2.

[4] Edited by Mr. F. B. Dexter and published in 1901.

the college in 1778. That appointment is a sufficient guarantee for Stiles's orthodoxy. Yet he approaches all the questions touched on in his diary—and since he was a man of wide and varied interests they are many—in the free, confident spirit of a man of the world. One never feels as one does in reading the earlier New England divines that one is moving in a restricted sphere, breathing an artificial atmosphere. More than once he mentions without explanation or comment that he has been reading Voltaire.[1] He defends Lucian against the charge of having dealt unfairly with Christianity[2] and he treats educational questions in the temper of a man who was a scholar first and a minister of religion afterwards. He deals in that spirit with a grotesque proposal for teaching Greek through a modern translation of the Psalms into that tongue. 'The design of the publication is to furnish a Greek classic which may instil Christianity at the same time as they are learning the Greek language.' Stiles sensibly points out that this attempt to combine two things will injure both. You would study divinity better in English. You would study Greek better by reading the classics. If a foreigner wished to learn English he would not use an English book written by a German or an Italian, but by Pope or Addison.[3]

Ezra Stiles.

The view may be obvious, but the directness with which it is expressed, the manifest sense that no qualification or apology is needed, belongs to an age very different from that of the Mathers.

Outside New England education suffered to some extent from apathy and indifference, but more from lack of trained teachers. The colonial legislatures were not backward in impressing the necessity for education on their citizens, nor in furnishing the needful funds. What they could not do

Education outside New England.

[1] *Diary*, vol. i. pp. 106, 179. [2] *Ib.* p. 136. [3] *Ib.* p. 99.

was to invest the calling of a teacher with sufficient importance to attract able men, in a society where industry and capacity opened many roads to wealth. Moreover in the Middle colonies, and even more in the South, the difficulty of communication in the rural districts must have made the proper organization of schools almost impossible. In the South, too, there was no class to profit by them. The college of Williamsburg never took any hold on popular sympathy; the young Virginian was sometimes sent to England for education, occasionally to Yale.[1] More often he had a tutor, in many cases a Jacobite who had been sent out as an indented servant. What respect could the young planter have for a man who but for a little book-learning would have been working with the negroes in the tobacco fields?

Schemes for a college in Maryland.

Projects there were, indeed, for a college in Maryland, one so grotesquely ambitious that it deserves notice. According to the prospectus of the would-be founders the pupils were to be instructed 'not only in the learning of the best Latin and Greek schools such as Eton and Westminster, but likewise the principal branches of the philosophy which a post-graduate' (presumably a bachelor of arts) 'learns at the University.' Also they were to be taught accounts, surveying, and navigation. All this was to be achieved with a staff of five teachers. At first they must be obtained from without; in a short time the college would be able to train up its own staff.

The teachers when old and infirm were to be pensioned off, on a system thoroughly consonant with the ecclesiastical ideas of the eighteenth century. The pension was to take the form of a benefice, the duties of which were to be discharged by a curate.

[1] Madison was sent to Yale because his parents distrusted the orthodoxy of the college at Williamsburg.

The scheme was brought before the Council, and by them, strange to say, transmitted to the House of Representatives with approval. After that we hear no more of it.[1]

In education as in other matters Charlestown rose to a higher standard. A modern historian of that colony has made a collection of over four hundred advertisements, which appeared in the 'South Carolina Gazette' between 1733 and 1734, dealing with education.[2]

Colleges in New Jersey and Pennsylvania.

About the middle of the eighteenth century a certain wave of educational enthusiasm seems to have passed over the Middle colonies. This apparently originated in a desire for a higher standard of education among the Presbyterian clergy. There was in existence a place of education, whose character may be in a measure judged by its title, the log-hut school. Certain presbyteries took the view that the log-hut standard of education was a sufficient qualification for the ministry. The central presbytery at Philadelphia refused to adopt this standard, with the result that the local presbyteries seceded. Probably as a consequence of this in 1746 a college was founded in New Jersey for the training of ministers of religion. The requirements for matriculation were Latin composition and an ability to translate Virgil, Cicero, and the Gospels.[3]

Four years later an academy was established at Philadelphia. Franklin was among those who interested themselves in the project, and the first Principal was one who might under more favourable circumstances have played a prominent part in the intellectual history of America. William Smith was one of those capable and well-trained Scotchmen who went to push

[1] Steiner, *History of Education in Maryland*, p. 26.

[2] McCrady, vol. ii. p. 490.

[3] Maclean, *History of College of New Jersey*.

their fortunes in the Middle colonies. His educational views were put forth in a work entitled 'A General Idea of the College of Mirania,' wherein the writer described his general conceptions of the aims and purposes of an educational foundation. For some a mere training of the business faculties must suffice. But the college must also minister to the wants of those whose future work needs a higher training. History must be studied as the practical comment on ethical theories. The perception and love of art must be developed. Latin is to be taught, but it must not be so used as to hinder the free developement of English speech.

It speaks well for those responsible for the college that they were willing to give the headship to one who must have seemed to many a vague idealist.

In 1754 New York was in some measure brought into line with Pennsylvania and New Jersey by the establishment of King's College. But the fact that it was exclusively a Church of England institution limited its benefits to a minority. It was not till the Revolution, when it changed alike its methods and its title, and became Columbia College, that it could be looked on as a national institution.[1]

[1] Smith, vol. ii. pp. 151–2

CHAPTER VI.

THE COLONISTS AND THE INFERIOR RACES.

THERE is no feature of colonial history with which moral and sentimental considerations have so closely combined themselves as the question of slavery. Yet there is hardly any which has been so largely determined by physical causes acting from without, so little by the deliberate volition of men. No reasonable man would underrate the force or reality of that moral sentiment which at last awakened the mind of the American people to the horrors and evils of negro slavery. But the causes which in the early days of the colonies promoted or restrained slavery had hardly anything in common with those which retarded or expedited abolition. The latter were moral, economical, and political. The former were almost wholly physical. In the seventeenth and eighteenth centuries the contest between free and slave labour was almost wholly decided by conditions of soil and climate.

Slavery in the colonies.

As we have already seen, there were, apart from minor differences, three zones each with its own physical conditions, and therefore with its own forms of industry. In each of the three, in New England, in the Middle colonies, and in the South, slavery existed. But in each the status of the negro as a portion of the social and industrial fabric had a distinct character of its own. In New England the negro differed from the white labourer or the white domestic servant only in social status, and in the sentiment with which he was regarded, and usually no doubt in the inferiority of his services. He had no special or separate place in the hierarchy of labour. The same may be said of Pennsylvania and the Jerseys. In New York, on the other hand, both in the country districts and the city, the negro was so largely employed as to form a distinct class presenting special dangers and needing special legislation. In the Southern colonies free labour did indeed exist. There were, as we have seen, yeomen farmers in Maryland, in Virginia, and in the western portions of South Carolina. White indented servants, too, were to be found, albeit in decreasing numbers. But negro labour so completely preponderated, that in considering the general structure of industry in the South all other forms may be disregarded.

The one exception to this was North Carolina. By the middle of the eighteenth century the proportion of negroes to the whole population was in Maryland about thirty per cent., in Virginia about forty, in South Carolina more than sixty. In North Carolina, on the other hand, whites outnumbered negroes as five to one. This assuredly brings home to one the truth that the presence or absence of slavery was a question of soil and climate, and that moral considerations, so far as they entered into the question, were effect and not cause. No section of the population could have been more ready to embrace the advantages of slavery such as they were than the shiftless and indolent population of North Carolina. Slave labour can, however, from its mechanical and unintelligent character, only be profitable when it is applied to the production of some one staple on a large scale. The slave gang must be large enough to make the work of supervision remunerative. Neither of these conditions could be fulfilled in North Carolina. Slaves could only be prevented from escaping where there is a well-organized system of gang labour, and the swamps and forests of North Carolina, with their scanty white population and absence of roads, made the position of the fugitive comparatively secure.

Legislation about the negro in New England.

The extent and importance of negro slavery in the different colonies may be gauged by the frequency and stringency of the legislation on the subject. It is to be noticed that this dealt fully as much with race as with status. The free negro was as much as the slave, or even more, the subject of special apprehensive restraint. References to slavery in the laws of the New England colonies are rare and unimportant. But in 1723 we find the Selectmen of Boston, acting under instructions from the town meeting, drawing up an elaborate code of regulations for the conduct of negroes, mulattoes and Indians, whether bond or free.[1] The freeman of colour[2] might not harbour a coloured slave under penalty of a fine or a severe whipping, and for the prevention of such an offence any two householders might search the premises of a suspected person. He might not have arms or ammunition. He might not sell liquor or provisions out of doors on training days. He might not receive any goods from a coloured slave or servant, and if any stolen goods were found in his possession it was assumed that he was guilty of theft. Such offenders were to be flogged and banished, and if they returned after such banishment, they were to be kept to hard labour for life. The negro might not work as a porter unless he could find security for fifty pounds. The dread of incendiarism as the negro's instrument of revenge, a dread which, well- or ill-founded, bore terrible results at a later day in New

[1] Boston Town Records, 1723, pp. 177, &c.

[2] I use this expression to avoid the cumbrous repetition of Indian, negro, or mulatto.

York, is shown by the provision that during the fire no negro might be out of doors unless his master's property was actually in danger. The violation of this rule was to be punished by whipping and imprisonment. All the above regulations applied to Indians, negroes and mulattoes, whether bond or free. They were supplemented by further special regulations applicable only to coloured slaves and servants. They might not be out of doors an hour after sunset in the summer, or half an hour in winter. They might not carry any weapon, nor even a stick, save in case of decrepitude. They might not 'lurk or idle' in or near the town in groups of more than two. They might not be present even with the permission of their master in the fields on public training days. All these restraints were to be enforced by the penalty of whipping, which in some cases was to be 'severe.' Once we read of death by burning in the case of a negro woman at Cambridge, convicted in 1749 of murdering her master.[1]

Even when he ceased to be the property of a master, a negro retained something of the servile status. In 1759 an order was made by the Selectmen on the subject of negroes working. The language of the order is so obscure that it is impossible to understand precisely what is enforced; but it is clear that some kind of compulsory work was contemplated.[2] In the same year an order was made by the town meeting that

[1] *Virginia Magazine of History*, vol. iii. p. 308.

[2] Minutes of Selectmen. The order runs thus:—'Whereas there is considerable work to be done this year on Boston Neck, and the free negroes of the town have been for many years exempted from any duty, therefore it was some time voted that they be ordered to attend the Selectmen, and on this day the following negroes attended: Bristol Jeffries, who will do what work he is ordered to do; Pompey Blackman, who agrees to pay half a dollar per day for so many days as he shall be ordered; Leicester Black, do.; Dick Tynge to pay half a dollar as above.' To pay must mean to be paid.

no negro or mulatto might buy drink without an order from his master.[1]

The absence of specific legislation about negroes in Rhode Island and Connecticut shows that the employment of them in those colonies was exceptional. In Rhode Island, indeed, we find an Act passed in 1715, providing that no slave be ferried over to the mainland without a certificate from his master, lest he should run away.[2] But as we find almost at the same time a statement that Indian slaves have been giving trouble, and that no more be imported,[3] it is not unlikely that they were the class named. The native once on the mainland would find it an easy matter to escape to the wilderness. In the Middle colonies, on the other hand, the presence of a negro population and the apprehensions caused by it meet us at every turn. An acute but not very trustworthy witness, before referred to, Mrs. Grant, draws an Arcadian picture of the relations between master and slave in one of the great New York families.[4] Each of the younger members of such a family had a negro boy assigned him to act as a body-servant, and we can easily believe that such an arrangement gave rise to strong and lasting affection.[5] We cannot, however, accept Mrs. Grant as a wholly trustworthy witness when we find her stating that the negro slave was exclusively employed in domestic work and not in husbandry, and then a few pages later mentioning reaping as one form of industry in which one particular negro outstripped his fellows.

She also describes how once a year a ship sailed to the West Indies with a cargo of refractory slaves, and

[1] Town Records, 1759, p. 20.

[2] R. I. Records, vol. iv. p. 179.

[3] *Ib.* p. 193.

[4] *Memoirs of an American Lady*, vol. i. pp. 51, &c.

[5] One is reminded of Gumbo in *The Virginians.*

how the dreaded threat of deportation was usually a sufficient security for good behaviour.[1]

Mrs. Grant's picture of the happy patriarchal relations which subsisted in a well-ordered New York household was probably true. Like pictures have been drawn of slave life in the South, even by those who were strongly opposed to slavery as a system. But the condition of a Leicestershire hunting stable does not prove that the Society for the Prevention of Cruelty to Animals is superfluous, and the records of New York and the adjacent colonies plainly show that there was a reverse side to the picture presented by Mrs. Grant. We have seen with what jealous suspicion the townspeople of Boston looked on the comparatively scanty coloured population. In New York the negroes were proportionately more numerous and the cosmopolitan character of the colony, the lack of mutual reliance, of rigid discipline and civic spirit, made restraint less easy. In a city largely constructed of wood, fire presents terrors which can hardly be understood by those to whom a town means a collection of stone houses, and a single incendiary could inflict wholesale ruin on the vast warehouses and shipping of New York.

The best proof that there was a side to the picture very different from that presented by Mrs. Grant is to be found in the various enactments of the legislature of New York about negroes. In 1702 it was enacted that no person might trade with a slave, that not above three slaves might come together except on their master's business. A master might chastise his slave so long as there was no injury to life or limb, and any township might appoint a public negro-whipper.[2] A runaway

[1] One is reminded of the threat which terrified Irus, how he was to be deported

Εἰς Ἔχετον βασιλῆα, βροτῶν δηλήμονα πάντων.

[2] Acts of Assembly.

negro would naturally make for the Canadian frontier, and to guard against this it was made a capital offence for a slave to be forty miles north of Albany.[1]

In 1712 a slave Act was passed prohibiting any free negro from entertaining slaves. At the same time it was enacted that a negro charged with felony should be tried by a jury of five, and have no right to challenge any of them. His master, however, might claim for him a jury of twelve provided he paid the jurymen.[2]

That was the precursor of an alarm nearly thirty years later far more extensive and also more terrifying through the element of vague mystery which entered into it. All that appears certain is that fire followed upon fire with such rapidity as to create a panic. There is no doubt that negroes were concerned in these, and there was strong reason to suspect that certain disreputable whites had instigated the crime for purposes of plunder. The very fact that the fires were successive and not simultaneous makes strongly against the theory of an organized plot for the destruction of the city. Public opinion, however, was carried away by a panic which may have been irrational, but which was certainly not unnatural or surprising. Fear was stimulated by a rumour that the fires at New York were the result of a scheme on the part of the Spaniards to destroy all the British towns on the American coast, and an unfortunate priest named Ury, against whom there seems to have been no proof of guilt, was hanged. Three other whites met with the same fate, among them Huson, the man originally accused of setting the incendiaries to work, and his wife. Twenty-nine negroes in all were put to death, several by burning.

The negro terror of 1741.[3]

[1] Acts of Assembly, p. 60. [2] *Ib.* p. 81.

[3] The chief authority for this is Clarke's Despatch to the Duke of Newcastle June 20, 1741. N. Y. Docs. vol. vi. p. 195.

The negro in Pennsylvania.

That same spirit of humanity which marked the conduct of the Quaker settlers towards the natives saved Pennsylvania from the possibility of any such horrors as befell New York. Yet the colony could not dispense with protective restrictions. In 1693 an Act had been passed forbidding negroes to 'gad abroad' on Sunday without their masters' consent.[1]

In 1705 magistrates were empowered in certain cases, with the concurrence of a jury, to pass sentence of death on negroes, and any negro carrying arms was to be flogged.[2] Free negroes were regarded as a dangerous class, and as setting an example of idleness to their brethren who were still in bondage. Their houses might not be used as meeting-places for slaves. No one might emancipate a negro without finding security that he should not become chargeable on the public, and any free negro who idled or wandered about might be arrested and bound to service.[3]

At the same time the Swedish traveller Kalm bears witness to the habitual humanity of slave masters in Pennsylvania, and contrasts it with the brutality of the West Indian planters. He admits, too, that the negro needed strict discipline, and could seldom use the gift of freedom for his own happiness. He also mentions the frequency of Obeah poisoning, used, he says, more often against some slave whose good conduct had earned for him confidence and a superior position than against the master.[4]

So, too, we read that in Delaware the haughty behaviour of those negroes who have been admitted into the fellowship of Christ's religion, combined with a want of zeal in masters, has hindered conversion.[5]

[1] Pennsylvania Records, vol. i. p. 380. [2] Laws of Pennsylvania.
[3] *Ib.* [4] Kalm, vol. i. pp. 390–400.
[5] Letter from Ross, the incumbent of Newcastle, March 1, 1727, in Perry Collection, Delaware, p. 43.

Kalm's account seems intended to apply equally to New Jersey and Pennsylvania. Yet the records of the former colony seem to show that, so far as the status of the negro and the feeling of the white towards him were concerned, New Jersey lay in a mean between the two colonies which bounded it. In the instructions issued to Governor Morris in 1738, the advisers of the Crown thought it necessary to insist on the principle that the arbitrary killing of a negro was murder.[1] In 1729 we read of a negro being burnt alive at Perth Amboy for murdering an Englishman.[2] Four years later a plot, real or supposed, was detected among the negroes in Somerset County, East New Jersey, for the murder of their master. This was punished with singular lenity. One offender was put to death, the rest were flogged and their ears cropped.[3] In 1755 a white man is arrested on the charge of killing his negro slave by undue castigation.[4]

The negro in New Jersey.

Economical causes served to keep down the negro population in the Middle colonies. The negro labourer was a more valuable commodity in the Southern colonies. The planter in Virginia or South Carolina could afford to outbid the merchant or landholder in New Jersey and Pennsylvania; and thus the stream of importation naturally flowed to the South.[5]

Passing southward into Maryland we are at once in the zone where organized negro slavery is the predominant form of industry. The rival system of white servitude, a system to which the climate of Maryland lent itself better than that of the colonies further south, did indeed still exist. Just before the outbreak of the Revolution the importation of indented servants during a period of thirty years was estimated at six hundred

[1] N. Jersey Papers, vol. vi. p. 15.
[2] *Ib.* vol. xi. p. 201.
[3] *Ib.* vol. x. p. 333.
[4] *Ib.* vol. xix. p. 451.
[5] Cornbury notices this in a report. N. Y. Docs. vol. v. p. 55.

a year. Yet if we take the average term of servitude as seven years, and allowing for deaths and escapes that is a liberal estimate, the number only reaches a trifle over four thousand, about one-tenth of the negro population.[1]

It may be safely said that on the whole the tone of legislation and administration in the Southern States showed less dread of the negro and more consideration in the treatment of him than that of New York. That is quite intelligible. Where slavery is the one pervading and almost universal form of industry, it carries with it almost of necessity an organized system of supervision and restraint which largely supersedes the necessity for public administrative control. The whole body of masters and overseers become an unofficial police, and thus escape is rendered almost hopeless in Maryland. In the middle of the eighteenth century a law was passed specially directed against riotous assemblies of negroes met together to burn tobacco warehouses. Arson and the murder of a master were punished not only by death, but by the added ignominy of quartering. It was further provided that runaway slaves should have their ears cropped. As 'boys and new-comers' were specially exempted from this, it is not unlikely that the Act included white indented servants.[2]

There is no trace in Virginian history of any organized outbreak on the part of the negroes. In 1710 we find Spotswood reporting to the Council of Trade rumours of a servile insurrection.[3] During the crisis of the French war Dinwiddie writes that the slaves are taking up a threatening attitude. 'The villainy of the negroes on any emergency of government is what I always feared.'[4] In 1723 a law was passed plainly designed to prevent criminal combinations

[1] Mereness, pp. 132–3. His authority is the *Maryland Gazette.*

[2] Acts of Maryland, 1724.

[3] Spotswood's *Letters,* vol. i. p. 42.

[4] Dinwiddie's *Letters,* vol. ii. p. 100.

among the negroes.[1] Not more than five of them might meet together unless they all belonged to the same plantation, and even then the meeting might not be at night nor on Sunday. A runaway slave or vagrant might be punished at the discretion of the County Court with dismemberment, and if he died under the punishment, the person inflicting it incurred no penalty. This last provision was re-enacted in 1748, at the same time it was provided that no white person might attend a meeting of negroes or harbour any negroes without his master's consent. No negro might be away from the plantation to which he belonged without written permission. Any planter or overseer who allowed a strange negro to be on his premises for more than four hours was to be fined four hundred pounds of tobacco.[2] In 1738 a special form of police was established, patrollers, as they were called, who were to visit negro quarters on any suspicion of an unlawful assembly, with power to arrest offenders and send them to the nearest justice, who might order a flogging.[3]

The dread of Obeah is shown by a special enactment against negro poisoners.[2] In 1753 an enactment was passed prophetic of future disputes, to the effect that 'a slave being in England shall not be undischarged from slavery unless there is proof of manumission.'[4]

Throughout the whole of this legislation in Virginia we see an increasing tendency to make the distinction not simply one of status, but also of race. In 1733 it was enacted that free negroes and mulattoes might not serve in the militia. We may be sure that this exemption was dictated not by consideration but by alarm. The Act of 1748 went further, and provided that no free negro

Increase of sense of race distinction.

[1] Hening, vol. iv. p. 118.

[2] *Ib.* vol. vi. pp. 104, &c.

[3] *American Magazine of History*, vol. xii. p. 542. Cf. Inglis, *Local Institutions of Virginia*, p. 88.

[4] Hening, vol. vi. p. 356.

or mulatto might have a gun. The same Act provided that no coloured man even if free could give evidence, except against a slave, and that any negro who assaulted a Christian could be fined merely on the oath of the person assaulted, unless that person were a negro, mulatto, or Indian. In other words the coloured man was placed under special disabilities whether he was to be regarded as violating the law or as protected by the law.

Yet it could not be said that in Virginia the negro was a mere chattel unprotected by law. One item in Spotswood's instructions from the Crown was to make the wilful killing of negroes and Indians a capital crime. Such a case arose. A negro, the property of a woman, died under what the apologists for the mistress called 'very moderate correction.' Spotswood pertinently answered that such language showed barbarous unconcern, and that it could hardly be called moderate correction under which a hail (*sic*) negro gave up the ghost. The owner's consciousness of guilt was shown by the fact that the corpse was suddenly and secretly buried. The coroner's jury, acting probably under the Governor's instructions, had the body exhumed, and found a verdict of wilful murder, whereupon Spotswood ordered the owner to be prosecuted.

When Spotswood's conduct in this matter was made subject of complaint, he laid down the doctrine that 'at the same time the slave is the master's property he is likewise the King's subject,' and that 'no master has such a sovereign power over his slave as not to be called to an account whenever he kills him.'[1]

A patriotic Virginian writer has taken the view that the restrictions on emancipation passed from time to time by the legislature of this colony were the

[1] Spotswood's *Letters*, vol. ii. The incident reminds one of the death of Hark in Mrs. Stowe's novel, *Dred*.

result of a humane desire to protect the old and worn-out slaves from being turned adrift by inhuman masters.[1] It is more likely that they were devised to check the increase of free negroes, a class always regarded with suspicion and dread.

Restrictions on emancipation.

We have already seen what a small proportion of the inhabitants of North Carolina were black slaves, and statistics on the subject are confirmed by the paucity of references to negroes in the records of the colony. Yet even there we find the Assembly deciding that a bill must be brought in to prevent a negro insurrection.[2]

The negro in North Carolina.

We find, too, a clause in the instructions issued to Governor Burrington, in 1729, bidding him to get a law passed for the protection of negroes, making the killing of them a capital crime and imposing a penalty for mutilation.[3] Like instructions were issued to Governor Dobbs in 1758.[4] But we should be crediting the advisers of the Crown with more detailed knowledge of colonial affairs than they often possessed if we assumed that this was necessitated by anything in the special conditions of North Carolina.

The one colony whose industry and social economy were wholly dominated by the presence of the negro was South Carolina. During the first half of the eighteenth century everything tended to the increase of the black population out of all proportion to their masters. As far as the wealthy classes were concerned, South Carolina was Charlestown, and Charlestown was, as we have seen, largely peopled by merchants and men of business whose

The negro in South Carolina.

[1] Mr. Moncure Conway, in the *American Magazine of History*, vol. xvii. p. 449.

[2] N. Car. Records, vol. iv. p. 364.

[3] *Ib.* vol. iii. p. 106.

[4] *Ib.* vol. v. p. 1105.

permanent homes and interests were in England. The movement already mentioned,[1] which led to the gradual introduction of a yeoman population in the inland part of the colony, did little or nothing to alter this. Till the downfall of slavery, South Carolina was dominated by the planter and merchant, though the ruling class was often replenished and invigorated by recruits drawn from the western uplands. The extended production of rice and indigo created a demand for negroes practically unlimited, and the prolificness of the black race would by itself have insured an abundant and increasing supply, even if it had not been supplemented by importation strenuously encouraged by the British Government in the interest of the English slave-trader. A contributory influence was to be found in the fact that the original settlers in South Carolina, or at least the most important body of them, came from Barbadoes, and brought with them the traditions of a society based on negro slavery. They also brought with them a code, one may almost say ready made, for the regulation of the system.

That code was one which clearly differentiated between the status of the white man and the slave, placing the latter under special disabilities, and withholding from him that protection which the law granted to the dominant race. No slave might be absent from his master's premises except when accompanying his master or bearing a special permit, to be renewed for each occasion; no slave might possess arms, and on suspicion of such possession his house might be summarily searched. The assault of a white man by a slave was punished by branding, mutilation, and, in the case of repeated offences, by death. Charges on which a white man would have been tried by jury were decided in the case of a negro by a special

[1] P. 210.

court consisting of two justices and three other freeholders.

No adequate protection was offered against an arbitrary and violent master. The master who out of mere passion or caprice killed his slave was liable to three months' imprisonment. If the mishap was caused by the infliction of punishment for some definite offence, the master went free.[1]

In 1720 the Lords of Trade reported that the increase of slaves in South Carolina was becoming a source of serious danger. It had nearly 'brought about a revolution which would probably have been attended by the utter extirpation of all the King's subjects in the colony.'[2] It was probably the alarm thus caused which induced the Assembly to pass an Act in 1726 designed to check the numerical supremacy of the negro. Every plantation must have at least one white servant. If the number of slaves exceeded ten, then for every ten there must be one white servant. The overseer, however, or, if resident, the master might count towards this number.[3]

What intensified the 'black peril' was that South Carolina had in its flank a watchful and unscrupulous enemy, who were doing their utmost to foster and utilize the discontent of the negro population. The Spanish Governor of Florida not merely received fugitive slaves, but organized them into a regiment under officers chosen from among themselves, differing neither in uniform nor pay from the Spanish soldiery.[4] This was well known to the negroes in South Carolina.

In 1739 the threatened storm broke on the colony.

[1] For the code see Statutes of South Carolina, vol. vii. pp. 343, &c. It may be compared with the Laws of Barbadoes, 1694. Mr. McCrady gives (vol. i. p. 360) a good epitome of the code.

[2] The report is in the North Carolina Records, vol. ii. p. 418.

[3] Trott's Laws of South Carolina, p. 471.

[4] McCrady, vol. ii. p. 185.

Early in September a party of negroes assembled, massacred whites and burnt houses, and possessed themselves of arms and ammunition. Since no support of any kind was received from the Spaniards in Florida, the affair would seem to have been an unpremeditated outbreak of fury, not an organized plot. It is scarcely possible that in the latter case the insurgents should not have in advance secured the help of their neighbours. It is even less likely that if the Spaniards had known what was intended they should not have seized the chance of dealing a blow at the English.

The negro insurrection.[1]

The rioters, too, had chosen their time ill. They began operations on Sunday. It was a custom—whether enforced by law or not seems doubtful—that the settlers should go to church armed. The result was that while individual plantations were unprotected, the male population of the colony was at once available for defence, and the negroes found themselves confronted by an armed force. The stores of rum found in the houses which were sacked were fatal to discipline, and the rioters fell easy victims. The short-lived nature of the outburst is shown by the fact that only twenty-one whites were killed. That only forty-four negroes lost their lives in the irregular fighting, and in the judicial proceedings which followed, shows that the settlers were not carried away by panic or vindictiveness.

It is noteworthy that the colonial records of the eighteenth century do not reveal much of that type of crime which in later days has been specially responsible for the terror and loathing with which the negro has been regarded. There are isolated instances of attacks upon the chastity of white women, and rape is among the

[1] The chief authority for the negro insurrection is Governor Bull's report to the Duke of Newcastle, October 5, 1739. There is an epitome of it in the South Carolina Collections, vol. ii. p. 290.

offences contemplated in some of the criminal enactments dealing specially with the negro. In the early records of Western Virginia we find a case where such a crime is punished by mutilation of a kind to make a repetition of the act impossible.[1] It is not unlikely that the substitution of this penalty for death was due to the fact that in the sparsely populated and inaccessible regions of the west, a negro was a rare and valuable commodity. On the tideway, where negroes were abundant, the crime would in all likelihood have been capital.

That such crime, however, was unfrequent may be inferred not only from the silence of the records, but even more, perhaps, from the absence of any special complaints on the subject in the writings of travellers, and in the correspondence of officials and of private persons.

Another repulsive feature of later times, intercourse between the races, taking the form of systematic concubinage by the large slaveholders, seems to have been unknown. That there was sexual intercourse between the races, mixed marriages, and in all likelihood illicit connexions, is shown by the legislation on the subject, and even more certainly by the frequent references to mulattoes. It is equally clear that such marriages were looked upon with disapproval, and as an evil grave enough to demand the intervention of the law. In Pennsylvania the Act of 1725, already referred to, made the marriage of a white with a negro punishable by a fine of thirty pounds. The negro, if free, relapsed into servitude. In Virginia any white intermarrying with a negro was imprisoned for six months and fined ten pounds, and the minister celebrating such a marriage was fined.[2]

The non-existence, or at least the unfrequency, of

[1] Peyton's *History of Augusta County*, p. 76. [2] Hening, vol. vi.

negro concubinage may be inferred from the absence of any specific enactments to prevent it, and perhaps even more from the silence of colonial officials and travellers. It is also significant that the critics and opponents of slavery, while dwelling on its moral and economical evils, do not cite this. If we may believe Mrs. Grant, such relations were unknown among the colonists themselves, and no mulattoes were to be seen. But she says, in somewhat magniloquent fashion, 'during the French war the progress of the British Army might be traced by a spurious and ambiguous race of this kind.'[1]

One writer, however, dating from Virginia about 1757, does state that 'many base wretches among us take up with negro women.' One would infer from the expression that the practice was disapproved by the social code of the better sort of planters.[2]

But, though the system of slavery might be as yet free from this special form of evil, its demoralizing influences were already perceived by those who had no interest in the maintenance of the institution. In 1745 we find an English traveller setting forth the demoralizing effect on the children of the dominant race.[3] They are brought up in the sight of cruel punishments, and in the society of those who in their sexual relations resemble the brute beasts. Woolman, one of the most rational and moderate of the opponents of slavery, dwells on the evil effects of slavery on the master.[4] Even then it was seen that the system could only protect itself by the infliction of punishments which must inevitably brutalize those who inflicted them. Slaves,

[1] *Memoirs of an American Lady*, i. 86. [2] Fontaine's *Letters*, p. 349.

[3] 'Itinerant Observations in America.' Originally published in the *London Magazine* for 1745. Republished in the *Georgia Historical Society's Collections*, iv. 38.

[4] Woolman's pamphlet entitled *Some Considerations on the Keeping of Negroes* was originally published in 1754. It was subsequently added as an appendix to his life, published at Dublin in 1794.

old and infirm it might be, often came into the possession of young masters wholly unfit for arbitrary power. Woolman, too, evidently sees, though he does not state it formally or definitely, one of the strongest arguments used against slavery in later days, that where toil was the badge of an inferior race there could be no wholesome reverence for industry.

It is assuredly no reproach to the American colonists that on the subject of slavery their moral standard was virtually that of the rest of the world. Stringent as was the moral sense of the New Englander in many respects, there was nothing to predispose him to look with any special aversion on slavery. By religious faith and by religious training he belonged to an oligarchy, and the training of an oligarchy leaves little room for tenderness towards those outside its pale. As we have already seen, physical conditions kept slavery in New England within very narrow limits. The New England virtues, self-respect and sense of justice, would have sufficed, even if slavery had been more widely extended, to avert its worst evils. They did not suffice to create any strong opposition to slavery when it only affected other communities. For the New Englander the evils of the plantation system were remote and unseen. Close familiarity with them might have hindered union, as at a later day it threatened to destroy it. In the South slavery was too closely interwoven with economic and industrial life to suffer men to question its fitness. Nor could the Established Church with any show of consistency condemn a system which the British Government had definitely taken under its protection. In almost every colony there were righteous and humane men of divers sects and classes found to protest against the abuses incident to slavery and its possibilities of arbitrary cruelty. Only among the Quakers in the Middle colonies, and there not till the middle of the eighteenth century, do we find a strenuous and comprehensive protest not against the abuses of slavery, but against the very system itself. Woolman in his autobiography tells us how, when a young man, he was exercised in mind because his employer told him to write a bill of sale for a negro slave. It was the common situation of a sensitive conscience suddenly brought face to face with a wide gap between the conventional standard of morality and his own unformulated and half-acknowledged convictions.

It was not long before vague distaste hardened into definite and convinced opposition. In 1759 Woolman and his fellow religionist Churchman were conducting a house-to-house visitation designed to bring slaveholders to a sense of the sinfulness of the practice. Then, as in later days, the cause of abolition was somewhat hindered by the overstrained scruples of its advocates. Some of those who were convinced of the guilt of holding slaves nevertheless did not emancipate their negroes at once. They would in that case have been bound to provide for them if destitute. To meet this they retained their slaves in bondage till they were thirty, considering that by that time their earnings would cover the risk which they were incurring. This Woolman condemned as an immoral concession. Yet it is characteristic of his temper, always more severe in judgment of himself than others, that his blame is directed not against his neighbours, but against his own conduct when, acting as an executor, he was a party to this arrangement.

Neau's negro school.

In the matter of slavery the Church of England can make no claim to have outrun the standard of morality usually recognised. What it may claim is that, while accepting slavery as an established and necessary institution, it did its utmost to secure for the slave humane treatment, and to deal with him, and to make others deal with him, as a being with a soul to be saved. The Society for the Propagation of the Gospel had a diligent servant in Elias Neau, a French Huguenot, who in 1704 established a missionary school for negroes at New York. In four years the number of catechumens in Neau's school had mounted up to two hundred.

The missionary labours of Elliot and Gookin in New England were frustrated by the outburst of indiscriminate fury against all Indians which followed upon Philip's war. So was it with Neau. When New York was put in danger by servile incendiaries, those restraints on negroes, which were dictated by necessity, or at least by common prudence, such as the prohibition to be in the streets at night without light, were some hindrance.[1] An even more serious hindrance to Neau's work was the indignation with which he was looked on as the friend of the negro. There was but the slightest personal connexion between his school and the incendiaries. Only one scholar, an unbaptized one, was implicated. Yet so violent was the feeling against Neau that he had for safety to avoid the public streets. Happily for him the Governor was one who understood the art of disregarding public folly without offending public feeling. Hunter, a Whig and a Scotchman, cannot have had any strong prepossessions in favour of Neau's work. It is the best proof of its value and of Neau's personal merit that Hunter stood by him in his trouble with unflinching loyalty. He paid the school a formal visit; he requested the clergy to advocate publicly from the pulpit Neau's claims, and he secured for him the support of the chief officials. The Council

[1] Anderson treats this as a grievance, urging that the negroes could not afford lanterns or candles. One would suppose that if there had been any real zeal among the settlers for the work that would not have been insuperable. The Society could have provided what was needed with no great drain on its resources.

of New York, the Mayor, the Recorder, and the two Chief Justices joined Hunter in a declaration that Neau 'had demeaned himself in all things as a good Christian subject,' and that his labours had served for the advancement of religion and the benefit of the negro slaves. Thus supported, Neau seems to have lived down his unpopularity. He carried on the school till his death in 1724, and bequeathed it to successors, under whom it prospered so long as New York remained a British dependency.[1]

The conditions of life in Maryland and Virginia, and the character and temper of the clergy in those colonies, made effective religious teaching among the negroes well nigh impossible. Ministers who had neither time nor energy adequately to fulful their duties towards their existing white congregations, were not likely to undertake missionary work which could only be carried out by continuous journeyings from plantation to plantation. In North Carolina if the slaves were heathens it was only a condition which they shared with the generality of their masters.

Negro conversions in South Carolina.

In South Carolina the case was different. Early in the eighteenth century one minister reports that he has taught twenty-three negroes to read. Another clergyman, writing in 1713, announces the baptism of fourteen slaves; and a third, writing twenty years later, reports that out of his thirty-one communicating parishioners nineteen were negroes.[2]

In 1727 Henry Gibson, then Bishop of London, and as such the diocesan of the colonies, issued a letter to shareholders urging the necessity of extending Christianity among the negroes. He takes successively

[1] For this affair see Humphreys' *History of the Society for the Propagation of the Gospel in Foreign Parts,* published in 1730. Humphreys was secretary to the Society. Cf. Anderson, vol. iii. p. 453.

[2] McCrady, vol. ii. pp. 49–50. He quotes several original authorities.

various objections that have been urged against the work and meets each of them.

Bishop Gibson's letters.[1]

1. It is said that the negroes being adults are unconvertible. This doctrine if accepted would make all missionary work impossible.

2. They cannot be taught since they know no English. At least they know enough for the practical purposes of life. The best can be chosen as interpreters and subaltern missionaries. In any case this difficulty need not hinder missionary work among the children.

3. Religious teaching will encroach on the time needed for work. To accept this view is to make Mammon everything and God nothing.

Finally the Bishop meets an objection which had always tended to hinder missionary work among the slaves—the belief that conversion to Christianity might be thought to carry with it a claim to freedom. Thus we find a clergyman in North Carolina, Taylor, reporting to the Gospel Society that he was doing good missionary work among the slaves in a certain plantation. The planter, however, was told that baptism would carry with it a right to emancipation, and he therefore stopped Taylor's ministration. Taylor suggested that this fear might be met by a declaratory Act.[2] That course had been adopted seven years before in South Carolina. There the legislature passed an Act setting forth that slaveholders might be deterred from having their slaves baptized by the belief that manumission of necessity followed; that this view was unfounded, and that the baptized slave still remained a slave.[3] A similar declaratory Act was passed in New York in 1709.[4]

[1] These are given by Dalcho, *History of the Church in South Carolina*, p. 104.

[2] N. Car. Records, vol. ii. p. 331.

[3] Statutes of S. Carolina, vol. vii. p. 352, quoted by Mr. McCrady.

[4] Acts of Assembly, p. 65.

Gibson enforces this view; St. Paul, as he points out, contemplated the possibility of slaves becoming converted to Christianity and still remaining slaves.

The Bishop also meets the objection of those who openly said that Christianity unfitted the slave for his work. That was probably thought by others who had not the courage to say it openly. Gibson's answer is that to say that Christianity and effective work as a slave are incompatible is to condemn Christianity. There was an alternative answer, but it was one which could hardly be looked for from an English public man in the first half of the eighteenth century.

This was accompanied by a short pastoral addressed to the ministry, exhorting them not to neglect the work of conversion among the slaves.

It has been made a matter of reproach to the British Government that by refusing to second the efforts of colonial legislatures for the restriction of slavery it rendered itself responsible for the continuance and extent of the evil. That is no doubt in a measure true. Before the middle of the eighteenth century various colonial legislatures had taken measures for checking the importation of negro slaves by the imposition of a duty. In 1738 such a measure was carried through the Lower House of the New Jersey Assembly. It was vetoed, not by the British Government but by the Council.[1] They probably were acting in the interests of the large merchants and landholders, while the Lower House represented the yeomanry tilling their own lands.

In South Carolina an Act was passed in 1740 laying a duty of sixty pounds on every negro imported. Furthermore a tax was imposed on all purchasers of negroes within six months of their importation. The duty was somewhat oddly graduated in proportion to

[1] New Jersey Papers, vol. vi. p. 219.

the height of the negro purchased. This Act was to be in force for ten years, and was then renewed for ten years more.[1] In 1756 Lyttelton, who came out as Governor, received instructions not to assent to any Act for taxing imported negroes. The existing Acts, however, remained in force. Lyttelton's instructions were repeated to his successor Boone, and probably in consequence the Act was not renewed.

Import duty on slaves in South Carolina.

The instructions given to Lyttelton expressly set forth that the imposition of duties on the importation of negroes operated to 'the great discouragement of negroes trading to the coast of Africa.'[2] The same policy is indicated in the instructions issued to Burrington as Governor of North Carolina, in 1728. Merchants trading to the colony were to be encouraged, 'in particular the Royal African Company and other our subjects trading to Africa. And as we are willing to recommend unto the said Company and other our subjects that the said Province may have a constant and sufficient supply of merchantable negroes at moderate rates in money and commodities, so that you are to take special care that payment be duly made.'[3]

The condition of public opinion in the mother country on this subject may be learned from a pamphlet written in 1709, but thought worthy of republication in 1745.[4] The title of the pamphlet somewhat fallaciously suggests care for the interests of the colonies. As a matter of fact the writer looks at the

Postlethwayte's pamphlet.

[1] Statutes of South Carolina, vol. iii. p. 566, quoted by Mr. McCrady.

[2] Quoted by Mr. McCrady, *South Carolina under Royal Government*, p. 378.

[3] N. Car. Records, vol. iii. p. 106.

[4] The pamphlet is entitled *The African Slave Trade the great Pillar and Support of the British Plantations in America*. It is attributed to one Postlethwayte, and was only one of a host of pamphlets and broadsheets called forth by the proposal to limit the trade in slaves to an incorporated company.

question solely as it bears on the commercial advantage of the mother country. 'Negro labour will keep the colonies in a due subservience to the interests of the mother country, for while our plantations depend only on planting by negroes and that of such produce as interferes only with the interests of our rivals not of their mother country, our colonies can never prove injurious to British manufactures nor become independent of these kingdoms, but remain a perpetual support to our European interest by preserving to us a superiority of trade and naval power.

'Were it possible, however, for white men to answer the end of negroes in planting, must we not drain our country of husbandmen, mechanics and manufacturers too? Might not the latter be the cause of our colonies interfering with the manufactures of these kingdoms as the Palatines attempted in Pennsylvania?' It is noteworthy that not only in Postlethwayte's pamphlet, but in all the controversial literature on the subject, we find no consideration of what would probably in modern times be regarded as the most important factor in the case—the moral and social aspect of the case as it affects the colonists and the slaves. The negro is just a commodity like any other chattel.

Nature of the opposition to slavery.

No doubt the policy of the British Government in this, as in all other matters, was to look primarily to the commercial interests of the mother country. But it would be assuredly a gross and unjust exaggeration to represent the colonies as struggling against a moral and social evil which the mother country was resolved to force upon them. Here and there were those who had scruples about tolerating slavery in any form. Such were to be found in England also, though no doubt they were more frequent in the colonies, where the moral and social evils of slavery were forced upon men's notice. But, taking the colonists as a whole, what they dreaded and resented was the presence among them of a barbarous population, outnumbering, or rapidly tending to outnumber, the white inhabitants. The negro imported fresh from Africa was far more an object of terror than the negro born on a plantation and reared under the eye of a white master. If the imposition of an import duty unduly lessened the supply of labour, that could be counterbalanced by an increased production of negroes in the colonies. Thus the taxation of imported negroes was an obvious and tempting method of raising revenue; it would leave the system of servile labour unimpaired, while it freed that system from some of its worst evils and greatest dangers. For if the thing was looked at purely from a humanitarian point of view the sufferings caused by the African trade were perhaps the worst features of slavery. Many who would have shrunk from such a far-reaching industrial revolution as would have been involved in the extirpation of slavery would have welcomed the abolition of that trade as a valuable instalment of justice.

The settlers and the Indians.

During the seventeenth century the proximity of the Indian was for the colonists an influence making for cohesion. Dread of the Indian, a dread intensely impressed on the settlers by the Pequod war, was the chief cause which brought about the one practical attempt at colonial union, the confederacy of the four New England colonies. That dread, kept alive by Philip's war and by the perpetual menace of a joint French and Indian invasion, helped to counteract that intense spirit of local patriotism which threatened to subordinate the state to the township. In the Southern colonies the proximity of the savage did something to check extension westward, and to force the settlers to develope to the full the resources of the sea-coast rather than seek new homes further inland.

One cannot say that this influence disappeared in the following century, but assuredly it lost its original force. In New England, indeed, it operated with more strength than elsewhere. Yet even there it had changed its form. What the New Englander in the eighteenth century had to dread was not the savage in English territory or on the border, who might at some unlooked-for moment fill the colony with the prospect of massacre, but the distant Indian—a weapon wielded by the unscrupulous and merciless diplomacy of Canadian Governors, adding enormously to the terrors of war, but not an independent source of danger. So far as it did operate, it was an evil which presented itself far more vividly to the inhabitants of scattered and thinly peopled villages on the verge of the north-western frontier than to citizens of Boston fenced off from danger by a belt of civilized country. A more far-sighted policy on the part of Great Britain might have turned to account the indifference of the government of Massachusetts to the danger of her more remote members. A well-organized military policy on the western frontier might have taught the settlers there that in union with the mother country lay hopes of safety which their own local government was powerless to give. In the South, too, the Indian peril had changed its character. The white invaders and the original inhabitants were no longer intermixed on the soil which the latter could claim as their inheritance. They stood confronting one another as two detached communities. The presence of the Indian so placed made for dissension rather than cohesion. It had been an important influence in forcing upon the Southern colonies, separately and individually, such union as they attained. It did nothing to further that wider union of colonies which was the crying need of the eighteenth century. Rather it hindered such union, and was a source of jealousy and mutual distrust. The troubles with the Indians in the Middle and Southern colonies were largely due to the lawless and brutal conduct of isolated settlers living on the western frontier, beyond the limits of civilization and authority. These were in many cases occupants of those debateable lands claimed by more than one colony, and they took advantage of the fact to ignore the authority of whatever government strove to control them. Thus the intercolonial bitterness which was engendered by territorial disputes was accentuated by the fact that such disputes were often attended by trouble with the savages as their direct consequence.

Changes among the Indian tribes.

The eighteenth century brought with it another change, specially felt in the Northern colonies. The English were no longer menaced in the same way by united communities large enough to be dangerous. The Pequods, the Narragansetts, the tribe or tribes that had formed the kingdom of Powhatan, had all vanished before the white invader. The hegemony of the Iroquois over all the tribes along the western frontier had become more complete. New actors indeed had appeared on the scene. No feature of Indian life is more noteworthy, and hardly any to the historian more bewildering, than the rapid changes in the relative importance of the various tribes. In the eighteenth century three tribes previously unknown or obscure in colonial annals come to the front and assert themselves, with relations to the colonists never cordial and at times hostile. These were the Shawnees, the Delawares, or, as they proudly called themselves, the Lenni Lenape, the Original Men, and the Miamies, sometimes called the Twightwies. These three tribes occupied a tract along the west banks of the Ohio, extending from the Monongahela to the Wabash, with the Delawares at the northern, the Miamies at the southern extremity. All of them had suffered in the seventeenth century at the hands of the Iroquois. The Miamies had been seriously reduced in numbers; the Shawnees had been for a while driven from their homes in the Ohio valley and become wanderers. The Delawares had been reduced to a state of degrading servitude. Yet in the eighteenth century each tribe had retained sufficient independence to have in some measure a policy of its own, and sufficient military strength to be a source of danger to the settlers.

Relations of New England to the Indians.

In dealing with the relations between the English and the Indians, we cannot do better than follow that division which has served us in other matters, and treat the colonies as falling into three groups, each occupying its own zone. The attitude of New England to the natives was now, as always, definite and free from complications. This was due alike to the composition and the constitution of the New England settlements. The sea-board towns, where the bulk of the population and wealth of the colony was to be found, were well outside the striking distance of any Indian raid. Danger could only come to them from a French invasion, in which the Indians might be auxiliaries. And even the inland, and therefore more exposed, portions of the colony were to a great extent exempt from all those influences which specially tended to embroil the colonists and the savages. The political system of New England, rigid as it was, could not wholly exclude the squatter, who wandered on his own account beyond the recognised frontier, debauching the natives with rum, and swindling them out of their furs and their land. But we may at least say that he was less frequent, and more easily and effectively controlled, than in the Middle and Southern colonies. The frontier was covered by a belt of forest, not indeed permanently occupied by Iroquois settlements, but in which the Canadian Indian invading from the north might at any time fall in with a Mohawk war-party. The loyalty of the Iroquois to the English alliance might be at times doubtful. His persistent hatred of the Huron might be reckoned on with unfailing confidence.

The Iroquois and the English.

There was, however, no such certainty about his relations to the French. Iroquois chiefs more than once told the English in formal conference that they could not answer for the fidelity of their tribe, that the younger warrior might be won over. The Five Nations were in constant danger of being alienated by the sloth and bewildered by the disunion of their white allies. The Mohawk was not a mere wild beast, loving indiscriminate carnage for its own sake. If he was to do the devil's work he expected the devil's wages, and there were times when he seemed far more likely to receive those wages from the French than the English. Was he, he more than once asked, to do all the fighting while his white ally sat quietly at home and enjoyed all the fruits of conquest? He was wholly bewildered, too, by the spectacle of communities, speaking the same speech, nominally belonging to the same nation, yet showing no unity of purpose or sense of common action. Could all the English, he asked, be really subjects of one King?

New England and the French Indians

Thus the security of New England depended more on her own geographical position and social conditions than on the somewhat precarious alliance with the Mohawks. Although, after the overthrow of Philip, New England never knew the full horrors of an Indian invasion, yet she did not wholly escape. But when the New Englander of the eighteenth century came into conflict with the Indian, it was not with the Indian as an independent enemy, acting for his own benefit and on his own responsibility, but with the Indian as the instrument of French aggression. Queen Anne's war, to give it the name which it bore among the colonists, brought as one of its consequences a conflict with the Indians. For ten years the frontiers of New England had to endure a continuous series of raids.[1] The burden fell upon the western frontier of Massachusetts and Connecticut, and on the scattered and sparsely peopled villages on the coast of Maine. The real heart of New England, the sea-board with its ports, its prosperous towns and its villages and farmsteads, near enough for mutual support and sheltered by the capital, were safe. There could be no stronger proof how weak and ill-considered was the policy of the French rulers of Canada and their priestly advisers than their attitude to New England. A war of raids, which merely harried the extremities and left the vital centre untouched, could only exasperate, without inflicting any permanent injury. In the Ohio valley such a policy might be unscrupulous, but it was at least effective. There France had to face an encroaching wave of population, and the Indian was no doubt the most effective weapon for repelling it. But no such danger menaced her from New England. There was not the slightest danger of Canada finding herself confronted with a belt of English population in the dreary forests and barren uplands which surround the sources of the Connecticut, the Androscoggin and the Kennebec. There nature had given New France an effective frontier; it was sheer folly to convert it from a neutral zone into an area of strife. Specially was it folly for the weaker side, which

[1] I have mentioned these and especially the destruction of Schenectady elsewhere: *The Puritan Colonies*, vol. ii. The chief authorities are Niles and Penhallow.

needed all its resources for the protection of its really vulnerable parts. Only an astonishing ignorance of the conditions of New England and of the temper of its citizens could have led to such an error. The New Englander was peaceful, not assuredly from cowardice, but from inertness, from a lack of the training and instincts which enabled him readily to take his place as part of a military organism. To him it was a matter of indifference whether the settlers of Pennsylvania and Virginia could find new homes on the banks of the Ohio, or whether France as one of the great Powers of Europe was crippled. Not for these objects was the New England yeoman going to leave his farm untilled, or the New England politician to deny himself the luxury of thwarting and insulting a royal Governor. But once bring him face to face with those two objects of hereditary and traditional hatred, the Indian warrior and the French priest, and a spring was touched which transformed the New Englander from a peace-loving trader and a disaffected politician into a tenacious and vindictive fighter.

It is but just to the secular rulers of Canada to say that the error which brought the fortunes of the colony to shipwreck was due far more to religious bigotry than to political miscalculation. It was a cruder and more brutal manifestation of that spirit which led to the revocation of the Edict of Nantes. That by alienating the very men who of all the population of France were best fitted for the task of colonization did much to bring about, or at least to accelerate, the fall of French Canada. The same spirit embroiled the colony in a wholly unnecessary and profitless struggle with New England. No one can withhold from the French missionaries the full meed of praise due to courage and self-devotion. Equally can no one deny that in nine cases out of ten the motives to which they appealed and the standard of life which they inculcated on their converts would have met with the most unsparing condemnation from the Founder of Christianity and the early teachers of the Christian religion. The Indian convert to Romanism was a recruit, bought at a price, and that price was unlimited opportunity for killing and torturing heretics.

No more typical instance of the militant French missionary could be found than Sebastian Rasle. In the last decade of the seventeenth century, he, then a man of about forty, was placed in charge of a missionary station at Norridgewock, on the Kennebec, hard by the frontier of Maine. In 1705, during Rasle's absence, a raiding party from New Hampshire fell upon the village and destroyed it, burning the church. The settlement, however, was not abandoned. The church was rebuilt, strange to say, by the hands of workmen hired from New England,[2] and by 1710 the village contained twenty-six houses within a wooden palisade.[3]

Sebastian Rasle.[1]

The conclusion of Queen Anne's war was the signal for a movement of English settlers into the valley of the Kennebec. There need be no doubt that, as in this case almost always, the influx of white settlers was more or less attended with forcible or fraudulent eviction of the natives from the lands which they claimed the right to wander over. It was not difficult for Rasle to represent the English advance as a deliberate scheme for the extirpation of the native.

In August 1716, Shute being anxious about the safety of the outlying settlements, summoned the Indian

[1] The best account of Rasle is to be found in Parkman's *Half Century of Conflict*, vol. i. p. 207. I have adopted Rasle's own spelling of his name.

[2] Hutchinson, vol. ii. p. 313.

[3] *Half Century*, vol. i. p. 210. Mr. Parkman quotes an inscription on a map dating from 1716.

chiefs to a conference at Georgetown, a fort situated on an island near the mouth of the Kennebec. Shute's somewhat overbearing manner, his ignorance of the Indians' habits of thought and his indifference to their severe regard for ceremonial form, nearly brought the conference to an untimely end. Matters were not improved when the Indians produced a letter addressed by Rasle to Shute, in which he said that the English could have no claim to lands east of the Kennebec, since no cession of such lands had been made by the King of France. This was practically a new and extended territorial claim. The Indians, however, were plainly anxious for peace. For all Rasle's ability and influence we may well believe that the French authority, represented and enforced by a solitary priest, was outweighed by the spectacle of the English Governor in uniform, coming in a frigate with a military retinue. The Indians, alarmed by Shute's threat of withdrawing from the conference, humbly granted all that he asked. An agreement was signed by twenty Indians, chiefs or elders, by which they accepted the sovereignty of the English Crown, and granted to the English settlers full rights of territorial extension. Shute on his side promised to set up trading houses, where the Indians might obtain goods on fair terms. They were also to have the services of an English smith to mend their guns. These provisions of the treaty are a good instance of the advantages which the English enjoyed for securing the friendship of the natives, if only the political condition of the colonies had allowed their rulers to play their cards to the best effect.[1]

The conference at Georgetown.

The Massachusetts Assembly did not confine themselves to warlike measures, but endeavoured to meet Rasle on his own ground and to countermine him by

[1] For these negotiations see Hutchinson, vol. ii. p. 219; Penhallow (ed. 1859), p. 84; N. Hants. Historical Collections, vol. ii. p. 242.

establishing a Protestant mission. A New England minister, Joseph Baxter, was sent out into the wilderness to preach Protestant doctrine to the savages. Rasle would have been probably well advised to trust to the Indian's indifference to a religion which offered them Calvinistic doctrine instead of Roman ritual, and which refused to bribe them by appeals to their worst passions. But his diplomatic powers were, as it would seem, marred by a hot and overbearing temper, and he entangled himself in a controversial correspondence with Baxter, carried on in Latin, in which each belaboured the other's scholarship after the fashion of two humanists of the Renaissance.[1]

A Protestant mission.

Rasle fared better in his attempts to keep alive anti-English feeling among his flock. In 1721 we find him writing complacently to the Governor of Canada that the teaching given at his mission had led the savages to threaten the English settlements and to destroy many of the cattle there. In reply, the Governor of Canada promised Rasle that the Jesuit mission should be strengthened and extended, and that hostility to the English should be inculcated. The Intendant[2] at the same time wrote that if the King would permit it, active help would be given to Rasle's followers. In any case they should be supplied with ammunition.

French intrigues with the Indians.

The Government of Canada, starved by the folly of the rulers in France, and honeycombed with internal corruption, could give little more than vague promises and verbal encouragement. Rasle's cause was better served by the misdeeds and follies of his opponents. Disreputable squatters on the border, acting after the wont of such folk,

Hostility between Massachusetts and the Indians.

[1] *Half Century of Conflict*, vol. i. p. 221. Mr. Parkman refers to unpublished papers.

[2] The official responsible for finance.

trafficked on the necessities of the Indians and their lust for firewater.[1] The Assembly of Massachusetts withheld from Shute the supplies necessary for carrying out his promises to supply the Indians with goods and with the presents which he had promised. Not only that, but by encroaching on the prerogative of the Governor, and claiming a right of independent action on a question of peace and war, they made a continuous and consistent policy impossible.[2] The settlers of Massachusetts were in the habit of using certain lands near Canso, in Nova Scotia, as summer pasturage for their cattle, during which time the owners or their herdsmen occupied *chalets* in that district. These were attacked by the Indians. Some of the occupants were killed; the houses were stripped, and the plunder carried off by small French fishing vessels from Cape Breton. Fortunately, an English sloop appeared on the scene and came to the rescue, capturing six or seven vessels with the plunder aboard.[3]

This was followed by minor outrages in the valley of the Kennebec: cattle were driven off and haystacks burnt.[4]

The Governor was still for peaceful measures, and his policy was approved by the Council. He sent instructions to the military officer in command of the district threatened to summon the Indians to a conference, and they promised to attend. On November 2, however, after the Governor's message had been sent, but before the day fixed for the conference, the Assembly voted that a hundred and fifty men be sent up to Norridgewock to make reprisals on the Indians and to capture Rasle. Whatever effect considerations of economy

Dispute between the Governor and the Assembly.[5]

[1] Belknap, vol. iii. p. 40; cf. *Half Century of Conflict*, vol. i. p. 223.

[2] Hutchinson, vol. ii. p. 238.

[3] *Ib.* p. 240.

[4] *Half Century*, as above.

[5] Hutchinson, vol. ii. pp. 240–1.

might have had was destroyed by that strange and unhappy delusion which haunted the New Englander, who thought that wealth could be called into existence by a mere stroke of the pen, and that an issue of paper money would enable the community to meet any charge without feeling the burden. Indeed, we may say that a desire, in some cases an interested desire, for the issue of paper money in itself furnished a motive for that warlike policy which made such an issue necessary. The Assembly also voted that a reward of five hundred pounds sterling should be offered for Rasle's head. This, however, was vetoed by the Governor and Council. That Rasle was well informed of the course of events at Boston may be inferred from his knowledge of this fact. At the same time he, in all likelihood deliberately, misrepresented the abortive proposal as an actual offer, and doubled the sum usually suggested.[1]

Second conference at Georgetown.

Whether Shute's policy or the policy of the Assembly was the better, it is at least certain that the interlacing of the two, the alternations of a policy of severity and a policy of propitiation, could only spell failure. For the time, however, Shute and the Council, exercising their constitutional right to veto the resolution of the Assembly, prevailed.

The Norridgewock Indians promised to pay two hundred beaver skins as compensation for the damages done, and to abstain from future hostilities. As a guarantee for the fulfilment of these promises they gave four hostages. A meeting was then arranged at Georgetown, the scene of the previous treaty, at which the beaver skins should be delivered.

Rasle and his supporters in Canada were resolved

[1] *Half Century*, vol. vi. p. 229. Hutchinson says (vol. ii. p. 265), 'his scalp would have been worth a hundred scalps of the Indians.'

that the issue should not be left in the hands of the now peacefully inclined Norridgewock Indians. As we have seen, Rasle was more or less acquainted with the course of affairs at Boston, and we cannot doubt that he succeeded in impressing upon his disciples that, whatever promises Shute individually might make, the policy of the English as a whole was one of uncompromising hostility.

On the day appointed there appeared at Georgetown two French officers, followed by a band of two hundred and fifty Roman converts, among them a sprinkling of Iroquois who had deserted the English alliance.[1] Accordingly there was little hope that a meeting thus composed and thus influenced would bring peace as a consequence. The anti-English party soon found a pretext for breaking off negotiations. The Indians demanded that on the payment of the beaver skins the hostages should be returned. To this it was replied that hostages were a guarantee not only for payment, but for future good behaviour, and must therefore be still detained. When their surrender was refused the Indian chiefs produced a manifesto, signed by themselves, but drawn up for them in readiness by the Jesuit superior for Canada. By this the English were ordered to leave the Indian country at once under pain of attack.[2]

France was now in the position, not unknown to the great Powers of the civilized world, of being openly at peace with a neighbour while intriguing with the barbarian occupants of a neutral zone. Vaudreuil, the Governor of Canada, would no doubt have adopted a more active policy of aggression

Policy of Vaudreuil.

[1] Penhallow, p. 86. He was himself at the conference. The presence of the Iroquois is shown by the fact that their totems are appended to the letter mentioned below.

[2] The letter is in the Mass. Hist. Collection, 2nd series, vol. viii. p. 259.

if he had not been restrained by the express desire of his own Government to avoid an open breach with Great Britain. In his letters to Rasle, and also to his own Government, he made no secret of his wish that the Abenakis should be supported in their attacks on the English by gifts of arms and ammunition, while at the same time he thought to escape responsibility by the somewhat transparent device of calling the Indians not subjects, but allies of France.[1]

Expedition against Norridgewock.

In September, a month after the conference, an Indian raiding party harassed the settlers on the Kennebec, and compelled them to take refuge in the fort at Georgetown.[2] Shute's hand was now forced, and a policy of peace rendered impossible. Three hundred men were sent against Norridgewock.[3] Their instructions were in the first instance not to attack the Indians, but to demand the surrender of Rasle and any other Jesuits that might be among the savages. If they were not given up quietly, they were to be seized by force, with as many of the Indian chiefs as the commander of the party should think fit. Before the English troops could reach Norridgewock, Rasle fled, leaving behind him his private papers. Among them were letters from Vaudreuil, giving definite proof of those intrigues with the Indians which had so far been merely matters of suspicion.[4]

Further disputes between Shute and the Assembly.

War had now definitely broken out between the settlers and the Indians. The constitution of the colony vested the control of the war in Shute. He was not without military experience, having commanded a regiment with credit in Marlborough's campaign. However obnoxious his previous desire for peace might have been to the

[1] Letter quoted by Parkman from the French Archives *Half Century*, vol. ii. p. 227.

[2] Penhallow, p. 93. [3] *Ib.* [4] Belknap, vol. iii. p. 43.

Assembly, it was clear that interference and divided counsels must be fatal to success. But it is seldom that a small republic, where self-government is a reality, a possession endeared by tradition and usage, can so far divest itself of its accustomed habits as to give a ruler a wholly free hand, even in military matters. Whatever the constitution of Massachusetts might be in name, more than half a century of charter government had imbued her citizens with all the instincts of a republic. It is but just, too, to say that one action of the Assembly which excited Shute's anger was prompted by a suspicion which, if not well founded, was at least natural. They demanded that inspectors appointed by themselves should have access to the various garrisons to ensure that the returns of numbers were correct, and that the exchequer of the colony was not being burdened with payments for non-existing soldiers.[1] The existence of such malpractices in the British army was a matter of notoriety, and Shute and the Council would have done well to welcome, instead of resenting as they did, such precautions.

It was a very different matter to insist, as the Assembly did, on regulating the disposition and movements of the forces actually in the field, and to require that an officer, Captain Walton, who had obeyed Shute's orders in preference to theirs, should leave his command and come to Boston to give an account of his conduct.[2]

The Assembly also showed a singular inability to perceive what were the essential conditions for success in diplomatic dealings with the savages. There were, as we have seen, symptoms of disaffection among the Iroquois. It was thought prudent to invite a deputation of their chiefs to Boston. Shute

Reception of the Iroquois.[3]

[1] Hutchinson, vol. ii. p. 79; cf. Penhallow.

[2] *Ib.* p. 281.

[3] *Ib.* p. 280.

wished that the speech which he was to address to the chiefs should be composed by himself and merely shown in advance to the Assembly. The Assembly demanded that it should be composed by them, that it should profess to come from the General Court, and they should be officially present when it was read. In New York and in Pennsylvania all diplomatic negotiations with the Indians were entrusted to the Governor as the representative of royalty, and there can be little doubt that Shute was right in believing that such a form of procedure was the best. It was all-important to impress on the savages the truth, so often obscured by the action of the colonists, that the English were not inhabitants of separate communities, but one nation under one ruler.

Shute, however, had neither the tact to outwit nor the firmness to defy the Assembly, and their wishes prevailed. Shute agreed to receive the Iroquois deputation as they proposed. Walton obeyed the summons of the Assembly and came to Boston. This, however, was only the signal for a fresh dispute as to the form of procedure to be adopted in dealing with him. Shute insisted that the inquiry should be held by the whole court; the Representatives claimed exclusive jurisdiction in the matter.

Shute's departure.

A New England historian, himself in his day the victim of mob violence, tells us that Shute had reason to fear assassination, a bullet having come into the room where he was sitting.[1] One is disinclined to believe in a crime so wholly at variance with the temper of New England. It is possible, however, that such a fear, albeit ill-founded, may have accelerated Shute's departure. At the same time, such action needs no special explanation in the case of a man of easy-going temper, with neither the inclination nor the

[1] Hutchinson, vol. ii. p. 287.

aptitude for strife, forced at every turn into trivial disputes with men in whom the taste and capacity for such disputes were almost morbidly developed.

The Assembly claim military authority.[1]

During the interregnum caused by Shute's retirement his authority devolved on the Lieutenant-Governor, Jeremiah Dummer. He was a Bostonian born and bred. But he had spent a considerable portion of his life in England, and in the eyes of Massachusetts patriots his good name was tainted by the fact that he was the son-in-law of the apostate Dudley. It was unlikely that there would be any change in the attitude of the Assembly. Hardly had Shute sailed before the Representatives proposed to follow the evil example of the Dutch Republic and to entrust the conduct of the war to a Committee. Dummer, however, stood firm in the assertion of his military authority. The Council supported him, and the proposal for appointing a Committee fell to the ground. But the Assembly so far prevailed that they obtained the dismissal of Walton and of another officer who was obnoxious to them.

On one point the Assembly were guided by a sound instinct. They understood how largely the policy of the Indians owed definiteness and cohesion to the influence of Rasle, and they made his capture or death their prime object. No doubt that purpose was largely due to the Puritan spirit, which, though modified, was far from extinct among the descendants of Dudley and Endicott.

Destruction of Norridgewock.

During 1723 nothing took place beyond indecisive skirmishes and attacks on frontier stations. But the following summer saw a decisive attack on Rasle's mission station. In August an English force of two hundred and eight men advanced in two equal divisions, the one to make a direct attack on

[1] Hutchinson, vol. ii. p. 293.

Norridgewock, the other to intercept the enemy's retreat. With a strange lack of precaution the village had been left unfortified, nor had the inhabitants even troubled themselves to make a clearing round it. Thus the assailants were able to reach the village unperceived, and to open fire at close quarters. The Indians fled to the woods. Rasle stood firm, firing on the English, and, refusing to surrender, was shot through the head.[1]

Embassy from Boston to Canada.[2]

In the following summer an embassy was sent from Boston to Canada to obtain the surrender of prisoners whom the Indians had handed over to the French, and also to obtain from Vaudrouil some effective assurance of neutrality. The first object was in part obtained. The French gave no help towards reclaiming prisoners still in the hands of the Indians. Some prisoners however had, so the French said, already been ransomed by them. These they would restore on the repayment of the ransom. The sum named was in the opinion of the English excessive; nevertheless it was paid, and the liberated prisoners brought back to New England.

But the attempt to neutralize the French and Indian alliance only resulted in total failure. All that the embassy could get from Vaudreuil was smooth words and disclaimers of any influence over the Indians. Yet at the very same time, in his despatches to France, he was taking credit to himself for keeping the savages firm in their hostility to the English.

Further trouble with the Indians.

The lack of any central authority among the Indian tribes was in one way a gain to the English, in another an added difficulty. It saved them from having to deal with a concentrated attack. Yet, on the other hand, the smouldering fire of hostility,

[1] Hutchinson (vol. ii. pp. 309–14) gives a detailed account of this.

[2] *Half Century*, vol. i. p. 243. The account there given is based on documents in the Massachusetts Archives.

trodden out in one place, might always break out in another. The death of Rasle and the destruction of Norridgewock no doubt did much to sap the strength of the Indians, and to strike general terror, but it did not end the war.

Lovewell's fight.[1]

In 1725 four Abenaki chiefs, each acting on behalf of his own clan, came to Boston and signed a treaty accepting the sovereignty of the English King, and pledging themselves to abstain from hostilities.[2]

Meanwhile, at the very same time in the northern portion of Massachusetts, a warlike drama was being enacted which found an abiding place among the traditions of New England. On the banks of the Saco, south of the White Mountains of New Hampshire, there lived a small, isolated Indian tribe, the Pequackets. In the autumn of 1724 they fell upon the adjacent English settlements of Dunstable, and carried off two prisoners. Ten of the settlers gave chase, but were entrapped into an ambush, whence only one escaped. Thereupon three of the Dunstable settlers offered to raise a company who should devote a whole year to clearing the neighbourhood of Indians. The Assembly accepted the offer, and promised payment of half-a-crown a day in Massachusetts currency—that is, about a shilling—together with rewards for Indian scalps. A troop of thirty men was raised. They chose as their captain John Lovewell. He had been one of the original three who started the scheme, and was the son of a man who had played a distinguished part in Philip's war. A small initial success gave encouragement. The troop was increased to eighty-seven, taken from five villages. In February 1725 they made their way in shoes to the

[1] Belknap gives a very full account of Lovewell's fight.

[2] Hutchinson, vol. ii. p. 316.

foot of the White Mountains, and cut off a raiding party of the Canadian Indians. The New Englander now, as always, was loth to leave his farmstead at a time when work was pressing, and when Lovewell mustered his force again in April, he could only raise forty-six followers. On May 8 Lovewell fell in with an Indian war party, of whose numbers estimates were formed varying from eighty to forty. The English force had been reduced to thirty-four by the necessity for leaving a sick man behind, with a small guard for his protection. A stubborn fight followed, lasting from ten in the morning to sunset. Fourteen of the English were killed and eleven seriously wounded. So severe, however, was the injury inflicted on the Indians, that they retired without waiting to scalp the dead, an omission which hardly has a parallel in Indian warfare. The small band of survivors found their way back unmolested, and the Pequackets, cowed by their defeat, made no further attacks on the English settlements. The other Indian tribes on the frontier, weary of profitless warfare, and getting no effective help from Canada, sought peace. By the end of 1727 they had all come to terms with Massachusetts. The policy of having Government trading-houses, which Shute had fruitlessly advocated, was now adopted, and till the outbreak of the great French war New England enjoyed peace.

It is clear that the concluding episode of the war—Lovewell's fight—made no little impression on the imagination of New England. It was commemorated in a contemporary ballad, and has furnished matter for later literary efforts.[1] That this should be so marks a change. An Indian raid hardly suggests poetical thoughts to those who are in personal danger of being

[1] *Half Century*, p. 261 *n*.

It was no doubt a gain to the English to have to deal with one solid body having a connected and continuous policy. Yet there were counterbalancing drawbacks. The situation was one which entangled the English in the complexities of Indian diplomacy and in issues with which they were imperfectly acquainted. The Iroquois alliance had to be purchased at the cost of alienation from the various tribes who resented the supremacy of the confederacy, possibly even at the cost of active hostility. The Catawbas, whose good will was essential to the peace of the Southern settlements, were strong enough to defy the authority of the Five Nations.

Nor was that all. There were undercurrents of jealousy within the confederacy itself. There was reason to think that the Mohawks, Onondagas, and Senecas formed in some measure a distinct party as against the three remaining tribes, and the jealousy of these rival factions was an embarrassment to the English in their diplomacy.[1]

Faced by an unscrupulous enemy, linked with a wavering ally, each strong enough for their friendship or enmity to determine the fate of the whole English frontier from the Hudson to the Mississippi, it was impossible for any of the colonies to stand alone. The difficulties of intercolonial action increased the danger. Yet, on the other hand, it was something to be reminded of the need for union, and to be forced into at least an approach to a solid national policy.

Importance of New York on the Indian question.

The key of the position was New York, for in the first place the most obvious and direct form of attack to which the English colonies were accessible was by way of the Hudson. There the French might, helped by the Indian alliance, drive in a solid wedge and separate the

[1] Colden, p. 167.

Northern from the Southern colonies. Secondly, the Indian trade was mainly in the hands of New York. It was by way of the Hudson that the Indian allies of the English received their supplies of clothes, fire-arms, ammunition and rum. The responsibility was laid on those who were ill-fitted for the discharge of it. As in Massachusetts the authority of the Governor was thwarted at every turn by political opposition, and all system or unity of policy was rendered impossible. But, factious though the leaders of the popular party in Massachusetts were, they never destroyed, they never sought to destroy, patriotism and self-reliance. Faction in New England, then and afterwards, was a means to something higher than personal advantage. It impaired authority, but it brought in its train a temper which did something to supply the absence of authority. That cannot be said of New York. Political faction there was the outcome of personal ambition and cupidity, the embodiment of personal intrigue. The New Englander might imperil the colony for the sake of thwarting a royal Governor. He would never have done so to advantage his own pocket.

Moreover, New York was, as we have seen, a cosmopolitan state, composed in a fashion almost of necessity fatal to any strong sense of corporate life. The trade of Massachusetts was mainly in the hands of her own citizens. The Boston merchant was in all likelihood a politician, and after his lights a patriot. The trade of New York, like that of Charlestown, was largely in the hands of merchants living in London, and their opinion and interests were a factor which the rulers of New York could not ignore.

One natural advantage which the English enjoyed in their dealings with the Indians was the great superiority in their opportunities for trading. Two commodities, which had become essential to the comfort of the Indian, spirits and clothing, could be supplied far more cheaply and abundantly from England than from France. The Indian, it is true, somewhat preferred French brandy to rum if it could be had on the same terms. But he cared more to get drunk cheaply, and therefore frequently, than to gratify his palate, and the English had a monopoly of the West Indian rum market. Moreover, France did not produce the coarse woollen fabrics which suited the Indians for winter wear. The French trade was also seriously hampered by the fact that goods could only be brought up to Quebec and Montreal during that limited period while the river was free from ice. The French sought to neutralize these natural advantages by buying the required goods from the English.

English and French trade with the Indians.

To check this the Assembly and New York passed an Act in 1720 prohibiting under heavy penalties any trade between the colony and the French.[1] The Act was neither formally approved nor disallowed by the Government at home, and it therefore remained in force for three years and then expired. It was, however, believed that there was a likelihood of the Assembly re-enacting such a prohibitory law. For it is clear that Burnet, then Governor, had a settled policy of securing the Five Nations and making them dependent for their supplies on the English. To that end a conference was held with the Indians at Albany in 1722. There Burnet utilized the influence of the Iroquois over their neighbours by persuading the former to threaten the eastern Indians with war if they did not desist from their raids on New England. He also established a trading-house at Oswego, and helped by the restrictions on French

[1] All the documents bearing on this dispute are printed in Colden's *History of the Five Nations.*

merchants succeeded in making Albany more and more a centre for Indian trade.[1]

There seemed every likelihood that the Council and Assembly would support Burnet's policy. Thereupon twenty merchants trading between London and New York presented a petition to the Crown asking that the royal assent should be withheld from any Act which interfered with the French trade.

The merchants' petition.

The only approach to an argument adduced was the audacious statement that the Iroquois were cut off from the English settlements by a belt of country occupied by Indians in the French interest, and that if the French and their allies were offended, they would make it impossible for the Iroquois to have any communication with the English settlements.

The petition was referred to the Commission of Trade and Plantations. One at least of that body, Bladen, had, as we have seen, given no little attention to colonial questions. The action of the Board shows what we see elsewhere, that, limited as its powers were, it did something for the security and well-being of the colonies, and might, if more carefully developed, have been of the greatest service in colonial administration.

The Commissioners summoned the petitioning merchants to appear before them and give evidence in support of their case. Their spokesman, with an extraordinary and audacious assumption of ignorance on the part of his hearers, declared that the Iroquois were settled in the valley of the St. Lawrence some three hundred leagues from Albany, and could only reach the English settlements by going down that river, where they might be cut off by the French!

The Commissioners thereupon reported, as they well might with perfect confidence, that the statements

[1] Smith, p. 205; Colden.

of the petitioners were open to doubt, and recommended that Burnet be instructed to give his views on the question.

Burnet passed the matter on to the Council. Their report was full and instructive. They had no difficulty in shattering the main foundations on which the merchants rested their case. Nor did they mince matters in dealing with the statements which had been made as to the position and distribution of the Indian tribes. There were no Indians under French influence between the Iroquois and the English settlements. To say that the road from the Iroquois country to Albany lay along the St. Lawrence was like saying that you must pass Edinburgh on the way from London to Bristol. 'These things the merchants have thought it safe for them and consistent with their duty to his sacred Majesty to say in his Majesty's presence, and to repeat afterwards before the Boards of Trade.'

Report of the New York Council.

They also pointed out that there was no such wish as the petitioners assumed wholly to deprive New York of the benefit of the Canadian trade. The restriction was only to apply to goods suited for the Indian market.

The Council, however, did not confine themselves to mere criticism on the views of the petitioners. They set forth very clearly the positive benefits which had resulted from Burnet's policy. One effect, they said, was to call into existence in increasing numbers a class of enterprising young men, who went into the Indian country to buy furs and thereby acquired a knowledge of the language, views, and policy of the Indians; a class, in short, answering to the Canadian *coureur de bois*. Besides, since the passing of the Act under consideration, over and above the effect on the Iroquois themselves, a number of the smaller Indian tribes had separately come in and voluntarily asked for the friendship of the English.

Colden's memorial.

One of the principal members of the Council was Cadwallader Colden. He was at this time a man of about thirty-six. A Scotchman of good education, he had started in practice as a doctor at Philadelphia. No Scotchman is ever backward in bestowing patronage on his fellow-countrymen. In 1718 Hunter invited Colden to New York and appointed him Surveyor to the Colony. He was a man of angular temper, somewhat prone to make enemies, not exempt from suspicions of self-interest, though probably not more amenable to them than most public men of his day. He was not wanting in public spirit, a shrewd observer and an untiring writer. He now, on his own responsibility, submitted to Burnet a memorial on the Indian trade. He begins by pointing out the design of the French to completely encircle the English colonies and make expansion westward impossible. As an illustration of this he refers to a French map, in which portions of New York and South Carolina are actually claimed as French territory. He points out that the two great instruments of French aggression are the fur trader and the missionary. The danger to be apprehended from the latter may be judged from the fact that a certain number of the Mohawks have already become converts of the Jesuits and taken up their abode in Canada, while many of the Shawnees who come to Albany wear crucifixes given them by the French priests.

Nevertheless, since England can and France cannot produce goods suited to the Indian market, and since the Hudson as a waterway for traffic is immeasurably superior to the St. Lawrence, the English ought to be able to defy rivalry. Colden points out, too, how heavily the French fur trader was weighed down by the duties imposed by his Government. As a consequence, the price given for beaver skins at New York is exactly double the maximum fixed by the Company in which the Canadian fur trade is vested, with the further result that many French traders who bought direct from the Indians actually brought their furs to Albany. Yet by the help of goods bought from English merchants the English were being ousted from their own markets, when, as Colden expresses it, 'in everything beside Diligence, Industry and enduring Fatigues' they 'have much the advantage of the French.' The rulers of Europe during the seventeenth and eighteenth century have often been justly accused of forcing trade out of its natural channels for the sake of imaginary political advantages. If the question had been merely one of commerce, it might have been best that the English manufacturers, the English shipper and the French fur trader should co-operate, each taking that part of the work for which his character and surroundings best fitted him. But no thinking man could consider the position of the two nations in America, the expanding energy and resources of the British colonies, the strenuous and unscrupulous resistance of the French to all such expansion, without feeling that the Indian trade was not an end in itself, but for England a necessary weapon in a defensive war.

Burnet's Indian policy.

The views of Burnet, backed as he was by his advisers, prevailed. Not only was the traffic with Canada in Indian goods prohibited, but a factory for the fur trade was established at Oswego, protected by a fort, built in part at Burnet's own expense.[1] Steps were taken at the same time to secure the Five Nations. Their chiefs met Burnet at Albany in 1722, and confirmed the formal surrender of their land to the King of England made in 1701. We

[1] Smith, pp. 205–21.

may doubt whether the Indians themselves had clear ideas at either time of the nature and extent of the obligations thus incurred. But the surrender might at least be taken as a definite pledge of friendship for the English and hostility to the French.

French retaliation.

There could be no better evidence of the soundness of Burnet's policy than the manner in which it was met by the government of Canada. Forts were established, serving also the purpose of factories, at Niagara, at Toronto, and at Crown Point. The building of the last named was a specially aggressive and audacious measure, little less than a declaration of war, since the fort stood on soil claimed by England. The French fort at Crown Point was in fact an *epiteichisma*, an advanced outpost thrust forward into the enemy's territory.[1]

Burnet's difficulties with the Assembly.

As with Shute in Massachusetts, Burnet's policy was hampered by his disputes with the Assembly, and especially by the jealousy and narrowness of that body in dealing with questions of finance. The defence of the frontier was allowed to languish for lack of funds, and even the work at Oswego had to be completed by Burnet at his own private expense, in the hope of repayment, a hope only in part fulfilled.[2]

In other ways Burnet more justly incurred popular displeasure. He somewhat indiscreetly acted as a partisan in a dispute between two sections of the French Protestant Church.[3] Among those whose displeasure Burnet thus incurred was James de Lancey, a leading politician, wealthy, able, and not over-scrupulous. Burnet, with a tactlessness which was perhaps hereditary, challenged in a somewhat offensive manner De Lancey's right to a seat in the Assembly on the ground that he was not a properly naturalized citizen.

[1] Smith, pp. 224–6. [2] *Ib.* pp. 221–3. [3] *Ib.* p. 228.

This not only offended De Lancey and his adherents, but was also looked on as an intrusion upon the privileges of the Assembly, who claimed the right to determine for themselves the qualification of members. Moreover, Burnet had made himself unpopular by his conduct as Chancellor, being, as even one of his supporters admits, ignorant of law and somewhat precipitate in his decisions.

The accumulated result of all these causes of unpopularity was the election in 1727 of an Assembly strongly hostile to the Governor. One of their first acts was to declare that the establishment of a Court of Chancery without the consent of the Assembly was illegal and a grievance. It was at the same time resolved that an Act should be passed declaring all the proceedings of the Court null and void.[1]

Burnet superseded, and his policy reversed.[2]

Two courses, and two only, were open to the British Government: either to support Burnet, even at the cost of a battle with the Assembly, or else to remove him. They chose the latter, and with Burnet's departure came the collapse of all that defensive policy which he had organized. His successor, Colonel Montgomerie, a respectable placeman, did indeed take measures for securing the friendship of the Iroquois by a conference held at Albany in 1728. But in the following year, through the pressure of those interested in the maintenance of the French trade, the policy of the Home Government was reversed, all restrictions were withdrawn, and the Canadians were again enabled to buy the alliance of the Indians with goods procured in British markets.

The relations of New York to the Indians were so interwoven with those of Pennsylvania, and also, though in a minor degree, with those of Maryland and Virginia, that it is impossible to deal with any of them

[1] Smith, p. 229. [2] *Ib.* pp. 233–5.

as an isolated subject. New Jersey, practically a peninsula, and screened on the landward side by Pennsylvania, was exempt from any possibility of Indian invasion, and stood outside any scheme for alliance or defence. The optimistic and peace-loving attitude of Penn towards the savages had left for his colony a mingled legacy of good and evil. It secured the colony in its young and struggling days against the hostility of the Indians. At a later time it gave a false gloss of religion to a policy which was largely the outcome of sloth, self-interest, and an indifference to all but material considerations, and it did much to prevent Pennsylvania from coming into line with the other colonies in any connected scheme of defence. Penn's policy of relying solely on forbearance and kindness in dealing with the savage was in truth only applicable to the commonwealth of Plato, and wholly out of place among the dregs of Romulus. An administrative ideal forced on men to whom its very phraseology is meaningless is doomed to failure. The practical result of Penn's humanitarianism was to furnish the prosperous citizens of Philadelphia with a pretext for leaving the frontiers of the colony to their fate, and as a necessary consequence to give the half-savage settlers of the frontier an excuse for shaping their policy according to their own standard.

Pennsylvania and the Indians.

One difficulty which confronted the government of Pennsylvania in its dealings with the Indians lay in the fact that they had to deal with a number of tribes, vaguely and uncertainly aggressive, responsible to no central power, influenced in some measure by the Five Nations, yet not under their effective control. And though the Five Nations might be friendly to the English, yet they had not the slightest intention of shaping their dealings with other tribes by regard to the safety or convenience of their white allies. The outlying districts of Pennsylvania, Maryland, and Virginia were of necessity incapable of any scheme of organized defence, and it was therefore all-important to their safety that they should stand well with the Catawbas and Cherokees, the two tribes whose position and power made them dangerous. It needed all the influence which the government of Pennsylvania could bring to bear to prevent the allies or dependents of the Five Nations from attacking these tribes and thereby involving the English in war.

In 1719 we find one French, a leading Pennsylvanian, sent as an ambassador to the Conestago Indians, warning them not to be led into war by the Five Nations, and also in the true spirit of the founder of his colony adjuring them not to torture prisoners.[1] Such conduct is, he told them, 'a violent affront to our government and contrary to the law of the great King, who will not suffer it.' He adds a comment which must have seemed strangely at variance with Indian habits of thought: 'men of true courage are always full of mercy.'

A conference which Logan held in the following year illustrates the same difficulty. Two years before the Governors of Virginia, Maryland, and Pennsylvania had just succeeded in restraining the Five Nations from attacking some of the English allies.[2] Now the trouble had recurred, with the added danger that the Shawnees were taking part with the Iroquois.[3] The account of the conference incidentally brings to light two factors which added to the complication: the lack of effective authority within the Indian tribes, and the evil effect produced by the spectacle of English disunion. The Indians plead that their older and more responsible chiefs would fain keep the peace but cannot control their young warriors. Logan finds it necessary to ex-

[1] For French's mission see Pennsylvania Records, vol. iii. p. 78.

[2] Spotswood's *Letters*, vol. ii.

[3] Pennsylvania Records, vol. iii. p. 92.

plain to the Indians that the English colonies are all one, 'as the Five Nations are.' The speaker, in likening the body of British colonies to a confederation, was formulating a political theory of which he was probably far from grasping the full significance.

Meanwhile hardly a year passed without the Indians receiving an object-lesson in English disunion, by the sight of those dissensions and contests which have been described in an earlier chapter.

Almost at the same date as the conference, the Susquehannah Indians were writing to the government of Pennsylvania to explain the difficulties of their situation. They would fain keep the peace with their southern neighbours, but the Five Nations will not suffer them to be neutral.[1]

If we may believe a letter written by Keith, the Governor of Pennsylvania, to the President of the Council of New York, these complications had for their ultimate cause French diplomacy.[2] The government of Canada had succeeded in so far influencing the Five Nations as to establish peace between them and the Hurons. The warlike spirit of the Iroquois excluded from its proper channel was directed against the Indians in the South. It was a specially ominous sign that one of the confederate tribes, the Cayugas, were protesting against alleged encroachments by Pennsylvanian settlers on the Susquehannah, and that they or their allies had actually been killing the cattle of the English.

Keith and the Indians.

In 1721 Keith held a conference with the Five Nations.[3] His language showed a singular inability to understand the feelings of those whom he addressed, or to grasp the real difficulties of the situation. His vague platitudes as to the evils of war must to Iroquois

[1] Pennsylvanian Records, vol. iii. p. 103.
[2] Keith's letter is in the Records, vol. iii. p. 99. [3] *Ib.* vol. iii. p. 125.

ears have sounded like the vapourings of imbecility or dishonesty. He acknowledged the difficulties which necessarily arose between the Indian and the unauthorized trader upon the frontier. But he could suggest no better solution than the obvious and wholly inapplicable statement that the trader and the Indian must each look after his own interest and make the best bargain he can.

The Indian diplomatist played a more creditable part than the English Governor. He pointed out the advantage which the French enjoyed from their intimate intercourse with the Indians and their mastery of the Indian language. He also showed that he understood the weakness as well as the strength of the French policy. If they had won the alliance of one party, they had made themselves hated and distrusted by the other. When asked whether his people had sold any lands to the French, he replied that they knew the French too well to treat with them.

Keith and Spotswood.

At the same time negotiations were going on between Pennsylvania and Virginia, which strikingly illustrate the injury inflicted on British interests by lack of intercolonial union and co-operation. Spotswood, the Governor of Virginia, proposed to Keith a system of passports for Indians. The Indians occupying the vacant lands which belonged to any colony were to be regarded as specially attached to that colony, and were not to pass into any other without a passport from the Governor of their own colony. The letter in which this suggestion is made also reveals a special danger to which the Southern colonies were exposed by the proximity of the Indians. The Shawnees have been helping negro slaves to escape; Spotswood trusts that Keith will co-operate in preventing this. This brings home to us one of the dangers of slavery, and also the need of some one central power to determine and control British policy. The sequel of the matter illustrates the latter truth even more forcibly. A proposal similar to Spotswood's had been made by Keith to his Council and approved. Yet now, when the scheme was suggested by the Governor of another colony, the same Council refuse to accept it. We cannot wonder that Spotswood should have written back indignantly, complaining that Pennsylvania was isolating itself from the other colonies and making his Indian policy of no effect.[1]

Gordon and the Indians.

In 1727 we find Gordon, the Governor of Pennsylvania, holding a conference with the Indians, at which he propounds views which would have made the founder of Pennsylvania turn in his grave. The Indians complained of being cheated by English traders. Gordon's answer even went beyond Keith's in its cynical avowal of the doctrine *caveat emptor*: 'As to trade they' (the Indians) 'know 'tis the method of all that follow it to buy as cheap and sell as dear as they can, and every man must make the best bargain they can; the Indians cheat the Indians and the English cheat the English, and every man must be on his guard.'[2]

John Penn.

Two years later John, the eldest son of William Penn, and one of three joint Proprietors, came out in person. The Indian has a memory which makes tradition a potent influence, and we cannot doubt that the son of an old friend and benefactor was a *grata persona.* He met representatives from three of the six confederated nations, who made friendly professions. They also warned Penn that if friendship was to be maintained between the English and the Shawnees, and the latter not to come under

[1] For this correspondence see Pennsylvanian Records, vol. iii. p. 203.
[2] *Ib.* p. 27.

French influence, unauthorized traders must be excluded from the valley of the Ohio.[1] Soon after Penn met representatives of the whole Iroquois confederacy. He expected them to use their influence to keep the Shawnees in the Delaware valley, and also not to harbour runaway negroes. In conclusion a treaty of friendship was proposed and accepted.[2]

Governor Thomas and the Indians.

Under Gordon's successor, Governor Thomas, the relations of Pennsylvania with the Indians enter for a term at least upon a new and far more satisfactory phase. In 1739 treaties were made both with the Shawnee and the Susquehannah Indians.[3] Not only did the colony work cordially with its neighbours in endeavouring to retain the alliance of the Five Nations, but Thomas seems to have in some measure informally stepped into the position of the representative and spokesman of all the colonies concerned. In 1742 he held a conference with the chiefs of the Five Nations at Philadelphia. The colony was represented by the Governor and his Council; the Indian spokesman was Conestago, the chief of the Onondagas.

The Conference of 1742.

The proceedings are recorded in the archives of the colony with a fulness and picturesqueness of detail somewhat unusual in official documents.[4] The metaphorical rhetoric of the Indians: the 'clearing of the path' between them and the white men by making due expiation for blood, the 'brightening of the chain' and 'keeping alive the fire

[1] Pennsylvanian Records, vol. iii. p. 433.

[2] *Ib.* p. 447. It is noteworthy that in the record of these proceedings the Mohawks are called Canynngoes, the Senecas Tsanandowans. The name each took seems to have had numerous variants. See Parkman, *Conspiracy of Pontiac*, vol. i. p. 6.

[3] Pennsylvanian Records, vol. iv. p. 333.

[4] *Ib.* pp. 449–578. I cannot help suspecting the hand of Colden. The reports and the subsequent conferences are printed by him as an appendix to his *History*.

of friendship by fresh fuel,' the 'sharpening of the hatchet' by the Governor of Canada, are all recorded with verbal exactitude. So, too, are the apologies for the dirty condition in which they had left the houses in which they had been quartered, 'by their different way of living from the white people,' and their applications on behalf of Conrad Weiser, the interpreter, who has so 'dirtied his clothes by living among them that he has become as nasty as an Indian.'

The proceedings were on the whole friendly; yet there are under-currents suggesting the possibility of dispute. The Indians apologize for their scanty offering of skins. The Englishmen's horses and cows have eaten the grass which used to feed the deer.

Three incidents especially illustrate the complications which inevitably resulted when there was on the one side a number of separate communities having to some extent common interests and acknowledging common sovereignty, but having no machinery with which to guard the former or enforce the latter; on the other side a confederacy exercising a vague and uncertain supremacy over a number of shifting tribes.

The Indians complained that certain persons had, without any right acquired by purchase, settled at Juniata, on the Susquehannah river. Thomas replied that officials had been sent to eject these intruders. The Indians then stated that these officials had actually committed the offence which they were sent to check, surveying the Indian lands with a view to occupation.

They also complained of certain encroachments on the Susquehannah made by settlers from Maryland. The Council thereupon decided that Thomas should at once write to the Governor of Maryland, telling of the wrongs of the Indians and of the danger of reprisals, which might be fatal to friendly relations between the two races.

On two other points the Indians had to apologize for the misconduct of their own people or allies. Certain young members of the confederacy had on their own responsibility sold land to squatters, thus violating the principle that all negotiations for land must be carried on with the government of the colony, not with indviduals.

Conestago also reported that when a party of Twightwy warriors were sojourning in a Shawnee village, their hosts had searched their bags, and there found two white scalps. This they had reported to the Iroquois, who in turn communicated it to the English. The Council thereupon sent a message to the Shawnees telling them that they ought to have thoroughly investigated the matter, ascertained who the natives were, and then reported to the government to which they belonged. Authority exercised in this exceedingly complex and vicarious fashion could not be effective.

In another instance the English had to take advantage of that indefinite sovereignty which the Iroquois exercised over tribes outside their own confederacy. Certain settlers of Pennsylvania were entangled in a territorial dispute with the Delawares. They had endeavoured to practise on that nation a most unscrupulous and unblushing fraud. The Indians had in the previous century made over to the settlers a tract of land. The transfer was called, from its peculiar conditions, the 'Walking Purchase.' The western boundary was to be a day and a half's march from a fixed point. This was no doubt understood by the settlers to mean an ordinary day and a half's march through the forest. The purchasers secured 'a well-girt man,' as Herodotus would have called him, who having been specially trained, helped by a level track laid out for him, and accompanied by horses carrying provisions, accomplished a forced march of eighty-six miles within the time named.[1]

The protest of the Delawares was at once silenced by the aid of Conestago. When the Council of Pennsylvania complained to him, he replied that 'the Delawares were an unruly people, but that we have concluded to remove them, oblige them to go over the river Delaware, and quit all claim to any lands on this side for the future.' He then turned to the Delawares, and in a tone of violent and contemptuous denunciation told them that in their statement made to the Iroquois they had fraudulently concealed the sale of those lands. Even the original sale was an act of disobedience to their superiors and the Iroquois who had conquered them, and in Indian language brought them to the state of women. What right have women to traffic in land? They must leave their habitations which they had usurped, and go either to Wyoming or Shamokin. 'You may go to either of these places, and then we shall have you more under our eye, and shall see how you behave. Don't deliberate, but move away.' It might be well that the unruly Delawares should be kept in order. It was hardly consistent with the dignity or safety of the English that they should delegate the task of control and correction to their Indian allies.

Conference of 1743.

In 1743 territorial disputes arose between the Five Nations and the governments of Maryland and Virginia. In the case of the latter colony a skirmish resulted in which lives were lost on both sides. The government of each colony wisely resolved to make use of the friendly relations already subsisting between Pennsylvania and the Five Nations as a foundation on which to build. A conference was to be held in the

[1] For the story of the 'Walking Purchase' see Hazard's *Register of Pennsylvania*, 1830, pp. 209–213.

following year at Lancaster, in Pennsylvania. Thomas was to preside, but Commissioners from Virginia and Maryland were to be present, and each set of Commissioners was to negotiate with the Indians separately, though not altogether independently. The Commissioners met, and before the conference actually began, Thomas addressed to them some weighty and well-timed words of monition. He pointed out how all-important was the friendship of the Five Nations as a barrier against French aggression, and how suicidal a policy it was to attack and weaken them. 'Every advantage you gain over them in war will be a weakening of the barrier of their colonies, and consequently be in effect victory over yourselves and your fellow-subjects. Some allowance for their prejudices and passions, and a present now and then for the relief of their necessities, which have in some measure been brought upon them by their intercourse with us, and by our yearly extending our settlements, will probably tie them closer to the British interest. This has been the method of New York and Pennsylvania, and will not put you to so much expense in twenty years as the carrying on a war against them will do in one. The French very well know the importance of these nations to us, and will not fail by presents and their other usual acts to take advantage of any misunderstanding we may have with them.'

The Commissioners for Maryland opened the case with a curious mixture of bluster and concession. The Five Nations, they said, had complained to 'Onas' of their treatment at the hands of Maryland, and had declared that if they did not get restitution they would exact it. Such a declaration was rash and inconsiderate. The colonists were well able to defend themselves. Nevertheless, the 'old and wise people' of Maryland had determined to hear the plea of the Five

Nations, and if a good case were made out to compensate them.

As to the lands in dispute, they had been bought ninety years before from the Susquehannah Indians. The Commissioners also pleaded that singular concession by which the Five Nations had thirty years before submitted themselves and their lands to the King of England. It is difficult to think that the Commissioners while arguing that plea can have really believed in its validity. Whatever the action of the Five Nations may have meant, assuredly it did not mean a complete territorial surrender.

The reply of the Indian chiefs was at once vigorous and dignified. They had not indulged in empty threats. They had made a just demand, and when it was refused they 'were resolved to use such expressions as would make the greatest impression on the government of Maryland.' The wisdom of their policy was proved, they said, by the fact that the Maryland Commissioners were now meeting them in conference, and had professed themselves ready to make compensation for any wrong done.

Conestago, who again acted as spokesman, admitted the purchase from the Susquehannahs. But it did not include, so he said, the lands now in question. Those had been conquered by the Five Nations from the Susquehannahs at a later date.

The Onondaga chief went further and took the opportunity to deliver himself as to the general attitude of the Indians towards the settlers. The Indians were sometimes told that they would have perished but for the arms, ammunition, and clothes that they received from the English. That was not so. Before the English came land was plentiful and game was plentiful; in those days stone weapons and bows and arrows sufficed for all the needs of the Indians. There was, the Indian chief said, pointing to the Secretary's table, too much pen-and-ink work for the well-being of the savage. He then illustrated his view by an account of a fraud which we shall probably not be wrong in attributing to Fletcher. The chiefs of the Five Nations were anxious to sell certain lands to Penn. The Governor of New York persuaded them not to do so, but to make him trustee for the lands. When at a later day they decided to sell the lands to Penn they found that the Governor of New York had already sold them to him. Penn, nevertheless, paid the Indians, and either abode by the loss or recovered the money from the fraudulent purchaser.[1]

On the following day the Commissioners for Virginia stated their case. They mentioned that in 1736 the chiefs of the Five Nations had, through Logan, then President of the Council in Pennsylvania, forwarded a demand for compensation for certain lands. But they did not make any references to the dispute of the previous year. What, they asked, was the title of the Five Nations to any land occupied now by Virginians? Nothing had been said about any encroachments at the conference of 1742. And in 1743 the representatives of the Five Nations had made a statement to the Governor of New York implying that they had no claim against Virginia? It does not seem to have occurred to the Commissioners that territorial claims, whether among civilized nations or savages, may be urged or withheld according to circumstances.

[1] I can find no other record of this transaction, but it is far more likely to have been perpetrated by Fletcher than invented by the Indians. Cornbury was morally capable of it, but he, unlike Fletcher, never seems to have taken any interest in Indian affairs. We know, too, that Fletcher was hostile to Penn. By the time that Cornbury was in office Penn was hardly in a financial position to buy land, and if the purchase had been an official one, made by the Governor of the colony, it is hardly probable that Penn would have borne the whole loss.

Conestago replied that the Five Nations had the best of all rights, that of conquest. That was met by the plea that the lands were now unoccupied and desert. Each side was probably right in its premises. The dispute illustrates the difficulty of establishing any sound test of territorial possession in the case of savages.

More discussion followed, of which the details are not important. Practically the victory lay with the Indians, who received from Maryland one hundred pounds in gold, from Virginia two hundred pounds in goods and two or three hundred in gold,[1] in satisfaction of all claims.

After the dispute had been settled the Virginia Commissioners suggested to the Indians that they should send a few of their children to be educated at the college at Williamsburg. They would not only learn English, but also teach some of the younger settlers their own language, and thus further communication between the two races. Weiser, the interpreter, was growing old, and a successor to him might soon be needed.

The suggestion met with a polite refusal. It was to be hoped that Weiser's life would be prolonged. The Indians loved their children too well to part with them, and they were ill-fitted for civilized life.

Spotswood's dealings with the Indians.

This proposal of the Commissioners was but the renewal of a scheme which had been tried thirty years before, not without success. Robert Boyle, the founder of the Royal Society, gave a substantial sum for the education of Indian children in the college of William and Mary.[2] The governors of the college, finding it impossible to attract the neighbouring Indians, complied with the terms of the bequest in a somewhat perfunctory and unsatis-

[1] There is a little ambiguity in the statement of the amount.

[2] Beverley, p. 232. He says, 'Large sums of money,' without specifying the amount.

factory fashion, buying a few children taken in war from distant tribes. Spotswood saw that such a system did little or nothing to improve the relations between the races. He was hindered by the indiscriminating hatred of the settlers for all Indians. But by bringing personal pressure to bear on the Indian chiefs, by inducing the Assembly to forgo certain dues of skins previously paid by the natives, and by spending money out of his own pocket, he secured a number of Tuscarora children, who served as hostages for the good behaviour of that tribe.

Spotswood's official letters furnish not a few striking illustrations of the difficulties which confronted English administrators in their dealings with the Indians. Speaking generally, we may say that those difficulties were threefold.

1. There was not a single colony, either Crown or proprietary, in which the local legislature, except at rare intervals and under the special pressure of some immediate danger, co-operated loyally with the Governor, or in which he could reckon with confidence on the support of the citizens.

2. There were perpetual hindrances due to intercolonial friction and disputes.

3. Though Indian alliances were necessary, yet it was impossible to control and regulate the policy of the Indian allies, or to avoid being entangled in the complications and disputes which arose from their own tribal jealousies.

We have already seen how Spotswood's policy of united action against the Indians was frustrated by the attitude first of North and then of South Carolina. Hardly was the Yamassee war over when the Virginians found themselves entangled in a dispute with the Five Nations. They had been molesting the Catawbas, a tribe friendly to the English.

Dealings of Virginia with the Five Nations.

Also they refused to hold any conference with the English except at Albany. This the Council of Virginia considered to be an insult to the English Government. They forgot that in the eyes of the Indians the phrase, English Government, was meaningless. To them the colonies were separate communities, speaking the same language, and sprung from a common stock, but having no political connexion with one another. Spotswood's recent exploration of the Alleghanies suggested to him the idea of utilizing the mountains as a frontier. The expediency of keeping the Indians beyond that boundary was to be explained to the British Government. A fort was to be erected. An annual conference, with a delivery of presents to the Indians, was to be held in alternate years at the fort and at Albany. It was to be impressed on the Indians that their presents were meant to secure the friendship of the Indians to all the British colonies, not only to that where they were delivered.

Nothing seems to have come of the project for confining the Indians within the bounds of the Alleghanies. But in 1720 the Assembly of Virginia adopted the same policy in a somewhat modified form. No one belonging to any of the tribes subject to Virginia was to go north of the Potomac under penalty of death or transportation. Likewise, no Indian of the Five Nations was to come south of that river.[1] It is difficult to see how such a restriction could be enforced. Who could track, arrest, or if arrested could confidently identify, every hunting party making its way through the forest? Moreover, the scheme implied an amount of co-operation on the part of other colonies which experience had clearly proved to be impossible.

The incident which finally secured for the English the friendship of the strongest and most warlike of

[1] Hening, vol. iv. p. 104.

the Southern tribes, the Cherokees, is among the most strangely romantic in American history. The savage is in many respects like the child, and in none more than this, that in managing him personality is everything, method by comparison nothing. Whenever the Indian was brought into relations of cordial and enduring friendship with either his French or English neighbour, it was through the influence of such an one as Rasle, Schuyler, Livingstone, at a later day Oglethorpe and Johnson. South Carolina found such an one in Sir Alexander Cuming. Had his sphere of operations been in the Northern or Middle colonies, Cuming would no doubt have appeared as a conspicuous figure in colonial history. But the contemporary chronicles of the Southern colonies are few and meagre, and the result is that we know less than we gladly would of one whose career transcends in its strangeness and variety the most daring conception of romance. What should we say of a novelist presenting to his readers a hero who inherited a Scotch baronetcy, became first an advocate, and then an officer in the Russian service, was elected a Fellow of the Royal Society, visited the Western mountains of America in obedience to a dream of his wife's, then became the adopted chief of one of the largest and most warlike among the native tribes, bound it by firm ties of friendship to the English; returned to his mother country with shattered fortunes, strove to redeem them by alchemy, found himself, for once by an obvious and natural consequence, in the Fleet Prison, and died as a Poor Brother of the Charterhouse? Yet such, with perhaps some deductions for the embellishment of details, was Sir Alexander Cuming's career. In March 1730 it became known that the Cherokees were being stirred up against the English by French or Spanish

Sir Alexander Cuming.[1]

[1] For authorities on Cuming see Appendix IV. There seems some doubt about the spelling of his name. I have adopted that used by himself.

emissaries, and also by a section of the neighbouring tribe, the Creeks. Cuming was then in America, having, as he himself avowed, gone thither because his wife dreamed that he did so. The cases of Gordon and Lady Hester Stanhope teach us that the temperament of the fanatic may carry with it an exceptional capacity for dealing with barbarians, and so it seems to have been with Cuming. The British Government, with a promptitude and a felicity in its choice of an agent which did not often mark their colonial policy, authorized Cuming to visit the country of the Cherokees and, if possible, to secure their friendship. In the spring of 1730 he departed from Charlestown. If his own story be true, he, accompanied by an interpreter and a few traders, entered a Cherokee town where a council of three hundred Indians was assembled. Without confiding his project to any of his companions, he walked straight into the council house, carrying arms but concealing them, and required the assembled chiefs to accept the authority of the King of England. They not only submitted, but agreed to summon a conference of the whole tribe to meet Cuming. Cuming visited some other Indian settlements and then returned to meet the conference. Apparently to make negotiations easier and more certain, the chiefs elected one Moytoy as head chief or, as Cuming expresses it, Emperor. The Indians did homage on their knees to the King of England, and offered eagles' feathers, scalps, and other like articles as a sort of symbolical tribute. A report of the conference was drawn up to serve as a permanent record of this acceptance of British sovereignty. It was signed by Cuming and his companions; the Indian chiefs appended their totems.

Cuming then, following the example of Schuyler, brought seven of the chiefs to England. Moytoy would have been of the party but for the sickness of his wife.

The Indians were presented at court and clothed from the royal wardrobe. A picture of them in their civilized habit is extant, or was so late in the nineteenth century. Attached to it is an account of the visit in which the Indians are described as 'remarkably strict in their probity and morality.' Before returning to their own country they accepted a treaty of alliance and commerce, drawn up and submitted to them by the Board of Trade.

Cuming may possibly have embellished the details of his proceedings in America. But the substantial truth of his story is proved by the presence of the Indian chiefs in England, as also by the steadfastness with which the Cherokees held fast to the English alliance. But for this the settlement of Georgia five years later would have been impossible.

General relation of the colonists to the Indians.

The Yamassee war of 1715 was the last occasion when Indian hostility, taken by itself and not regarded as an instrument in French hands, was a source of serious danger to any of the colonies. The presence of the Indian tribes on the frontier, allies of a Power every whit as cruel as the savage, and far more politic and unscrupulous, no doubt did something to hinder extension westward. That it should have been so was in all likelihood a gain to the English. It was well that the tide of westward emigration should not flow lax and unrestrained, that the pioneers of the movement should be forced to regard themselves as a picked vanguard, who could never with impunity cut the bond which united them to the older settlements. As concerned intercolonial relations, the presence of the Indians and their intermittent hostility were influences at once for good and for evil. They forced upon the colonists the need for co-operation and union. At the same time, the habitual failure, at best the partial and incomplete success, which attended all attempts at co-operation must have disheartened those who looked forward to a time when the colonies should be bound together as one organic whole. The latter influences which severed were probably stronger than those which united. The need for union must have been obscured, and its advocates disheartened, by the dissensions which attended every practical attempt at union.

Lack of missionary zeal.

Despite brilliant instances of individual zeal and self-sacrifice, despite much patient and well-organized labour among heathen races who have come under British sway, no one would claim that missionary zeal has been among the special endowments of the English Church or the English nation. Nowhere was that weakness more fully disclosed than in America. The brilliant dreams of extending Christendom which animated the efforts of the Elizabethan colonizers live on only in faint and conventional references among the instructions of royal Governors to the need of mission work. Moreover, if the English colonies as a whole started with a certain natural and inherited lack of aptitude for missionary work, assuredly that deficiency was in the case of each separate colony, or group of colonies, intensified by special causes. The religion of New England was in its essence unbending, exclusive, repellent to all save those whom inherited tradition and early associations had reconciled to its harsher aspects. The Southern colonies had not enough of spiritual enthusiasm or ecclesiastical organization to serve their own needs, far less to undertake work beyond their own borders. South Carolina was ecclesiastically the best equipped of the Southern colonies, and there communication with the inland districts was rendered impossible by physical difficulties, by a belt of impassable swamp and impenetrable forest.

If we turn to the Middle colonies, New York was beyond any of her sisters devoured by the cares of the world and the deceitfulness of riches. In Pennsylvania, indeed, a certain sympathetic tenderness for the savage was an abiding legacy from the days of the founder. Yet even there the zeal and energy of the English settlers would have been wholly unequal to the task, if it had not been supplemented, as we shall see, from a foreign source.

Moreover it is a truism that those elements of civilized life with which the savage must constantly come in contact were just those least fitted to impress him with any respect for the white man. He saw little of the respectable Boston and New York merchant, of the planter in Virginia or Maryland. His dealings were with the poor trader, who cheated him over the sale of fire-arms and powder and debauched him with rum, or with the squatter who had often betaken him to the frontier, because the jurisdiction of a colony over its westward territory was frequently doubtful in theory and always inapplicable in practice.[1]

The repeated enactments in various colonies against the sale of rum to the Indians prove at once the honest desire of the better class of the colonists to check the traffic, and the futility of their efforts. There is indeed something pathetic in the entreaties of the more intelligent and self-respecting of the natives that they and their countrymen should be protected against this prolific source of mischief. In 1733 an Act was passed in Connecticut against the sale of drink to the natives, at the special request of an Indian chief, Ben Uncas.[2] So too, Conrad Weiser, the Indian interpreter for Pennsylvania, reports that in the eyes of the better sort of natives the importation of rum is an abomination before God and man.[3]

[1] For an illustration of this see North Carolina Records, vol. ii. p. 94.
[2] Connecticut Records, 1733, p. 472.
[3] Pennsylvania Records, vol. v. p. 166.

Mrs. Grant points out too, how, even when these causes of demoralization were absent, the mere contact with the life of the white man impaired that of the savage. He became dependent on the trader for clothes and for the fire-arms and ammunition which use had made necessary to him. He lost the primitive virtues of the savage without acquiring the civilization of the white man.

Here and there it may be he put on some semblance of civilization. As early as 1717 the legislature of Connecticut, at the same time that they prohibited all private persons from either buying land from the Indians or selling spirits to them, arranged that the remaining natives in the colony should be formed into agricultural communities, each with a tract of land which might not be alienated.[1] What was the result of this experiment history does not tell us. A like attempt was made in Massachusetts with some success. There, in 1749, a township of Indians was established at Stockbridge, which appears to have lived on for more than a century with a fair share of prosperity.[2]

No doubt in these instances and elsewhere, as the Indian became more or less absorbed into the life of a civilized community, his conversion followed as a consequence. Thus we find the Mohegan Indians making a rather pathetic request for the services of a Christian minister. They cannot do much for him, but they will give him a few oysters and some fish, and a piece of venison if they have luck in hunting.[3] Occasionally, too, we find among the instructions to a Governor a somewhat slight and conventional response to the duty of furthering the conversion of the natives.[4]

[1] Connecticut Records, 1717, pp. 17, 31–2.

[2] Holmes, vol. ii. p. 144.

[3] Hawks and Perry, p. 299. The petition is undated, but apparently is between 1750 and 1760.

[4] *E.g.* the instructions to Morris. New Jersey Archives, vol. vi. p. 15.

That movement was made under the sudden impulse of strong religious feeling. Save under such conditions, there was little likelihood that the Principality would swell the tide of emigration. Fitted though the Welshman is by energy and versatility for colonial life, yet his deep-seated love for the land of his birth and for the associations that surround his home, and his reluctance to be merged in an alien population, would always make banishment distasteful. It could only be endurable when, as in Pennsylvania and Delaware, the colonist carried Wales with him, and remained one of a community speaking Welsh, and inhabiting a home with a Welsh name. It was only under exceptional conditions that such a state of things was possible. Moreover, there was nothing in the material condition of Wales to prompt men to emigrate. Population was scanty, and in proportion to population the resources of the country were abundant. The country, too, was almost purely pastoral, and gave its inhabitants but little training in the arts of tillage. Such emigration as there was from Wales would inevitably tend to attach itself to the existing nucleus, and the presence of Welsh communities in Pennsylvania and Delaware would be an effective bar to their appearance elsewhere. Neither in New England nor in the Southern colonies does the evidence of names suggest the presence of any Welsh element.

The Welsh in South Carolina.[1]

To this, however, there is one exception. In 1736 a body of emigrants from Pennsylvania, mostly but not wholly Welsh, settled in South Carolina. The tract originally granted to them was near the northern boundary of the colony, in the fork formed by the greater and lesser Pedee rivers. Their first home was near the confluence of the two streams. That, however, was soon forsaken for a higher and more

[1] McCrady, vol. ii. pp. 136–7.

wholesome position. The name of the Welsh Neck, commonly applied to the tract which they occupied, showed what was the dominant nationality. The presence, however, of several undoubtedly non-Welsh names, two at least of them French, shows that if the nucleus of the settlement was Welsh, it had, not improbably in the very act of migration to Carolina, taken up and assimilated foreign elements. That did not weaken, but, on the other hand, intensified the effect of the migration in the life of South Carolina. It contributed to that cosmopolitanism which distinguished South Carolina from every other of the Southern colonies, and which saved it from becoming a community made up of English planters and merchants on one side of the line and negro slaves on the other. There was, too, as we have seen, a scheme started in Maryland for introducing Welsh settlers.

Celtic Irish in the colonies.

If the Welsh Celt contributed but little to the population of the colonies, the Irish Celt contributed even less. American politicians in the eighteenth century knew nothing of the troubles of that Irish vote which has weighed so heavily on their successors. This is easy to understand. The Celtic Irishman was unfitted for colonial life, and unacceptable to those already in occupation. The Irish gentleman, smarting under intolerable indignity and injustice, betook himself not to dependencies where the hand of his oppressor might still lie heavy on him, but to some country where the career of a soldier offered him prospects of revenge. The peasant, ignorant, slothful, and unenterprising, had neither the temperament which makes colonial life attractive nor the resources which make it possible. From New England the Irish Papist would have found himself rigidly excluded. Elsewhere there was enough Protestant feeling to make him unacceptable to a large section of communities. The Quaker emigrant either went out as one of a congregation or found a place in such a congregation awaiting him ready made. Moreover, in one respect the Quaker had the advantage over the New England Puritan. He belonged to a society more flexible in its organization. A man passed more easily and readily from one community to another. There was not that intense and exaggerated spirit of cohesion, of which we see the more heroic side in the emigration from Brainford, the narrower and weaker aspect in the opposition to the settlement of Connecticut. From 1682 the tide of Quaker migration from Ireland to America flowed steadily. It has been already said that Quakerism took a far stronger hold in Leinster and Munster than it did in Ulster. Yet it is a noteworthy fact that the number of Quaker emigrants from Ulster was nearly equal to that from Leinster, and more than four times as great as that from Munster. This may have been in some measure due to a personal cause. James Logan was an Ulsterman, and it is not unlikely that the position which he held and the influence which he exercised may have helped to draw emigrants from his own province to Pennsylvania. But over and above that, the men of Ulster, living in an isolated atmosphere of Protestantism, were already marked off by cohesion and tenacity of purpose from the Protestant invader in those districts where even the heavy hand of Cromwell had not wholly crushed out the creed of Rome or the temperament of the Celt.

This migration from Ulster had most important and far-reaching consequences. The Quaker set an example which was speedily followed by the Presbyterian. That the population of Ulster would, under the pressure of material causes, have thrown off swarms, that those swarms would in any case have sought the New World, is probable. But it

Migration of Ulster Presbyterians.

is hardly probable that but for Quaker influence their choice of a home would have been Pennsylvania. As it was before 1721 Presbyterians from Ulster had established themselves in that colony. The uniting power of race was stronger than the separating power of religious differences. We may ignore the latter, and during the period with which we are concerned, that between 1720 and 1760, look upon the emigrants from Ulster as a homogeneous body with a common destiny.

Economical influences favour migration.

Economical causes were at work confirming the results which religion had brought about. In 1699 the English Parliament, in a selfish spirit of monopoly, had destroyed the Irish woollen trade. On none did this blow fall more heavily than on the hard-working Protestant handicraftsman. Further distress was created by failure of crops. Among such that of 1729 stood out in tragic prominence. Moreover the economical disease of the Irish Celt, land hunger, was beginning to make its influence felt. As the crushing force of the Cromwellian conquest passed away, as the policy of James and his servants tended not indeed to redress, but to avenge the wrongs of the Papist population, so the Celtic Roman Catholic, creeping back to the soil from which he had been evicted, tended to raise rents and to break up by competition the profitable land monopoly of the invader.

The original Quaker migration contained two elements, one urban, one rural. It consisted in part of tradesmen and artisans from Dublin, in part of farmers and husbandmen from the north. The former for the most part settled in Philadelphia and were absorbed in the city population. It was through the latter that Irish emigration played so important a part in the history of the colonies.

In none of the colonies was the process of expansion

westward so easy and so spontaneous as in Pennsylvania. The deep indentation of Delaware Bay enabled Philadelphia to combine the advantages of a sea-board and an inland situation. In Pennsylvania, too, the Blue Mountains dip to a somewhat lower level than elsewhere, and thus the capital was at once an Atlantic seaport and an easy and natural starting-point for the backwoods.

Moreover that migratory impulse, which is almost certain to make itself felt among the more energetic and enterprising members of a young population, could find a vent only in one direction. The north-east frontier of Pennsylvania, faced as it was by the Catskill Mountains, and by a country which even now retains much of its primitive wildness, repelled migration just as much as the south-western section of the colony invited it.

The movement not wholly from Pennsylvania.

It is not to be assumed that this movement, which did so much to people the western portions of the Southern colonies, and to leaven those colonies with a new element of incalculable value, was exclusively Irish, or that it had its one and only base in Pennsylvania. There is every likelihood that the Ulster pioneers as they moved on attracted to themselves recruits of kindred opinion and temper. There is direct evidence that congregations both of Irish Quakers and Irish Presbyterians existed in Virginia and in the Carolinas who had made their way direct from the mother country. Thus in 1732 a body of Irish Presbyterians came out, obtaining from the Council of South Carolina a free passage and a tract of land twenty miles square, in what one may call the border land between the swamps of the seacoast and the western hills. There after many hardships they grew into a prosperous community. The name of the settlement was Williamsburg, so named in honour of the hero of the Boyne.[1] But, though these influences may have helped and strengthened the movement, they were not essential to it. As was said before, Pennsylvania was the gateway through which the Ulster migration made its advance.

Importance of the movement.

The importance and value of that migration can hardly be overrated. It leavened the South with a social and industrial element of incalculable value, a witness that the slave plantation was not the only normal and possible form, perhaps not even the best form, of labour. It garrisoned the western frontier with a population very different from the hunters and traders who might otherwise have monopolized it: a population of disciplined and organized communities, trained in an austere creed and in the habits needful for self-government; a population far more akin to the Congregationalists of New England than to the slaveholders of the Southern sea-board. Even into the lawless barbarism of North Carolina the Quaker and Presbyterian immigrants imported some element of cohesion and definite purpose. One can hardly overrate the importance of a movement which tended to break down the barriers between the slaveholder of the South and the yeoman of the North, and to infuse into the members of the future republic something of that unity of principle and sentiment so much needed and so largely absent.

In another way, too, the Irish emigrant did much to unify the colonies by being the first to overcome the more material and mechanical difficulties of communication between the colonies. We can never understand the social and industrial, any more than the military, history of the colonists unless we clearly grasp the fact that before the colonist could move in a line parallel to the Atlantic he must move inland. There

[1] McCrady, vol. ii. p. 132.

could be no easy or expeditious transport along a coast deeply indented with bays and navigable rivers, and lined with dismal pine-barrens and pestilential swamps. Westward these obstacles disappeared; others took their place: pathless forests, wild beasts, Indian ambushes. These the Ulster emigrants overcame, and in the process became a trained and disciplined force, an advanced guard in the conquest of the west.

Scotch settlers.

There was no collective and corporate migration from Scotland similar to that from Ireland. Scotch settlers did indeed, as we have already seen, find their way into the Middle colonies. But the Scotch wave of migration to New Jersey soon came to an end, and there was no renewal of any similar attempt elsewhere. Scotch colonists no doubt there were, but such migration was isolated and as one may say accidental, neither continuous nor organic. There were causes enough in the condition of Scotland to explain this: military service in the continental armies of Europe had traditional attractions for the Scot, as it had for the Irish Celt, and furnished a vent to relieve that pressure which was at times caused not by over-population, but by lack of resources. The experiment of Darien, too, had made the very name of colonization under the English Crown odious in Scotland, and that rapid increase of commercial prosperity which followed the Union found full employment for all the capital and all the labour which the country could provide. The Highlanders in Georgia were a garrison rather than a settlement. After the 'Forty-five a body of Jacobite refugees, Flora Macdonald and her family among them, took refuge in South Carolina, and there proved as loyal to the House of Brunswick as they had been to that of Stuart. But as far as the general temper and character of the community went their influence was non-existent.

As was just said, the Middle colonies were in some measure an exception. The names of Hunter, Burnet, Montgomerie, Colden, and William Smith remind us how large a part men of Scotch blood played in the official life of New York and New Jersey. There was also a scheme on foot in 1739 for a Highland colony which if carried out might have had far-reaching effects. Clarke, who was then Lieutenant-Governor of New York, proposed to establish a settlement of Highlanders at Wood Creek, a point a little east of Lake George, and commanding one of the chief passages from Canada to New York. Unfortunately there was a delay, and before the project could be put in force the Commissioners for Indian Affairs reported that the French had occupied the spot.[1]

Two explanations of the delay have been given. Colden, then Surveyor to the Colony, stated at a later date that the Assembly were lukewarm in their support of the scheme and dilatory in finding the needful funds.[2] But if we may believe a leading public man who took part in the dispute, the refusal was made through a suspicion that Clarke and Colden favoured the scheme for the sake of the official fees which it would bring with it.[3] Be that as it may, it is clear that here, as so often in New York and in other colonies, the inability of the citizens and the officials to work together was fatal to a measure which might have done much to strengthen the frontier and curb French aggression.

Of the various non-British[4] elements which entered into the composition of the colonial population, that

[1] New York Documents, vol. vi. pp. 144–6.

[2] Colden's letters on the subject are printed in the second volume of the New York Historical Society's Collections.

[3] Smith, vol. ii. p. 50.

[4] It is almost needless to say that British is here used in its later political, not in its earlier ethnological, sense.

contributed by French Protestantism was, though perhaps not the most numerous, by far the most important. The influences under which the Huguenot had been trained were not unlike those which had moulded the character of the Ulster Presbyterian. Each held the same creed. Fatalism, whether it be the fatalism of Calvin or the fatalism of Mohammed, is the creed which of all others breeds and sustains fighters. The austerity, the persistence, and the self-reliance which are begotten of Calvinism were in both the Ulsterman and the Huguenot confirmed and intensified by the discipline of life. Both had fought and suffered for their creed. The persecution of the Huguenot had, it is true, been far more severe and more persistent. But he had never, any more than the Ulsterman, sunk into a state of passive martyrdom. Like the Ulster Presbyterian, he had been a strenuous combatant, holding to his faith as to a fort hard pressed by a hostile majority, actively as well as passively daring, as ready to inflict pain as to bear it. Yet, along with these points of likeness, there were points of difference hardly less strong or less essential. In the Scotch Presbyterian, Calvinism had been grafted on to a stock already predisposed to all that was most characteristic in the creed. In the Huguenot the oyous and versatile temper of the Frenchman was overlaid but not destroyed by Calvinistic teaching, and might revive in brighter and happier surroundings. Nor had the French Protestant ever become to the same extent as the Ulster Presbyterian separated from the surrounding world. He had not formed one of an isolated community amid an alien, a hostile, and as he deemed an inferior, race.

The Huguenot in the colonies

Moreover the Huguenot was for the most part a townsman, as the Ulster Presbyterian was a tiller of the soil. Thus the Frenchman had neither the training nor habits which could have enabled him to do the work which was done by the Irishman, to lead the way in a migration steadily moving forward in organized communities. The task for which the Huguenot in America was fitted, and which he fulfilled, was to leaven the industrial and commercial life of the seaboard with his own qualities—versatility, enterprise and manual skill.

Moreover, while the Ulsterman seldom brought more than his one form of labour and the small capital needed by the colonial farmer, the Huguenot was not unfrequently a well-to-do man of business. Huguenot merchants play a leading part in the commercial life of New England and New York. Two of the most conspicuous figures in Boston commerce during the eighteenth century were Peter Faneuil and Amory. To the gratitude of the former towards his adopted country Boston owes the building of Faneuil Hall, associated with so many stirring scenes and with political battles whose issues were felt far beyond the precincts of Massachusetts. His business records do more than those of any among his contemporaries to throw light on the nature and extent of New England trade in pre-Revolution days. The history of the Faneuil family also well illustrates the ubiquity and the versatility of the French Huguenot, and the fashion in which he served to link together the various colonies of British origin. Two Faneuil brothers emigrated from France, the one to New York, the other to Boston. The former again moved his abode to Rhode Island, while his son, the well-known Peter Faneuil, joined his uncle at the capital of Massachusetts. Well may an American writer call the family history an epitome of cosmopolitanism.[1]

Beside the Faneuils the names of Bowdoin and

[1] Weedon, p. 608.

Sigourney remind us of the part played by descendants of the Huguenots in the political and intellectual activity of New England. So, too, in New York, the De Lanceys were foremost among those great capitalist families whose action so largely influenced the history of the colony not always for good.

Germans in the Southern colonies.

Over and above these various migrations of religious bodies there was much isolated and, as one may call it, secular migration, in some cases due to the attempts of English administrators to introduce a new industrial element. Of the Palatines brought in by Hunter I have already spoken. In 1714 Spotswood established a settlement of German miners in the Tuscarora county.[1] In 1735 two hundred Palatines were imported to South Carolina—as they were technically called, Redemptioners.[2] They were in the same position as the indented servants of Maryland and Virginia. The importer was paid so much a head by the purchaser, and the persons imported then earned their freedom by a period of service.

The district which they occupied was formed into a county, entitled Orangeburg. Irish emigration, as we have seen, gave birth to a Williamsburg, and thus the hero of British and continental Protestantism was doubly celebrated in South Carolina.

The Swiss in South Carolina.

A far less successful attempt at settlement was made by certain Swiss, under the leadership of a sanguine or dishonest projector, Jean Pierre Purry. So resolved were the colonists to identify themselves with their new abode that they were accompanied by two ministers of their own nationality, probably Lutherans, who obtained episcopal ordination in England.

[1] Letters, vol. ii. p. 70.

[2] The *South Carolina Gazette*, quoted by McCrady, vol. ii. p. 129.

Swiss mountaineers might, if transported to the uplands of Vermont or the banks of the Hudson, have formed a valuable addition to the population of the British colonies. But, as might have been foreseen, the climate and the industries of South Carolina were wholly unsuited to them. A proposal was made to transfer them to North Carolina, but nothing seems to have come of it.[1] So disastrous was the result of the settlement, called after its founder, Purrysburg, that the cantonal governments of Zurich and Berne forbade further emigration.[2] The original settlers died or dispersed.

Germans in Pennsylvania.

In Pennsylvania the migration of Germans was so extensive and at the same time so wanting in system and control as to be a serious embarrassment to the government. Apparently Keith allowed them to settle on Indian territory without any attempt at purchase or compensation, and thereby endangered the relations of the colony with the natives. In 1727 Gordon complains that four hundred Palatines are making their way into the colony without leave from the Crown or the Proprietors, and probably as the result of his complaint in 1728 he reported to the Assembly that he had orders from Great Britain 'to provide against those crowds of foreigners who are yearly poured in upon us.'[3]

That the evil continued or recurred is shown by an enactment passed in 1749. This set forth that Germans were unwholesomely crowded together and were thus a cause of sickness, and it compelled shipmasters bringing such emigrants to provide proper food, and to limit their number of passengers in proportion to their stowage room.[4]

[1] Memorial from Rodolph in N. Car. Records, vol. iv. p. 139.

[2] This is stated in Rodolph's memorial.

[3] Pennsylvania Records, vol. iii. pp. 282, 324, 342.

[4] Laws of Pennsylvania, 1749.

pauperism, a safety-valve for that poverty and misery which seems the inseparable accompaniment of rapid material prosperity, a refuge for the so-called 'breakages of society.' Furthermore the battles of the Old World were to be fought in the New. Our colonies were to balance and control the Transatlantic empire of Spain. We see into what strange and unlikely channels that stream of thought had run when we find a little band of persecuted Brownists pleading to be allowed to settle in Canada, that they may there 'annoy the bloody and persecuting Spaniard.'[1] Lastly, the colonist was to be a missionary. That Gospel light which had succeeded to centuries of Romish darkness was to be spread among the yet heathen natives of an unexplored continent. Such were the aspirations which have come down to us in countless sermons and pamphlets.

Constraint between the ideal and the actual.

The actual course of English colonization dealt with lower motives and contented itself with more commonplace successes. Its aims, its methods and its results had nothing in common with those imagined by Gilbert and his fellows. Spain ceased to be a source of danger; the meagre resources of the English colonies gave them no scope for a policy of extension or aggression southward. The crusading dreams of the Elizabethan age were exchanged for the dreary realities of the Pequod war, of the struggle with

the Progress of Georgia, 1743. The case of Oglethorpe's opponents is stated with some cleverness, but much acrimony, shallow sarcasm and obvious misrepresentation in a pamphlet entitled *A True and Historical Narrative of the Colony of Georgia*, 1741. Two authorities of considerable value are: *A Voyage to Georgia*, by Francis Moore, 1744. Moore was for some time store-keeper to the colony. *History of Georgia*, published in Dr. Harris's *Collection of Travels*, vol. ii. pp. 323–47. London, 1764. The journals of John and Charles Wesley are valuable authorities for those events in which they took part. Wright's *Life of Oglethorpe*, 1867, and Jones's *History of Georgia*, 2 vols., 1883, are careful and laborious works, based on very full research. Mr. Wright's admiration for Oglethorpe makes him at times somewhat uncritical.

[1] *Puritan Colonies*, vol. i. p. 36.

Philip, of inroads, sieges and skirmishes on the Canadian frontier, often fruitless, never adequate in their results.

Nor was the material gain less widely at variance with what was expected. Every feature of colonization presented to the Elizabethan age had in its foreground visions of El Dorado. The experience of thirty years of actual colonization served wholly to dispel them. The men who sailed with Winthrop had learnt to look on such hopes as no better than the dreams of the alchemist. Nor was that all. With those visionary hopes had been joined others, seemingly more sober, yet in real truth almost equally doomed to disappointment. The early experience of Virginia showed that the New World with all its resources and advantages could never become on any large scale a refuge for the thriftless and unprosperous. All colonial history was the confirmation of Bacon's warning against planting with 'the scum of people and wicked condemned men.' It was soon seen that those who really made the strength and backbone of our colonies were men who at home would in all likelihood have won for themselves by patience and enterprise a fair share of the world's good things. Our plantations had done but slight and indirect service in relieving those grosser forms of poverty which are bound up with ignorance and suffering, and are the parents of crime.

No one with the history of New England before him can dispute that the colonies had done a definite religious work of reality and importance. But assuredly it was not the work contemplated by those who first designed and directed our colonial system. The Churches of New England had been conspicuous as the homes of individual piety, and, though with limitations and drawbacks, as centres of corporate spiritual life. But they had done nothing to enable Protestant Catholicism to face Roman Catholicism as a compact and organized whole. On the other hand they had done much to develope the opposite tendency, to break up the Church of the Reformers into opposed and discordant sects. Those missionary hopes which had filled the minds of such men as Crashaw and Copland had been hopelessly scattered to the winds. The attitude of the settlers to the savages had ranged from merciless hostility to half-contemptuous kindness. Here and there we had given them some small share of the material gains of civilization, more than balanced by the degradation which accompanies its baser side. The pious labours of isolated men such as Gookin and Eliot, the spirit of justice and humanity with which Penn imbued his followers, had done something to redeem the credit of their countrymen, to brighten the dealings with the savages, and to lighten the inevitable misery of the conflict between barbarism and civilization. But the heathenism of a continent remained unbroken, almost untouched.

The settlement of Georgia.

For more than a century the colonies had gone on in the varied paths which their material conditions seemed to mark out for them, with destinies determined by outward conditions of coast line, climate and soil, by the habits and beliefs which the settlers brought out with them, and by the wishes and theories of statesmen at home. The projects and hopes which in the sixteenth century filled the minds of all those who thought about America at all seemed dead and buried. Suddenly a historical cycle seems to re-open. In the colonization of Georgia the old schemes seem to revive in a narrower field and in less ambitious forms. To curb the Spaniard in Florida, to carry a knowledge of Christian truth to the savage, to find prosperous homes for those whom vice, thriftless folly, and the harshness of the world, working together, had made wretched and homeless—these were the tasks which the founder of Georgia set before him, and in which he won some share of success, greater assuredly than had followed the more venturous schemes of earlier days, as much, one may fairly say, as the inherent difficulties of the various problems permitted.

James Oglethorpe.

The period which lies between the Revolution and the accession of George III. is peculiarly an age of biography. Pope's doctrine that the proper study of mankind is man had been accepted, and applied not to man as a philosophical abstraction, but to individual men and women. The crude, transparent advocacy of Burnet, the better veiled though more partial advocacy of Swift, have furnished us with pictures of their contemporaries often, it may be, misleading, but never lacking in life. What they did for their own generation, Hervey and Walpole have done more artistically for the next. Even writings which would usually fall into more abstract forms have not escaped the general tendency. The social and moral speculations of Sterne and Addison, the satire of Pope, even the spiritual teaching of Law, have left us vivid pictures of actual men and women. Thus in studying the drama of eighteenth century history we move among the actors as among familiar friends. It is seldom, however, that colonial history comes in any way into contact with this full-flowing stream of biography. But if he had never crossed the Atlantic, if Georgia had never come into being, Oglethorpe would still live for us in the pages of Boswell and Walpole, and other less known social chroniclers.

By birth James Oglethorpe belonged to what one may call the constitutional and moderate wing of the Jacobite party. His father, Colonel Theophilus Oglethorpe, the head of an old Yorkshire house, did good service at Bothwell Bridge and against Monmouth.

He played a part against the Prince of Orange active and conspicuous enough to lead to the loss of his commission. But he appears to have kept free from the political intrigues of his party, and he twice sat in Parliament during the reign of William. Two at least of his children drifted further into Jacobitism than their father. Theophilus, the eldest son, lived as an exile and figured in the Jacobite peerage of St. Germains. His sister Anne earned like rank by a connexion which she did something to redeem by loyalty and good sense, too rare among the advisers of the Old Pretender. The support given by James Oglethorpe to the fallen cause was of a soberer type, and after the Hanoverian accession he enlisted himself among the followers of Windham. The outward conduct and policy of Oglethorpe reflected the more rational and reputable side of Jacobitism. His temper and character, and they are not hard to decipher, remind one of all that is best in that creed, as disclosed to us by the writer who above all others understood its strength and weakness. The genial courtesy, the ready wit, the fearless simplicity of Oglethorpe, tempered by a vein of wayward eccentricity, would have furnished Scott with a companion figure to the Baron of Bradwardine. It is well for such men when party obligations do not sit too heavily on them. The men who can render effective service under a system of party politics are either those whose principles are held so loosely that they can be pared down or extended as needful, or those who hold a few great principles with such overwhelming and tenacious conviction that the sacrifice of all that is not essential seems as nothing. Oglethorpe assuredly rose above the one type. He hardly attained to the other. The condition of his party suffered him to play the part for which he was best fitted, that of a free lance.

Of the three features of special interest which attach to the colonization of Georgia, two do not come before us till the colony is fairly launched on its career. The utility of the settlement as an outpost against the Spaniard in Florida, the part which it played as a centre for the missionary operations of the Wesleys, these were minor and incidental objects quite secondary to the main purpose for which the colony existed. The supreme interest of Georgia in its early days lies in the fact that it was the first attempt to devote a colony systematically and exclusively to the relief of pauperism. One may go further and say that it was the first attempt by any one definite organized scheme of industry to cope with the problems of poverty. Here lies the real interest of the story, an interest by which in colonial history it stands alone.

His colonial policy.

A figure like that of Oglethorpe seems to stand out among the corrupt and place-hunting officials of the Hanoverian age, like Max Piccolomini among the intriguers of Wallenstein's camp. Yet Oglethorpe did not so much rise above his age, as reflect a side of it which is often overlaid by its more striking or more obvious characteristics. In many respects the eighteenth century deserves the stigma laid upon it: in a certain sense it may be fairly called prosaic and unimaginative. Its literature was confined and one-sided; its art, looked at as a whole, lacked grace, fancy and imagination; its religion was cautious, superficial and unspiritual. We, living in an age which has freed itself from these failings, which, when it errs, errs in ways widely different, see only these things, and are blind to the better aspects of that century. It has suffered from its very admirers and advocates. They have dwelt on the outward features of the time, features which they would describe as 'quaint,' and have been unjust to that vein of real heroism which runs through the public life of the time. If the eighteenth century was the age of Addison and Horace Walpole, it was in a far more abiding sense the age of Chatham and Wolfe and Clive. Oglethorpe's career was on a small scale the foretaste of that adventurous and public-spirited heroism to which we owe our Canadian and our Indian empires.

In one respect, however, Oglethorpe undoubtedly did rise above his age. It is hardly an exaggeration to call him the founder of modern philanthropy. Hitherto public men had acquiesced in the existence of vice, ignorance and squalor combined, not as isolated plague spots, but forming what one may call a solid phalanx in the midst of our social life. They were prepared so far to accept Mandeville's doctrine of the utility of private vice, as to believe that much social evil was an inevitable accompaniment, probably a needful condition, of material prosperity. Men accepted as inevitable a condition of things such as we see in Hogarth's Gin Alley, in the perversion of justice and the administrative tyranny at the expense of the poor painted for us by Fielding.

Oglethorpe first, and for a while alone among public men, saw and acknowledged that the community was largely responsible for the suffering of its poorer members, that to remedy and prevent such suffering was a task which needed, if not the interference of government, at least some systematic and organized effort.

It is worth noting that Oglethorpe's labours in this matter moved on lines somewhat different from those who in later days have followed in his footsteps. It was not the condition of the wage-earning classes that chiefly excited his pity. Both for the peasant and the artisan, the first half of the eighteenth century was a time of rapidly increasing prosperity. The evil which specially stirred up Oglethorpe to his work of reform was the suffering of the imprisoned debtors. That mania of speculation which soon after the accession of George I. ran through all trading classes, great and small, of which the South Sea Bubble was but the most noteworthy and widespread instance, must have filled the debtors' prisons with victims, often deserving of no moral blame, yet exposed to the wrath of creditors themselves half-ruined, and therefore necessitous and vindictive.

Oglethorpe's first appearance as a public man was in obtaining a Parliamentary inquiry into the condition of the debtors' prisons. The results of that inquiry forced upon him the conviction that for the victims there could be no hope save a fresh start in a new world.

Sir Robert Montgomery's project.

The relief of the distressed was not, however, the only motive which urged Oglethorpe to take up colonization. The presence of Spanish neighbours to the south had long been a source of danger to South Carolina. It was a danger, too, which the colony was ill-fitted to face. The population was sparse, the Indians on the western marches were warlike and unfriendly, the slaves were constantly escaping to the Spaniard, and serving to replenish a negro regiment which might at any moment be used against the colony. More than one project had been set on foot for a military colony, designed to cover the frontier of South Carolina. One of these was at least ambitious enough to deserve special notice. Among the followers of Lord Cardross in his ill-starred attempt to colonize in South Carolina was a Nova Scotia baronet, Sir Robert Montgomery. His son and successor, also Sir Robert, undeterred by his father's misfortunes and by the tragic results of the Darien settlement, revived Lord Cardross's project in a vague form. He obtained from the Proprietors of South Carolina so much of the province as lay beyond the Savannah. To this province or, as he not unfittingly called it, Margravate, he gave the name of Azilia. Colonial history can show us not a few wild schemes of fortunes to be made without risk or effort out of the boundless resources of the New World. But of all such schemes, those of Sir Robert Montgomery are probably the wildest and most extravagant. They are set forth by him in what may be called in modern language a prospectus, inviting subscriptions. In this the soil of the Margravate is offered in lots of five acres or more, at forty shillings an acre. The purchasers, however, are not to be in the position of colonists or landowners, so much as shareholders. As far as one can understand Sir Robert's proposals, he was to administer the agriculture and trade of the colony for the joint benefits of the whole body of subscribers. Only half the capital subscribed was to be called up. In addition to a dividend on their capital every subscriber of five hundred pounds was at a future day to receive as a bonus, six hundred and forty acres of land with a house. The province was to be parcelled out into symmetrical departments, each securely fortified against Spanish invasion. The colony was to make the English consumer independent of foreign markets. Coffee, tea, figs, raisins, currants, almonds, olives, silk, wine, cochineal, 'and a great variety of still more rich commodities,' 'all these,' the Proprietor announced, 'we shall certainly propagate.' At the same time he modestly admits that these are distant views. For the present the profits of the shareholders were to come from potash and rice. The labour of a single man is to cost the shareholders thirty-three pounds a year, and will in either of the industries produce fifty pounds. The ordinary cost of boiling potash was to be greatly reduced by some process not explained, whereby all metal would be dispensed with.[1]

Nothing in this wonderful document is more amazing than the unquestioning confidence with which the projector appeals to the public. One is reminded of Subtle's promises to Sir Epicure. There are no doubts, no hints at the possible need of modifying his schemes in the future. Sir Robert describes his province of a hundred and sixteen squares each a mile on every side, the four great parks filled with all kinds of cattle, and the city with 'a large void space affording a fine view of the city in drawing near it,' and with 'the Margrave's house containing all sorts of public edifices for dispatch of business.'

Montgomery anticipates, only to dismiss with magnificent scorn, the suggestion that it might be well to have trustees, or as we should rather call them directors, to look after the interests of the shareholders. And it must be admitted in justice that Montgomery argues with some shrewdness against the evils of divided counsels, and illustrates his point effectively from the early history of colonization. Intending shareholders might probably have felt that, though the government of a directorate might be bad, that of one who was either a wild enthusiast or an unscrupulous projector would be worse. No attempt was made, as far as history shows, to put Montgomery's schemes into practice. The design itself is an episode of some little interest as illustrating the wild projects of speculation which were floating in the air. As far as colonial history goes, it has but a negative importance. If

[1] Montgomery's Prospectus, entitled 'A Discourse concerning the designed establishment of a New Colony to the South of Carolina, the most delightful country in the Universe,' was published in 1717. It is reprinted in Force's *Tracts*, vol. i.

Montgomery's schemes had been a little more sane or more sanely expressed, if they had had in them just enough show of reason and sobriety to enlist any followers, they might have discredited Oglethorpe's projects and laid practical difficulties in his way.

Inception of Oglethorpe's scheme.

The scheme of a colony south of Carolina, a mark as one may call it, appealed to Oglethorpe's two ruling passions, philanthropy and soldiership. He saw that the projects of a pauper colony and a military outpost might be combined, and he doubtless felt that each scheme would strengthen the other by enlisting different supporters and appealing to different sets of motives. His first step was to get partners and capital. On June 9, 1732, a body of trustees, twenty-one in number, was incorporated by charter.[1] Two only of the names besides that of Oglethorpe meet one in the general history of the time. One was George Heathcote, a member, though not a prominent one, of the constitutional Jacobite party who followed Windham ; the other Lord Percival, afterwards Lord Egmont, an independent and somewhat wayward politician. It would seem as if the colonial scheme had the good fortune not to be identified with any party, political or ecclesiastical.

The charter described the partners as trustees, and their functions were strictly limited in accordance with that description. They were expressly debarred from enjoying any direct pecuniary interest in the colony either as landholders or as paid officials. A careful system of audit was enforced, whereby the accounts of the trust had to be annually submitted to the Lord Chancellor, the two Chief Justices, the Chief Baron, and the Master of the Rolls. Private contributions

[1] The charter is printed in the *True and Historical Narrative.*

came in to the amount of rather more than three thousand seven hundred pounds.[1]

Although the military side of Oglethorpe's scheme counted for something in his own mind and that of his supporters, yet the establishment of the colony as a means for the relief of distress came first. Elsewhere in the gallantry of Oglethorpe and his Highland soldiers, in the mingled self-devotion and self-will of the Wesleys, we have incidents full of dramatic and biographical interest. To those who study colonial history in a serious and scientific spirit, the special importance of Georgia in its early days lies in the battle between industry, organized and guided by benevolent intelligence, and pauperism. Regarded thus the history of Georgia in its first years has a unique value. For the most part the conditions of colonial life were so simple and so favourable, and its economical problems therefore so easy of solution, that from that point of view colonial history does not carry with it much profitable instruction. The efforts of the legislature in the early days of New England to control wages and prices show the hopeless and unpractical nature of such attempts. Later colonial history reminds one of the economic evils of a reckless issue of inconvertible paper money. But in neither of these instances can we say that colonial history does more than illustrate what all sane men recognise as true. No one believes, no one but a party politician pretends to believe, that the ordinary laws of demand and supply can be suspended for his own special benefit. But the problem which the founders of Georgia set themselves to solve lies in that debateable land between politics and economics, where every ray of light which can be gained from practical experience is valuable.

Special interest of the history of Georgia.

[1] *Account showing the Progress*, &c., p. 13.

It is one of those questions where the teaching of abstract economy fails, because many of the premises lie wholly outside its sphere. Political economy will tell us what will be the ultimate result of certain conditions if things are left to themselves. But it may be that the matter which concerns the legislator and the man of affairs is not the ultimate result, but some intermediate stage. That does not make it otherwise than folly to ignore the plain teaching of economy. But it should remind us that political economy only teaches, while public morality or public expediency commands.

To gather together those who form the waste and wreckage of society, to form them into an industrial community isolated more or less from the world in which they have lived and failed, to give them a fresh start, free from the evil influences which have surrounded them, is a project which has commended itself in one form or another to successive generations of social reformers. The dangers and drawbacks are too obvious to need stating. It is no exaggeration to say that they are enough in the eyes of any thinking man to make complete success unattainable. But the problem is one where something very far short of complete success may be worth aiming at. The questions which a practical man will ask himself in considering any such scheme are: whether the industrial machine thus constructed will work at all, and whether the relief given will in the long run find those relieved happier and more prosperous than they would have been otherwise; lastly, and perhaps most important, what will be the effect on those outside the scheme, how far the need for thrift and shrewdness in business must be enforced by the visible consequences of their absence. How far did Oglethorpe and his allies understand these difficulties, face them and overcome them? Therein lies the main interest of the early life of Georgia. The last question, the measure of success reached by the colony as a social and economical experiment, is practically answered in the events which lie before us. The views of Oglethorpe and his fellow-trustees are clearly shown in the provisions of the charter and in the pamphlets issued by Oglethorpe himself.

It is to be noticed at the outset that the scheme was at least free from certain dangers to which projects of the kind are liable. It did not profess to be very wide-reaching in its aims. The colony was to start with but a little over a hundred settlers. Even if it failed, failure could not be very disastrous in its consequences when the experiment was made on so modest a scale. There was ample room for careful selection of emigrants. No one could fear that the terrors of the debtors' prison would be sensibly lessened by such slight alleviation. More plausibly might it be urged that the relief thus given covered so small a field as to be well nigh worthless.

This, too, was an advantage in another way. Benevolent schemes of the kind always reach the stage of danger when they outgrow individual supervision, and become dependent on official machinery. But here the colony was of a size which would allow of the control of a single man of strong will and active intelligence, and such an one was forthcoming in Oglethorpe.

Details of the scheme.[1]

The original instructions to emigrants fenced in the colony with precautions, and show that the founders were alive to some of the special dangers ahead. The object aimed at was the creation of a number of small independent freeholders. It is always a manifest objection to such a scheme that the distribution of land will be determined not by legislative

[1] For what follows see *Account showing the Progress*, and the History in Harris's voyages.

enactment but by economical causes. Where the small landholder is the natural product of such causes he will hold his ground; where he is the artificial creature of legislation he will sell or mortgage his holding and vanish. To guard against this every precaution was taken to check such alienation. Not merely was it forbidden save under special permission, but the estate granted was not one in fee simple, but in tail male. Failing male issue the holding was to revert to the trustees, who in re-granting were to have special regards to the sons-in-law or maternal descendants of original tenants. The reasons given for these restrictions are instructive. Free sales of land would be fatal to the general design of the colony. Lots would get consolidated, men would own more land than they could clear, and their uncleared ground would be a nuisance to their neighbours. The thriftlessness which had brought the colonists into their present case showed that they were unfit to be trusted with discretionary control over their own estates. Moreover it was needful that the trustees should continue to enjoy the right of admission and exclusion to the colony, a right plainly inconsistent with the free sale of land. The main objects of the colony would be frustrated if Spanish or French Papists found their way in.

Partly on these grounds the importation of negroes was absolutely forbidden. It was apprehended that if slaves could be bought there would be a temptation to landholders to mortgage their estates. In all likelihood the military danger from the presence of a slave population and the general interference with the special industries of the colony were equally strong motives. The trustees had before their eyes the examples of Carolina and Virginia, and they saw from those that slave labour almost inevitably begot a system of large estates, the existence of which would undo the very objects for which the colony was formed. The poorer settlers would prefer the post of an overseer to the life of a small yeoman working on his own holding. Large plantations might encourage the existence of absentee landholders. Again the peculiar industries which suited slave labour, such as the rice plantations of South Carolina, would interfere with silk-growing and the other resources on which the trustees relied. The founders of the colony also clearly saw that slavery if it is to exist must stand alone, and that the slave and the free labourer cannot stand side by side.[1] Moreover the yeoman farmer tilling his own land would never work with his own hands among a gang of negroes as he would with his free labourers.

The restriction of the holdings to tail male illustrates another side of the intended life of the colony. The system was feudalism on a small scale, tenure of land by military service. The main purpose of the colony might be thwarted and disarranged if one of the holdings passed into the hands of a woman. Throughout, as was said above, the trustees did much to ensure success by the sober modesty of their aims. They did not hold out to those who contributed money the faintest hope even of ultimate profit. The colony was to support itself by its own industry; that was enough. The foundations were to be laid tentatively with a party of emigrants small enough to be under the direct control of Oglethorpe. They might in some sort be looked on as pioneers. The trustees, too, abstained from committing themselves in advance to any elaborate projects of industry or trade. So, too, the character and dimensions of the colony released the founders from the need of making any present arrangements as to its constitution. For the present Oglethorpe was to be Governor, with the powers of a magistrate. All judicial machinery

[1] This is clearly expressed in *The Impartial Inquiry*.

might be created by the trustees as the growing wants of the colony should make it needful. For military purposes the Governor was in the event of joint operations to be subordinate to the Governor or Commander-in-Chief of South Carolina.

The authority, or rather the official existence, of the trustees was strictly limited in time. After twenty-one years Georgia was to become a Crown colony. Thenceforth the nomination to all offices, the formation of all judicial and legislative machinery, and the division of powers between officials and departments were left to the discretion of the Sovereign.

The task of selecting emigrants was left to two committees of the trustees. One was to visit the debtors' prisons and choose such persons as seemed specially suitable. The other was to receive and investigate applications.[1] This mode of proceeding allowed the choice of settlers specially suited for the various needs of the community. The trustees could in fact construct a carefully organized labour gang. By October 1732, a hundred and fourteen emigrants were selected, formed from thirty-five families.[2] Unfortunately no record is extant to show what number over and above the heads of these families were able labourers. But we can at least see that the colony was designed to be a complete, organic, self-sufficing community.

Selection of emigrants.

Oglethorpe's writings show that he was not likely to err in overrating the competence of his settlers. He did not delude himself into the idea that there was any magic in colonization which would transform thriftless paupers into prosperous and industrious citizens. Opponents of the colony had argued that if men had a mind to work they could work in England. Oglethorpe scoffs at the idea that those who have never

[1] This is stated by Mr. Wright, p. 53. I have failed to trace his authority.
[2] *Account showing the Progress.*

learnt manual work by practice can suddenly turn to and compete with regular labourers. Let those who argue thus try their own powers. One of them will soon find that he is less than the fourth part of a labourer.[1] If there is anything over-sanguine in Oglethorpe's calculation, it is in his estimate of the resources of the colony. Ten acres of land will maintain a settler when he gets it rent free. Oglethorpe appears to have forgotten that the family had to be maintained too, and that the constitution and objects of the colony made every settler liable at any moment for military service.

Considering the latitude of the colony it was probably wise that the settlers should time their arrival at the beginning of the year. Save for the death of two children, the vessel bearing the emigrants reached America without mishap. On January 13, 1733, Oglethorpe landed in Charlestown. There he obtained from the Governor what was needful in the way of guidance and convoy. With a pilot from Charlestown, the emigrants sailed to Port Royal, an inlet some eighty miles to the south.

Arrival of the colonists.

When Port Royal was reached Oglethorpe himself landed, and having arranged that huts should be made ready for the settlers, he set out to choose a site for his town. Twenty miles above the mouth of the river rose a bluff. Standing a good deal higher than the stream it was free from the danger of malarious fogs; opposite was a rich meadow suited for cattle pasture. From the summit of the bluff the whole course of the river could be traced as far as the sea. Thus the approach of a hostile fleet could be at once signalled. To the west and south, too, the country

Settlement at Savannah.[2]

[1] *New and Accurate Account.*

[2] For this see Oglethorpe's two letters quoted in *Account showing the Progress.*

could be seen for six miles, and thus there was little fear of a surprise either by natives or by Spaniards. Moreover, the swampy character of the land to the south, making the march of troops difficult and the transport of stores and artillery well-nigh impossible, was in itself a protection.

Oglethorpe did not in his choice of a name show any wish to commemorate either place or person in the Old World, and the future city kept the Indian name of the adjoining river, Savannah.

Before allowing his settlers to occupy their new home Oglethorpe took measures to secure the friendship of his savage neighbours. For once the frontier trader, associating with the Indians and adopting their habits, was a help instead of a hindrance. An Englishman named Musgrove had settled among the tribes south of the Savannah and had married an Indian squaw. She now acted as an interpreter and envoy from Oglethorpe to her own people. The principal tribe in the country was that of the Creeks. They appear to have been divided into two confederations of about a thousand men each, known to their English neighbours as the upper and lower Creeks. There was also a smaller tribe, the Uchees, some two hundred strong. The village nearest to the site chosen by Oglethorpe was that of the Yamacraws. They appear to have been one of the subdivisions of the Creek nation. Their chief, Tomochichi, had we are told been banished from his own people, probably the Creeks, and it is not unlikely that the insecurity of his position made him welcome the alliance of the strangers. Through the agency of Musgrove and his wife friendly relations were established between Tomochichi and Oglethorpe, and the native chief made over to the English whatever rights he himself may have had in the land required for the new settlement.

After a week's sojourn at Port Royal, while Oglethorpe was exploring the country, the emigrants landed at their new abode on January 30. Oglethorpe's first report to the trustees was sent on February 20, followed by a better one three weeks later. His statements are supplemented and confirmed by the evidence of a party from Charlestown who visited Savannah, and published an account of what they saw there.[1] It is noteworthy that their account of the progress and prosperity of the little community is decidedly more favourable than Oglethorpe's own. He reports in a somewhat apologetic tone that though the public magazine and the needful preparations for defence were complete, there were as yet but five wooden houses built and that the people were living in tents. This, he says, is all that could be done from the small number of the settlers, of whom many, too, were unused to labour. The Carolina visitors, on the other hand, marvel that so much has been done in so short a time and with such scanty resources. The town is palisaded, some wheat has been sown and already shows above ground, and two or three gardens have been stocked with herbs. Unused as the settlers are to manual labour they work cheerfully; all, even the children, bear their part, and there are no idlers. Oglethorpe is described as a kind of paternal despot, nursing his settlers if sick, settling all disputes by his arbitrary judgment, and exercising such control that not an oath was to be heard nor a drunken man to be seen.

Prosperous beginnings.

That things should have gone well at first is no matter for surprise. We may suppose that the emigrants had been chosen with a special view to their deserts and good character. They were just set free

[1] In the *South Carolina Gazette*. Reprinted in Harris, p. 327.

from what had seemed a year ago a life of hopeless misery. For the time mere promise of material prosperity was enough, and the presence of a ruler such as Oglethorpe, hopeful, genial, masterful and practical, would keep in check any symptoms of discontent. The real difficulty would come when the first pinch of material distress had been overcome, when the increasing size of the colony made it no longer possible for the Governor to exercise direct personal influence over each settler, and when with the increase of material prosperity different degrees of wealth began to show themselves. Not utter misery but a condition of slowly increasing prosperity is the seed-bed of discontent.

Dealings with the natives.

As we have already seen from the outset Oglethorpe, warned one may well believe by the recent experiences of South Carolina, saw the need for standing well with his savage neighbours. Tomochichi showed that he valued the English alliance. He wished to be taught the religion of his neighbours, and the members of his tribe asked that they might bring their children to be trained at the English schools. The southern Indians seem for the most part to have still retained the system of female succession. The next heir, the chief's nephew, held a recognised position like the Tanist of an Irish chief. From the importance which evidently attached to Tomochichi's nephew, Toonahowi, it is probable that he held this post. He seems to have been as zealous as his uncle in his desire for the teaching and faith of the white men.

Oglethorpe used the ground thus gained to extend his influence over the native tribes further inland, and with the help of Tomochichi he summoned the heads of the various Creek villages to a meeting.[1] On May 21

[1] This interview is described in the *Brief Account*, pp. 10–13.

the Creek chiefs to the number of fifty met Oglethorpe at Savannah. They were near enough to South Carolina to have heard something of the power and resources of the English, and of the disasters which their enmity had brought on the Yamassees. Moreover, there was as yet ample room for the Englishman and the savage. A belt of some fifty miles in width along the coast seems to have been unoccupied. The Creeks opened the interview, according to their interpreter, by a formal acknowledgement of the superior strength and wisdom of the white men and by a present of skins. Tomochichi then appealing, as was the wont of the Indians, to visible symbols, laid before the meeting a buffalo hide, tricked out with eagle's feathers. The English, he said, had crossed the great water with the speed of the eagle, and they possessed the irresistible might of the buffalo. They had, moreover, Tomochichi said, shown themselves kind to the Indians. Instead of using their strength to drive him from his lands, they had given him and his followers food from their own stores. Finally a treaty was drawn up. The Indians were presented with clothes, guns and ammunition. They ceded all their right in the soil bounded by the sea and by the tidal waters of the Savannah and the Alatamaha. The natives reserved a few islands for hunting and fishing, and a tract as camping ground whenever they visited the neighbourhood of Savannah. Regulations, too, were framed controlling the intercourse and trade between the two nations.

Oglethorpe visits Charlestown.

Just before the Indian conference, Oglethorpe had visited Charlestown. In a speech to the Assembly he reminded them of what their colony had but lately suffered from Indian violence and from threats of Spanish invasion. Already, he told them, had the good effect of a strong colony on the southern frontier made itself felt. Large tracts had been occupied and the value of land had doubled itself.[1]

In June Oglethorpe, accompanied by an officer and troop of soldiers from South Carolina, set forth to explore the south-western portion of his province and to take such steps as were needful for defence. A site was chosen about fifteen miles south of the capital, commanding the valley of the Ogechee, a river parallel to the Savannah. There Oglethorpe designed a fort and left a garrison to build and man it, while a small party of civilians was sent up from Savannah to help at the work and to raise supplies. In the following January, Oglethorpe renewed and extended his explorations as far as the mouth of the Alatamaha. The success of his defensive schemes at a later day showed with what strategic wisdom he had studied the character of the coast. On his return he found his fortification on the Ogechee, Fort Argyle as he named it, defensible and mounted with cannon. There does not seem as yet to have been any road through the forest, and the outpost was connected with Savannah only by water.

Provision for the defence of Georgia.

Oglethorpe and his associates must now have seen, if they had not indeed seen before, that the relief of pauperism could only be one incident in their colonial scheme. If the colony was to have any military value, even if it was to be materially and economically prosperous, other elements must be introduced. It had long been a principle with the English Government, imperfectly carried out, but plainly in keeping with the foreign policy of England, to make our colonies a refuge for the persecuted Protestants of Europe. As we have seen, the dealings of

Introduction of the Salzburgers.[2]

[1] The speech is given in the *Brief Account*, p. 13.

[2] The best authority for the migration of the Salzburgers is the diary of Commissary Van Reck who conducted them. It was published in London in 1734 and republished in Force's *Tracts.*

Louis XIV. with the Huguenots and the devastation of the Palatinate had helped to swell that tide of miscellaneous emigration which had peopled the valley of the Hudson. Between 1729 and 1733 a number of the inhabitants of the Salzkammergut were made homeless by the persecuting policy of their Romanist bishop. In 1733 the trustees of Georgia opened negotiations for receiving a number of these into their colony. The introduction of a small alien community, with its own usages and pursuits, was rendered more easy by the absence of any rigid constitutional provisions. At the same time the very ease with which such incorporation could be made was in itself a hindrance to the ultimate unity of the colony and to its corporate life. The trustees were enabled to carry out this part of their scheme without diverting any of those funds which had been contributed for the special relief of distress. In 1726 the missionary zeal of Berkeley had so far won upon a reluctant Ministry and an indifferent Parliament that ninety thousand pounds had been voted as an endowment for a college in the Bermudas. Sordid indifference to the interests of the colonies, an indifference which was among the worst faults in the public policy of the Hanoverian age, and which forty years later bore its own retribution, brought Berkeley's scheme to nought. Payment was delayed; wearied out with hope deferred, Berkeley returned to his career in the English Church and to his studies as a philosopher. Of the ninety thousand pounds, eighty thousand was appropriated to the dowry of the Princess of Orange; the rest was with Berkeley's assent voted to help Oglethorpe and his associates in their benevolent objects.[1] The Act of Parliament by which

[1] 6 George II. c. 25. Mr. Wright (p. 51 *n.*) states that Oglethorpe obtained Berkeley's consent. I have not found any proof of it, but the friendship between the two men and their respective characters make it probable.

this money was granted contained a clause which allowed it to be appropriated to the help of foreign Protestants. The trustees entered into negotiations with the pastor of one of the exiled churches, that of Berchtesgaden, and in March 1734 seventy-eight emigrants sailed firstly from Rotterdam and then from Dover. Early in April they reached Savannah, and after a short halt moved up the river some thirty miles, to the site of their new home. We are told that the river was as wide as the Rhine, and the woods full of the sounds of spring filled them with joy. To us of the present day, trained to take an almost exaggerated delight in natural beauty, and to seek in its wilder and sterner forms a relief from monotony and over-civilization, it would seem a poor exchange to leave the shores of the Königsee, and the stern glories of the Untersberg and the Dachstein, for the pine-clad sands and the sluggish, swamp-girt streams of Georgia. But the native of mountains loves them with a love begotten of instinct and habit rather than deliberate preference, and we may well believe that the new home, with its promise of security and material prosperity, seemed more than a compensation for what they had left behind them.

Oglethorpe returns to England.

Oglethorpe had no sooner seen the Austrian emigrants settled than he sailed for England to report to the trustees, and to take up in Parliament certain questions connected with the colony. With him he took Tomochichi and some eight other Creek Indians. Their arrival created some of the same interest which at an earlier day had been awakened by Pocahontas and by the Mohawk chiefs who accompanied Schuyler. Tomochichi and his companions were taken in their war-paint and feathers to Kensington Palace, to Lambeth and to Eton, where, after the approved fashion of foreign potentates, they asked for a whole holiday, and doubtless furnished a pretext for much hearty shouting from admirers to whom the names of Georgia and Savannah conveyed very vague ideas.[1]

Underlying the reception of Tomochichi and his followers by the fashionable world there was something more than the mere idle curiosity of sightseers. The Evangelical movement was then in its dawn, and missionary zeal, eager, if not at all times well-judging or practical, has always been a mark of that school. The modern spirit of humanitarianism too was awakening. Thus the savage was something more than a mere curiosity. The presence of the Creek chiefs suggested serious, if somewhat vague, reflections on our responsibilities towards the savages on our borders. Not only did Tomochichi furnish the subject for an ode,[2] but Wilson, the Bishop of Sodor and Man, whose scholarly Churchmanship linked him to the age of Laud and Andrewes, as his earnest piety anticipated the coming revival, applied himself to the task of preparing a simple manual of devotion suited to the use of the savages, and capable of being rendered into their language.[3]

Meanwhile the trustees had been using the legislative powers conferred on them by the charter to give the force of law to certain provisions already adopted by Oglethorpe under their instructions. They had prohibited the importation of any spirits. This provision had been violated by the Carolina traders. An Act was now passed imposing the same restraint. But it should be noticed that not only was beer freely imported from England and wine from Madeira, but also molasses from

[1] Tomochichi's visit to Court is told in the *Gentleman's Magazine*. Mr. Wright describes the visit to Eton. I have not found his authority for it.

[2] The Ode, a pompous production, is printed in full by Jones, vol. i. pp. 175–8.

[3] Published under the title *The Knowledge and Practice of Christianity made easy to the meanest capacity, or an Essay towards the Instruction of the Indians.*

that, the settlers gave to the territory assigned them the name of Darien, as though to declare that they did not accept defeat, and that the scheme which had come to ruin thirty years earlier was yet to revive and prosper.

Extension of the colony.

In some respects the growth and life of Georgia had more in common with that of the New England colonies than of the Southern plantations. The absence of slave labour and the special conditions of land tenure prevented the growth of large estates. Thus there did not spring up, as in Virginia, Maryland and South Carolina, isolated plantations, each a self-supporting and in many respects an independent community. Nor were the settlers suffered to straggle over the country as in North Carolina. On the other hand the colony extended itself as in New England by regular steps, each forming part of a methodical and organic scheme of expansion. And the various settlements were to some extent as in New England little coherent bodies, starting with a life of their own, not chance accumulations of settlers. But whereas in New England each onward movement was taken by the free choice of those who made it and each little society had in it the capacities of self-government, the expansion of Georgia was a mechanical scheme imposed from without.

It is a truism to say that a community whose life is thus ordered for it must lack much of the energy and self-reliance of one which chooses and shapes its own destiny. The exigencies of her lot, the very purposes for which Georgia existed, cut her off from such hopes. As we shall see, the colony fulfilled honourably and effectually the military purposes for which she was created. When we contrast the promptitude and success of Oglethorpe's operations against the Spaniards with the years of weary harassing warfare on the Canadian frontier, hindered by jealousies, bickerings, selfish and narrow disregard to imperial interests, we cannot but feel that the colony had put on that form of life which best fitted it for its appointed work.

And even if the military necessities of the colony had not hindered its free growth, one may almost say that its composition rendered such growth impossible. Bankrupts and paupers are not the material out of which to make a self-governing state. Georgia fulfilled the two functions for which she was created: she served as a bulwark against the Spanish invader, as a safety-valve for the pauperism and misery of England. Discontent there was, as we shall see; there may have been even suffering: and so far those who planned the colony missed their aim. But the real praise which attaches to Oglethorpe and his colleagues lies in this: that their colony, while serving as an asylum for distress, was also able to take unto itself the elements of healthy national life, that a better class of settlers were not repelled by such association, and that thus alongside the community of paupers and bankrupts, of the thriftless and discontented, at Savannah there grew up other types of colonial life, able in due time to contribute elements of value to the life of the republic.

In 1736 the colony received a fresh accession of two hundred and two settlers. Among them was a fresh instalment of German Protestants and a congregation of twenty-five Moravians under their own bishop. It was a hopeful sign that an English gentleman of good position, Sir Francis Bathurst, had been willing to make the colony a home for himself and his family.[1]

This inflowing tide of immigration enabled Oglethorpe to take another step forward in his defensive policy. The mouth of the Alatamaha is commanded by an island about twelve miles long, pear-shaped and narrowing towards the south. Here Oglethorpe

[1] Bathurst announced his arrival in a letter to the trustees, Feb. 17, 1734.

planted a fortified town, the southernmost point as yet of his colony. The settlement, to be called Frederica, stood on the western shore of the island, in a meadow about a mile long by half a mile wide, flanked and backed by almost impenetrable woods.[1]

Organization of the colony.

With the influx of fresh settlers the tide of emigration flowed up the valley of the Savannah. The township of Abercorn and the smaller villages of Hampstead and Highgate were established between Savannah and Ebenezer. Settlements sprung up along the broken chain of islands which face the coast between the Savannah and the Alatamaha.[2] This process of growth brought out a defect almost inevitable in the composition of the colony—the want of any constitutional machinery to bind together its scattered members. It is not easy to make out clearly under what system of law and administration the colony lived. Oglethorpe appears to have exercised a certain general and not precisely defined authority over the whole colony. A soldier and a disciplinarian such as Oglethorpe, kindly but peremptory, unsparing of himself and expecting the like energy and self-denial of others, could not fail to incur the charge of harshness in his exercise of arbitrary power.

The Highlanders and the Salzburgers in all likelihood found, the one in the patriarchal usages which they had brought with them, the other in their ecclesiastical organization, an adequate substitute for any civil magistracy. The English settlements along the Savannah presumably lived under the common law of England. We hear nothing of any magistrates in the country districts. If any civil or criminal business arose it was probably dealt with either by Oglethorpe

[1] It must be remembered that in Georgia, as in South Carolina, a wood is usually a great tract of swamp.

[2] For these, see *The State of the Province of Georgia* and the *Account*.

or by those whom he had left in authority at Savannah. There in his absence he had vested power in three magistrates or bailiffs. Here at once the difficulties inherent in the scheme made themselves felt. With the three bailiffs was associated in office a public storekeeper. The holder of this post, Thomas Causton, appears to have been both corrupt and unjust. He is charged with making a profit out of the public stores, with interfering with the course of justice and with using the authority which his position gave him to intimidate juries. Neither the trustees nor Oglethorpe showed any wish to screen Causton. The charges against him were, as we shall see, fairly investigated.[1]

Discontent among the settlers.

But one can plainly see that the difficulties were not caused, but only increased and brought to the surface, by the personal failings of Causton. In their first moments of exile and relief, the emancipated debtors and paupers might throw themselves with temporary zeal into their new life of industry. But the failings which had brought them to ruin in the Old World were sure to make themselves felt. The allotments were, as might have been surely foreseen, a source of jealousy and discontent. The resources of the trustees did not allow them to carry out public works, lighthouses, fortifications, the laying out of streets and clearing of woods by hired labour. All this had to be done by the settlers in return for supplies advanced. Can we wonder or blame them if, with no hope of direct personal reward, they shrunk from toils under the burning sun of Georgia? Their intercourse with South Carolina was a constant spur to jealousy and discontent. There they saw planters living in sloth and luxury by the toil of their negroes,

[1] Beside the official reports there are several references to Causton in private letters, among the Georgia Papers, in the Record Office, all unfavourable.

and able to carry on trade with the English merchant by mortgages of their estate and stock. In Georgia slavery was strictly forbidden. Repeated petitions and remonstrances were met by the answer, in all likelihood a reasonable one, that the military exigencies of the colony made slavery dangerous. It is plain, too, that Oglethorpe was a man of somewhat despotic temper, one who would make his neighbours happy, but in his own way, with whom a position once taken up had to be defended as a matter of principle and conscience. With him and his co-trustees in England the exclusion of negro slaves became at once a dogma not to be questioned, and resistance to slavery a matter of personal dignity. To the settlers on the other hand, at least to a section of them, Oglethorpe's stubborn resistance to this and to the importation of spirits seemed a wanton and purposeless exhibition of self-will. His politic kindness to the Indians was another grievance. Money was wasted on the support of 'useless vagrants' when 'many poor Christians were starving for want of bread.' Oglethorpe in short thought of the future security and stability of the colony, the Savannah settlers of their present ease. He would make it a bulwark against the Spaniard, they a paradise for thriftless idlers.

The Wesleys in Georgia.

Religious dissensions came in to complicate and intensify these disputes. Among those whom Oglethorpe took out with him on his return to Georgia in the autumn of 1735 were John Wesley and Charles Wesley. The latter was to act as the Governor's private secretary. It is somewhat noteworthy that the Wesleys do not seem to have rushed into the venture in any sanguine spirit of missionary zeal. The trustees wanted two clergymen to serve the parish of Savannah, and the town to be built on St. Simon's Island. Oglethorpe was slightly acquainted with the Wesleys: another trustee who knew them more intimately made overtures to them. John Wesley, not without hesitation, accepted their offer. His example was followed by Charles, and by two young laymen of the same way of thinking.[1]

There is nothing to show whether Oglethorpe was attached to any ecclesiastical party, or what were his theological convictions. He was politically an ally of Atterbury. He may have been a Nonjuror, if not avowedly at least in his sympathies, or a free-thinking Jacobite of the school of Bolingbroke. But be his religious opinions what they might, it is very certain that the personal tempers and characters of John Wesley and Oglethorpe would have made harmonious action impossible. Both were impulsive, masterful and benevolent, eager to hurry men to their own good, by short cuts, rather than let them find their own way to it slowly by the discipline of failure. Each in a measure would be working by like methods and in a like frame of mind to different ends. It was Oglethorpe's task to drill, encourage and coerce the citizens of Georgia till they become prosperous farmers and an efficient militia. It was Wesley's task to bring them by similar means to the salvation of their own souls. The obligations were sure to conflict, and with two such men the conflict must inevitably mean personal quarrel. Moreover the Wesley with whom Oglethorpe had to deal was not the Wesley of mature years, the founder and ruler of a sect, disciplined in tact, in forbearance, in knowledge of human nature, but a passionate, self-confident young enthusiast of twenty-six. Such a man could hardly fail to wound Oglethorpe's personal dignity. He would be absolutely certain to outrage his sense of military discipline. Yet Oglethorpe was not a man to be blind to real moral worth, and the stamp of such worth on Wesley's character was too plain to be mistaken.

[1] Southey's *Life of Wesley*, vol. i. p. 75.

There were sure to be conflicts, the conflicts were sure to be tempered and modified by an undercurrent of mutual respect and mutual love.

The Wesleys were allotted as pastors to the two chief settlements, John to Savannah, Charles to the new town on St. Simon's Island, Frederica.[1] Danger by this time threatened from Spain, and Oglethorpe's presence was needed in the southern part of the province. Accordingly during the summer of 1736 he made Frederica his head-quarters. Each of the newly arrived ministers took upon him the part of a social reformer and a moral dictator, and the result was to bring Charles Wesley into conflict with the Governor. Wesley soon made enemies. In one case at least the hostility was deserved; while living on avowedly good terms with Oglethorpe, he gave credit and apparently publicity to rumours which accused the general of an intrigue with a married woman. This incidentally betrayed a certain want of faith on Charles Wesley's part in his brother's judgment, since the lady in question was described by John Wesley as 'a hopeful convert.' Her husband was the doctor to the settlement. An order had been issued by Oglethorpe against any shooting on Sundays. Once during the course of Wesley's sermon a shot was heard; the doctor was found to be the culprit and was by order of the preacher arrested, to the injury of an unlucky woman who was in need of his services. This incident seems to have raised the first open breach between Oglethorpe and Wesley. If, as is likely, the general heard of the injurious suspicions attaching to his name one cannot wonder that his feelings were bitter.

For what followed we have only the evidence of Charles Wesley. The details as given by him are so

[1] For what follows I have used Charles Wesley's journal. But it must be remembered, as I have tried to point out, that this is only evidence for what Wesley, no doubt honestly, believed to have happened, not for what actually did happen.

strangely improbable that one feels sure that one has not the whole story. There may well have been matters unknown to Wesley himself which entered into it.

If he is to be believed Oglethorpe was guilty of the pettiest tyranny, depriving Wesley of the ordinary necessities of life, hindering the washing of his linen, taking away his bedstead, and giving express orders that the public carpenter should not replace it. In all likelihood Oglethorpe had used harsh and passionate language; Wesley's enemies, and we cannot doubt that he had made plenty, would take advantage of the situation and would wreak their spite by interpreting Oglethorpe's orders in the severest fashion. The time was a critical one in the life of the colony. The danger of a Spanish invasion hung over it; Oglethorpe was busy palisading the town, providing a public bakery, laying in by the help of the Indians supplies of food, testing the vigilance of his garrison by false alarms, taking every precaution in almost daily expectation of a siege. Such cares left him no time to think about one whom he can only have regarded, and with a good deal of justice, as an ungrateful and self-willed young enthusiast. Wesley's own mode of describing the matter shows that he was not without a morbid craving for martyrdom. In all likelihood he was priding himself on the endurance of suffering, which would have been removed if a word of remonstrance had reached the ears of the supposed oppressor.

The relations of Wesley to the Governor were not the only matter which was going wrong. The Austrians at Ebenezer were dissatisfied with the site of their settlement. Their cattle and their garden gave outward evidence of prosperity, but they found fault with the soil as ill-suited to corn-growing. The real motive of their discontent, so Oglethorpe suspected, was a desire to

The Salzburgers discontented.

get possession of land specially reserved for the Indians. Without granting that, Oglethorpe so far humoured the settlers as to allow them to shift to another spot.[1]

Danger of Spanish invasion.

To all these administrative difficulties was added the fear of foreign invasion. The difficulties which beset the colony were the same which had embarrassed the New Englanders in the days when the Dutch held the valley of the Hudson, and which were perpetually arising on the Canadian border. In an uninhabited and imperfectly explored country, a frontier line can always be made a bone of contention if either party is in quest of one. An even more certain ground of dispute is the presence of savage allies on each side. Possession of territory by savages hardly admits of strict definition and thus charges of encroachment are hard to disprove. A civilized power if it wants a pretext for war can always incite its savage allies to acts of violence, and then on their behalf resent the infliction of punishment. The dangers of the situation were increased by the peculiar code of international morality which during the eighteenth century had been gaining ground among the great Powers of Europe. Two nations might be ostensibly at peace, yet each might have alliances which would involve it in active hostility with the other. Thus in 1718, when Byng was shattering the Spanish fleet at Passaro, there was in theory friendship between the Courts of St. James and Madrid. Thus Oglethorpe might at any moment find his colony threatened with invasion, and yet be unable to depend with certainty on the help of the mother country.

The occupation of Georgia made it needful for the English Government to confer with the Spaniards in Florida as to some more precise line of demarcation

[1] Christie, a leading settler, writing to the trustees in 1735 admits that the land on which the Salzburgers were settled was very sandy.

than had yet existed. To this end a commissioner, Charles Dempsey, was sent out from England with Oglethorpe in 1735. Early in the following year Dempsey went, escorted by an officer of militia, Richards from South Carolina, to St. Augustine. The length of their absence made Oglethorpe uneasy. Accompanied by Tomochichi and other of his Indian friends, he coasted as far as the frontier.

Difficulties with the Indian allies.[1]

The conduct of Oglethorpe's allies must have enlightened Oglethorpe as to some of the difficulties and dangers before him. The Indians had learnt enough to know that the English and Spaniards were unfriendly. In all likelihood they looked on the whole expedition as simply an ingenious scheme for getting within striking distance and then making a destructive raid into Spanish territory. As soon as the frontier was reached Tomochichi pointed out to Oglethorpe the Spanish guard-house. The Spaniards, he said, had long since crossed the frontier and done wrong to the Indians. Now was the time to retaliate. Oglethorpe saw the need for divesting himself of these dangerous followers. He persuaded, as he thought, the Indians to turn back, and lest they should evade him he sent one of his boats to attend them. Tomochichi soon escaped the escort. The next night he rejoined Oglethorpe, declaring that he had seen a party of Spaniards advancing and clamouring to attack them. Oglethorpe could only so far prevail as to persuade the savages that the attack should be deferred till morning. Tomochichi pointed out what he regarded as the insane folly of allowing an enemy the advantage of daylight, but he did not care to attack unsupported. When the day came the party proved to be an escort bringing back Dempsey and Richards. The latter

[1] The authorities for what follows are Oglethorpe's own despatches and journal, and Moore. Mr. Wright follows his authorities closely.

returned with Oglethorpe, the former remained as an official English representative in Florida.

The despatches which they brought from the Governor of Florida were avowedly friendly. But he complained of the conduct of the Creeks and begged Oglethorpe to restrain his allies, in a tone which implied that the English might be held responsible. The English envoys, too, had learnt privately that the Spanish Governor was making hostile preparations. He expected reinforcements from Havannah, and he looked for increasing his supply of arms to the unpatriotic greed of traders at Charlestown. He was also organizing a force among the Yamassees, already the enemies of the Creeks, and owing the English a debt of revenge for their defeat by South Carolina.

A twofold task was now laid on Oglethorpe. He had to press on with the defence of his own colony, and at the same time to do everything to restrain his Indian allies and give the Spaniards no pretext for an attack. As yet the colony was receiving no military help from the Crown. It was defended only by the Highlanders and by a force of mercenaries paid by the trustees, and commanded by a German soldier of fortune named Hermsdorf. The whole of the force was devoted to garrisoning outposts towards the south. Everything was done by earthworks and palisading to make Frederica secure. The actual task of defence was left to the Highland inhabitants. To the south of St. Simon's was an island some twelve miles long, to which the Spaniards had given the name of St. Peter's. Tomochichi when he went southward with Oglethorpe renamed it Cumberland, as a special mark of the gratitude to the Duke for his courtesy and kindness to the savages on their English visit. Forts called respectively Fort St. Andrew and Fort William were placed at the northern and

Oglethorpe's measures of defence.

southern extremities of this island. Further south, at the mouth of the river St. John,[1] were found the remains of a fort ascribed by an improbable tradition to Drake. This was repaired, and the task of guarding it entrusted to Hermsdorf. At the same time the valley of the Savannah was protected from a Yamassee invasion by a fort called Fort Augusta, some two hundred and seventy miles up the river, which also served as a station for Indian trade and a means of communication with the inland districts of South Carolina. Boats were stationed to guard the various inlets south of St. Simon's.

In the meantime Tomochichi was instructed to explain matters to the Creeks, and to promise that if they would hold their hands, Oglethorpe would do his utmost to obtain justice for them from the Spaniards. To prevent any further breach a guard-boat was posted on the river St. John with orders to suffer no Creek to cross into Spanish territory.

In April the General sent Richards with one of the chief settlers, Horton, bearing letters to the Governor of St. Augustine. Scarcely had they gone when a despatch arrived written by Dempsey, but at the order of the Spanish Governor. The Indians, he said, had attacked a Spanish outpost. It was impossible that they could have done this without the approval of the English. In taking this ground the Spanish Governor virtually declared that Oglethorpe would be held responsible for the action of any of the tribes north of the St. John. With that doctrine accepted the Spanish authorities could never want a pretext for an attack.

Threatening attitude of the Spaniards.

Events soon showed that they hardly had the decency to wait for any pretext, and that the English settlers might at any moment have to face an invading

[1] The river appears to have been called somewhat indiscriminately the St. John or the St. Matthew.

force. News reached Oglethorpe that a fleet of seven Spanish vessels was threatening the Sound to the south of St. Simon's Island. He seems to have contrived that the extent of the danger should not be known to his settlers. On April 24 he sailed south to watch over the safety of the menaced settlement. Before his departure he was reconciled to Charles Wesley. He, it is plain, was deeply touched. Oglethorpe, so Wesley records in his diary, listened patiently to his solemn disavowal of the charges which had been brought against him. When he had heard it 'he seemed entirely changed; full of his old love and confidence.' He did not think it prudent to tell Wesley at the time the full ground of his apprehensions. He seems rather to have left the impression of a man who could not define his danger, but had a vague foreboding of evil. Afterwards on his return he explained how matters really stood. He added, so Wesley tells us, that he was depressed by vague omens of evil. His servants twice brought him out a mourning sword instead of that which he called for. At last they brought him the one meant; it had been his father's. A characteristic touch of the knight-errant broke out: 'With this sword I never was unsuccessful.'

The whole scene as described by Wesley is not inconsistent with Oglethorpe's kindly, impetuous, demonstrative nature. Yet one also feels that the story may have been unconsciously coloured by the young enthusiast, worked into a half hysterical state by suffering and self-reproach, and the prospect of a last parting from one whose kindness he had repaid somewhat ungenerously.

The winds and waves fought for the threatened colony, and the Spanish fleet after a stay of three weeks withdrew. The garrison at Frederica was cheered by the arrival of a party of volunteers from Savannah and of a man-of-war. Oglethorpe himself returned in five days, having inspected and strengthened the defences of the southern forts.

Rumours of danger soon called him southward again. It was reported that Richards and Horton had been seized by the Spaniards and were being kept as prisoners. Oglethorpe heard, too, that the garrison under Hermsdorf had mutinied, and forced their commander to evacuate the fort. Both rumours proved exaggerated. A day's sail brought Oglethorpe to the southern point of Cumberland Island. There he met the fugitives. Their action did not seem to be so much a mutiny as a panic, the work of a single alarmist. The offender was punished and the garrison returned to their fort.

Meanwhile a Spanish force had actually crossed the frontier, passing Oglethorpe and leaving Fort George in its rear. A vessel, having on board four cannon, thirty foot soldiers and some Yamassee Indians, had sailed against St. Simon's, while a force of fifty horsemen and a hundred and sixty infantry supported them from the land. They had no expectation of finding the English position so strongly defended. After reconnoitring St. Simon's Island they decided to abandon the attempt on Frederica, and to content themselves with destroying Fort George.

Oglethorpe knew neither their numbers nor their exact position. But fires lighted along the coast showed that the enemy was about. Accordingly on the night of May 3 he sent his artillery up into the woods, and discharged it in such a fashion as to create the belief among the enemy that a ship at sea was saluting and being answered by a battery on the mainland. Throughout this expedition Oglethorpe's attitude was strictly one of defence. It was all the easier for him to preserve this, since while the Spanish

Governor was actually threatening the English settlements, he was at the same time keeping open the door of negotiation. Dempsey, Richards and Horton were still at St. Augustine's, really it may be as hostages, but ostensibly at least as official representatives. Dempsey as the spokesman for the British Government seems to have been throughout treated with respect. Horton and Richards were arrested on a charge, unfounded as they themselves said, of taking plans of the Spanish fortifications, and Horton was actually threatened that he would be sent as a prisoner to the mines if he refused to answer questions as to the position and resources of the English. On May 3 Oglethorpe, having landed on the Spanish side of the river, met a messenger bringing letters from Richards and Horton to the commander of Fort George.

Two days later Oglethorpe again started to cross the St. John, hoping to receive a letter from the Governor of Florida. Before he could reach the southern bank he saw a Spanish vessel. He had on board twenty-four men; the Spaniard appeared to outnumber him by nearly three to one. Nevertheless she showed no wish to come to close quarters, and after unsuccessfully trying to conceal herself in the bends of the river she made for the open sea and turned southward.

Oglethorpe then, seeing the passage of the river clear, crossed and stood on to the Spanish bank. Two horsemen drew out of the woods to meet him. They warned him not to land on Spanish soil. Otherwise the interview was friendly, and Oglethorpe sent on a letter to St. Augustine to say that if Horton and Richards were sent down, a boat should be ready to meet them. Oglethorpe then recrossed, strengthened the defences of Fort George and his batteries along the river and took his way back to Frederica.

A fortnight later the Spanish Governor sent his

secretary to Oglethorpe, accompanied by the chief military officer at St. Augustine. With them were Dempsey and Richards. Horton had been already released and had returned to the colony. Oglethorpe, not wishing that the enemy should have the opportunity of examining and reporting upon Frederica, resolved to receive the embassy on shipboard. At the same time tents were pitched for their reception on Jekyll Island, thus keeping them wholly aloof from St. Simon's. Everything was done to impress the visitors with an exaggerated idea of the resources of the colony. The tallest and most warlike of the Highland emigrants were brought on board, and were drawn up on deck with unsheathed claymores, and successive salutes were fired from all the forts. The Spaniards, we are told, marvelled at the completeness of the English defences. They now understood, they said, the rapid retreat of their invading force.

A Spanish embassy at Frederica.

The conference gave Oglethorpe the opportunity of propitiating his Indian allies by figuring as their benefactor and protector. Some of the Creek chiefs came on board and demanded satisfaction. Their men, they said, had been slain in time of peace, not by the Spaniards themselves, but by their native allies. The Spaniards explained that this had been done without their consent or knowledge. The offending chief should if possible be arrested and put to death. In no case should arms or ammunition be supplied to his followers.

The real discussion between Oglethorpe and the Spaniards turned on the question of boundary. Oglethorpe's fortifications to the south were, so the Spaniards said, an encroachment. Oglethorpe denied that the Spaniards had any title to territory north of the river St. John. All he had done was to secure what had hitherto been an asylum for pirates and marauders.

The matter was plainly one which could only be

settled by the two Home Governments. Pending such settlement, Oglethorpe pledged himself to abstain from hostilities. Dempsey was to be sent back to St. Augustine, to obtain a like undertaking from the Spanish Governor.

The result of the interview and of the preceding campaign, as one may call it, may have relieved Oglethorpe from present fear. The military policy of the Spanish colony was, it would seem, controlled by the cavalry commander, Don Pedro Lamberto, and he seems to have been genuinely desirous of peace. Yet Oglethorpe must have seen plainly enough that his position was a precarious one. His anxiety that the Spaniards should not spy out the real condition of Frederica shows that he considered the defences inadequate. Moreover, the policy of forbearance was merely dependent on the good-will of an individual. There was but little likelihood that it would be recognised and approved by the Spanish Government.

To say that Oglethorpe had only secured a respite for his colony is in no way to belittle his work. For a community like Georgia, growing every year in resources, in cohesion and self-reliance, a respite was everything. Moreover Oglethorpe's campaign of 1736, if we may call it by that name, cannot have failed to give him a hold on the confidence of the settlers. There they saw clearly illustrated his mixture of audacity and practical resource, his power of inspiring his subordinates with his own enthusiasm, of at once utilizing and controlling his savage allies. This it is which gives importance to the incidents related. They make us feel, too, how much allowance must be made for Oglethorpe as a civil Governor if one so beset with responsibilities was at times guilty of haste and infirmity of temper.

Soon after this Charles Wesley resigned the secretaryship and returned to England. His parting with

Oglethorpe was not unfriendly, but the latter, it seems clear, did not regret nor try to hinder his secretary's departure.

Oglethorpe soon found himself confronted with one of those intercolonial difficulties arising out of trade which play so large a part in American history, and illustrate so strongly the need for union and central administration. Not only had the trustees placed a veto on the importation of spirits for the protection of the Indians and the security of their own frontier, they allowed no one to trade with the natives unless he held a license. Before the settlement of Georgia traders from South Carolina had been wont to deal with the natives along the southern bank of the Savannah, importing amongst other things rum. They had no mind to give up this gainful trade at the bidding of Oglethorpe, or to exercise it only with his consent. Accordingly unlicensed vessels continued to ply between the mouth of the river and Fort Augusta. The magistrates at Savannah stopped the vessels, staved the casks of rum, and in some instances put the traders in prison.[1]

Difficulty with the Carolina traders.

The aggrieved traders brought the matter before the Assembly of South Carolina, and a committee of that body was appointed to obtain redress. They so far succeeded that the officials of Savannah made restitution for the goods destroyed. Oglethorpe, however, would not abandon his right to control trade within the borders of Georgia, nor would the Carolina settlers accept any such restraint on their dealings with the natives. Such a question could only be settled by a reference to some superior and independent authority.

The prospects of a peaceful settlement with Spain were soon overcast. In October 1736 a treaty was signed with the Governor of St. Augustine confirming

[1] See documents in third volume of the Georgia Historical Society's Collections.

all those concessions which had been informally made by Lamberto. But in less than a month it was made clear that the Spanish Government had no intention of being bound by the acts of the Governor. A commissioner from the West Indies visited St. Augustine, and thence coming to Savannah, served an order of eviction on the English settlers. They were to evacuate everything south of Port Royal. No plea of occupation or of any previous treaty would be listened to, and the tone adopted clearly showed that if the English settlers held their ground it would be deemed a legitimate *casus belli*.

Further trouble with the Spaniards.

It must have been plain that if war broke out between Spain and Great Britain, Georgia would have to bear the first brunt of the attack. It must have been plain, too, to anyone who knew the course of English politics and English public opinion, that peace with Spain hung by a thread. Spanish officials harshly enforcing the right of search, English traders defying and evading the provisions of the treaty of Madrid, kept alive a smouldering spirit of discontent which might at any moment burst out into a blaze. It was an accepted article of the Tory creed that the treaty of 1730 was a shameful concession of national rights, and that Walpole was 'the mastiff of England and lap-dog of Spain.' The prolonged ascendancy of the Prime Minister rested on the solid support of the trading classes; to raise the cry of the wrongs of English merchants might shake the chief stronghold of his influence, and a card of such value in the party game was sure to be played. Hot-headed patriots and unscrupulous place-hunters would be united in a common policy.

For Georgia the whole question was a vital one. Whether the British policy was one of peace or of war, her interests were deeply involved. In any negotiations the curtailment of her territory and her defences was certain to be among the demands of Spain. On the other hand a declaration of war would at once leave her in the very forefront of the battle. Apart, too, from the interests of Georgia, Oglethorpe's local knowledge would be of special service both to his party and his country. Clearly a crisis was at hand which called for his presence in England.

Simultaneously Oglethorpe received a summons from the trustees urging him to be in his place when Parliament met in January. They did not lay any stress on the Spanish question. They could not, they said, carry on the colony without financial help from Parliament, and the presence and advocacy of Oglethorpe would be the best means of obtaining such help. Oglethorpe at once obeyed the summons, and early in January he was in England.

Oglethorpe returns to England.

There is nothing to show that Oglethorpe took any part in the debates which through the session of Parliament raged over our dealings with Spain. Indeed the question of Georgia entered but slightly into the discussions on the subject. That this should have been so is nowise creditable to the Opposition, for there beyond doubt was the strongest point in our case against Spain. To admit the claims of Spain was to abandon all the principles on which our colonial policy had been grounded. She could show nothing in the nature of regular and continuous occupation; even a claim based on discovery was uncertain. She had suffered the trustees of Georgia to sink capital in the soil without protest. The very means adopted to harass and hinder the colony, raids without any declaration of war, were themselves an outrage. Yet the patriots who denounced the right of search, and raved over Jenkins's ear, do not seem to have troubled themselves about claims fully as insulting and far more threatening to the future of the British Empire. One could hardly find a stronger illustration of the small space which colonial questions occupied in the consideration of English statesmen.

Supine though Parliament was in its regard for the interests of Georgia, the English Government must have seen that the colony was to be the battle-field of the coming struggle. In 1737 a memorial was presented from the Spanish ambassador demanding that Georgia should be evacuated, and that Oglethorpe should not be suffered to return. News too came that all English residents had been ordered to leave St. Augustine, and that the barracks there were being enlarged.

Measures were taken to meet these dangers. Men were sent from Gibraltar to Savannah, and a regiment of six hundred men and a company of grenadiers was raised and placed under the command of Oglethorpe for the defence of the colony. In addition Oglethorpe took out at his own charge a small body of volunteers and supernumerary officers.

Measures for the defence of Georgia.

The trustees decided to bind the soldiers to the colony by a permanent tie of interest and connexion. To each of them was assigned an allotment of five acres of land. Each too, if at the end of seven years he received his lawful discharge from the service, was to receive twenty acres more.

The presence of Oglethorpe in England made itself felt in the action of Parliament toward the colony. In 1736 there was no Parliamentary vote of money to the colony. But in 1737 ten thousand pounds was voted, and in the following year this was doubled. A portion of this was applied by the trustees to a further emigration of German Protestants. What with these emigrants, with the Highlanders at Darien and Frederica.

and the better class of independent planters who had been joining the colony, the original scheme of a pauper settlement was more and more falling into the background.

Later in the year the trustees took a step which still further modified—one might almost say which abandoned—the original conception of the colony. They found that many of the paupers whom they had exported would not work for their livelihood. Nor was that all; the original composition of the colony at Savannah made it necessary to grant supplies to everyone out of the public store. This drew idlers and adventurers from other colonies, many who had gone out without any definite intention of applying themselves to settled industry. Thus, within four years of the foundation of the colony, the trustees found themselves confronted with the danger which is in the very nature of things inherent in any such experiment. To meet this they issued an order that the benefit of the public store should be withheld from all who had without due reason neglected the cultivation of their land. This we are told cleared off many of the incomers from other colonies, and also not a few of those who had never really understood what would be the hardships and privations of colonial life.

Changes in the regulations for settlers in Georgia.

At the same time a modification was introduced into the original conditions. It was now clear that the defence of the colony would no longer depend on its own population organized as a militia. Accordingly the restriction by which all lands were to go in tail male was removed. Succession was at first thrown open to females, then all legal limitations to alienation were removed.

On another point, however, the trustees held fast to the principles which they had laid down. A number of settlers at Savannah were clamouring for permission to import negro slaves. In December a petition to this effect reached the trustees, signed by upward of a hundred and twenty of the settlers. Without negro labour they pointed out they could not raise the corn needful for their subsistence, nor compete in trade with their northern neighbours. The country was full of timber; this might be made a source of profit, if only the felling and shipping of it could be done by slave labour.

Demand for the importation of negroes.

Economically, no doubt, the petitioners had a good deal of reason on their side. But the very objects for which the colony had been created debarred the trustees from considering exclusively the economical aspect of the matter. Such an application was singularly inopportune at the very time when danger threatened from Florida. The southern settlers who would be exposed to the first brunt of the attack saw this, and sent in a counter-petition against the change. The Germans, too, at Ebenezer petitioned against it. Their opposition was mainly economical. They could grow, they said, more than enough produce for their own subsistence. They could not have purchased negroes, and they probably saw that a small community of peasant proprietors could not subsist alongside a system of slavery.

If the trustees had any thought of relaxing their original policy, the turn which events took in South Carolina must have decided them to stand firm. The Spanish Government had offered protection to all runaway slaves. Tidings reached the government of South Carolina that the whole body of slaves in the colony, forty thousand in number against some seven thousand English, had resolved to accept this offer. Several had already escaped to St. Augustine. Three representatives were sent to remonstrate with the Spanish Governor and to demand restitution of the fugitives.

That was refused; the Governor pleaded the orders of his superiors, and declared his intention of receiving all such runaways.

In May 1738 the questions at issue between Georgia and South Carolina came before the Board of Trade. The independent action of the South Carolina traders had been approved and supported by the legislature of the colony. It passed a bill raising a sum of money to indemnify any traders who should suffer by the action of Georgia, and in conjunction with the Council of the colony it lodged a petition against the action of the Georgia trustees. The interests of each colony were represented by counsel. Murray appeared for Georgia. A characteristic touch illustrates Oglethorpe's temper. Disgusted for some reason with Murray's advocacy, in the middle of the hearing he sprung up and rushed out of court.[1] The question was referred on by the Board of Trade to the Privy Council. This decision was an evasion of the difficulty rather than an authoritative settlement. It started with accepting the general principle that the navigation of the river should be open to both colonies. At the same time it approved the policy of the trustees in excluding spirits. The task of drawing up enactments which would secure both objects was left to the trustees of Georgia and to the Assembly of South Carolina. The death of the Governor of the latter colony, Samuel Horsey, through whom the instructions of the Privy Council were sent, enabled the Assembly to shelve the question.

It is a characteristic illustration of Oglethorpe's versatile and unresting energy that at the very time when all these cares lay heavy upon him, he could find leisure to advocate the claims of the unknown writer who had just produced the poem of 'London.' In that

[1] Charles Wesley's Journal, quoted by Wright, p. 172.

well-judged patronage were laid the foundations of a friendship by which, apart from Oglethorpe's public services, his name would live.

Over and above the danger of foreign invasion, matters within the colony were causing anxiety to Oglethorpe and the trustees. John Wesley's strenuous activity, his personal courage and his indifference to the comforts of life, had raised among the trustees who selected him great hopes of his services as a missionary among the Indians. On that side his career in America came to nothing. Like Goldsmith's hero when he went to teach English in Holland, neither the trustees nor Wesley seem to have reflected that a certain knowledge of the language spoken by his disciples was essential in a missionary. Nor indeed did Wesley's temper, especially in his young days, nor his conception of religion fit him for dealing with savages. The successful missionary must be yielding and compromising in non-essentials. Wesley's inclination was to make everything an essential. The missionary must be patient in his hopes, valuing and cherishing every tendency towards amendment, every stage in moral growth. The chief failing of such teaching as Wesley's is to overlook the gradual nature of moral growth, and to treat everything which falls short of moral perfection as worthless.

John Wesley.

Wesley, too, at once found himself hampered by the evil influence of the South Carolina traders, as yet the only specimens of English Christianity whom the natives had met. The French missionary, content to accept mere outward conformity when he could not secure moral conversion, seldom troubling himself to hold up to his disciples any high standard of conduct, did not feel this difficulty. Wesley must have constantly felt that the nominal Christianity of which the savages had before them examples was no better than heathenism. He must have fully felt the weight of the well-known protest of an Indian: 'Christian drunk. Christian beat men. Christian tell lies. Devil Christian. Me no Christian.'

Nevertheless the Wesleys seem to have entertained the idea of conducting a mission among the Indians of the Mississippi valley. The Moravians, by whom the Wesleys were guided, thought that the neighbourhood of the French would make such an attempt both useless and dangerous, and that there was plenty of spiritual work for ministers to do among the settlers at Savannah, and these views were supported by Oglethorpe.[1]

The tranquillity of Savannah would have gained something, and Oglethorpe would have been spared no small share of anxiety and vexation, if John Wesley had neglected this advice and chosen another sphere of activity.

In John Wesley's conduct at Savannah we see many of the same failings which had marred his brother's colonial career, intensified as might be expected by a more strenuous, self-confident, and uncompromising temper. An honest desire to bring about moral and spiritual reform was thwarted and made almost useless by a despotic, egotistical, and somewhat suspicious temper, and by a want of perfect directness and simplicity in action. To use Southey's words, 'he drenched his parishioners with the physic of an intolerant discipline.'[2] He insisted on baptism by immersion. When a would-be communicant was not a member of an Episcopal church, Wesley insisted on his re-baptism as a needful condition. He refused to read the burial service over a Nonconformist. Yet in other respects he claimed and exercised a discretionary power by dividing the services of the Church in a

[1] Southey, vol. i. p. 94.

[2] *Ibid.* p. 96.

manner certainly unusual and of doubtful legality. The result was naturally bewildering to those whose knowledge of creeds and ordinances ran in a few simple and familiar channels. One witness—a party pamphleteer indeed—tells us that 'all persons of any consideration' believed Wesley to be a Roman Catholic. One remonstrance addressed to him is reported by Wesley. 'The people say they are Protestants, but as for you they cannot tell what religion you are of; they never heard of such a religion before, and they do not know what to make of it.'[1] That we may well believe was the ordinary, obvious view of plain men.

It is clear too that Wesley, like his brother, aimed at that direct personal influence and control over individuals which is almost inevitably fatal to family peace and social quiet. If such a policy can ever be innocuous it can only be so where the person who aims at such power possesses exceptional insight into character, and an absolute freedom from egotism and from the love of power for its own sake. Wesley's most enthusiastic admirer could not justly claim for him the first-named virtue. The others, so far as they came at all, came with the discipline of maturer years.

The discontent and unpopularity which surrounded John Wesley were brought to a head by one special act of indiscretion. Causton, the store-keeper, had a pretty and accomplished niece, Sophia Hopkins. Her charms one may well believe were emphasized by the squalor and roughness of life at Savannah. To a cultivated young man, fresh from University life and from the decorum and peace of an English parsonage, they would easily be irresistible.

The girl presented herself to Wesley as one in need of spiritual guidance and consolation. She nursed him through a fever. Wesley, as one can see from constant

[1] Southey. Cf. *The True and Historical Narrative,* p. 30.

references in his diary, was one of those who delight in regulating their neighbours' life in small outward matters. At his bidding she gave up wearing colours and accepted his dictation as to her meal times.

A vague story, possibly true in its outlines, most improbable in its details, connects Oglethorpe with the affair. He, it is said, had made up his mind that marriage would be the proper cure for Wesley's moral and mental infirmities. Accordingly he incited Sophia Hopkins and another young lady to lay siege to the young clergyman. Whether the reserve wing of Oglethorpe's force was ever brought into action does not appear. But we are told that soon after she married, and then becoming smitten in conscience she presented herself to Wesley and confessed the plot against him, adding that she and Sophia Hopkins had instructions from Oglethorpe to win him by any concessions, even she said at the expense of virtue.[1]

This strange confession is told on the authority of information privately communicated to the biographer of Wesley. The confession may have been recorded; it may even have been made. Neither morbid and exaggerated confessions, nor the exaggerated interpretation of confessions, are uncommon phenomena where emotional religion comes into action. The one thing we may be sure of is that Oglethorpe never laid such a plot in the form in which it was thus imputed to him. One may safely go further and say that Wesley can never have deliberately believed such a charge, or wished others to believe it. He was not the man to remain on terms of courtesy, still less of affection, with one who could have imagined such a scheme.

On the other hand there is nothing unlikely in the belief that Oglethorpe was ill-judging enough to attempt

[1] Southey (vol. i. p. 111 *n.*) refers to this strange story, but very reasonably refuses to accept it.

the part of a match-maker. His was just the restless benevolence which delights in shaping other people's destinies for them, and his sanguine energy would blind him to the very serious dangers of adopting such a course with a man of Wesley's temper and character. If it were so, his indiscretion was fully punished by the annoyance which he brought on himself and the disturbance inflicted on the colony.

So far Wesley had dealt with Sophia Hopkins as a spiritual adviser and director.[1] He now combined with that the character of a wayward and exacting lover. Not indeed that he was carried away with passion. He gravely weighs her fitness to become his wife and solemnly records the result in his diary, without so far as one can judge the faintest perception of absurdity. The docility with which she abandoned the pernicious habit of late suppers turned the scale in her favour. Wesley was not, however, carried away by any enthusiastic conviction of the lady's merits. He consulted his friend and companion, Delamotte. He was of opinion that Sophia Hopkins was thinking of her prospects of a husband rather than aiming at spiritual perfection. Wesley then laid the matter before the Moravians. They appear to have been influenced by Delamotte's judgment. Wesley placed himself unreservedly in their hands, and their decision was against the marriage. Thereupon he gave up all further thoughts of it. In less than a year the lady married one of the chief settlers, Williamson.

One cannot doubt that Wesley is recording his own feelings with perfect sincerity when in his diary he describes his act as one of genuine self-sacrifice in the cause of duty. But other passages in Wesley's life show that his feelings to womankind were neither

[1] For this part of the story and for the rest of Wesley's sojourn in the colony see his journal,

deep nor abiding. He soon satisfied himself with obvious and commonplace sources of consolation. 'God,' he records, 'has shown me yet more of the greatness of my deliverance by opening to me a new and unexpected scene of Miss Sophy's dissimulation.' But though he withdrew from the position of a lover, he still felt it incumbent on him to fill that of a spiritual adviser. Mrs. Williamson's conduct in certain matters struck him as blameworthy and he reproved her, and she not unnaturally showed resentment. Wesley then punished her contumacy by the extreme step of excluding her from communion. It would be a gross injustice to the kindliness of Wesley's temper to suppose that the act was not painful; it would be equally unjust to his intelligence to suppose that he did not foresee the consequences. But in the morbid and self-torturing frame of mind which Wesley's diary at that period discloses to us, the pain and the danger of the measure would be overwhelming arguments in its favour.

In spite of all that had come and gone, Causton and his wife seem to have retained a friendly feeling to Wesley. They now sought to persuade him to adopt more moderate measures. He, however, remained obdurate, and thereupon the lady's friends took up an attitude of open hostility. Williamson brought a civil action against Wesley for defaming his wife's character. At the same time he was prosecuted for various alleged irregularities in the conduct of divine service, and on the exceedingly vague charge of speaking and writing to Mrs. Williamson without her husband's consent. Causton also published extracts from Wesley's letters to his niece, and affidavits made by the latter of what Wesley had said to her; while Wesley retaliated by recording a statement of his case in church to his congregation.

It would seem as if the legal proceedings were rather designed to annoy and humiliate Wesley, and so to drive him from the colony, than to lead to any formal sentence. The prosecutors themselves interposed delays, in spite of Wesley's repeated demands to have the matter brought to trial.

If the object was to make Wesley's position in the colony untenable, his enemies (and he had many) could plausibly represent him as an unscrupulous hypocrite, who had first made love to a pretty woman, then jilted her, and finally sought to bully her. His friends must have felt that his own lack of discretion had put him in a position where it was hard to refute such charges. And, worst of all, we may be sure that Wesley himself must have known that, though he might find a controversial defence for his conduct at each successive stage, yet really the matter as a whole was to his discredit. Denounced, suspected and self-reproachful, he could no longer play a useful part in the colony.

Wesley's enemies were not content with destroying his influence and driving him from Georgia. They were determined that no drop in the cup of humiliation should be spared him. When he announced his intention of leaving the colony he was told that he must stay till the charges against him had been settled. He protested that he had been repeatedly ready to answer the charges, and that as often proceedings had been delayed. Nevertheless the magistrates insisted that he must give bail for his appearance. He refused, and thereupon an order was issued to all officers and sentries bidding them prevent his escape, and prohibiting all other persons from assisting at it. Yet it seems clear that there was no real intention to detain him. Only he was to be humiliated by the appearance of a clandestine flight from justice. On December 2 he left the colony on foot with three companions, men according to his enemies of no very good character.[1] After

[1] Stephens writes, 'If the parson had taken a few more with him of such

enduring hardships and losing their way in the woods they reached Port Royal. Thence they went by boat to Charlestown, where Wesley took ship for England.

Spanish intrigues.

In July 1738, Oglethorpe with his regiment set sail from Plymouth. Before they had left England they were reminded of what they might expect from an unscrupulous enemy like Spain. The two nations were at peace. Yet Oglethorpe found that more than one Spanish spy had enlisted. Among them was an Irish Roman Catholic, who had served under Berwick. His unsuccessful efforts to seduce his comrades led to the discovery of the plot. He was allowed to sail with the regiment in the hopes that more discoveries might be made. On September 18 the fleet reached Frederica. A court martial was formed; those who were found guilty were with singular, and one cannot but think unwise, lenity sentenced to expulsion and flogging.[1]

Oglethorpe's first care was for the military security of the colony. The newly arrived troops were dispersed for garrison duty at the various fortified outposts. This arrangement made it necessary to secure effective communication between Frederica and the southern portion of St. Simon's Island. To this end a road was cut through the woods and along the west coast of the island, flanked on one side by water and swamps, on the other by an impenetrable forest. The whole male population of the island was employed in the work, and the result was complete in three days.

Over and above his military cares Oglethorpe found himself beset with difficulties arising out of the social and economical condition of the colony. The fear of invasion from the south had hindered cultivation. The

as he then made his companions, provided their creditors did not suffer, the colony would be the better without them.' Journal, vol. i. p. 46.

[1] Oglethorpe to the trustees; written on shipboard, July 3, 1738, quoted by Wright.

native allies in the western part of the colony had been attacked. The Spanish authorities in Florida laid the blame of such attacks on their own Indians whom they were unable to control. For once Oglethorpe's sanguine courage showed some signs of failing him. In September he reported to the trustees that the northern part of the colony had lost two-thirds of its population. Some have fled because of their debts, others for fear of Spanish invasion. 'If,' the General wrote, 'there is not a supply from Parliament this year, those brave fellows who stood the worst, and also till the arrival of the regiment were forced to be almost a whole year under arms, must starve with their families, since they could not do their duty and work at the same time.'[1]

Economical and administrative difficulties.

Later on in the same year we find Oglethorpe writing to a friend in England: 'I am here in one of the most delightful situations as any man could wish to be. A great number of debts, empty magazines, no money to supply them, numbers of mouths to be fed, mutinous soldiers to command, a Spanish claim and a large body of their troops not far from us.' He ends up by pointing out that the trustees have been at great cost for national objects. These ought to be paid by Parliament.[2]

The military operations against the Spaniards had not only hindered the industry of the colony, but had also compelled Oglethorpe to disregard the principles which had guided him in his choice of settlers. In 1741 he sent one of his officers to Virginia to get recruits, with the result that he brought back, as we are told by a not unfriendly witness, 'all the scum of Virginia.'[3]

[1] Letter to the trustees. Georgia Hist. Soc. vol. iii. p. 49.

[2] *Ibid.* p. 62.

[3] *Itinerant Observations,* p. 62. The writer says that he sailed in the same ship as these recruits.

Nevertheless the better prospect of safety which Oglethorpe's return brought with it improved matters, and the settlers could till their fields in safety. The real difficulty was at Savannah. There it is plain the settlers had allowed themselves to become dependent on the eleemosynary aid given by the trustees. The hopes that they would struggle upward to the condition of a self-supporting community had not been fulfilled. And now this act of ill-timed parsimony on the part of Parliament cut short the help on which the settlers had been taught to rely. In consideration of the grant of a regiment, the money vote for the colony had been cut down from twenty thousand pounds to eight thousand.[1] With these tidings Oglethorpe had to face the already discontented settlers at Savannah. He had to explain to them that the town, or at least that portion which was supported from the public store, must be treated somewhat like a city on siege allowance. Everything approaching a superfluity must be retrenched, and the public resources economized for those who were absolutely dependent on them. At the same time Oglethorpe explained to the settlers that no blame would attach to any who might leave the colony in the hopes of faring better elsewhere. This permission does not seem to have been taken advantage of by many. It must be remembered, however, that the colony had already been weeded by secessions.[2]

It is also probable that the repeal of the strict system of inheritance in tail male originally enforced had done something to pacify the discontented party among the settlers.[3]

[1] This was stated by Oglethorpe in a speech which he made to the settlers at Savannah. Wright, p. 208.

[2] *V.s.* p. 461.

[3] Letter-book of Trustees.

Something Oglethorpe was able to do in supplementing the resources of the trustees out of his own private purse. He also set on foot a much-needed investigation into the conduct of those officials who controlled the public funds and stores. Causton, it was plain, had been guilty of maladministration, if not of actual dishonesty. He endeavoured to evade the charges against him by pleading that he had only carried out Oglethorpe's instructions; that the trustees were now dissatisfied with the conduct of the General, and that he, Causton, was being made a scape-goat. Neither the independent testimony of Stephens, who was now the secretary to the colony, nor even the partisan statements of Oglethorpe's enemies, in any way bear out this view.

Dismissal of Causton.

Causton was dismissed, but his dismissal does not seem to have pacified the malcontents at Savannah. According to them Jones, his successor in the administration of the store, instead of selling them goods at cost price, made the utmost profit that he could on behalf of the trustees. In fact, if we may believe their complaints, the only change was that Causton put the profits into his own pocket, while now they went into the public exchequer. The difficulty was simply that which must inevitably arise when a government undertakes the work of distribution instead of leaving it to the free action of individuals in open market.

Other troubles even more threatening as matters stood beset Oglethorpe. In addition to the regiment which he took out, a small force had been sent in advance, drawn from the garrison of Gibraltar. They seem to have been unfortunate in their officers. Some of the men, too, had during their stay at Gibraltar learnt Spanish. As we have seen, the enemy was alive to every possible chance of stirring up sedition among our troops, and there was reason

The soldiers mutiny.

to think that intrigues were on foot. Moreover the Government in its contract with these troops had agreed that they were to receive rations only for six months; after that they were to supply themselves out of their pay. This created discontent, and when in November Oglethorpe visited the fort at St. Andrew's he found the garrison ready for mutiny. An application to him for redress insolently made was followed by an altercation. If an attack had not been arranged, it is at least clear that the mutineers only wanted a signal to act together. The officer in command of the company, Captain Mackay, enraged by the insolence of the soldier who now acted as spokesman, drew his sword. The mutineers wrested it from him and broke it, and then rushing to barracks raised the cry of 'One and all!' This as it would seem was taken as the watchword for rising. Two men aimed at Oglethorpe; one gun missed fire, the bullet of the other grazed the General's head; a third drew his sword. Oglethorpe parried the blow and an officer ran the mutineer through. The others were arrested, tried and sentenced to death, but Oglethorpe, always lenient, and as some thought in this case unwisely so, spared all but the ringleader.[1]

Before long further disputes arising out of the rations question broke out. Oglethorpe's own regiment was required to find its own supplies out of pay. His lieutenant-colonel, Cochrane, was charged with making a profit of this, 'following merchandise to the neglect of his duty.' His accuser was Captain Mackay. Accusations were exchanged between him and Mackay, and it was necessary to send both to England to stand their trial.[2]

Meanwhile it became painfully clear that the whole

[1] Wright, pp. 203–4. He quotes a letter from Oglethorpe to the trustees, and refers to Stephens's Journal and the *Gentleman's Magazine*.

[2] Oglethorpe to Newcastle, quoted by Wright, p. 211.

safety of the colony hung on the stability of the alliance with the Creeks. The Spaniards were doing all that could be done by bribes and intrigues to kindle disaffection, and their efforts were seconded by the misconduct of the traders from South Carolina. There was, too, yet another source of danger. As early as 1735 the French occupants had made it abundantly clear that they were prepared to resist any attempt of the English to ally themselves with the Indians in the Mississippi valley. A letter is extant, written from Mobile by Bienville in fairly good English, and addressed to the Governor of Georgia, in which he complains that a certain Englishman 'who has the inspection of the traders has been setting the Indians against the English; telling them that he is to be termed the man of valour, and that the French ought to demolish their forts.'[2]

Dealings with the Indians.[1]

As early as the summer of 1736 the Chickasaws had sent a deputation to Savannah to inform Oglethorpe of French plots and to ask for protection. This address contains a curious specimen of Indian rhetoric, and Oglethorpe's answer shows how he could adapt himself to the requirements of Indian diplomacy. The Indian orator told Oglethorpe, probably as a compliment, that they regarded him as 'the son of a red woman.' He replied that he was at least an Indian in heart.[3]

About the same time we read in the archives of Georgia of two unsuccessful attacks by the French and their Indian allies on the Choctaws and Chickasaws' villages.[4]

Two years later, however, the colonists were made anxious by the news that the Chickasaws were being

[1] Oglethorpe's letters to the trustees, and to Newcastle, in the Colonial Papers.

[2] In the Colonial Records.

[3] Report of conference in Colonial Papers, July 13, 1736.

[4] Letters from Samuel Eveleigh in the Trustees' Letter-book.

driven out of their country by the French, and were taking refuge in South Carolina.[1]

Impetuous enthusiasts of the type of Oglethorpe are none too often judicious in their choice of subordinates. We have seen this in the case of the Wesleys. It probably was so in the case of Mackay whom Oglethorpe had intrusted with the management of Indian affairs in the Chickasaws' country. A man was not likely to make a successful Indian diplomatist who set out with the conviction that an Indian 'has no idea of gratitude; in a word I cannot observe that they are governed by any virtuous principle.'[2]

He was, moreover, a thorough-going advocate of a 'forward' policy and would fain have seen the French cleared out of the Mississippi valley and the Spanish out of Florida: counsels of perfection, it may be, but perilous as practical doctrine to be acted on by the authorities in Georgia.

He also was undoubtedly responsible for stimulating, if not creating, hostile feeling between Georgia and South Carolina, by the summary fashion in which he sought to eject the licensed traders from the latter colony. They pertinently remarked that when the government of South Carolina gave Georgia seven or eight thousand pounds wherewith to build a fort and to protect Indian trade they did not look to see their own citizens debarred from that trade.[3]

In one way Mackay showed a power of intelligent observation. He at once recognised the superiority of the western highlands over the sea-board as a habitation for Europeans.

The French were gathering a force at Montreal which was to march through the valleys of the Ohio and

[1] Stephens's Journal, vol. i. p. 187.

[2] Mackay to the trustees, March 23, 1735.

[3] Letter from Broughton, Deputy-Governor of South Carolina, to Mackay, July 1735.

Mississippi, accumulating native allies by the way, and whose aim was either to crush the Creeks or at least to detach them from the English alliance. Fortunately the Creeks were an extensive, homogeneous, and well-organized power, with whom it was possible to negotiate. Moreover, the two neighbouring tribes, the Chickasaws and Choctaws, though independent of the Creeks, seem to have been united to them, if not by formal alliance, at least by recognised and habitual friendship. Thus the three tribes were to our Southern colonies much what the Five Nations were for New York. Early in the summer Oglethorpe arranged to meet the native chiefs in their own country. The spot chosen was Coweta, a stronghold of the Creeks, three hundred miles inland near the head waters of the Alatamaha, on what is now the northern frontier of Alabama. It had to be reached by paths through the forest, three hundred miles from the German settlement at Ebenezer.

The account of Oglethorpe's conduct at the conference reminds one, save that it was followed by no unworthy concessions to savage usage, of those rulers of French Canada who won the hearts of the Indians by a partial adoption of their customs. He smoked the calumet with them and drank their black drink, a brewage of mysterious virtues, reserved for chiefs and medicine men. The Indians pledged themselves to keep friendship with the English, and to respect their wishes by abstaining from any attack on the French.

Within a few weeks of his return from the conference, Oglethorpe lost his chief Indian ally, Tomochichi. He was said to be over a hundred years old,[1] and the colony had passed the stage when the friendly influence of a single savage was of vital

[1] Stephens, vol. ii. p. 153. For obvious reasons statements of age among savages are never much to be trusted.

importance. But the military honours paid to his corpse, when it was borne by his English allies from the landing-place at Savannah and buried in the chief square of the town, were not undeserved. Missionary accounts of savage virtue are apt to be misleading. But one may really believe that Tomochichi possessed those better qualities, that steadiness of purpose and constancy in friendship, that superiority to merely personal and sordid aims, in which the best specimens of his race could at times rise above the common level of the barbarian.

To Oglethorpe and to the settlers in Georgia the declaration of war with Spain in 1739 must have come as a relief from intolerable suspense. Hitherto their hands had been tied by restraints to which their enemies were unscrupulously indifferent. While Oglethorpe was restraining his savage allies, the Governor of Florida was intriguing to undermine their loyalty and that of the English garrison, and to stir up a servile insurrection among the negroes in South Carolina.

The circumstances which attended the outbreak of the war illustrated forcibly how the English colonies were hampered by the lack of some common administrative system. Before Oglethorpe knew that war had actually been declared, he heard that the Governor of Rhode Island was fitting out privateers.

At the same time the alliance of the Indians had been a danger. The presence of certain unlicensed traders from South Carolina among them had been followed by an outbreak of sickness, in reality small-pox, but thought by the natives to be the result of poisoned rum. Oglethorpe succeeded in allaying their suspicions, and promised more efficient control over the traders for the future.[1]

[1] This statement and that in the previous paragraph are taken from

The war began with a petty raid by the Spanish troops on the southern frontier, having for its result the killing of two unarmed Highlanders. Oglethorpe saw that a scattered population living by agriculture would do best to act on the offensive. An effective invasion might destroy or cripple St. Augustine's. Otherwise all the outlying planters would be compelled to keep within the defences of Frederica and the colony would be starved.

Measures of defence against the Spaniards.[1]

Oglethorpe's first measure was to make a reconnoitring expedition in boats, rowed by the soldiers themselves and by some of the Highland settlers. He landed on the southern side of the St. John's river, and marched within some ten miles of St. Augustine. At the same time he did his best to prevent the Spaniards crossing the St. John's by destroying every boat on which he could lay hands. The southern forts had, in obedience to the orders given by Newcastle in expectation of continued peace, been suffered to fall into ruins. Oglethorpe now proposed as soon as Frederica was put in a defensible condition to go on with the refortification of St. Andrew's and Amelia.

There were special reasons for pressing on with hostilities. Havannah was now blockaded by an English fleet, and thus the Spaniards in Florida were cut off from their chief source of supplies and troops. To seize this opportunity of striking an effective blow it was needful to have the help of South Carolina. There does not seem to have been any wish on the part of that colony to shirk her fair share of duty. But, as was usual in such questions, the difficulties of

Mr. Wright's book, pp. 218-9. I have verified both, but I regret to say that I omitted to make a note of the precise reference.

[1] The operations previous to the joint invasion of Florida are described in letters from Oglethorpe to the trustees and to the Duke of Newcastle, quoted or epitomized by Mr. Wright, pp. 227–32. When Mr. Wright does not give the text I have verified it.

communication and the want of ready and cordial co-operation between the different members of the legislature caused delays. South Carolina, too, was suffering from the cost of suppressing the negro rebellion, and from the destruction of property and hindrance to industry which had accompanied it.

Negotiations with South Carolina.

In the winter of 1739 Oglethorpe sent to Bull, the acting Governor of South Carolina, a series of letters explaining his own intentions of attacking the Spaniards and asking for help. The Assembly referred the matter to a committee. While this committee was sitting a further communication came from Oglethorpe. He had, he said, enlisted the services of the Indian allies, and was expecting at least a thousand Cherokee and Creek warriors to be ready in March. This went far to force the hand of the South Carolina government, for an Indian force once raised had to be used without delay. If long held in leash they were sure to be troublesome, and might even join the enemy rather than remain inactive.[1]

Oglethorpe attacks the Spaniards.

Meanwhile, without waiting for the decision of the sister colony, Oglethorpe had taken independent action against the enemy. The treaty of Utrecht bound the Spaniards to abstain from any occupation of territory north of the river St.

[1] In my account of the invasion I have relied on Oglethorpe's own despatches and on Mr. McCrady. His description is based on the report of a committee appointed by the Assembly of South Carolina to inquire into the conduct of the war. The report is published in the South Carolina Historical Society's Collections, but unfortunately the volume that contains it is not in the British Museum.

Mr. Wright's account shows a strong bias in favour of Oglethorpe. He dwells on the fact that the South Carolina commander, Van der Dussen, was a man of bad private character. That may be so. Mr. McCrady admits that he was by tradition a severe slave-master. But 'the trade of war needs no saints,' and Oglethorpe's moral superiority to his colleague does not prove that the former was a good soldier or the latter a bad one.

Matthew. Nevertheless they had before the declaration of war built a fort, St. Francis, on the north bank of the river exactly facing another Spanish fort called Piccolata. By this means they commanded a passage across the river into the Creek county. The place might be a dangerous refuge for fugitive slaves who made their way across land from South Carolina. Furthermore, the Spaniards could thus establish land communication with Mexico, and bring troops thence either to reinforce St. Augustine or to invade Georgia from the west. Early in January Oglethorpe embarked a detachment of his own force and some of the Highlanders, and ascended the river. The attack was supported by a strong body of Indians, who made their way through the woods along the southern bank. Without help from their civilized allies the Indians fell upon Piccolata and burnt it. On the same day Oglethorpe invested and attacked St. Francis with his whole force. At the second cannonade the place surrendered. Oglethorpe now might safely invade, without any fear of leaving his colony open to a flank attack from the land.

Further negotiations with South Carolina.

In February Oglethorpe communicated these successes to Bull, and on March 23 he appeared in person at Charlestown, to press on the Assembly the need for instant and united action. Oglethorpe urged strongly on his hearers the weakness of St. Augustine, a weakness which, as later events showed, he greatly underrated. There was also present at the conference Commodore Pearce, who was in command of a squadron of six ships and expected to be joined by three more. He promised co-operation and shared Oglethorpe's sanguine view. Whatever reluctance there may have been was overborne by these assurances, and the Assembly agreed to raise a force of four hundred rangers, and to contribute twenty-five thousand pounds. There was among the Carolina troops one at least who had special experience fitting him for the task now at hand. Captain William Palmer can have hardly yet reached middle life. Nevertheless he had twice played a brilliant part in the frontier warfare of his colony. In the Yamassee war of 1715 he had had a scaling party which captured an Indian fort. In 1720 he had been sent out against his ancient enemies at the head of three hundred men. But interpreting his commission liberally he had harried and destroyed all the outlying Spanish settlements, laying the country waste up to the very gates of St. Augustine. He now accompanied the expedition as a volunteer, and was appointed by Oglethorpe his aide-de-camp.

It was much, no doubt, that South Carolina was willing to co-operate. Yet one may doubt whether the conditions under which that co-operation was agreed to promised well for success. The Carolinians may well have felt that they were being hurried into action by the dominant will of Oglethorpe. The older colony was being forced, in reality if not in name, into a position of subordination to a younger community, which in the eyes of South Carolina planters and merchants with their aristocratic traditions was little better than a penal settlement. Seldom, too, could a colonial force officered by provincials work smoothly and effectively under a commander whose military experiences were wholly European.

The allied colonies invade Florida.

On May 10 Oglethorpe began his advance with two hundred men of his own regiment, a hundred South Carolinians and a hundred and three Indians. The expedition began with a small initial success. A wealthy mulatto, Don Diego Spinola, had a ranche with a fortified dwelling-house half-way between the St. John's river and Fort

Augustine. The place was valuable as supplying St. Augustine with cattle. On the appearance of Oglethorpe's force it surrendered. But any good gained by the success was sacrificed by the credulity, the failing no doubt of a magnanimous temper, with which Oglethorpe afterwards allowed himself to be influenced by the advice of his prisoner, Spinola.

Three weeks appear to have been now spent by Oglethorpe in somewhat erratic and uncertain movements, in feints and reconnaissances. There may have been justification for this, but one may confidently say that on the face of it Oglethorpe's best policy would have been to keep his ill-compacted force together by a policy of prompt attack. The delay gave the underlying elements of disunion time to develope. The South Carolinians thought they were unnecessarily marched and countermarched. They demurred to having to pay Spinola for his cattle, and there were disputes as to the terms on which runaway negroes, the property of Carolina slaveholders, and recaptured from the Spaniards, were to be restored. Nor was this the only evil which resulted from delay. A small Spanish fleet succeeded in evading the English vessels which were co-operating with Oglethorpe, and reinforced St. Augustine's with two thousand men.

On the last day of May Oglethorpe resumed his advance, and on June 2 the invading force were within two miles of St. Augustine. Palmer and another volunteer officer from South Carolina eagerly urged Oglethorpe to make an immediate assault on the town. Oglethorpe, however, was determined not to attack till the fleet could co-operate. That no doubt was sound policy, granted that such co-operation was possible.

Unfortunately, Oglethorpe appears to have been ill-informed as to possibilities of approach from the sea. On that side the place was practically impregnable.

The bar across the harbour mouth forbade the access of large vessels, and the Spanish batteries were so placed that no small boats could run in under their fire. The land force met with no opposition. Such external defences as existed were abandoned by the Spaniards, and on June 4 Oglethorpe found himself under the walls of the town. But his signal of attack to the fleet was unanswered.

Though he did not till later know the cause of inaction Oglethorpe saw that the fleet either could not or would not attack. With such resources as Oglethorpe had, to assault the town by land without support from the fleet was clearly a hopeless policy. The Indian allies were practically useless for such warfare. There were no sappers or siege apparatus, only at the outside a thousand infantry. The garrison was double that number, the fortifications were strong and in good repair, mounted with fifty cannon. The only hope was to starve out the place, blockading it by sea and land. This, however, involved cordial and prompt co-operation between the land force and the fleet. Commodore Pearce had already plainly warned Oglethorpe that the fleet could not stay beyond July 5. At that date the hurricanes were expected. It was even possible that easterly winds might compel the fleet to quit the coast earlier.

That declaration might well have been the signal for the withdrawal of Oglethorpe's force, and it is impossible to acquit him of blame for obstinately clinging to his original plan when the one vital condition of success was changed. It was probably unfortunate that he was encouraged by obtaining one small success.

He succeeded in capturing a Spanish battery which as he believed would command St. Augustine. On the strength of this he summoned the Spanish Commander to surrender. He only received for answer a taunting message: 'The Spanish Governor would be delighted to see the English General inside St. Augustine.' The utter futility of Oglethorpe's attempts to bombard the town from the position which he had seized fully justified his enemy's confidence. Meanwhile the English experienced a reverse in another quarter: a reverse, too, for which it is impossible wholly to absolve Oglethorpe from blame. The English had in their advance occupied without resistance an advanced post of the enemy called Fort Moosa, some two miles from St. Augustine. Oglethorpe had made the place indefensible by breaching the walls in three places, fearing, as he himself expressed it, that it might at a later day become 'a mouse-trap' for his own troops. Nevertheless he sent back a detachment under Palmer to occupy it, or rather to use it as head-quarters. They were to harry the enemy in that direction, and to lie out in the woods. It is exceedingly difficult to see what effect Oglethorpe expected this operation to have on the siege. Palmer plainly had no liking for his task. He told Oglethorpe that the force allotted to him, about one hundred white men and thirty-five Indians, was wholly insufficient and ought to be doubled. High words passed, and Palmer left with the feeling of a man who is bound by obligations of soldiership to accept a task which he himself believes to be hopeless.

There was apparently no clear understanding as to the extent of Palmer's authority and responsibilities. He was nominally in command. But when he insisted that the troop should take full advantage of the cover of the woods and should on no account shut themselves up in the fort, his orders were wholly disregarded. The result was that the party was attacked and shut in. Palmer himself was shot down. Nearly all the regular troops shared his fate; the Carolinian militia were for the most part taken prisoners. This mishap was in no way calculated to bring about any friendly feeling between the constituent parts of the force. An incident arising out of this illustrated the dangers and drawbacks of the savage alliance. An Indian prisoner was given over to the Spanish allies to be tortured and burnt. The Cherokees had a Spanish prisoner. Their chief by Oglethorpe's instruction sent a message to the Spanish Governor that as the Yamassees dealt with their prisoner, so would the Cherokees with theirs. As a result of this an agreement was made that all Indian captives should be treated as prisoners of war. It is said that Oglethorpe's attempts to enforce this cost him the alliance of the Chickasaws.

Towards the end of June Oglethorpe made a last attempt at a combined attack, but the fleet again was unwilling or unable to co-operate. The invasion was abandoned and the land force withdrew across the frontier, the Carolina troops it is said in disorder, while Oglethorpe with a portion of his own regiment brought up the rear and, in spite of more than one sally by the enemy, secured the retreat.

The materials at our disposal hardly justify us in apportioning with confidence the blame of this failure.

Causes of Oglethorpe's failure.

According to Oglethorpe and his friends, the commodore of the fleet was at best supine, the Carolina soldiers ill-disciplined. One may doubt whether it was wise of Oglethorpe as things were to persist in the policy of invasion. He urged in his own defence that if the Carolina Assembly had sent troops at once the blow could have been struck in January, before supplies could arrive from Havannah, and while St. Augustine therefore was defenceless. That may be an effective condemnation of the government of South Carolina for its tardiness, but it does not prove that Oglethorpe, who must have known or at least suspected how matters stood, was then right to keep to his original policy. If a commander disregards the conditions under which he has to work, it is no excuse to say that some one else is to blame for the existence of those conditions. The truth would seem to be that Oglethorpe, while a brave and not unskilful soldier, was but an indifferent organizer, and ill-fitted to concert and control operations which depended on the harmonious working of incongruous and conflicting elements. To his buoyant, hopeful temper the difficulties of concerted action seemed small till they were actually present, and then the very sanguineness which had gone before brought on a confusing and paralysing reaction. It is impossible to acquit Oglethorpe of failure in foreseeing and providing for difficulties, of a lack of forethought and judgement in allocating duties to subordinates, and as a consequence of inability to inspire them with confidence. It has been urged that he was harassed and unstrung by the perpetual activity required in controlling operations scattered over a wide field. But that was so, largely because he chose to be ubiquitous, and showed no ability for delegating work.

The best defence that can be urged for Oglethorpe is that he played for heavy gains and did not risk much. Let St. Augustine be captured, and all danger either to Georgia or South Carolina from that quarter would be at end. The defence of those colonies would no longer be a drain on the pockets and industry of the inhabitants, nor on the naval resources of England. And Oglethorpe might at least plead that his conduct of the expedition had involved no irreparable loss and had not thrown the colony open to attack.

Discontent at Savannah.

While the cloud of invasion was hanging over the colony, and while Oglethorpe was fully employed in strengthening the defences of Frederica and of the adjacent islands, the malcontents at Savannah were doing all in their power to hamper and embarrass him. There was no doubt much distress among the poorer settlers at Savannah, and probably a good deal of discontent. But the attacks on Oglethorpe and the clamour for change did not come from them. There is nothing to show that the ordinary run of settlers there had any wish for the importation of negroes. That demand came from those independent settlers with enough land to make slave labour useful, or enough capital to make the slave trade profitable. Some were landholders, who however did not live on their plantations, but settled in the town either as traders or idlers. Their temper and position are illustrated by the fact that they formed a club intended at once to give voice to popular discontent and to promote sport. The streets were converted into a race-course.[1] In short, their aim was to create a poor and squalid imitation of the idle and pleasure-seeking life of the Charlestown planters.

Their grievances found utterance in a long and cumbrous pamphlet.[2] There was no doubt in the condition of the colony ample material for a picture of misery and failure. Composed as it was, threatened from without, its energies and resources drawn off to resist foreign invasion, how could it be otherwise? The permission of slavery too was a point which might fairly be argued. But whatever strength there was in their case Oglethorpe's opponents wholly threw away by their statement of it. For one thing they sought to prove far too much. According to them the resources of the soil did not admit of free industry at all. The free labourer could not subsist, they said, by growing rice and corn; the idea of supplementing their industry by the production of silk and wine was a delusion. The experience of the Salzburgers and of the Highlanders pointed all the other way, and clearly showed that the

[1] Letter-book of Trustees, p. 38. [2] See introductory note.

small freeholder might subsist by the labour of his own hands. That could only be met by alleging that the reports of such prosperity were given by interested witnesses, suborned by Oglethorpe. But if it were so, the case needed remedies far more radical than those proposed. If the colony could only prosper by slave labour, then the main object for which the trustees existed and had laboured was futile, and had better be at once abandoned. For it was very certain that whoever might profit by slave labour, bankrupt traders brought out at the public cost could not. And this cuts the ground from under the feet of the malcontents. Their condition very possibly was a poor one. They might have been better off in South Carolina or Virginia. But they had deliberately chosen to attach themselves to the colony knowing the purposes for which it was created. There was nothing but impudence in the demand that all those purposes should be abandoned and the whole policy of the founders reversed for their convenience.

Attacks on Oglethorpe.

But that which was far more certain to discredit the attack than anything in the substance of it, or even than its ponderous irony and dreary iteration, was the malevolence of its tone to Oglethorpe. Oglethorpe no doubt had faults of temper and character. But it was as plain as daylight that he was a man of vigorous mind and of a singularly generous, kindly and unselfish nature. His assailants painted him as a dull blunderer, wicked with the peculiar wickedness of a Domitian or a Surajah Dowlah. All the world could see that he had impaired his private fortune, given up the ambition of a hopeful career and turned his back on a fashionable and literary society of singular charm and brightness, only for the benefit of his country and for the relief of the poor and neglected. It was a hard task to persuade anyone that he had in reality done all this merely to inflict suffering on his fellow-men, and to play the part of an incompetent despot.

There is nothing to show that these malcontents spoke for any but themselves, or that they had any hold over the inhabitants of Savannah. The demand for negroes and for the importation of rum was no doubt largely supported. But it was quite possible to make those demands without calumniating or assailing Oglethorpe. His chief assailants saw so little chance of playing the part of successful demagogues that, in the autumn of 1740, they broke up the club, withdrew from the colony to Charlestown, and thence issued their manifesto.

A good deal of light is thrown on the question of introducing negro slavery by a letter in the Georgia archives addressed to Oglethorpe.[1] The writer is Samuel Eveleigh, a Charlestown merchant who took a keen interest in the affairs of the new colony. He may have looked to benefiting somewhat himself by the prosperity of Georgia. But the general tone of his letters justifies one in thinking that his interest in Georgia was prompted by a desire for the economical welfare of the whole body of colonies. He points out that from a merely material point of view slavery would be a gain. But he frankly admits that there may be other superior considerations.

The struggle was that ever-recurrent one between the sectional aspect of the community as an industrial machine, and the wider view of it as a complex organization with aims and demands transcending mere material needs. The conflict was all the more difficult to settle because of the special purposes for which Georgia had been created.

[1] Eveleigh to Martin, September 10, 1735. For a remarkable declaration by the Highlanders on the subject of slavery see Appendix V.

There is yet another point to be noticed. It was said before that the limitations of slavery were determined more by material considerations than by moral convictions. Georgia was no exception. Those who advocated slavery dwelt in the northern half of the colony, flanked by a community in which slavery was a carefully organized institution, and where therefore escape was difficult and unfrequent. To those on the southern frontier slavery presented itself as a real danger, since in Florida the escaped negro could always find a refuge, and would become an almost certain source of danger.

An element of discord soon arose from another quarter to vex Oglethorpe. In 1738, after Wesley's retirement the trustees appointed as the parish clergyman of Savannah one Norris, a respectable and apparently somewhat commonplace person, whose conceptions of religion did not probably rise above the ordinary level of the day. With him was associated as assistant George Whitefield, then a young deacon. The weaker points in his character, his contentiousness, his intolerant denunciations of all religious methods but his own, did not yet show themselves. During his first year at Savannah he was only known as specially strenuous in carrying out the services of the church and in impressing on the settlers the need of private devotion. Wesley's indiscretions must have inclined the inhabitants of Savannah to look with distrust on anything like exceptional zeal. Whitefield seems to have excited no suspicion or hostility. That this was so, that he should have laboured as he did and remained on good terms with his flock, shows that at this time at least there was no want of discretion and self-restraint in his conduct.

Whitefield in Georgia.

Whitefield was struck with the need for an orphanage house in the colony, where children without parents might be brought up under the control of some responsible person. To gain the support of the trustees for his scheme and to receive priest's orders he returned to England on September 6, 1738. It was during this stay in England that the world discovered—one may probably say that Whitefield discovered in himself—those peculiar powers by which his name has lived. In little more than a year he had shown by his work among the most brutal and profligate the power of awakening religious enthusiasm in vast masses, never equalled by any man speaking the English tongue. He had aroused the jealousy and hatred of those who felt that a great spiritual awakening within the Church would imperil the easy and indolent security in which they dwelt. He had awakened the more just suspicions of many who doubted whether sudden and violent emotion was a needful or healthy condition of spiritual life, whether indifference to the methods prescribed by the Church would not inevitably pass into hostility.

It is clear that there must have been among the trustees of Georgia a strong spirit of sympathy with the Evangelical revival. In spite of Wesley's failure, and undeterred by the symptoms of coming strife between Whitefield and the rulers of the Church, they appointed him to replace Norris as the parish clergyman at Savannah.

In certain ways Whitefield was undoubtedly a fitter man for the post than Wesley. His fibre was coarser, his nature less sensitive. He was perhaps better able to enter into the feelings of commonplace men than Wesley, certainly at that time better able to appeal to their emotions and control their wills. Yet recent events had shown elements in his character unfitting him for the post to which he was called. A man who had just played such a part on such a stage would not be content with the simple pastoral duties of a small community like Savannah. He would be sure to use his position in Georgia as a stepping-stone to far-reaching schemes of spiritual revival. Nor would it be in keeping with his character and views to remember and accept the various purposes for which Georgia had been founded. Religion was not with him an element in life, concurrent with others: it must absorb in itself the whole of human life; its rights as against other human emotions and obligations were not civic but despotic.

One may doubt, too, whether Whitefield's teaching, even the better side of it, was just that which such a society as Savannah needed. It was his mission to remind men that they might be conforming in a very respectable way to the standard of morality recognised by the world wherein they lived and yet be lacking in all the real elements of spiritual life. Assuredly England in the reign of George II. gave ample scope for such teaching. There in almost every walk of life a man might be a fairly respectable and law-abiding citizen and yet a very bad Christian. One may doubt whether that was so in Georgia or whether the settlers there stood in much need of Whitefield's warnings. There was no need there to expect men to turn their backs on the world. Ordinary civil and industrial life was itself a school of self-denial and self-sacrifice. The best teacher would be the one who could show most clearly how every-day life might be made a means of spiritual discipline, and how the duties of the citizen and of the Christian were consistent and largely identical.

The altered temper in which Whitefield returned to the colony was shown at once. During his first stay he seems to have worked harmoniously with Norris. Now Norris was not even to be allowed to withdraw from the colony peaceably. His evil influence was such that it must be counteracted by public denunciations. Norris was musical and occasionally played cards. He had been doing the work of the devil. He preached falsehood. To this Norris replied that he had at his ordination fully satisfied Gibson, the Bishop of London, of his orthodoxy. Norris knew very little of his man if he thought that any such formal test of religious truth would satisfy Whitefield. Gibson, Whitefield replied, was a disciple of the arch-deceiver Tillotson. The works of the master and the pupil alike had sent thousands of souls to hell. One can trace the gross and crudely expressed exaggeration of a truth. But it was not a truth needed by the settlers at Savannah. There was no doubt many a comfortable canon and rector in England, many a squire or trader who went to church or chapel on Sunday and thought no more of religion for six days in the week, who needed to be reminded that decorous morality was one thing and spiritual life another. But the dangers of morality were not the dangers to which the Savannah settlers were exposed. There a man who followed the teaching of Tillotson was in all likelihood taking a step upward. Mere morality might need to be supplemented, it certainly did not need to be quelled.

Whitefield's proceedings in South Carolina have already come before us. They cannot have been without their effect in the relations between that colony and Georgia. Georgia was chiefly known to the settlers at Charlestown by the report of those who had left Savannah discontented or unsuccessful. The present incident must rather have confirmed the feeling of those who looked on the new colony as a hotbed of anarchy and wrangling.

Whitefield, too, was not merely a spiritual enthusiast; he was a philanthropist, and like most strenuous and one-sided men he was in his philanthropy unscrupulous and almost merciless. Having obtained from the trustees a grant of five hundred acres he founded his projected orphanage, and his management of it soon brought him into direct conflict with Oglethorpe.

The orphanage.[1]

Whitefield would assuredly have been indignant at anyone who found points of likeness between his system and that of the Church of Rome. Yet he had much in common with the founders and upholders of monasticism. The world was evil and corrupt: if men could be entirely withdrawn from its influences so much the better for them. Accordingly in administering his orphanage it was Whitefield's policy to sweep into his net all whom he could.

According to Oglethorpe's view the trustees had established and endowed the orphanage in order to relieve themselves of the responsibility of maintaining those who were left destitute. According to Whitefield's view he was empowered to seize upon all orphans and force them in as inmates. He applied this doctrine to the case of a boy of fifteen who had been brought up by a settler named Parker. Parker not unnaturally contended that, having had the expense of rearing the boy, he was entitled to his services. Whitefield replied that the very fact of the boy being fit for service made him all the more useful as an inmate of the orphanage, and his superior obstinacy and power of assertion carried the day.

Soon after Whitefield broke up a home of orphan children, who were living together, and subsisting by the labours of the two eldest. The younger ones were carried off to the orphanage. Thereupon the eldest brother, acting by Oglethorpe's advice, demanded that

[1] Stephens tells very fairly and temperately, as far as one can judge, these proceedings of Whitefield. It argues in favour of his justice that he admits that Parker, the aggrieved employer, spoke with too much warmth. Mr. Wright's view seems to me exaggerated. He describes the orphanage as a sort of joyless penitentiary. I expect he was misled by Whitefield's ill-chosen language. Habersham, who may, I think, be regarded as a fair witness, gives a much more favourable account.

the others should be allowed to come home. Whitefield replied that they were in their own home. 'I know no other home they have to go to.' The message was to be sent on to Oglethorpe. The latter had already declared that Whitefield's claims to a general right of wardship over all orphans in the colony on whom he could lay his hands were unfounded. He now ordered that the children should be removed. An open scandal was avoided by the execution of the order in Whitefield's absence.

Be the merits of Evangelicalism what they may, the education of the young has never been its strong point. Whitefield tells with complacency how the whole time of the children was taken up with steady, useful work or meals, and that as a consequence of the total absence of play, the seventy inmates made no more noise than an ordinary private household. Such merits as the establishment had did not commend it to the colonists, and we hear of conflicts between the managers and the magistrates. Whitefield, and those who acted for him in his absence, wished to keep promising scholars, while the magistrates, acting in the interests of employers, thought more of supplying the labour market of the colony.

While Whitefield's general attitude must have put him out of harmony with the majority of the settlers, on one important matter he was at issue with the trustees. He strongly supported the case of those who were for importing negro slaves. Among the permanent triumphs of the Evangelical party, none has been more conspicuous and unquestioned than its opposition to slavery. It is singular that in one of the earliest battles over the system a great Evangelical leader should have been among its defenders.

Whitefield advocates negro slavery.

The arguments used by Whitefield were the ordinary

ones, based on the inadequacy of free labour to satisfy the wants of the colony. Though abolition was not yet an accepted article with his party, there was certainly nothing in Whitefield's experience of slavery to prepossess him in its favour. So far his evidence may be taken as that of an intelligent and disinterested witness against the views of the trustees.

With all these elements of internal strife distracting the colony, there ever hung over it the almost immediate prospect of invasion. The danger which threatened our Southern colonies from Spain was of a different kind from that which threatened New York and New England at the hands of French Canada. In the North we had to fear systematic and gradual aggression, preparing the way for ultimate conquest. Spain had no real wish for any permanent extension of territory north of Florida. Her operations therefore would be strictly military; they would aim solely at harassing and distracting England, by striking a blow at her settlements. The Spaniards might seek to occupy points on the coast of Georgia, but if they did so they would hold them merely as advanced outposts for military purposes, not as part of a continuous territory.

Difference between Spanish and French aggression.

Thus in a certain sense Spain was a far less dangerous rival in America than France. The whole future of the English-speaking race on the American continent was not involved in the same fashion. But if the ultimate danger to the whole body of colonies was less, the immediate danger to the colonies specially threatened was for that very reason greater. The danger from Canada was such as to unite all the colonies from the Kennebec to the Chesapeake for purposes of resistance. Their joint action might be blundering, hesitating, imperfect; still the necessity for such action was recognised. And as the danger extended, as the basis of the Ohio and the Mississippi became the scene of French aggression, so did the spirit of resistance extend too. Every public man who thought about the colonies at all had in his mind some scheme of federal action, which should take in the whole body of colonies. Such schemes found as much favour in Virginia as they did in the colonies which had actually suffered at the hands of the French and their savage allies. And remiss as English statesmen were in their dealings with colonial questions, yet there is no doubt that the danger of a rival power which should hold the line of the lakes and the St. Lawrence, and the valleys of the Ohio and Mississippi, was becoming more and more present and obvious.

The danger to Georgia involved no such extensive or abiding issues. It concerned only Carolina and Georgia. The other colonies might not unreasonably feel that the question was a purely military one which might fairly be left to the home authorities. War on the Savannah or Alatamaha was little more to the citizens of Boston and New York than war on the Senegal or on the coast of Bombay.

Nor was there any hearty spirit of co-operation between the two colonies threatened. The failure of their joint attack on St. Augustine had sown the seeds of mutual distrust. The government of Georgia had for military purposes the inestimable advantage of being practically a despotism. All political authority, military, financial, diplomatic, was centred in the hands of Oglethorpe. Thus placed he could hardly make allowance for the delays inevitably imposed by a constitutional government. In June 1742 we find him writing to Bull, in a peremptory fashion, demanding that succour should be sent without delay to Frederica, and reminding him that if there was any 'trifling,' and ill came of it, he (Bull) would be held answerable.[1]

[1] Letter quoted by Wright, p. 297.

He apparently forgot that the unlucky Bull could not feed a single soldier or hire a single transport vessel without the approval of his Assembly.

The Southern Indians and the Five Nations.

Military action against Spain was not the only matter in which co-operation was needed. The help which the Spaniards received from the Indians of Florida could only be counterbalanced by the active alliance of those tribes whom Oglethorpe had brought together and pacified at Coweta. But they in turn might at any moment find their hands full in defending themselves against the Five Nations. Thus it became an object of great importance with the English to reconcile these hitherto hostile confederacies. The Cherokees and the Creeks plainly told Oglethorpe that if the English would ensure them against an attack from the Five Nations they would each send contingents to help Georgia. Clarke, the acting Governor of New York, clearly saw the need for carrying out such a policy.[1]

Oglethorpe and the Home Government.

Oglethorpe's biographers have not altogether unjustly heaped anger and contempt upon the English Government for its slowness and supineness in backing him up. They tell us how his application for help was handed about from department to department, from the Secretary of State to the Lords Justices, acting in the King's absence as a Council of Regency, from them to the Master of the Ordnance and the Lords of the Admiralty; how, while coil upon coil of red tape was thus strangling his cry for help, Oglethorpe with a bankrupt exchequer, a half-armed garrison, and empty ammunition boxes, was every day looking for the sails which should bring the invaders upon his colony.[2]

In this, however, Oglethorpe was but suffering from a spirit which in that day pervaded the whole policy of

[1] Oglethorpe to the trustees, quoted by Wright, p. 289. [2] *Ibid.* p. 280.

England. Something no doubt was due to the individual statesman who was then responsible for our colonial policy. It is no small set-off to the general merits of Walpole's rule that so large a share in determining the destinies of our colonial empire should have drifted into the hands of an ignorant jobber such as Newcastle.

But the evil had a deeper root than the shortcomings of any individual. The apathy which imperilled Georgia was but an instance of that torpor which had come over the whole of our public service, and from which the nation was only to be roused by the quickening spell of Pitt's genius.

Nor must we forget that the peculiar circumstances under which Georgia had come into existence did to a certain extent absolve English statesmen from responsibility for the fate of the colony. The trustees had for good purposes of their own, purposes in which no doubt the public interest was involved, created the colony. It would be a perilous doctrine to admit that a private corporation might on its own responsibility create a dependency, and then make unlimited demands on the imperial government for its defence. To leave Georgia to its own resources would have been at once cruel and short-sighted. But the apportionment of the cost of defence between the trustees, the colonists and the English exchequer was a matter for careful consideration, not one to be settled off-hand at the dictation of an interested party.

Oglethorpe's military policy.[1]

From the outset Oglethorpe evidently took the view that the best mode of defence was by an aggressive policy, that he must not simply sit still and strengthen his defences, but harry and embarrass the Spaniard. For one thing he could by such a policy best utilize the Indian alliance.

[1] The chief authorities for the Spanish invasion are Oglethorpe's own despatches. There is a report by Lieutenant Sutherland. I expect from

Moreover an invasion from Florida even if successfully repelled would do irreparable material injury. The whole population would have to be gathered within the defences of Frederica, and their plantations left to the mercy of the enemy. The forts, too, towards the south were really designed for attack rather than defence. To hold them continuously would detach a large body of men, and it would be no easy matter to keep up communications with Frederica. But they might do good service used as advanced points designed to support and protect parties of invaders.

It was however an essential condition of Oglethorpe's aggressive policy that the English fleet should co-operate, and should make it impossible for St. Augustine's to receive reinforcements and supplies by sea. This was not fulfilled. In June 1742 Oglethorpe learnt that the failure of the English operations against Havannah had set free a large force. The garrison of St. Augustine's was strengthened to a point which made attack hopeless. Nor was that all; in the presence of such a Spanish fleet it would have been fatal folly of Oglethorpe to detach any portion of his scanty force from the defence of the colony. His policy of defending himself beyond his own frontiers had to be given up perforce. Instead he adopted a policy of concentration.

On June 22, a Spanish fleet of fourteen vessels threatened Fort William, the English fort at the south point of Cumberland Island. The guns of the fort supported by an English schooner beat them off. They then turned northward, and sailed up the strait between the mainland and the island.[1]

The island was guarded by Fort St. Andrew at the

its tone and its agreement with Oglethorpe's own report that it was substantially written by the Governor, and that Sutherland was little if anything more than an amanuensis.

[1] This and the following operations are described in Oglethorpe's despatch of July 30, 1742.

northern and Fort William at the southern end. Oglethorpe now decided to abandon the former, and to concentrate all his defending forces within the latter. It is not quite easy to see why the preference was given to the place farthest from Frederica, nor why the execution of the scheme should have been postponed till it had to be done under the guns of a Spanish fleet.

To carry out his policy Oglethorpe embarked a detachment of troops in three vessels, and manœuvred his way through the Spanish fleet. The officer in command of one boat lost heart, took refuge in a creek, and then sailed to St. Simon's with the tidings that Oglethorpe had been surrounded and killed. His account was confirmed by those who had watched the fight from the defences of Frederica. In real truth Oglethorpe had not only made his way through safely, but had inflicted such damage on the Spanish fleet that it put back to St. Augustine's for repairs, while it is said that four of the vessels actually foundered on their homeward voyage. Oglethorpe took advantage of this to carry out his policy of evacuating St. Andrew's and strengthening Fort William. Then he returned to Frederica, and took possession of some of the merchant vessels in the harbour. From these he arranged a fleet of three vessels, one with twenty, the others with fourteen guns. The little fleet moved to St. Simon's, and was there drawn up for the defence of the harbour, while eight gun-boats moored close to the shore were to act as floating batteries. One is reminded of the versatile heroes of the Elizabethan age, as one reads of Oglethorpe thus playing the part of soldier and seaman. Nor was that all: the absence of his two engineers compelled Oglethorpe to place his regiment under the command of a deputy, while he himself took command of the ordnance.

On July 5 thirty-six Spanish sail appeared before

Whitefield say that 'the deliverance of Georgia is such as cannot be paralleled but by some instances out of the Old Testament.' Humanly speaking we may say that the colonists owed their safety to the skill with which Oglethorpe had chosen the site of Frederica and laid out its approaches, to the strategy with which he turned to account the peculiar powers of his Indian allies, and to the well-contrived and fortunate devices which enabled him to deceive his enemies as to his own resources and prospects.

The Spanish defeat.

From St. Simon's to Frederica the only approach was along the narrow path which Oglethorpe had laid out, belted by swamp and jungle. Small parties of Indians and light infantry posted in the woods harassed the advanced columns of the Spanish force, and for a while made their advance impossible. After a day of such harassing skirmishes Oglethorpe saw that the time had come to strike a direct blow at the head of the advancing force.

The strategy adopted was not unlike that which was used thirteen years later with such terrible effect against Braddock. The advancing enemy was thrown into confusion by flanking parties firing from ambush,[1] and then an attack was delivered in front. Oglethorpe's charge was effective, and the advanced guard of the enemy was routed and fled in confusion for a mile. But the English force was far too small to push an attack or to attempt a general engagement. He himself returned to Frederica to bring up reinforcements. His troops were placed as before in the woods where their fire would command the path.

An accident precipitated the engagement. One of the Spanish horses took fright; the noise which he made convinced the Spaniards that the enemy was on them and

[1] In Braddock's case the frontal attack was delivered first and supported from the flanks.

they rushed to their arms. Immediately the English opened fire. Through the thick summer foliage the invaders could not see a foe; nearly every shot that they fired wasted its force on trunks and boughs. Instead of attempting a deliberate and orderly retreat along the narrow path, the Spanish force broke and fled through the forest, where many fell victims to their Indian pursuers. Oglethorpe himself hurried from Frederica at the first fire. A small party of fugitives whom he met told him that the English were routed. He rallied them and pressed on, only to find on his arrival at the scene of action that the victory was complete. The Spaniards did not halt till they reached the ruined works of St. Simon's. There they encamped under the guns of their vessels. Oglethorpe wisely made no attempt at an assault, but returned to his policy of harassing the enemy by skirmishing parties.

There was little likelihood that the Spaniards would renew their land attack. They had lost six officers and six hundred men without gaining a single position or advancing a step nearer their main object. The attempt which had thus failed by land was now renewed by water, and the Spanish fleet made its way up the creek which separated the island from the mainland. In this attempt the Spanish commander no doubt relied on his treacherous ally within the walls. The defences of Frederica were now strong enough for her guns to keep the enemy's fleet at bay. Attempts to land troops at points beyond the fire of the fort were thwarted by the Indians who were ambushed along the shore.

One more resource remained to the Spaniards. Both forms of assault had failed. But they might blockade Frederica by sea and land. The ill-victualled state of the fort made this a serious danger. Oglethorpe had laid in what he reckoned to be a year's supplies. But he was short of storage room at Frederica. A portion of the supplies was still on shipboard, and some in a house beyond the town. When the Spaniards advanced, Oglethorpe deemed it better to destroy all this portion of the stores rather than risk it falling into the hands of the enemy.

On the other hand the condition of the Spaniards themselves was hardly such that they were likely to carry through a prolonged blockade effectively. They lacked water and had no accommodation for their wounded. Above all they were crushed down by the demoralizing effect of their defeats. Nothing is more depressing to a civilized force than to be unable to bring any of its resources into action, to be perpetually harassed by attacks of a wholly unfamiliar kind. There was also dissension in the camp, and the commander of the reinforcements from Florida refused to co-operate with troops from St. Augustine's, and even occupied different camping ground.

Oglethorpe now decided to strike a more decisive blow than he had yet attempted. Mustering his whole force he marched on the enemy. The attempt was frustrated by treachery.[1] A Frenchman had been unwisely suffered to attach himself to the expedition as a volunteer. He gave the alarm by firing his gun and then fled to the enemy. Oglethorpe's attack had been designed for a surprise. To attack with greatly inferior numbers when the enemy was fully warned would have been madness. Versatility and resource were the most marked characteristics of Oglethorpe as a soldier, and he now devised a scheme for turning the treachery of the Frenchman to good account. After what had happened there was little fear of a decisive attack either by sea or land. But a blockade might still be effective and, straitened as

Oglethorpe's counter-attack.

[1] This is told by Sutherland.

the English were for provisions, any prolongation of operations was to be dreaded. To get the Spanish force off the island was the supreme object with Oglethorpe. With this view a Spanish prisoner was hired to convey a letter to the Frenchman. The letter exhorted him to encourage the Spanish commander to make an attack. He was to represent to him that the English were weak, and he was to pilot the Spanish fleet into a position where gunboats placed in ambush were ready to receive it.

If he could not do that, at least let him keep them at St. Simon's. If he could only delay them for three days Oglethorpe would have a reinforcement of two thousand men from Carolina and a squadron of six or seven ships, and would be ready to attack the Spaniards. Moreover, the English fleet under Vernon was about to attack St. Augustine. To the success of his attack it was vital that the Spanish force should be withheld from retreating.

As Oglethorpe anticipated, the messenger was seized and the letter discovered. One need not suppose that the Spaniards were ingenuous enough to have no suspicions of such an obvious trap. But they could not be sure that the correspondence was a mere pretence. To advance under such circumstances would be rash. Fortunately, too, for the English some strange sails were seen out to sea. The Spaniards saw in this the confirmation of Vernon's intended attack, and it was judged prudent to act as though the Frenchman was actually in English pay, and as though Oglethorpe really wished to lure the invader on to destruction.

The retreating Spanish force endeavoured to strike a blow at the garrison of Fort William. But the determination of the Commander, Stuart, and the judgement with which Oglethorpe had chosen the position of the fort and constructed its defences, made their efforts fruitless. For three hours the Spaniards assaulted it both by sea and land, then learning that Oglethorpe was marching up with reinforcements they continued their retreat.

Supineness of the British Government.

The spirit of faction which had engaged us in the war was hardly more discreditable to English public men than the purposeless and ineffectual fashion in which it was conducted. In vain Oglethorpe urged the Ministry to concentrate its efforts on crushing the Spanish power in Florida. In vain he pointed out that the conquest of Georgia would bring with it the ruin of our whole colonial empire in America.[1] Not only was the garrison of St. Augustine's strongly reinforced, but the Yamassees were molesting the English settlements on the upper waters of the Alatamaha, and there were rumours of a French attack from the north-west. To strike a defensive blow at Florida was the one effective means of meeting the danger.

Besides the supineness of the English Cabinet Oglethorpe had to contend with the jealousy and shortsightedness of his neighbours in South Carolina. In the autumn of 1742 a detachment was sent from Jamaica to co-operate with the colonists against the Spaniards. The commander had orders to consult either Oglethorpe or the acting Governor of South Carolina as to his operations. Unfortunately the first point he touched at was Charlestown, and he was there told that all danger was at an end. No doubt as far as South Carolina itself was concerned that was in a measure true. In all likelihood the Spaniards would be satisfied with the destruction of Georgia. In any case that colony would have to bear the brunt of the blow. Her fate would at least give Carolina time to prepare for defence. The policy of the trustees, a

[1] As I have said before (p. 498) I do not think that this view can be accepted. But it was quite natural that Oglethorpe should take it.

policy which economical considerations may have made needful, had checked the growth of any cordial good-will or mutual self-reliance between Georgia and South Carolina. Such joint military operations as there had been had only left feelings of jealousy and dislike.

We have already seen how the skill of a Charlestown pilot was near being exerted to the destruction of Georgia. It was currently reported in Georgia that the traitor was to be seen walking abroad in the streets of Charlestown. Spanish prisoners, too, were suffered to study the navigation of Charlestown harbour and then returned by way of exchange. It was even added, though only on the authority of Indians, that merchant vessels from Charlestown were delivering stores of food and even of ammunition in St. Augustine.

Unsupported as he was, Oglethorpe could only keep to his policy of harassing the Spaniards by inroads, and thus making the best use of his Indian allies. If there was vagueness in the English policy and want of spirit in the execution of it, assuredly the same might be said of Spain. A force was sent from St. Augustine to reinforce San Mattheo. But it was not strong enough to face the detachment, mainly of Indians, which Oglethorpe sent against it, and it speedily retreated to St. Augustine, and not without loss.

Daring as Oglethorpe's operations often were, he showed plainly that he was no mere knight-errant, fighting in light-hearted gallantry, but a shrewd strategist, who could adopt a Fabian policy when needful. His Indian allies were allowed to believe that the inaction of the Spaniards was due to cowardice. Oglethorpe's own operations were based on the assumption that the Spaniards were only seeking to draw him into an ambush.

Oglethorpe had hardly secured his colony against invasion when he found himself confronted with trouble of a different kind. In July 1741, Sir Robert Walpole had, as Chancellor of the Exchequer, notified Oglethorpe that he must draw no more bills on the exchequer till further orders. If he should draw any bills between the issue of this order and the reception of it, the matter was to be referred to the Lords Justices, then acting as a Council of Regency. Verelst, Oglethorpe's representative in London, acted on this instruction. The Justices not only agreed to meet the liabilities which Oglethorpe had incurred, but also sanctioned a further outlay of eight thousand a year. When however Oglethorpe's bills were presented at the Treasury they were dishonoured, on the ground that Walpole had issued an order forbidding further expenditure. Verelst had no difficulty in showing that this order was overridden by that issued by the Justices. The Treasury then took new ground: they had no available funds, and Oglethorpe's bills were not drawn direct on the Treasury, but on English merchants. The discussion was protracted into the summer of 1743.

Oglethorpe's financial difficulties.

By this time the colony was in a sufficient state of security to allow Oglethorpe to return to England and fight his own battle. The financial question was not the only one which demanded his presence. His conduct of operations against Florida and his civil administration were both challenged, and the clearing of his character seemed to demand a public inquiry.

Oglethorpe never returned to Georgia. Those responsible for the colony may have felt, he may himself have accepted the view, that he was better fitted for the task of calling into existence a young community under peculiar conditions, than for the humdrum work of administering it when once established. The danger of invasion, a danger best met by the rule of a dictator, was at an end.

Oglethorpe's work as a whole.

Spain and England were at peace, and the rulers of Florida had been taught a lesson which made any isolated attempt on their part most unlikely.

There is so little of subtlety or intricacy in Oglethorpe's character and policy, so little below the surface that calls for analysis, that his work may well be left to speak for itself. Impetuous and self-confident, beyond doubt he made errors, alike administrative and military. At times, as with the Wesleys, he gave his confidence with indiscreet haste, and withdrew it with a precipitance which led him into injustice. As a commander he seems to have been somewhat lacking in definiteness of purpose, of continuity of policy. Like many energetic captains he was prone to expect too much from his men in the way of endurance. He marched and countermarched his troops in a fashion which might have been tolerable in Europe, but which was little short of merciless under a torrid sun, and amid the swamps of Georgia or Florida.

To say this is only to say that Oglethorpe had the defects of his qualities. The same temperament which made him unable to delegate authority effectively, whether in military or civil matters, also made him the strenuous, ubiquitous organizer that he was. Nothing is more striking than the way in which when overwhelmed with administrative cares, he yet found leisure for minute examination of details. He disapproves of the coats supplied to settlers, 'they shrink intolerably.' He inspects and condemns the pork, and suggests the substitution of other articles of food.[1]

Whatever may have been Oglethorpe's defects and failures, whether as an administrator or as a commander, looked at broadly, his work in both characters was a success. Had anyone foretold that within ten

[1] See his letters in the third volume of the Georgia Historical Society's Collection.

years of its foundation the little settlement, built out of the worthless *débris* of over-civilization, would repel a foreign enemy, and serve as an efficient bulwark against the tide of invasion which menaced the English colonies, he would have seemed a sanguine man. More sanguine still would it have been to prophesy that such a community would without any violent convulsion put on some measure of self-government, and should in less than half a century be fit to take its place as one of the constituent members of an independent republic. We may see in it a strong illustration of that underlying fitness for citizenship which through generations of training has become inherent in the English character. But a large share of the praise due for that success must be put down to the chivalrous courage, the single-minded devotion, the genial and contagious energy of Oglethorpe.

Introduction of slavery.

With the departure of Oglethorpe and the cessation of the Spanish terror, the chief elements of dramatic interest disappear from the history of Georgia.[1] For seven years the colony went on under the simple form of executive government which has been already described. The trustees in England exercised occasional control, but without any representative of their authority resident in the colony in the place of Oglethorpe. The first important change came in 1749, when the exclusion of slavery had to be abandoned as hopeless. Such a restriction made social and commercial connexion with the other colonies difficult, and when in defiance of such difficulties intercourse began, the situation became at once complicated and unmanageable. The very difficulties which a hundred years later threatened to rend the United States asunder

[1] For what follows I have relied on the Georgia Papers in the Record Office. Many of the most important are printed in the Collection of the Georgia Historical Society.

arose. Settlers from the other colonies migrated into Georgia and took their negroes with them. Did the owner retain his rights or were those rights overruled by the restrictions imposed by the trustees? These regulations were evaded by contracts whereby negroes from other colonies were nominally hired, but practically bought. The attempt to keep Georgia as an isolated stronghold for free labour, difficult under a dictator such as Oglethorpe, was impossible when his strong hand was removed, and in 1750 the trustees gave up the attempt and repealed the anti-slavery ordinance.

Thomas Bosomworth.

Meanwhile, those friendly relations with the natives which had been so invaluable to the colony in its early and struggling days were being endangered in a somewhat strange fashion. It will be remembered that Oglethorpe had at the very outset profited by the good offices of a trader, Musgrove, and his wife. She appears to have made some claim to the position of a native princess, though if we may believe one competent witness she was only herself a half-bred Indian.[1] After Musgrove's death she became the wife of one Matthews, and then becoming a second time a widow she married one Thomas Bosomworth, a missionary. He, it would seem, wished to exchange the lot of an English clergyman for that of an Indian chief. We read of him riding round the Indian villages, stirring up their occupants to support him in freeing his wife's territory from the English invaders. Nothing came of Bosomworth's strange enterprise, but there was danger in anything which suggested to the Indians the notion that their invaders were not a people at unity among themselves.

[1] Stephens's Journals. Several of Mrs. Musgrove's letters referring to her own claims and her past services are among the Colonial Papers. They are moderate and reasonable in tone.

In 1753 the colony acquired a somewhat important accession. In 1696, when Presbyterianism was beginning to gain a foothold in South Carolina, that colony received as immigrants a congregation from Dorchester in New England. True to their accustomed usage they had given to their new home the name of the settlement they had left. In 1753 they or a majority of them again moved, crossing the border into Georgia. As was said elsewhere, one of the most important though not the most conspicuous processes of change which were at work in the colonies during the eighteenth century was the leavening of the South by the civic and religious influences of Presbyterianism. It brought qualities of which plantation life stood in need: cohesion, austerity, self-restraint; and in no colony were such more needed than in Georgia.

Presbyterian immigrants.

In 1752 the trustees resigned their charter. The Lords of Trade drafted a constitution for the colony which was approved by the Crown. There was to be a Governor, with the usual staff of officials and a council of, at first, eleven members. There was to be a representative Assembly. Members must be qualified by the possession of five hundred acres; electors by fifty. Apparently the formation of electoral districts was left to the Governor. He could convene and dissolve the House of Representatives, and veto any of their bills.

The new constitution.

The first Governor under the Crown was John Reynolds, of whose antecedents nothing can be learnt save that he was a captain in the army. He was appointed in August 1754. His letters at the outset were businesslike, and show real anxiety for the well-being of the colony. But he soon entangled himself in a dispute with the Assembly. He nominated three Representatives as Councillors, and then issued writs for election of three new members. The fact that

John Reynolds as Governor.

one of his three nominees refused the appointment raises a presumption that Reynolds's object was not to promote the three Assembly men, but to create three vacancies. The vacant seats were filled, but the Assembly refused those elected, and carried on business with a house of only twelve, described by Reynolds as containing 'a majority of very troublesome people.' He goes on to say that he gave them time enough by short adjournments to recollect that they were wrong, and in a message explained to them that they were so, but nothing would do, for 'they expect to have the same privileges as the House of Commons in Great Britain.'

If we may believe Reynolds's opponents, one of his objects in dissolving the Assembly was to burke an inquiry into the conduct of the Secretary for the Colony, a personal favourite of the Governor. He is even said for this purpose to have falsified the journals of the Assembly. It is tolerably safe to assume that there was good ground for the charges brought against him from the fact that he resigned instead of defending himself, and also from the total absence of any testimony in his favour.

The unfavourable opinion of Reynolds was held not only by the settlers, but also by his successor, Henry Ellis. He was, like Spotswood in Virginia, a strenuous explorer of the unoccupied territory in the west. Like Spotswood, too, he earns gratitude from the student of colonial history by the fulness and vivacity of his despatches. His term of office ended in 1760, and he escaped the troubles which overtook his successor James Wright, perhaps the ablest, and certainly the staunchest and most resolute, of all the public servants in the colonies who clung to the mother country in the great struggle.

CHAPTER IX.

THE CONQUEST OF CANADA.[1]

How far it forms a part of colonial history.

THE conquest of Canada was from one point of view by far the most important event in the collective history of the American colonies. It liberated them from an attitude of continuous and watchful alarm. It insured that possibility of expansion westward on which all their future greatness depended. It carried with it, if not as an inevitable consequence, at least as a likely one, foreseen and foretold by observant men, separation from the mother country.[2] Yet it would be hardly a paradox to say that the war itself in its details played but a subordinate part in the history of the colonies. It would be indeed unjust and ungrateful to refuse full recognition to the military services rendered by colonial troops. From first to last they represented at least one half of the fighting power of the British armies engaged.[3] Without colonial troops Forbes would never have

[1] It is hardly needful to say that Mr. Parkman's writings, *Half a Century of Conflict* and *Montcalm and Wolfe*, are the standard authorities for the relations between Canada and the English colonies during the period which is dealt with in this chapter. Where he deals with unpublished documents or inaccessible authorities I have never scrupled to rely upon him. For so much as directly concerns New York the second part of Smith is useful. Hutchinson is a valuable authority for the part played by New England in the first war. A careful study of the Pennsylvanian Records and of Dinwiddie's official correspondence and of the pamphlet literature of the time is necessary.

[2] One such prophecy is well known. John Adams, with a characteristic touch of pomposity, wrote 'if we can remove the turbulent Gallics the seat of empire might be transferred to America.' Adams's *Works* (ed. 1856), vol. i. p. 23.

[3] For the proportion engaged see Appendix VI.

penetrated to the valley of the Ohio. But the control of those troops and the conduct of the war were entirely in British hands. The war, no doubt, did something to supply the colonies in the struggle against the mother country with troops who had been under fire, and something, though less, to supply competent officers. It did but little to teach the colonists strategy, and still less to familiarize them with military organization. Nor can one even say that the war was waged in the territory of British colonies. Virginia and Pennsylvania were the only colonies which at any time stood in danger of invasion. Even there the danger was but an aggravated form of that terror from which the colonies had always suffered, a possibility of an Indian inroad. If the conquest of the English colonies by France ever came about, it would come not as an incident of the war, but as a remote and indirect consequence.

Thus a writer who deals exclusively with the history of the colonies is only concerned with the war from certain special and limited points of view. He is not a little concerned with it as it affected the administrative relations between the colonies and the mother country. Difficulties about financial and administrative control, which under other conditions might not have got beyond the stage of chronic dissatisfaction, became acute. The political life of the colonies had a better and a worse side. Self-reliance, jealous distrust of authority, vigilance in detecting, persistency in resisting, every attempt at usurpation—these are vital conditions of freedom, and therefore of real and abiding national greatness. But to English administrators they presented themselves in the present case as a spirit of sullen isolation, of evasive and persistent factiousness. And if the war on its political and administrative side served to alienate English statesmen from the colonies, not the less on its military side did it destroy whatever respect and confidence the colonists felt towards the mother country. Unhappily, too, the successes of British arms were comparatively distant, and were not forced upon the notice of the colonists as a whole. To the men of Virginia and the Carolinas the crowning triumph of the war, the capture of Quebec, was something remote, almost as remote as would have been a victory won in the West Indies. What had been brought close to their eyes was the opening phase of the war, with its mistakes and disasters: the defeat of Braddock, with the panic and destruction which it brought in its train, the blundering of British commanders and the discomfiture of British arms wherever they were concerned with those problems of backwoods warfare, with which hundreds of colonial militiamen were familiar. The colonists saw British soldiers toiling through the forests in bearskin caps and cumbrous uniforms, where hunting shirts and leggings would at the very least have doubled their efficiency. They saw Braddock driving his soldiers to their death, by refusing to let them adopt those methods in which the colonists had learnt to imitate their savage enemies. They saw British officers as a class, though not without honourable exceptions, bound fast in military matters by unquestioning adhesion to conventional and outworn methods, in social matters by Old World traditions of narrow exclusiveness, by aristocratic pride which utterly lacked any real basis of moral or intellectual worth.

A writer whose subject is the history of the colonies is bound therefore to consider the war as it affected the colonies. He is concerned with the result as affecting colonial interests, and with those special incidents which illustrate colonial feeling. With the general history of the war he need only deal so far as is needful to keep those incidents in their proper order and position.

It will be well, however, to sum up briefly those earlier incidents in colonial history when the colonists took a part in the military operations conducted by the mother country. By a most unhappy fatality in every instance where the American colonists acted in conjunction with British troops there was disastrous and discreditable failure, failure which beyond question was largely due to the incompetence of British commanders.

Part taken by the colonists in earlier wars.

I have elsewhere described the mismanaged and fruitless attack on Canada in 1711. The colonies, too, had their share in the ill-conceived and ill-executed attack on the Spanish West Indies in 1740. The men of Massachusetts might be factious, and politically even unscrupulous. But, to give them their due, their colony was the one of the whole body which most readily responded to any military call. Moreover the war with Spain was essentially a Protestant war and a merchants' war, and in both of those aspects it appealed to the descendants of the Puritans, the foremost of all the traders on the Atlantic sea-board.

The war with Spain.

When, on April 21, 1740, Belcher publicly announced to the people of Boston the declaration of war, he was received with such a display of popular enthusiasm as might have made him wish that campaigns against Popish idolaters were things of more frequent occurrence.

The colony did not limit itself to cheering. It contributed a contingent of five hundred men, of whom it is said only one-tenth ever saw New England again.[1]

Even inert and peace-loving Pennsylvania felt some enthusiasm for what was essentially a war for trade.

[1] The action of Boston in this matter is dealt with very fully in a paper by Mr. Ellis Ames, published in the Proceedings of the Massachusetts Historical Society for 1881, pp. 364–78. It is mainly based on local records.

In 1740 we find the Proprietor, Thomas Penn, writing from Philadelphia that the scheme for raising a colonial force is progressing. Eight companies have been enlisted and eight transports are in readiness to carry them. The success of the undertaking is, according to Penn, largely due to the personal influence of Thomas. He inspects and drills the volunteers, delivers patriotic addresses to them, and encourages them by bonuses out of his own pocket.

Action of Pennsylvania.

One point of Penn's eulogy on the Governor is a curious illustration of the accepted standard of morality among the public men of that day. Thomas 'deserves the best government in the King's gift: great care has been taken to get the best provisions for the men at the very lowest rates, the Governor scorning to make a profit for himself.'[1]

In the result of the expedition the colonists saw nothing to inspire them with confidence in Britain as an ally or respect for her as a superior. Colonial co-operation in the war with Spain has left indeed one trace of a somewhat curious kind. Among the volunteers from Virginia was Lawrence, the elder brother of George Washington. He apparently enjoyed the friendship and confidence of Admiral Vernon. Of the countless pilgrims who visit the home of the first President probably but a few know that its name commemorates that boastful and self-asserting sailor, the 'brave and happy Vernon' of partisan poetry.

By a strange and perverse fate, the one exploit wherein colonial soldiership covered itself with glory and achieved definite and substantial success served, alike through its conception, its execution and its con-

[1] Letter from Penn to Paris, Hist. MSS. Comm., xl. app. iv. p. 302. William Smith, writing in 1755, speaks of the Assembly as opposed to Thomas in the matter. *Brief State of Pennsylvania*, pp. 10 and 26. I am inclined to think that he only refers to the Quakers, not to the whole body of colonists, though this is not quite clear.

sequences, to separate rather than to unite the colonists and the mother country. Louisburg, the fortified town which guarded the harbour of Cape Breton, was founded in 1713. Year after year the defences were strengthened, and till its capture it remained a nest of privateers and a perpetual menace to the trade and fisheries of New England. It was evident, too, that whenever open hostilities between England and France broke out, Louisburg might serve as the basis for an attack on the English colonies. The reality of this danger was at once shown when in the spring of 1744 France declared war against England. As soon as Duquesnel, the Commander at Louisburg, received the news, he fitted out an expedition which captured Canseau, a British fishing-station at the north-east end of Acadia.[1] This was followed up by an ill-conducted and unsuccessful attack on Annapolis.[2]

Scheme for an attack on Louisburg.

The men of New England resolved to retaliate with a vigorous counterstroke. There seems to be some little doubt as to who the individual was by whom the proposal for an attack on Annapolis was first definitely made.[3] But according to the most trustworthy authorities the scheme originated with William Vaughan, a native of New Hampshire, trained at Harvard, who owned an important fishing station off the coast of Maine and also drove a thriving trade in timber. But though the scheme of attack may have first taken definite form in Vaughan's mind, we may be sure that it was 'in the air.' Like the expedition against Carthagena, it appealed to the sentiments and interests of a community of Protestant traders.

Shirley was at this time Governor of Massachusetts. He listened with approval to Vaughan's suggestion and

[1] Hutchinson, vol. ii. p. 364. [2] *Ibid.*

[3] This question is fully discussed by Parkman, *Half a Century of Conflict*, vol. ii. p. 52 *n.*

resolved to do all in his power to give effect to it. His strength and his weakness alike fitted him for this task. He had a taste for soldiering and a confidence in his own military capacity, in a measure justified by events. He at once proceeded to make full inquiry from all those who knew Louisburg whether from trading voyages or from having been imprisoned there, and to learn the resources of the place, its weak points, and the most favourable time and means for an attack. A joint fleet might be obtained from Massachusetts and other colonies, strong enough to co-operate with an invading land force and to cut off relief. There was also a chance of obtaining naval assistance in another way. An English fleet under Commodore Warren was at the Leeward Islands. They might perhaps co-operate. Shirley also wrote to the Government in England, not disclosing his design, but suggesting that a fleet should be sent to protect Annapolis and if opportunity offered to seize Cape Breton. The following words were underlined in his despatch: 'We are at the crisis, and our only hopes are on what succour your Excellency may promise for us, proportioned to the circumstances.'[2] Newcastle does not seem to have held out to Shirley any hopes of acceding to his request. In making the attack on Louisburg without any definite promise of help from England the sanguine Governor showed himself not unwilling to leave a good deal to chance.

Governor Shirley.[1]

Fortunately Shirley understood better than any of his predecessors the temper of the men with whom he had to deal. He knew that they must be treated with perfect confidence, that if they were to throw thenselves heartily into a scheme of attack they must be made to feel that it was wholly of their own devising, that so the

[1] I have relied mainly on Hutchinson and Parkman for the capture of Louisburg. Parkman refers to various unpublished documents.

[2] See Shirley's letters to Newcastle, November 9 and December 28, 1744, in Colonial State Papers.

project would acquire an interest and an attraction which would be lacking if it were thrust upon them by any higher authority. Shirley was fortunate, too, in that those fierce administrative battles which had raged in the days of his predecessor were ended. The colonists could now in the completeness of their victory abandon their attitude of watchful jealousy.

The strength of Shirley's hold on popular opinion was best shown by the fact that he secured that most difficult of all conditions to obtain under democratic government, secrecy. When the Assembly met in January 1745 Shirley, before broaching his project, told the members that they must swear not to divulge what he was about to disclose. Shirley then unfolded his scheme. To some it seemed a wild dream. But the personal influence of Shirley, the hereditary hatred of New England for French idolaters, and the belief that Louisburg, strengthened as it soon might be by the conquest of Acadia, would be a continuous menace to colonial trade, were motives strong enough to secure consideration for Shirley's project, and a committee was appointed to report on it. Those who advocated the scheme pointed out that the garrison at Louisburg was ill supplied and disaffected, the Governor old and unskilled in war, the defences out of repair.

The Assembly consulted.[1]

These statements were denied by others. Moreover how could a raw colonial militia hope to prevail against regular troops? The foggy nature of the coast would make it impossible to exclude supplies by any kind of naval blockade. In undertaking on their own responsibility so daring an enterprise with such slender chances of success the colonists would incur the displeasure of the Government at home. The men who used that argument were curiously inept in judging of the temper of their fellow-countrymen.

[1] Hutchinson, vol. ii. p. 361.

Finally the committee reported against the scheme, and in consequence it was thrown out by the house.

An attack decided on.

Shirley, however, had no intention of sitting down defeated. His policy was still 'delenda est Carthago,' but with that sound judgement which had marked his conduct throughout he made no attempt to use his personal influence in the matter. Working more subtly he enlisted the support of a number of merchants from Boston, Salem and Marblehead. They addressed a petition to the Assembly for the adoption of Shirley's scheme, urging more especially the inevitable destruction of the New England fisheries which would ensue if Louisburg were left in French hands. A second committee was appointed to consider the petition. They reported in favour of the scheme. The House of Representatives debated the matter. One of those who was opposed to the scheme was, it is said, incapacitated by an accident, and the recommendation of the second committee was confirmed by a single vote.[1] The words in which Hutchinson, himself no doubt present at the discussion, records the matter are worth noting: 'Never was any affair deliberated upon with greater calmness and moderation; the Governor indeed laid the matter before the court, but left the members free to act their judgement (*sic*) without any solicitation, and there appeared to be no other division than what was caused by a real difference in opinion (*sic*) the true interest of the province.'[2] There is implied a significant condemnation of the methods adopted by Shirley's predecessors, and a condemnation, too, of the factious temper of their opponents. The words are also valuable as an illustration of the writer's temper and an explanation of his attitude at a later day. The man who wrote that passage could hardly have been the

[1] Parkman mentions this as a tradition, but gives no authority. Hutchinson says nothing about it.

[2] The word 'on' has evidently been omitted by Hutchinson.

supporter of arbitrary power, that Hutchinson's enemies would have us believe him to be.

Preparations for attack.

The scheme for reducing Louisburg may have been adopted with hesitation and reluctance. When once it was adopted there was a spirit of unanimous zeal and energy in furthering it. Hutchinson tells us with justifiable pride that 'those who opposed the scheme before were employed upon committees, and exerted themselves with zeal equal to that of the principal promoters.' He says further that Shirley 'had set his heart so much upon the expedition that many points were conceded by him which he would not have given up at any other time, and the people of the province submitted to compulsory measures from the government which at another time would have been grievous and not very patiently borne.' Shirley, regardless of official opinion in England, made no opposition to the issue of paper money. In the appointment of officers, Hutchinson tells us there was complete unanimity. The democracy of New England was never tender in its dealings with individual rights, and the government now took to itself powers for the compulsory purchase of stores. Help was sought from New York, New Jersey and Pennsylvania, but without success. When we remember the difficulties which had attended almost every scheme for military co-operation between the colonies we cannot feel that the refusal prejudiced the expedition. Even within New England the help given to Massachusetts was but scanty. Her own contribution was three thousand two hundred and fifty men. Connecticut sent five hundred and sixteen, New Hampshire three hundred and ten. Rhode Island promised three hundred, but so dilatory was the government that Louisburg had fallen before that contingent arrived.[1] Thus Massachusetts was the

[1] For the contingents see Hutchinson, vol. ii. p. 371.

backbone of the enterprise. In all likelihood the loss of numbers was more than compensated for by unity of purpose, by the strenuousness and self-reliance engendered by the feeling 'alone we did it.'

Shirley's insight into the peculiar conditions of the case was further illustrated by his choice of a commander. If the leader of the expedition was to enjoy the confidence and good-will of the troops he must be a New Englander, able to enter into the views and feelings of that peculiar and isolated community, able to understand and work upon that intense local patriotism which had to make amends for the lack of regular soldierly training. Under those conditions it was idle to think of obtaining the services of a skilled officer. The best that could be done was to find a man whose general character and civic virtues would inspire confidence. Such a one was found in William Pepperell, a sober-minded merchant living at Kittery, prosperous in trade and a large landholder. It has been already pointed out how the business of a New England trader fostered, not merely ordinary business capacity, but likewise versatility and resource. Pepperell was also a colonel of militia in Maine. The time, however, had been a peaceful one and the distinction was little more than titular. There is nothing to show that Pepperell had learnt the arts of the backwoods fighter, and even if he had they would have profited him little in conducting operations against Louisburg. More serviceable in all likelihood was his political experience as first a representative and then a councillor. That at least had given him some administrative training, some insight into the temper and views of his fellow-countrymen, and some perception of the motives through which they could be influenced.

The command given to Pepperell.

When the command of the expedition was offered by the Governor to Pepperell, he hesitated in accepting.

He was asked to neglect his business and to abandon his peaceful home life. Moreover, he was fully conscious of the inadequacy of his own experience and training. Pepperell was a devout man, a hearer, and in some measure as it would seem a disciple, of Whitefield. To him he now turned for counsel. Whitefield did not at first give much encouragement. At length, however, he so far approved the scheme as to suggest a motto for the flag, 'Nil desperandum Christo duce.'[1] To give a religious sanction to the scheme, to present it as a crusade against the idolatrous adherents of the Scarlet Woman, was the surest way of securing for it the sympathy and good-will of the New Englanders.

Nor can we doubt that Pepperell's hesitation finally overcome was in itself a serviceable influence. It brought home to the minds of men that their commander was not influenced by any craving for military glory, that he was putting aside the good things of life in obedience to the call of duty. The professional soldier and the citizen soldier have each his own set of motives and his own moral standard; the relative merits and efficiency of each may be matter of doubt. But the campaign against Louisburg had to be undertaken by men of almost exclusively civil training, and it was fortunate that special circumstances as well as inherited instinct had made them strong in the peculiar virtues needed by the citizen soldier.

One thing no zeal or energy on the part of the citizens of Massachusetts could supply. Unless the besieging party was secured against an attack from the sea, the expedition might at any time be frustrated. That security the colonists had no means of providing for themselves. Thirteen small vessels, the largest of twenty-four guns, was all the naval force that

Naval help.

[1] Belknap, vol. ii. p. 160.

New England could supply to co-operate with the land attack.[1] For anything more they must depend on the help of the mother country. Here they were followed by the same good fortune which gave them Shirley for a Governor at this crisis. Commodore Warren, who was in command of the English squadron in the West Indies, was bound to the colonies by special ties. He had married an American wife and was himself a large landowner in New England. Nevertheless when Shirley applied to him for help he felt that the responsibility of giving it was more than he could undertake. Luckily however before the Louisburg expedition was decided, Shirley had, as we have seen, represented to the Government at home the unprotected state of Acadia and the fisheries. In compliance with this warning orders had been given to Warren to sail to New England and co-operate with Shirley in checking the action of French privateers. Warren acted on this promptly and made for Boston. On his way he met a vessel from that port and learnt that the expedition had sailed. The schooner not only furnished the needful information but also the means of taking advantage of it. She had on board a capable pilot, who it is said had embarked in her to avoid being pressed for the Louisburg fleet. Warren now appropriated him. Without such guidance it was thought that the British commander could hardly have ventured to make for Louisburg.[2]

The expedition, filling about ninety transports with their convoy of thirteen small vessels, set sail from Boston on March 24, and on April 30 the troops landed off Louisburg. It is very clear that the skill in managing small sea boats which the New England sailors had learnt in the whale fishery

The landing.

[1] Williamson's *Hist. of Maine*, vol. ii. p. 227. He gives the name of each vessel and the number of guns that it carried.

[2] Hutchinson, vol. ii. pp. 370–1, is my authority for these proceedings.

now stood them in good stead. It is equally clear that there was a most culpable lack of promptness and energy on the part of the defenders, both in opposing the actual landing, and then in allowing the troops to take up a strong position and to destroy a large quantity of naval stores. The landing of supplies, and even more the transport of the cannon, were tasks which brought into full play all the best qualities of the New Englanders: perseverance, physical endurance and resource. The cannon had to be hauled for two miles over ground so swampy that horses or oxen would have sunk in. Flat timber sledges were constructed, under the direction of a New Hampshire ship-builder, and dragged by teams of men, two hundred to a sledge, forced constantly to choose a fresh track so as to avoid the slough created by their predecessors.

Pepperell was justified in praising the cheerful spirit of his men 'under almost incredible hardship.' Yet we may well doubt whether all their resource and determination would have profited them but for the singular inertness of the defenders.

Capture of the Vigilant.

On May 18 the Vigilant, a French man-of-war, carrying sixty four-guns and laden with stores, appeared off Louisburg and was captured by Warren's fleet. Security against a seaward attack was not the only good service which Warren did the besieging force. The colonists were but imperfectly supplied with artillerymen, and, as in the late Boer war, the land force was largely beholden to the skill of gunners transferred from the fleet.

Feeble resistance by the garrison.

There can hardly be a doubt that more strenuous resistance at the outset would have frustrated at least the land attack. The New Englander was better fitted to bear mere physical hardship than the British soldier. But the zeal of the citizen combatant more easily evaporates under discouragement, under the strain of mere passive resistance, unsupported by the excitement of effort and incident, than the more automatic courage of regular troops. Moreover, prolonged service, and especially foreign service, is always more irksome to the civilian with engrossing cares, pursuits and interests elsewhere than to the professional soldier. It is clear, too, that there was among Pepperell's men a lack of discipline, a craving for independent action, often showing itself in grotesque forms, which could never have stood the strain of initial disappointment. There would have been no chance left save that of a naval blockade, and one may well doubt whether that could have been effectively maintained on that stormy and fog-bound coast.

But when once the attacking force had been allowed to take up a position from which it could seriously threaten the defences of the town, success was nearly won. By June the garrison was straitened for supplies and exhausted by the prolonged strain of the siege. Their stock of powder was reduced to thirty-seven barrels. The New Englanders had worked the artillery so vigorously and so successfully that not only were the defences severely injured, but the town itself was well nigh a ruin. 'Never,' Pepperell wrote to Shirley, 'was a place more mal'd [*sic*] with cannon and shell.' On June 13 Pepperell and Warren made all their arrangements for a general attack. The citizens, however, were nowise minded for profitless martyrdom. They petitioned Duchambon, the military commander, to surrender. He acceded, and on June 17 Pepperell and Warren took possession of the town.

The surrender.

An inhabitant of Louisburg used significant words in a letter describing the capture. 'It was an enterprise less of the English nation and its King than of the inhabitants of New England.'[1] That view unjustly ignores the co-operation of Warren and his fleet, without which all the brilliant daring of the New England troops would have availed nothing. But though the view was greatly exaggerated, yet it had in it an element of truth. The capture of Louisburg did nothing to bring the colonists and the mother country into closer union. It did not a little to strengthen those influences which at a later day made for separation. It taught the colonists that what one may call civilian virtues and attainments could go a long way to winning military success.

General effect of the conquest.

At the same time it blinded them to the value of technical training in the art of war. It begot the spirit of fearless self-reliance which made Bunker Hill possible. It equally begot the spirit of misplaced trust in mere untrained courage which we see in the writings of Adams and the speeches of Warren, and which by an exaggerated reaction begot futile confidence in such men as Lee, Gates and Conway. What is strange is that the lesson taught by the siege of Louisburg should have been so utterly lost on British statesmen and legislators. It seems hardly credible that within thirty years of that event, men should have been found who could stand up in the English Parliament and describe the colonists as slothful cowards.

In its effect on the relations between the mother country and the colonies, the last act in the Louisburg drama was the worst. The peace of Aix-la-Chapelle gave back Louisburg to France. A mutual restitution of all places taken during the war was insisted on by France as a preliminary condition of peace. Without that condition England would have had to leave Madras in the hands of the enemy. Her Indian empire either would never

Louisburg restored to France.

[1] Quoted and translated by Parkman, vol. ii. p. 155.

have come into being or would have been won at the cost of many added years of bloodshed and destruction. That brought but little justification or consolation to the minds of Boston merchants whose ships were taken by French privateers, of New Hampshire farmers exposed to the raids of the Indian allies of France. For them the truth lay in the saying attributed to George II., that Louisburg had been won by the colonists and was not his to give up.[1] The abandonment of that view under the pressure of diplomatic necessity was in the eyes of the colonists an unscrupulous betrayal, and a manifest proof of total indifference to colonial interests. It gave a sting to the words of colonial demagogues and cut the sinews of colonial loyalty.

Attack on Acadia thwarted.[2]

Indifference to colonial interests was all the worse because the mother country had derived one substantial and lasting good from the capture of Louisburg. In July 1745, just when all New England was rejoicing in the prosperous issue of the campaign, a fleet of seven ships sailed from France, with orders to touch at Louisburg and then attack Acadia. The French population of that province were in a supine and inert fashion disloyal to their new masters, and it may be doubted whether the British naval force then in American waters could have coped with the enemy's fleet. But the latter on its way captured an English vessel with letters on board. They then learnt for the first time of the fall of Louisburg. Thereupon the French commander abandoned the expedition and sailed homeward.

One compensation, and that of no little importance, the British Government did grant to the colonies. The energetic representations of Shirley succeeded in obtaining for the New England colonies a substantial

[1] N. Y. Col. Docs. vol. x. p. 147.

[2] Hutchinson, vol. ii. p. 423.

money payment from the English exchequer. The whole sum came to a little more than two hundred and thirty-five thousand pounds, of which about three-fourths fell to the share of Massachusetts.[1]

Even those who in his own time and since have belittled Hutchinson's patriotism have never cast any doubt on his clearness of vision in matters of finance. He saw that the subsidy about to be received might be so used as to liberate Massachusetts from that incubus of debt which lay so heavy on her, and his advice was accepted.[2]

Warlike policy of Clarke and Clinton.

The capture of Louisburg was an isolated incident in the war of which it formed a part. There were hostilities on the New England frontier, attended with loss and suffering, but they hardly did more than intensify a trouble which the colonists had learnt to look on as chronic. The only other colony which was brought face to face with the problems created by the war was New York. In that colony there were at least two among the officials representing the Crown who saw clearly the nature of the dangers threatened by French aggression, and had definite ideas as to the best means of checking it. Clarke was a conspicuous advocate of what would be called in the language of Indian politics a forward policy. We have already seen how he conceived the scheme of planting a Highland garrison at Wood Creek, and how that scheme was frustrated by causes for which in all likelihood he was himself to blame. In 1743 Clarke sent reports to the Board of Trade and the Duke of Newcastle urging the need for a bold and comprehensive policy against the French.[3] It was an error to have allowed them to fortify Niagara and Crown Point. We must build a fort on Lake Ontario,

[1] Hutchinson, vol. ii. p. 380.
[2] *Ib.* pp. 391–5.
[3] N. Y. Docs. vol. vi. p. 225.

so as to secure the communication with the Mississippi, and we must put a flotilla on the lake. When once the Five Nations see that we are in that position, they will not hesitate between England and France.

He also anticipates Shirley's policy and recommends an attack on Cape Breton. Here the New England militia will do good service. They have a direct interest in the capture of Cape Breton, and their unrestricted indulgence in field sports makes them valuable as irregular troops.

Clinton followed up the line which had been taken by Clarke. His despatches show that, while he did not personally like Clarke, he was in full accord with his Canadian policy.[1] All his own efforts against Canada, he says, are thwarted by a party opposed to war mainly on two grounds. A successful war would make him popular. Moreover if the colony hangs back it will not really suffer. The English Government will in its own interest do all that is needful. There was a section of the opposition who went further, and who actually resisted the war because they had an interest in the trade with Canada. They supplied the French with those very goods which enabled them to maintain their alliance with the savages. The leader of the opposition, according to Clinton, was the Chief Justice, De Lancey. While his appointment to that office was still a matter of uncertainty he had made a show of loyalty. Once secure in his position he became an avowed opponent of Clinton. How deeply the spirit of faction had eaten into the life of the colony is shown by the fact that the chief legal dignitary of the colony was regarded by friend and foe as an important political power.

The conquest of Louisburg was followed up by one of those numerous schemes for a confederated attack on Canada which form so large and so unhappy a chapter

[1] N. Y. Docs. vol. vi. *passim.*

in colonial history. Newcastle, acting under the advice of Shirley, sent a circular to all the colonial Governors to invite their respective Assemblies to raise contingents. All but Pennsylvania and the three southernmost colonies responded, and seven thousand eight hundred men were raised, together with four hundred volunteers from Pennsylvania. Massachusetts contributed nearly half the force, New York seventeen hundred, Connecticut a thousand. The smallest contingent was that from Virginia, numbering only a hundred. The Home Government promised to assist with a naval force and eight battalions of regulars.[1]

Projected invasion of Canada.

If a Pitt had directed the counsels of England it might well have been that the colonists, flushed with the success of Louisburg and united with an effective British force, might have anticipated the triumph of Wolfe. The dilatory and spiritless government of Fox and Newcastle was a reed which pierced the hand of him who leant on it. Newcastle wrote to Shirley admitting that the demands of the continental war for men and money made it impossible to help the colonists, and adding somewhat superfluously that the troops had been detained by adverse winds.

Dilatory policy of the British Government.

Anything like a comprehensive attack on Canada had to be abandoned. The two chief advocates of the expedition did not however sit down contentedly and accept discomfiture. Shirley and Clinton agreed to use the troops already raised in their respective colonies for a joint attack on Crown Point.

Clinton's efforts were thwarted by the factious conduct of the Assembly, who refused to provide transport for troops beyond Albany.[2] The opposition which Clinton had to fear was not only that of the professional politicians or of the merchants who were interested in the trade with Canada. When there was an

[1] Hutchinson, vol. ii. pp. 380–1.

[2] Smith.

alarm of invasion on the frontier the Governor ordered the militia to march to the threatened point. Every one of them refused to march on the ground that such an order was unconstitutional, and that the control of the militia was vested not in the Governor, but in the Assembly.[1] The result of all this disaffection was that Clinton, so far from being able to conduct active operations against Canada, was forced to weaken the defences of the colony by first abandoning and then burning Fort Saratoga, a display of weakness which sank deep into the minds of the Mohawks.[2]

Clinton thwarted by the people of New York.

In Massachusetts a wholly different spirit prevailed. There Shirley succeeded in raising a force of fifteen hundred men for the attack on Crown Point.[3] But just as they were ready to start news reached Boston which showed that all the resources of the colony would be needed for self-defence. The capture of Louisburg was to be met and avenged by a counterstroke. A fleet was fitted out, which from its size and the terror which it inspired was likened by a New England historian to the Spanish Armada.[4] The same writer frankly admits that 'our dependence under God was upon a squadron from England.'

French naval attack expected.

The colonists were better befriended by storms and sickness than by the tardy counsels of Newcastle and his colleagues. Almost at the outset the fleet met with bad weather, and had to reduce its pace to that of the slowest vessels. Then calamities followed thick on one another. The fleet was becalmed off the Azores; then several ships were struck by lightning. After that a pestilence broke out. Lastly, fogs seemed to make it

[1] Clinton to Lords of Trade, Nov. 10, 1747. Board of Trade Papers.

[2] N. Y. Docs. vol. vi. p. 374. 'You burned your fort and ran away,' was said by an Indian at a conference at Abbey in 1754. *Half a Century of Conflict*, vol. ii. p. 227.

[3] Hutchinson, p. 425. He is also the authority for what follows.

[4] *Ibid.* vol. ii. p. 385.

impossible for them to reach the American coast. This difficulty was at last overcome by the skill of a New England pilot who was captured on the voyage, and in September, three months after leaving France, the fleet anchored in Chebucto Bay, near Cape Breton. Yet more disappointment was in store. A small contingent from the West Indies was to have joined the fleet, and the misfortunes of the voyage had made such a reinforcement even more important than it originally seemed. But the French admiral, Danville, could get no tidings of them, and it was afterwards found that their commander, after waiting for about a fortnight, had despaired of Danville's arrival and departed.

The hardships of the voyage, intensified no doubt in their effect by continuous disappointment, had broken down Danville's health, and on September 27 he died, it was said of apoplexy, though there were hints of suicide by poison.

Deaths of Danville and Destournel.

Danville's successor, Destournel, was for abandoning the expedition. His officers opposed him and, being outvoted in a council of war, he stabbed himself. The pestilence from which the crews had suffered during the voyage so increased as to render the fleet powerless for attack, and the terror of invasion which had hung over New England passed away.

An incident happening at Boston in this same year showed that, though the men of Massachusetts were willing to play their part against France, they would only do so in their own fashion and on their own terms. Commodore Knowles, the commander of a squadron lying at Boston, found his crew considerably weakened by desertions. Thereupon he proceeded to make good the deficiency by

Impressment of seamen at Boston.[1]

[1] Hutchinson's account of this dispute is very full, and I have followed him throughout. He was a witness of the first order, as he took part in the whole affair himself.

impressment. The press-gang was an institution which the New Englanders not unnaturally detested. Seamen disliked it as taking them away from lucrative employment at the fisheries. The wealthier classes disliked it, exactly as they disliked the measures for the protection of ship-timber, because they valued the commercial prosperity of the colony more than the naval supremacy of England. There was, too, what one may call the hereditary dislike of New England for anything which savoured of arbitrary power. Hardly had Knowles accomplished his impressment than a mob assembled, armed with clubs and the like, to demand the release of the men pressed.[1] Their proceedings were marked with something of that method and self-restraint which usually distinguished a Boston mob.

At the outset they fell in with a naval lieutenant who chanced to be on shore and apprehended him, but released him on learning that he was in nowise concerned in the impressment. Then, hearing that several naval officers were in the Governor's house, they surrounded it. The officers appeared on the stairs with fire-arms ready to defend themselves, and there might have been an anticipation of the Boston massacre. A diversion, however, was created which can best be described in the words of Hutchinson, himself in all likelihood a spectator. 'A deputy sheriff attempting to exercise his authority was seized by the mob, and carried away in triumph and set in the stocks, which afforded them diversion and tended to abate their rage, and disposed them to separate and go to dinner.'

In the evening, however, a crowd assembled and began by breaking the windows of the Council house. The riot. Shirley thereupon appeared on the scene, expressed his disapproval of Knowles's proceedings, and

[1] Some, according to Hutchinson, were armed with 'pitch mops,' whatever they may be.

promised to secure the release of the men impressed, but at the same time 'gently reproved the irregular proceedings' of the mob.

Undeterred by Shirley's 'gentle reproof' the crowd seized a boat supposed by them to belong to a King's ship, was really private property, and were about to burn it in front of the Governor's house. But when the danger of burning down the town was pointed out, the rioters performed the *auto-da-fé* in a place of less danger. They also seized several naval officers, but liberated at least one of them on parole. The best part of three days, as it would seem, the mob was left uninterrupted and unchecked. But then, as later, a Boston mob had in it much of the temper of an organized force, and we hear nothing of outrage or purposeless riot. On the third day the House of Representatives met and passed a series of trimming resolutions. These set forth that there had been, and still was, 'a tumultuous and riotous assembling tending to the destruction of all government and order; that it was therefore the duty of all civil and military officers to do their utmost to suppress all riotous proceedings, but that at the same time they would do everything in their power to redress the grievance which had given rise to the riots.'

These resolutions were confirmed in substance by the town meeting. Knowles, dealing with his opponents in a spirit of concession, released the men pressed and departed, as Hutchinson says, 'to the joy of the town.'

Yet the matter did not end without a slight renewal of hostilities. Shirley wrote two letters to a Boston newspaper, the 'Post-boy,' on the subject of the riot. There could be little doubt of the unwisdom of the Governor's conduct in thus stepping down into the arena of partisan conflict. Shirley's action was at once made the subject of a protest by

Shirley's letters to the 'Postboy.'

the town meeting. He had in their judgement 're-presented the town in a light very much to their disadvantage.' A copy of this was sent to the Governor. He replied that he had written not to accuse the town, but to vindicate his own conduct from certain misrepresentations, and he ended up with the perilous admission that the conduct of the town 'appeared to him in a favourable light.'[1] This answer was voted satisfactory, and the formal thanks of the town meeting were accorded to the Governor.

The incident has a double significance. It at once brings home to us the difficulties which stood between any effective military co-operation between the mother country and the colonies. In none of them was the dread and hatred of the common enemy so vivid and so unmodified as in Massachusetts. Yet even there the sense of hostility to Romanist idolaters who hounded on the savage to destroy frontier homesteads and massacre women and children was balanced by a morbid suspicion of external control. Nor should it have been hard to foresee how that suspicion would act when the motives which checked and controlled it disappeared. The rioters of Shirley's day, uncompromising and unscrupulous, yet self-restrained in their violence and never losing their capacity for organized action, the politicians outwardly decorous and law-abiding, yet careful not to lift a finger in support of authority, these have each their exact counterpart in the revolutionary drama enacted by the next generation at Boston.

To the natives of the Old World the Peace of Aix-la-Chapelle at least brought a breathing space. It did hardly as much as that for the British colonies. For them peace between France and England had never

[1] Shirley's actual words were 'this affair appears to me in a favourable light.' For the proceedings of the town meeting and Shirley's answer see Boston Town Records, 1747, pp. 128–30.

brought with it any immunity from attack. The peace was signed in 1748. In less than three years from that time French and English officials were exchanging unfriendly messages, and asserting claims which if pressed could only lead to open war.

The peace of Aix-la-Chapelle.

Jonquière, the Governor of Canada, was with the approval of his own government seeking not merely to alienate the Five Nations from the English, but to stir them up to active hostility. The Fort at Oswego was a constant menace to Canada. The Indians must be incited to destroy it as an encroachment on their own territory. French authorities too, military and civil, saw far more clearly than their English opponents what was the real issue, and acted on their view far more promptly and decisively. They saw that the whole future of the French and English respectively in America turned on the maintenance or severance of the communications between Louisiana and Canada.

This meant an entire change in the theatre of war. French invasion of New England, naval attacks on Boston, retaliatory blows at Cape Breton, were only important as weakening or strengthening one or other of the combatants. The central issue had to be fought out in the valley of the Ohio. In one way this change stood the French in good stead. It enabled them to bring into full play the most potent weapon in their arsenal, their gift for working on the superstition, the vindictiveness and the cupidity of the savage.

Struggle for the Ohio valley.

It was fortunate for the English colonies at this juncture that they had among them one strong in those very gifts in which they were usually outmatched by their rivals. William Johnson was an Irishman, gifted fortunately for his special task with

William Johnson.[1]

[1] Mr. Parkman gives a good description of Johnson, *Half a Century of Conflict*, vol. ii. p. 227.

that dash of barbarism which still clave to the Ireland of the eighteenth century. He lived in a fortified house on the Mohawk river, acting as factor for his uncle, the sailor, Sir Peter Warren, who owned a large tract of land in those parts. We do not anywhere find him charged with duplicity or wanton severity. On the other hand, he appears to have kept up his authority among the savages by a studious observance of equity. But he was like the French Canadian in his power of adapting himself to the ways and tastes of the savage, and of winning their confidence by a genial compliance, not with their crimes, but certainly with their grosser tastes and habits. He married a squaw, danced the war dance, suffered his allies to paint his face, and joined them in their feast upon a whole ox.

The change in the field of contest brought with it as an inevitable consequence a change in the personality of the actors. The stress of the contest would now fall on the colonies whose western frontier was menaced by the French extension, namely on New York, Pennsylvania, Maryland and Virginia.

Change in the attitude of the English colonies.

New York, as we have seen, was torn through and through by faction. Effective help in any regular operations conducted by the mother country was not to be looked for there. All the more fortunate was it that the safety of her frontier was so largely in the hands of one like Johnson, not only fitted for the task both by natural temper and by training, but also standing aloof from the intrigues and entanglements of local politics.

New York.

In the situation of Pennsylvania there was no such redeeming feature. Her politics were as factious as those of New York. Her once holy places were now a sanctuary for sloth, cowardice and sordid self-interest. The humanity of Penn, the peace

Pennsylvania.

principles of the early Quakers, were a cloak behind which the factious and indolent citizen with no sense of public responsibility could always screen himself. Her frontiers were infested by men in whom the traditional treatment of the Indian had begotten a violent reaction, men as unscrupulous and brutal as the worst French Canadian, without that which did something to redeem the misdeeds of the Canadian, persistent policy and devotion to the public cause. The Philadelphian politician and the border desperado between them must often have tempted reasonable and patriotic men to wish that Penn had never been born. Moreover in all the three Middle colonies the large influx of German settlers and the remains of Dutch and Swedish population stood in the way of any strong and distinct corporate feeling, or even more of any real devotion to the cause of Britain as a whole. For these the conception of a united English-speaking commonwealth was as remote as for the New Englander, and if imagined would have been fully as distasteful though for less worthy reasons.

Maryland.

Maryland, like the Church of Laodicea, blew neither hot nor cold in the coming struggle. She made no show of zeal, but she did not at any time actively hinder the operations of war. Moreover the position of her western frontier, screened as it was by Pennsylvania and Virginia, saved her from being brought into close contact with the war.

Virginia.

Virginia has incurred severe—it may reasonably be contended exaggerated—condemnation for the part which her citizens played. She has been reproached for her tardy co-operation, for her inadequate grants alike of men and money. The blame has probably been the more freely bestowed because the antecedents of Virginia and the conditions of life there justified other expectations. The training and temper of the

Virginian planters might have been thought to ensure a certain aptitude for military duties. Where could better fighting material be found than in a population trained to outdoor life, seasoned in hardships and perils by love of sport, bearing themselves with the pride and self-reliance of an aristocracy? The exploits of 'Light-horse Harry' and William Washington, and at a later day of Stuart, showed that there would have been no error in such an estimate. Yet undoubtedly in the struggle against France the help of Virginia was given grudgingly and inadequately. That was largely due to causes for which individual Virginians of that day could not fairly be held responsible. These were two. Firstly, there was the dread of a servile insurrection. At the most critical stage of the war we find Dinwiddie writing, 'The villainy of the negroes in any emergency of government is what I always feared.' The Virginian who marched to the western frontier might be leaving his wife and children at the mercy of an enemy as unscrupulous as the Indian. This danger was greatly increased by the lack of communication among a widely dispersed population. The same cause, too, helped in other ways to paralyse the military life of Virginia just as it paralysed her economical and religious life. It was no easy matter to organize a system of defence in a country where there was no regular administrative unity.

Governor Dinwiddie.

Nor can it be gainsaid that the supine and unpatriotic attitude of Virginia was in a measure due to failings of temper and character in the Governor. There was much in Robert Dinwiddie to admire—clearness of perception, tenacity of purpose, a capacity for plain speech and forcible reproof when they were needed. Nor is there proof that Dinwiddie was actually corrupt. But he was keenly alive to his own rights, tenacious of his opinion in small matters, often unwilling to smooth over difficulties by compromise and by concession in non-essentials. Moreover he had before entering on the Governorship incurred the ill-will of the settlers. He had held the post of surveyor of customs. The occupant of that post was sure to be unpopular, and Dinwiddie's harsh and unconciliatory temper was certain to intensify the dislike earned by his office.

His perception of the real issue at stake and of the need for prompt action was shown at the very outset of the struggle. In 1753, while France and England were yet at peace, Dinwiddie learnt that a French militia force had secured the communication between Lake Erie and the upper waters of the Ohio, and had either gained the friendship or extorted the submission of the chief Indian tribes in those parts. A fort at Presqu'Isle on Lake Erie, and another, Fort le Bœuf, between fifteen and twenty miles further south, gave the French the command of the Alleghany river, and thereby secured them an easy access to the Ohio valley. They moreover seized an English trading station at Venango, the site of the present town of Meadville, and converted it into a fortified outpost.[1]

Dinwiddie's despatches show how thoroughly he understood the nature and how justly he rated the importance of the coming struggle. He at once acted with a promptitude and with a fearless acceptance of responsibility not too common among colonial statesmen of that age. It was indeed fortunate for Great Britain that two points, one of vital importance to the very existence of her empire, the other by its position playing a conspicuous part in any scheme of military action, should have been in the hands of two such men as Dinwiddie and Shirley.

Dinwiddie's task, however, was at the outset a far

[1] *Montcalm and Wolfe*, vol. i. pp. 128–33.

easier one than Shirley's had been eight years before. He did not need for the present to obtain the consent of the colonial legislature nor to enlist popular enthusiasm on behalf of his policy. All that was necessary was that an envoy should be sent to warn the French commander that he would be treated as an intruder. To that end Dinwiddie drafted a letter asking the French commander by what authority he had occupied English soil, and warning him to depart.

Washington's first mission.

The letter contained no reference to the possibility of hostile action. Dinwiddie, however, had at his back the authority of the Crown for using force. His instructions sent from England in August commanded him to require any intruders who had erected a fort on the soil of Virginia to withdraw. If in spite of such warning they remained, they were to be forcibly ejected.

Dinwiddie in conformity with this instruction for the present confined himself to words. Yet it can hardly have been by chance that Dinwiddie's choice fell on a man untrained indeed as a soldier, yet full of the military spirit, and gifted with what one may call the capacity for military observation. Not indeed that we can credit Dinwiddie with perceiving the full character of his choice, or all its consequences. No one short of an inspired prophet could have foreseen that Dinwiddie's selection of Washington was putting the young land surveyor on the first step of a career full of greatness. All that we can say is that out of all the young and enterprising Virginians available for such a mission, Dinwiddie chose the one fittest.

The despatch which Washington was instructed to deliver to the French commander was perfectly firm and definite. The fort which the French had been occupying stood upon land 'notoriously known to be the property of Great Britain.' 'It is my duty to require your peaceable departure.'[1]

Virginia now reaped the benefit of the policy initiated by Spotswood. He had foreseen the importance of the communications with the Ohio valley, and had understood how they should be secured by developing and organizing the Indian trade and encouraging exploration westward. The policy which he had initiated was followed up by the formation in 1750 of a trading company, holding a charter from the British Government, and purposing to develope the trade with the Indian tribes in the Ohio valley. One Christopher Gist was sent by the Company to explore and to report upon the attitude of the Indians.[2] At the same time the Governor of Pennsylvania had sent an agent, George Croghan, on a like errand.[3]

The Ohio Company.

There was no little jealousy between the two colonies, Pennsylvania and Virginia, as to the respective rights to the unoccupied territory in the west. Fortunately, however, this feeling does not seem to have extended in any way to their agents. Gist and Croghan united their parties and together penetrated as far as the Miami river in what is now Ohio, securing the friendship of the Indian tribes by the way.

This expedition might, if followed up and utilized, have laid the foundation of a secure friendship with the native tribes in the Ohio valley, and saved the frontiers of Pennsylvania and Virginia from years of terror and suffering. But all that the Assembly of Pennsylvania could do to thwart and nullify the action of Gist and Croghan they did. They refused to accept Croghan's report or to be at any cost in securing the alliance of the Indians.

Supineness of Pennsylvania.

[1] *Montcalm and Wolfe,* vol. i. p. 135.

[2] Pownall, *Topographical Description of N. America* (Appendix VI.).

[3] N. Y. Col. Docs. vol. vii. p. 267.

Next year Croghan was again sent out by Hamilton with presents for the Indians, and so far won their good-will, that they sent a petition to the government of Pennsylvania asking that a fort might be built in their territory. When the Proprietors of Pennsylvania heard of the scheme they with somewhat unwonted liberality offered to contribute four hundred pounds, but the Assembly was obdurate and nothing was done.[1]

The Pennsylvanians were even worse than inert. Not merely did they refuse to act themselves, but did their best to neutralize the action of Virginia. When the Ohio Company built a fort at Wills Creek, on a tributary of the Potomac, on a site occupied somewhat later by Fort Cumberland, the traders from Pennsylvania warned the Indians that this was part of a scheme for robbing them of their lands.[2]

Washington reaches Fort le Bœuf.[3]

Yet the little that had been done by the two colonies counted for something in smoothing the way for Washington's expedition. It furnished him with a starting point in the fort at Wills Creek, and in Gist with a guide familiar with the country and its savage occupants. With him, a French and an Indian interpreter, and four attendants trained to the hardships and difficulties of the woods, Washington set forth on November 15. About a hundred and seventy miles of wilderness severed him from the French outposts on the Alleghany. On the 30th Washington reached Venango. His progress had been delayed by exceptional falls of rain and snow which had flooded the creeks. But as a compensation he had been able to win allies among the Indians through whose territory he passed. Some of these accompanied him and strengthened his party. Their guidance and protection

[1] Pennsylvania Records, vol. v.

[2] *Montcalm and Wolfe,* vol. i. p. 59.

[3] Washington's own journal of this mission is published in Sparks's edition of his works, vol. ii., appendix.

were no doubt useful, but one may doubt how far it was wise to bring them into contact with the French and make them the object of French intrigue. Armed neutrality was an attitude altogether foreign to the Indian mind, and the spectacle of Washington being received in friendly fashion by the enemy must have bewildered the savages as to the real relations between the two nations. At Venango Washington was hospitably entertained by the three French officers stationed there. The presence of a visitor seems to have stimulated them to conviviality, and after dinner they told Washington that they meant to occupy and hold the Ohio. The English might outnumber them, but their greater energy and promptitude of action would counterbalance that.

There could be no pretext for detaining one who was at least in form only a peaceful envoy from a friendly Power, and the French officers contented themselves with hindering Washington's progress by privily creating discontent among his Indian companions. After some delay thus caused Washington started and in four days reached the principal French station, Fort le Bœuf.

The commander, St. Pierre, like his fellow-countrymen at Venango, received Washington courteously. In his answer to Dinwiddie he abstained from committing himself or incurring any responsibility. He would send Dinwiddie's letter to the Governor of Canada. Till he received further instructions he must remain at his post.

We may be very sure that St. Pierre knew perfectly well that Dinwiddie's remonstrances would count for nothing alike with Duquesne and with Duquesne's superiors in France. During Washington's absence Dinwiddie had been endeavouring to secure the support of his Assembly in preparing for active hostilities. Most unhappily he was at the same time, by conduct in which it is difficult to acquit him alike of obstinacy and cupidity, alienating the burgesses, and furnishing them with a pretext for refusing his demands. Certain official fees legally authorized by the Assembly had to be paid whenever a patent was taken out for unoccupied land.[1] Dinwiddie now claimed the right to impose at his own arbitrary discretion a further fee of a pistole for the use of the public seal in such cases. In this he was supported as he alleged by his Council. The reply of the Assembly was perhaps the most definite avowal that had yet been heard from any colonial body of the doctrine, no taxation without representation. 'The rights of the subject are so secured by law that they cannot be deprived of the least part of their property but by their own consent.' Dinwiddie's answer was as weak in substance as it was confused in expression. 'The establishment of the fee complained of relates solely to the disposal of the King's lands, and which it is conceived may be deemed a matter of favour from the Crown, and not a matter relative to the administration of government.' If that doctrine meant anything it meant that the Governor might impose a fee of any amount at his own discretion. How, too, could it be said that the necessary condition of expansion, and therefore of corporate life, was a matter of royal favour?

Dinwiddie and the pistole fee.

Dinwiddie added the somewhat disingenuous plea that he was influenced by his care and concern for the improvement of his Majesty's revenue of quit-rents. It is not easy to see how that was affected by an addition to the Governor's personal emoluments.

[1] For this dispute see the Dinwiddie Papers, vol. i. pp. 45–48, and elsewhere. According to the Editor of the Dinwiddie Papers, a pistole was equal to about eighteen shillings in English money. In Massachusetts in 1720 it was reckoned at twenty-four shillings. See Crosby's *Early Coins of America*, p. 116.

Failing to come to any terms with the Assembly Dinwiddie prorogued them. At the same time he took such steps for the security of the Ohio valley as were possible with his limited resources, acting with a promptitude and energy which went far to redeem his administrative errors. Washington was to be despatched to the Ohio valley with a force of two hundred militiamen, and with definite instructions to build a fort and to use force against anyone who hindered him. In the meantime Dinwiddie was sending friendly messages to native chiefs in anticipation of the support of the Assembly, and was taking steps to embody troops and to secure supplies and transport for a stronger expedition later in the year. He also sent despatches to the Governors of Massachusetts, New York, New Jersey, Pennsylvania, Maryland, and both the Carolinas, giving a very full account of what the French had done and were doing, and of his own measures and intentions.[1]

Dinwiddie's military policy.

In February the Assembly met again, and so far put aside their differences with Dinwiddie as to vote ten thousand pounds for military purposes. North Carolina also contributed a subsidy, enough for the maintenance of three or four hundred men, and the Governors of New York and South Carolina sent each a contingent, troops maintained in the colony but at the cost of the Crown.

It is a significant illustration of the imperfect knowledge and confusion of thought on colonial subjects which prevailed among British officials that the Secretary of State, Lord Holderness, sent instructions about the independent company to Dobbs, the Governor of North Carolina, when as a matter of fact there was no such force in that colony.[2]

[1] For all this see the Dinwiddie Papers, vol. i. pp. 48–88.

[2] *Ibid.* vol. i. p. 97.

Joshua Fry was appointed captain of the composite force, with Washington as his second in command. Here we probably see the working of a prejudice which at a later day wrought no small evil to the American cause in the struggle with the mother country. Fry was an Englishman, an Oxford graduate.[1] Washington's military ability in any wide sense of the word was absolutely untested. But he had shown himself a skilful explorer and competent in dealing with the Indians, observant, watchful and strenuous. It is probable that the same feeling operated in Fry's favour which afterwards made the colonists lean on such broken reeds as Gates and Lee. It might, too, have been a dangerous experiment to put a composite force under the command of an imperfectly educated young land surveyor. Dinwiddie's policy was not merely to dispossess the French force now established in the valley of the Ohio. He proposed to grant two hundred thousand acres of land there free of rent in the hope that the soldiers who formed the expedition would settle there, and thus form a garrison. The occupation was to be secured by two forts, and a thousand acres adjacent to one of these was to be laid off under the name of garrison land, and allotted at Fry's discretion to the officers and soldiers under his command.

Washington was at once despatched to the trading house at Wills Creek, and a party of forty men, a force utterly inadequate for the purpose, was sent to occupy a post at the junction of the Ohio and Alleghany where Pittsburg now stands, and to build a fort there. They reached the spot and began their works, but were almost immediately met by a French force more than twelve times their own number, with artillery. The Virginians surrendered and were then suffered to with-

[1] *Montcalm and Wolfe*, vol. ii. p. 142.

draw; the French commander built a fort on the spot called after the Governor of Canada Fort Duquesne.

Fight at Great Meadows.[1]

The next incident was important. It was the first instance in the present struggle in which blood was shed. It was virtually a declaration of war, the inception of that contest which ended with the annihilation of French power in America. Yet the skirmish at Great Meadows probably owes its notoriety far more to the later celebrity of one of the chief actors than to any sense of its integral importance. While Fry was waiting at Alexandria, on the lower Potomac, for his whole force to assemble, Washington with a hundred and fifty men was pushing forward through those forest paths of which he now knew something, accompanied by a party of friendly Indians. On or about May 25 he reached Great Meadows.

Having encamped there, Washington heard first from Gist, now settled in those parts, and then from an Indian, of the proximity of a French force. He thereupon advanced with a detachment of forty men and some friendly Indians as guide. Meanwhile the French commander had also sent out an ensign, Coulon de Jumonville, at the head of a detachment with orders to require the withdrawal of any English whom he might meet. Jumonville's force failed to conceal themselves from the well-trained eyes of Washington's savage allies and were taken by surprise. On what followed there is a conflict of testimony. According to the English version, the French on seeing the enemy stood to their arms, whereupon Washington gave the word to fire. The French themselves declared that Jumonville was reading his commission when he was fired upon.

[1] Washington's journal of this expedition is unhappily lost. It was captured by the French when Braddock was defeated, and a translation of it into French is in existence. Mr. Parkman's account is based on this and on the French official documents.

The only fact beyond doubt is that he, with nine of his men, was killed and the rest of his force captured.

That the testimony of the actors should be too conflicting to make any confident judgement of the matter possible was inevitable. Was there ever any transaction from a battle to a football match, involving a rapid succession of stirring incidents, on which it was possible to get a clear consensus of testimony, or on which men honest, and as far as intention goes truthful, will not make absolutely conflicting statements? Of two things, however, we may be sure. No conceivable motive, no desire for the advancement of his country, and still less any thought of personal safety, would have led Washington into an intentional breach of faith. But, on the other hand, Washington was not the man to be morbidly scrupulous or exaggeratedly sensitive on any question of honour. All through his career as a soldier he played the game honestly but strictly, never hindered by any self-imposed restraints of so-called chivalry. We may be sure, too, that he could in no way regret any incident which made war inevitable. The young land surveyor could not have clearly grasped all that was involved. But he knew, as every intelligent colonist knew, that he was face to face with an enemy whose methods were methods of extirpation. At a later day Washington showed a considerable capacity for merciless indignation when he is writing about Tories, and we may be sure that the French soldier and the French Jesuit, with their allied hordes of scalping and torturing barbarians, were just as much the objects of his detestation. Many colonists, and perhaps even more colonial officials, must have felt profoundly thankful for an incident which no longer left the relations between France and England in that nebulous condition in which they had been before, which of necessity committed each to a policy of open and avowed war.

The prompt daring of Washington, the reckless self-confidence of Jumonville had given the English colonists an initial success. But it was very certain that the inadequate resources at Dinwiddie's disposal, the supineness of the other colonies in co-operating, and the alacrity and military strength of the French would at once throw Washington on the defensive, and that even so, he would have but a faint chance of success. Immediately after the death of Jumonville, Washington returned to the camp at Great Meadows. He had left Fry ill, and after a few days he received news of his death. This left Washington in command. Fry's men soon reported themselves at Great Meadows, and with them the independent Company from South Carolina. There was also a small troop of Indian allies.

Camp at Great Meadows.

Washington soon learnt what troubles and difficulties wait on the commander of a mixed force. Mackay, the commander of the independent Company, refused to take orders from Washington, pleading that he was commissioned directly by the King. His men would not be content with the pay of eightpence a day which was all that the Virginian troops got. Partly to escape from this difficulty Washington advanced with his own troops to the place where Gist had formed his settlement. There however rumours of an impending attack became so alarming that he had first to send for Mackay, and then to fall back to Great Meadows.

From the Ohio valley a mixed force of French and Indians, outnumbering Washington's by about three to one, was advancing towards Great Meadows. It was under the command of Jumonville's brother, Coulon de Villiers. There they found the Virginians and their allies in a feebly constructed fort, to which Washington had given the dismal name of

The camp attacked by the French.

Fort Necessity. It was appropriate, since he was ill supplied with ammunition and had no bread.

It would seem as if the death of Jumonville had imbued his brother with an exaggerated respect for his enemy's power. One can hardly doubt that prompt and resolute assault would have carried the fort and made prisoners of the whole British force. De Villiers was content to open a distant fire from a position of comparative security. If his object was to save his men he seems to have failed, since from the best accounts the losses on each side were about equal. The effect of the fire on each side was impaired not only by the fact that each side was more or less protected by cover, but also by continuous rain. At eight in the evening, after an exchange of shots which had lasted nearly all day, the French commander proposed a parley.

Washington surrenders.

Hopelessly outnumbered as Washington was, and straitened for food and ammunition, he could not have been blamed if he had offered an unconditional surrender. To hesitate in accepting the overtures of the French commander would have been suicidal. The terms offered were such as Washington could hardly have looked for from an enemy who seemed to have him at his mercy. The British troops were to march out with the honours of war, carrying off their effects and one of their field-pieces, and were to be protected against attacks from the Indians. The French prisoners captured in the first fight at Great Meadows were to be restored.

Effect on the Indians.

That Washington's opening campaign should have ended thus had in it something as it were prophetic. Initial defeats, manfully borne and patiently retrieved, were strewn thickly along his career as a soldier. The worst result of the British discomfiture was the effect upon the Indians. The tribes in the Ohio valley were not, like the Five Nations, bound to one of the combatants by a traditional, and to some extent a durable, tie. There had been continually under their eyes the very worst aspect of colonial policy: inertness, dissensions, border feuds, men of the same race and speech shedding one another's blood and violating one another's homes. And now a strong and united power was stepping in to seize upon the inheritance which their rivals had, as it seemed, despised and neglected. Could there be a doubt which side would command the allegiance of the savage in the coming struggle?

One gleam of light there was, indeed, through this darkness. Two such incidents as the death of Jumonville and the surrender of Fort Necessity must at least put an end to any pretence of peace. Every colonist or British resident with any sort of insight into the future must have felt it a relief that the inevitable conflict was no longer delayed. As Dinwiddie put it in a letter to Sharpe, the Governor of Maryland, 'If the misfortune attending our forces has aroused the spirit of our neighbouring colonies, it has done more than probably a victory could have effected.' [1]

Prompt action by Dinwiddie.

Dinwiddie may have been rapacious, and at a later stage of the trouble he showed himself contentious and dictatorial. But Britain, and even more British America, owes him no small debt for his conduct at this crisis. He at once summoned the Assembly and laid before them the urgency of the need for active measures, and therefore for a vote of money. Twenty thousands pounds was voted. But the Assembly could not resist the temptation of securing an advantage over the Governor, and tacked on a supplementary vote of two thousand five hundred pounds towards defraying the cost of an agency sent to England to state their

[1] Dinwiddie Papers, vol. i. p. 258.

case over the pistole fee. Dinwiddie grumbled but gave way.[1]

Dinwiddie did not limit his efforts to his own colony. He did all that could be done to organize collective action on the part of the Middle and Southern provinces. A letter written by him about this time to Sir Thomas Robinson, the Secretary of State, is the best comment on the need for such action. While Frenchmen were occupying and annexing British territory, New York and Pennsylvania were supplying Canada with the necessaries of life, such as beef, pork and flour.[2] Loyal colonists for whom Hindostan was a vague name might well be wroth at the policy which had bartered away Louisburg, since that port was the head-quarters of this suicidal trade.

The Albany conference.[3]

In the previous September a circular letter had been sent by the Home Government to each colonial Governor in America bidding him arrange with his Assembly for a conference of colonial delegates, who should take steps to secure the alliance of the Indians. In conformity with this instruction the seven colonies north of the Potomac, New Jersey and Delaware excepted, sent commissioners to Albany. They were met by an embassy from the Five Nations, headed by a chief named Hendrick, who told the English some very plain truths about their supineness and vacillation in dealing with the French.

The value of personal influence in dealing with the savages was forcibly illustrated by the demand of the envoys that the management of Indian affairs should be vested in Johnson.

Fair words and rather vague expressions of good-will passed, but little was done to put the relations between the colonies and the Indians on a surer footing.

[1] Dinwiddie Papers, vol. i. p. 344. [2] *Ib.* p. 473.

[3] N. Y. Col. Docs. vol. vi. pp. 853–92.

The really memorable incident in connexion with the Albany conference was that there the project of a colonial union, which had slept for half a century, once more took definite shape. We have seen how Penn had broached such a scheme, and how vague suggestions tending in that direction had constantly floated before the minds of colonial administrators and their critics. The mechanical difficulties, as we may call them, of communication would have been fatal to Penn's scheme. The intervening years had done something to remove those difficulties. But they had done nothing to lighten the equally serious obstacles: the lack of common feeling and common interest, the jealousies begotten of boundary disputes, the total absence of any comprehensive ideal of nationality.

Franklin's scheme for a colonial union.

Franklin was a member of the Congress. The somewhat reckless young agitator had sown his wild oats; the old distaste to control and the old gift of sarcasm were in no wise impaired, but they were disciplined by a sense of responsibility and of serious and sustained purpose. He now came before the Congress with a detailed and carefully thought out scheme of confederation. Though it bore no fruit, yet it is full of interest as showing the views and wishes of one who had so large a share in bringing about a wider and more complete union.

There was to be a colonial Council of forty-eight members, elected by the various Assemblies. Each colony was to be represented in proportion to its population, Virginia and Massachusetts coming at one end with seven members each, New Hampshire at the other with two. They were to be elected triennially, and to meet once a year, or if needed oftener, and twenty-five was to be a quorum. Over them was to be a President appointed by the Crown. The appointment of officials was to be divided between the two powers; military officers were to be chosen by the Crown, civil by the Council, with in each case a reciprocal right of veto. This was evidently on the ground that the mother country was specially interested in defensive measures, the colonists themselves in administration. On the same principle dealings with the Indians were to be under the control of the President.

The right of taxation was one which was sure to be viewed with suspicion, and Franklin's language on that point shows a curious wish to propitiate the opinion of his fellow-colonists. 'They' (i.e. the President and Council) 'may levy general duties as shall appear equal and just, considering the ability and other circumstances of the inhabitants in the several colonies, and such as may be collected with least inconvenience to the people, rather discouraging luxury than loading industry with unnecessary burdens.'

The scheme was criticized by Shirley on the ground that it unduly impaired the authority of the Crown. One cannot but reflect that within less than a quarter of a century the King and his advisers would have been thankful for as much as Franklin's scheme left them. The proposal, however, found favour with neither party. This fact has been claimed as a proof that it hit the happy mean needed in a compromise.

The weak points of Franklin's scheme were two. There was no machinery, such as was afterwards introduced into the Federal Constitution by the creation of the Senate, to secure the rights of the smaller provinces. Still more serious was the total absence of any coercive machinery.

Weaker even than Franklin's scheme was that put forward by the British Government shortly after. A circular letter was to be sent to the various colonial

Governors, instructing them to recommend each Assembly to appoint Commissioners, to be approved of by the Governor. These Commissioners were to meet as a board to consider measures for defence and to apportion the cost. Each colony was to pay any special expense involved in its own defence. Such a method was certain to be fruitful in disputes. Moreover, by making the defence of each colony a special and local charge, it emphasized that very view which the British Government should have aimed at dispelling. Everything should have been done to impress on the colonists the belief that French encroachment, whether in the valley of the Ohio or on the frontier of New Hampshire, was one and the same thing, and threatened the colonists with common danger.

Scheme proposed by the British Government.[1]

Dinwiddie clearly saw that the spirit of union must come first, the machinery for giving effect to it afterwards, and that to bring home to the British Government and to the neighbouring colonies the need for common action was a more practical task than to devise schemes for a confederation. Early in the year, before Washington had returned discomfited from the Ohio, Dinwiddie had written to the Governors of Maryland, Pennsylvania and New York, telling them of his intended policy and urging them to make ready for the coming struggle.[2] At the end of July Dinwiddie returned to the charge. He asked Sharpe, the Governor of Maryland, to build a magazine at Wills Creek, while Hamilton, the Governor of Pennsylvania, is to do his share by filling it with flour.[3] From both these colonies and also from New York Dinwiddie hopes to get a military contingent. In short, pending action by the Home Government,

Dinwiddie endeavours to secure joint action.

[1] N. Y. Docs. vol. vi. pp. 903-6.

[2] Dinwiddie Papers, vol. i. pp. 83-6.

[3] *Ibid.* pp. 255-8.

Dinwiddie was, although without any definite commission or authority, controlling the military operations not only of his own but of the adjacent colonies.

Acting on his authority as Governor he placed James Innes, a fellow-countryman and friend who was colonel of the North Carolina militia, in command ot the whole combined force of the different colonies. It was his intention that they should at once re-establish themselves to the west of the mountains.[1] This scheme, however, was frustrated partly by the conduct of the North Carolina troops who stood out for higher pay than the Virginians,[2] and partly by the refusal of the Assembly to comply in full with the Governor's demand for money.[3]

Dinwiddie did not, however, relax his attempt of secure the co-operation of the other colonies. His communications were not of the nature of formal circulars. He made a direct personal appeal to each Governor, urging special arguments applicable to his case.[4] Only in one quarter does he seem to have met with a hearty response. Sharpe, as may be seen from the correspondence which passed between them, threw himself zealously into Dinwiddie's plan and succeeded, though not without delay and difficulty, in persuading his Assembly to vote six thousand pounds towards the common cause.[5]

In the other cases Dinwiddie must indeed have felt that he was 'stirring a dish of skim milk to an honourable action.' As he complained in his despair to Hamilton, the Governor of Pennsylvania, 'there appears to be an infatuation in all the Assemblies in this part of the world. They are not affected with the imminent danger they are obviously exposed to,

Action of Pennsylvania.

[1] Dinwiddie Papers, vol. x. pp. 194–6.
[2] *Ibid.* vol. i. p. 306.
[3] *Ibid.* pp. 283, 285.
[4] *Ibid.* pp. 259, 303, 306.
[5] Dinwiddie to Robinson, Papers, vol. i. p. 279.

but seem satisfied to leave the French at full liberty to perpetrate their utmost designs to their ruin.'[1] To Morris, Hamilton's successor, he writes hoping that, though the colonists 'may plead some religious tenets for their excuse, yet they will show themselves good subjects and attend to the first law of nature—self-preservation.'[2]

The attitude of Pennsylvania throughout the war was a dismal comment on Dinwiddie's words.

In all the colonies save one the difficulty lay with the popular representatives. From the Governors Dinwiddie met with cordial replies and promise of co-operation. The one exception was South Carolina. There the attitude taken up by Governor Glen was one of absolutely selfish isolation, one which would have been fatal to Dinwiddie's policy of holding the Ohio against the French. That was to be effected by securing the alliance of the chief Indian tribes in the southern valley of the Ohio. This Glen resented as likely to disturb the relations of those tribes with South Carolina. They were in his own language 'our Indians,' and as such were not to be taught that Virginia or the English colonies as a whole had any claim on their friendship. Glen would not even accept the claim of Great Britain to the valley of the Ohio. The attempt to enforce that claim might expose South Carolina to a French invasion. It was suspected that Glen, like the merchants of Pennsylvania and New York, was not influenced solely by regard for the peace and safety of his own colony, but also by a personal interest in the Indian trade.[3] If we may believe Dinwiddie, Glen even went so far as to tell the Catawba Indians, after they had actually promised to meet

Governor Glen, of South Carolina.

[1] Dinwiddie Papers, vol. i. p. 306. [2] *Ibid.* p. 395.

[3] The letter to Dinwiddie in which these views are expressed is quoted textually by Mr. McCrady, vol. ii. p. 303.

Dinwiddie for a conference, to stay away.[1] Could there be an incident more certain to impress the Indians with a sense of British disunion and helplessness?

We cannot wonder that Dinwiddie did not mince matters answering Glen. His 'letter and arguments would have been more proper from a French officer than from one of his Majesty's Governors.' Such a reply was no doubt a pleasant safety-valve for Dinwiddie's feelings, but it did nothing to secure the carrying through of his policy.[2]

Shirley's letters.

Dinwiddie was not the only colonial Governor who was labouring to bring home to the minds of the British Government the dangers of the situation and the need for prompt action. Shirley was not only animated by recollections of the Louisburg campaign, but his own recent experience had brought him in contact with Frenchmen, and in all likelihood given him an opportunity of learning the nature of French colonial policy. He had been in Paris on a boundary commission, a business in itself likely to open his eyes to the danger of French territorial claims, and while so employed he had married a French wife. He now wrote to the Secretary of State pointing out that the Ohio was not the only quarter from which danger threatened. There was the ever present danger of a servile insurrection. There were numerous Roman Catholics, many of them indented servants, who would probably take the part of the French. The French might even invade the valley of the Hudson, a danger made all the more real by the inertness of Pennsylvanian Quakers and the cupidity of New York traders.

Seldom has there been a stronger illustration of the unreality of diplomatic formalities than was now to be

[1] This is stated in the letter referred to below.

[2] Dinwiddie Papers, vol. i. p. 378.

seen in the relations between Great Britain and France. In November, at the opening of Parliament, the prevalence of peace was mentioned in the King's Speech as a subject for congratulation. At that very time a thousand men were embarked for Virginia, to be strengthened by the enlistment of four hundred more in America. Their commander was Edward Braddock. His character as a man has been made the subject of more controversy than it is perhaps intrinsically worth. He was abused by the colonists, among whom he fought and fell; he has been handed down to us by a great master of social satire as 'a very Iroquois,' and the picture set with appropriate ornaments. His reputation has profited by reaction. It has been held that the colonists who suffered by his errors as a soldier are tainted witnesses, and that Walpole would never scruple to sacrifice a character to an epigram. Against the latter plea it may be urged that gallantry and patriotism never appealed to Walpole in vain, prone though he was to hide generous enthusiasm under a thin veil of cynicism. Nor should it be forgotten that Walpole expressly admits that Braddock was 'adored' when he commanded at Gibraltar, and that he tells a story of him illustrating a certain magnanimity which rose above mere brute courage.

General Braddock.[1]

Braddock as a soldier offers an easier problem. His private secretary, a son of Governor Shirley, delivered himself of a not wholly undiscriminating condemnation of his chief: 'We have a general most judiciously chosen for being disqualified for the service he is employed in, in almost every respect. He may be brave for aught I know, and he is honest in pecuniary

[1] In my account of Braddock's expedition and death I have mainly followed Parkman, and Washington's letters, printed by Sparks. The Dinwiddie Papers also are valuable. I have besides consulted Mr. Sargent's monograph.

matters.' The events of the coming year left little doubt as to the soundness of Shirley's judgement.[1]

The really most effective condemnation is to be found in Franklin's measured words. Braddock 'might,' he thinks, 'have made a good figure in some European war. But he had too mean an opinion of Americans and Indians.'[2] That was an error which was not merely calculated to bring about, as it did, a crushing disaster in the field. No general could hope to succeed in the task set Braddock unless he could excite the enthusiasm and command the loyal co-operation of the colonists. Inability to do that would have made military talents of a higher order than Braddock's useless.

The council of war at Alexandria.

Braddock's first step on landing was to hold a council of war at Alexandria. It was attended by Dinwiddie, Shirley, Sharpe, and three other colonial Governors. A plan of campaign was produced by Braddock in conformity with his instructions. The attack was to be on four lines. Braddock himself was to advance into the valley of the Ohio. Three separate bodies of troops, all colonial, were to be sent against Niagara, Crown Point, and Acadia.

The general conception was a sound one. Braddock was taking into his own hands what was no doubt the most essential part of the campaign. It was all-important to wipe out the effect produced on the savages by Washington's defeat. A blow struck at French power on the lakes or in the valley of the St. Lawrence might isolate the Ohio valley, and make it difficult or even impossible to replenish the garrisons there. But supplies might be got from the country itself, and a mere handful of Frenchmen would be enough to keep alive the hostility of the savage to the British.

[1] Letter to Morris, quoted textually by Mr. Parkman, vol. i. p. 188.

[2] Franklin's autobiography in his works, vol. ii.

Braddock and his advisers were no doubt right, too, in their belief that the Ohio campaign could only be of service as part of a connected scheme of operations.

British forces insufficient.

The real error lay not in the choice of operations, but in the scale on which it was proposed to conduct them. To open a campaign with wholly inadequate resources, and thus to create difficulties which have to be redeemed at a heavy price alike in blood and in money, has always been the besetting sin of British Governments. So it was now. Even for the immediate task in hand fourteen hundred men was a wholly inadequate force. If the Ohio valley was to be secured, it would have to be secured, as Dinwiddie saw, not by one decisive blow, though that might be needed, but by systematic military occupation, and for a while at least by a chain of forts, securing not only the valley of the Ohio but the communications with the settled parts of Virginia. To do that securely and effectively needed a far larger force than Braddock had at his disposal.

Even more short-sighted was the notion that operations on the scale intended could be effectually conducted by provincial troops without aid from the mother country. There it is probable that Shirley had been unconsciously misleading the Home Government. His strenuous and sanguine mind, flushed with the success of Louisburg, may well have overrated the task in hand. He may have imagined that a large proportion of the colonists were as courageous and enduring as his New Englanders, that all New Englanders were as zealous and public-spirited as himself.

Yet the general scheme of the war conceived at the outset was a sound one, as was shown by those who succeeded to the responsibilities of Robinson and Braddock. The merits of Pitt and Wolfe and Forbes were not that they saw things which had been concealed from their predecessors, but that they measured their difficulties and their resources justly, that they did resolutely and persistently what others had only attempted feebly and incompletely.

If Braddock imagined that the temper of Dinwiddie and Shirley would be reflected in that of the colonists he was speedily undeceived. All that the Assembly of Pennsylvania would do was to vote twenty thousand pounds, with a special clause attached to the vote making the Proprietors' lands liable to taxation. To permit this was in direct opposition to the Governor's instructions. His remonstrances are best quoted in his own words. In December he addressed the Assembly on the subject: 'Upon the whole you will consider, gentlemen, in what light you will appear to his Majesty and a British Parliament, who are expending great sums of money for the defence of these colonies, while you, the very province most concerned, as being invaded, instead of contributing towards your own defence, are entering into an ill-timed controversy concerning the validity of royal instructions which have been determined long ago, and may be delayed to a more convenient time without being any the least injury to the rights of the people.'[1]

Again, on the first day of the new year, he spoke in the same strain. 'It gives me particular concern that you should purposely enter into a dispute about the instruction, and choose to express and publish such sentiments of his Majesty's Government, at a time like this, when a French army are fortifying themselves in your country; and I earnestly recommend it to you to consider whether such expressions may not have a tendency to alienate the affections of the people of this province from his Majesty's person and Government, and thereby greatly obstruct the measures he is taking

[1] For this and the following speech see the Pennsylvania Records.

at a vast expense for the preservation and protection of his subjects upon this continent.'

There is, he points out, danger of invasion. The French have a thousand soldiers on the Ohio, and they will attack Pennsylvania, as it is 'the most plentiful and only defenceless part.'

'I must therefore, gentlemen, once more entreat you to lay aside everything that may admit of dispute between us till a more favourable season, and enter seriously into the consideration of the danger to which your country is exposed, and not only grant the supplies recommended by the Crown, but enable me to raise a considerable body of men to be employed in conjunction with the troops his Majesty has destined for this service, and, by establishing a regular militia and providing the necessary stores of war, leave us no longer for want of discipline an easy prey to a much weaker body of men than are now encamped within a few days' march of the city.'

The curtailment of the needful supplies was not the only way in which the slothfulness and disloyalty of the Pennsylvanians had a prejudicial effect on Braddock's operations. He might advance to the Ohio through either Pennsylvania or Virginia. If one looked merely at the map, there was little difference. But the route through Virginia traversed a wilderness, that through Pennsylvania lay for a considerable distance in a civilized country, with good roads and abundant supplies of transport and food. Braddock, however, could not be expected to know that. It was but natural that he should choose his route through the loyal colony rather than the disloyal. It is said, too, that his choice was prompted or confirmed by the members of the Ohio Company, who took the view that a military road made by Braddock would afterwards profit their speculations. If that be so, it would be hard to find a stronger instance of the harm done to the common cause by sectional interests.

As it was, Braddock soon learnt what difficulties resulted from a march through a backward and sparsely populated country. No means of transport could be found and the expedition was at a standstill. Franklin, who was with Braddock, heard of the difficulty and went to get what was needed from his own colony. The Pennsylvanians might object to voting money towards a British army even for their own protection. But they had no scruple about making profit out of the General's necessities, and Franklin returned with a hundred and fifty waggons and a sufficient supply of horses. By May 10 Braddock reached Wills Creek. Beside his own two regiments he had now four hundred and fifty Virginians. With these he dealt characteristically. They were handed over to one of his officers to be 'made as much like soldiers as possible,' in other words to be transformed from efficient backwoods fighters into a poor imitation of regulars. In a despatch to Robinson he described them as slothful and languid—probably because they did not take kindly to parade work, which was not likely to advantage them much in the woods.

Braddock's advance.

In the same spirit Braddock refused the help of a small party of frontier men, painted like savages, and headed by a leader whose house had been burnt and family murdered by the Indians, and who had sworn a vendetta against them.

These errors of Braddock's may not have affected the result of a campaign, though that is far from certain. They did affect the conduct of the war as a whole. The refusal to accept such help wounded the pride of the colonists. The spectacle of a British General undertaking a forest campaign without a notion of the special conditions and requirements, fighting on the banks of the Potomac as he would have fought on the banks of the Rhine, filled the colonists with contempt. Conduct such as Braddock's begot a tradition, too often kept alive by his successors, of an impassable barrier between Briton and colonist. The French war might have done much to break down that tradition. It did much to create and perpetuate it. When the Virginians are reproached for supineness and lack of patriotism these things ought to be borne in mind.

One set-off against this must not be forgotten. It was owing to Braddock that Washington reappeared on the field. He had sent in his resignation, indignant at the regulation which gave colonial officers inferior rank to those who held the King's commission. Braddock recognised that Washington's experience and courage, tested it is true only by one campaign, yet fully tested, would be of service to him, and appointed him one of his aide-de-camps.

On June 10 Braddock resumed his march through the wilderness. The tragedy that followed is one of the most familiar incidents in history. The French and Canadian troops were established at Fort Duquesne, on the site of the present town of Pittsburg, with four hundred Indian allies.[1] From Wills Creek to Fort Duquesne was a distance of about eighty miles as the crow flies. In any case progress would have been slow, since a track had to be cut through the forest. Beside that, the march was retarded by the sickness alike of men and horses. Washington seems to have been the one colonial soldier whose judgement carried weight with Braddock. By his advice before the march was half accomplished Braddock lightened his column by leaving behind his heavy baggage with a rear-guard, under the command of General Dunbar, and advancing

[1] There does not seem to be any evidence as to the exact number of French troops.

with a force reduced to twelve hundred men. Yet even so his progress seemed slow to the active and hardy land surveyor, accustomed to scramble amid forest tracks and streams, with his equipment in a pair of saddle-bags. 'They halted,' Washington complained, 'to level every molehill and to erect bridges over every brook.'

Military pedantry, however, was not the only influence at work to delay Braddock's progress. His transport was weakened, firstly by the worthless character of the horses supplied by the colonists, and secondly by the parties of horse stealers who hung on to the line of his march.[1]

On July 3, Contrecœur, the French commander at Fort Duquesne, heard of the approach of Braddock and decided to attack him while still in the forest. That movement, one on which the whole fate of the campaign turned, was on the brink of being frustrated by the caprice of Contrecœur's savage allies. The tact of the Frenchman in dealing with savages, his patient bearing with their caprices and his power of stimulating their enthusiasm, now came into play. The Indians at first refused to leave the fort. An English officer of the type of Braddock would have sworn, grumbled and given up the native alliance as a broken reed. One of Contrecœur's lieutenants, Beaujeu, declared that he would in any case go forth single-handed. Would the Indians suffer their white father to fight unaided? The appeal was not made in vain and Beaujeu, himself in Indian dress and war paint, sallied forth, at the head of over six hundred Indians and two hundred and fifty Frenchmen.

The French and the Indians.

Beaujeu's intention was to wait for Braddock in ambush, but that plan was frustrated by the capricious self-will of the Indian allies, half of whom went off to fight independently according to their own ideas.

The battle.

[1] This is stated by Mr. Sargent. He quotes his authorities.

The result was that Beaujeu, instead of concealing his forces in the wood and taking the enemy in flank, was compelled to make a direct attack on the head of Braddock's advancing column. At the outset the English behaved both with courage and good discipline. It was no easy matter to form line under fire amid the foliage and undergrowth of an American forest in July. Indian marksmanship was not conspicuously accurate, and the savage could not be relied on to persevere when the first fury of his attack was spent.

As it was, after the English delivered their first fire, it was all that the French officers could do to rally their savage allies.

There can be little doubt that, if Braddock's men had been in any way familiar with the methods of bush fighting, all might have gone well. But to a man of Braddock's training and temper it was better to be defeated in conformity with orthodox methods than to win by conduct which seemed lacking in courage, and by imitating the hitherto unknown tactics of colonials and barbarians. When his men would fain have followed the example of the Virginians and fired from behind trees, Braddock drove them into the open, beating them, it is said, with the flat of his sword.

It was little reproach to a force thus handled, fighting under wholly unfamiliar conditions and against a mysterious and unseen foe, that they fell into hopeless confusion, and fired upon the colonial skirmishers, mistaking them for the enemy.

Hopeless confusion and a complete rout ensued, and the defeated British fled through the forest, leaving behind baggage and cannon. Braddock, after doing all that mere individual courage could do to repair his errors of generalship, was carried off the field yet breathing, but stricken to the death; most of the wounded were less fortunate, and were left on the ground to be tomahawked and scalped.

Braddock's defeat put an end to any present operations against the French in the Ohio valley. It did, though it need not have done so, expose the English settlements to invasion. Both these consequences, however, were reparable. Every year that the French remained in the valley of the Ohio made their ultimate eviction more difficult. But the possession of the Ohio was an issue to be settled in other fields than the banks of the Ohio itself. A savage inroad might be a terrible scourge, but it was a passing one. It was a raid for plunder and blood, not an invasion for conquest.

Consequences of defeat.

But one consequence of the defeat was not transient. It helped to imbue the colonists with a contempt, never wholly eradicated, for British generalship and a distrust of English courage. The latter was beyond doubt unjust. What European force would not have been demoralized, hemmed in on a narrow track with unseen foes firing upon them from every side? We are so used to England's 'small wars' that we have almost come to look on a bush fight with savages as the normal kind of engagement. The soldiers of Braddock's day had never seen a savage in the field. They might have fought on Indian plains or Scotch moors. But the military methods of the Indian troops were not those of barbarians, rather of an incomplete and clumsy civilization. It was a long step from a kilted Highlander to a Shawnee in his war paint. On the battlefields of the Old World it might be true that:

'Trained through steadfast work and drilled,
Till as one thought they moved along,
By the old land's old memories filled,
Our English lads were calm and strong.'

But what calmness could be looked for in a man reared in an English village, exposed to the fire of an enemy dimly and vaguely discerned through the trees, painted till he looked like a wild beast, and yelling like a fiend let out of hell? The colonist forgot these things. He forgot that to ask an English regiment to engage in a bush fight was like asking a band of backwoodsmen to stand a charge of cuirassiers in the open. But though the contempt might be unjust and unreasonable, that did not make it one whit less of evil consequence.

How far blame attached to Braddock.

Contempt for English generalship was better founded. A historian usually in nowise favourable to Braddock acquits him of having led his men into an ambush.[1] Technically that may be so, since no deliberate ambush was attempted by the enemy. But beyond doubt he did place his troops in a position where they were exposed to a most perilous form of attack. It may be true that he threw out reconnoitring parties on each side of his track. If they failed to report an enemy, that revealed deficiencies which Braddock ought to have known and guarded against. Nor can one suppose that under any conditions it would have been safe to move a column of nearly a thousand men along a path twelve feet wide, flanked by thick wood. There might have been excuses for Braddock if there had been urgency, if he had been moving to the relief of a besieged garrison. The only argument that could have been used in favour of haste was the danger of supplies failing and the difficulty of transport. It may be said, and plausibly, that Washington gave bad advice when he urged Braddock to press on without his heavy baggage. But Washington's own words show that he expected from that plan a rate of progress far beyond that attained, and one can hardly deny that he was justified in

[1] Mr. Parkman's *Montcalm and Wolfe*, vol. i. p. 214.

expecting it, though he might not have done so if he had known English troops better.

Probably Braddock's best policy would have been to follow Washington's advice, only in a much more thoroughgoing fashion, and to secure his own troops with temporary log-huts and earthworks, sending Washington with all the Indians and backwoodsmen that could be raised to reconnoitre and skirmish. They might have so dealt with the French and their allies as to make an advance safe; at the worst they would have fallen back, possibly with lessened numbers.

Perhaps the most unhappy phase of the whole matter was that the colonists should have seen a British general pedantically clinging to the inappropriate methods of the Old World, and refusing to let even the irregular troops make the attempt which might have won safety for themselves, possibly even for the whole force.

A contemporary pamphleteer expressed the view, and it has been accepted and approved by a modern writer, that Braddock's defeat was a blessing in disguise, since it forced upon the colonists as nothing else would have done the need for united resistance. It is a somewhat obvious answer that Braddock's defeat did not have that effect, that it left the colonies as it found them, disunited and unorganized, distrustful of the mother country, yet not atoning for that distrust by any spirit of self-reliance and self-help.[1]

Dinwiddie's energy.

Something might have been done even after Braddock's defeat and death to redeem the situation and re-establish the good name of the British army. The stout-hearted Dinwiddie in the spirit of Varro refused to despair of the state. There

[1] This contention is to be found in a pamphlet published at Boston in 1755. It is entitled *Two Letters to a Friend on the present Critical Conjuncture of Affairs in North America.* Mr. Sargent adopts the same view.

might yet be time for a counter-stroke. With characteristic energy he showered despatches upon all from whom help might be looked for: on the Governors of North Carolina, Maryland, Pennsylvania, New Jersey, New York and Massachusetts, urging the need for action, and telling them what he could himself do in the way of raising troops.[1] The letters were not mere reproductions of a circular or a common form, but personal appeals differing in every instance. Glen is told very plainly that if he had induced the Cherokees and Catawbas to send auxiliary forces, as he might have done, the French Indians would have been held in check and the disaster averted.[2]

Firmness was naturally to be looked for from Dinwiddie. In his dealings with the Assembly he showed what was less to be looked for, patience and forbearance. In his address to them, when they met in August, there are no reproaches as to the past, no attempt to fasten on them responsibility for failure, nothing but forcible representations of the imminent danger, and an assumption that it would be dealt with effectively.[3]

The Governor's confidence was not misplaced. In less than a week from meeting the Assembly had voted forty thousand pounds, and would, Dinwiddie believed, have made the sum up to a hundred thousand more if they could have been promised that offensive operations would be resumed at once.[4]

Unhappily the apathy of the colonists themselves was no longer the chief obstacle to be overcome.

It is shown from the tone of Dinwiddie's letters that he had misgivings as to Dunbar's firmness. He adjures him at least to stand fast in such a defensive position as would enable him to guard the frontier

[1] Dinwiddie Papers, vol. ii. pp. 126–31.
[2] *Ibid.* p. 125.
[3] *Ibid.* pp. 134–6.
[4] *Ibid.* p. 176.

Dunbar's action more than justified the Governor's fears. In Braddock's case the colonists had witnessed the spectacle of British presumption and lack of soldierly skill; they were now to see the spectacle of something which suspiciously resembled cowardice, and of gross indifference to their own safety.

Dunbar's retreat.

On July 26 Dinwiddie wrote to Dunbar, advising him to hold his ground and wait for reinforcements.[1] Dunbar called a council of war, but, if we may believe Dinwiddie, told them nothing of this letter.[2] He then, presumably with their approval, marched off to Philadelphia, carrying with him all his artillery, and the three independent companies which had been raised for the defence of the colony, and were of right under Dinwiddie's command. The colony was thus left to such precarious protection as it could get from a hastily organized and ill-equipped militia. All that the colonists had gained from Braddock's expedition was the construction of a road at present useless to themselves, but certain greatly to facilitate an invasion of their own territory.

That followed which might have been looked for: the western frontier of Virginia and Pennsylvania was transformed into a blood-stained wilderness. Two men alone conspicuously retained not only their courage, but their self-possession amid the pervading panic. Dinwiddie's untiring pen kept pouring forth petitions and remonstrances in every quarter. Washington, now commissioned as colonel of the militia, showed then at the age of twenty-four the same temper which a quarter of a century later won independence for the colonies in the face not only of hostile forces, but of lethargy, selfishness and cowardice within. As he was at Valley Forge, so was he now, strenuous

Washington's action.

[1] Dinwiddie Papers, vol. ii. pp. 118–20.

[2] Letter to Sharpe, vol. ii. p. 169.

without petulance, patient without illusions. In his letters to Dinwiddie he complains that no orders issued to civilians are obeyed unless enforced by a party of soldiers or by his own drawn sword, that without such means he cannot so much as obtain a single horse. The conduct of the soldiers was little better than that of the civilians. Washington complains 'of the growing insolence of the soldiers, the indolence and inactivity of the officers.'[1] When one reads these things one feels that Washington's command in the west was giving him the very discipline and experience which he needed for his future career. There was a touch of unconscious inspiration in the words of Samuel Davies when, in a sermon preached at this time, he described Washington as 'that heroic youth whom I cannot but hope Providence has hitherto preserved in so signal a manner for some important service to his country.'[2]

Dinwiddie and Washington might have grounds for complaining of the attitude adopted by the settlers.

Factious attitude of the Pennsylvanian Assembly.

But the shortcomings of the Virginians were as nothing to those of Pennsylvania. Various causes were at work paralysing the action of the government in that colony. There was that averseness to war, that shallow and optimistic refusal fully to believe in the ferocity of the savage which had become traditional in Philadelphia. There was the equally traditional determination to meet all exceptional expenditure by an issue of paper money. There was the view, not wholly unreasonable in itself but wholly ill-timed, that the main share of the cost of the defence should fall on the Proprietors since their interest in the unoccupied lands was greater than that of the colony at large.

[1] For this see Washington's letter to Dinwiddie, October 11, 1755. Dinwiddie Papers, vol. ii. p. 237.

[2] Quoted in a note to Sparks's *Washington*, vol. ii. p. 89.

There was also the fear that the western lands might, if redeemed from the French and the Indians, fall to the share not of Pennsylvania but of Virginia. In short the citizens of Philadelphia and the inhabitants of the Eastern counties entered upon the struggle solely as Pennsylvanians, not as British subjects nor with any sense of allegiance to the body of colonists as a whole.

We have already seen how the persistent and immoveable selfishness of the Pennsylvanian legislature had driven Braddock and Morris to despair. It might have been thought that the spectacle of wholesale devastation on the western frontier would have alarmed and shamed them into a more compliant attitude. Indifference to the future of Virginia, jealousy of the possible gains of the Proprietors, might have been pardonable in time of peace. It was a very different matter when men's eyes were so blinded by faction and cupidity that they would rather see their fellow-citizens massacred and plundered than bate one jot of their financial rights.

All through 1755 the wearisome struggle between the Governor and the Assembly went on. At first the Assembly were ready to raise a loan. The British Government, however, would not allow Morris to accept any bill which did not provide for redemption within five years. Considering the past action of the Pennsylvanian legislature in the matter of paper money, that could not be looked on as an unreasonable restriction. The Assembly, however, refused to attach any such condition to their vote.

Obstinacy of the Assembly.[1]

Morris made two attempts to turn the flank of the Assembly. First he proposed that the necessary funds should be raised by a voluntary subscription. But according to his own account 'so many difficulties and

[1] For this, as for the disputes in the previous year, I have depended on the Records, vol. vii.

objections were raised to this proposal that it was dropped.' Then with the approval of the Council he suggested that military service in the west should be rewarded by grants of land there. Considering how far the bear was from being killed this prospective gift of his skin could hardly be looked on as a tempting offer.

At last the Assembly consented to raise the needed funds by a tax on land. To this, however, they attached a condition. The waste lands belonging to the Proprietors must bear their share. This Morris pointed out was absolutely at variance with his instructions, and the result was a deadlock.

The difficulty was in part due to the diversity of elements which entered into the population of the colony. The Ulster emigrants believed that the Quakers were indifferent to their fate. One of that sect was reported to have said, that there were only some Scotch-Irish killed who could well enough be spared.[1]

The German section of the population were worked on by a newspaper published in their own language. This impressed upon them that war would bring with it cessation of business, heavy taxes and compulsory service. As a result many of the Germans who had hitherto taken no interest in politics attended the election of Representatives and voted for Quaker candidates.[2]

Can we wonder that an old Indian chief, a faithful adherent of the English, warned the settlers that, if they delayed any longer to take decisive action or as usual put their allies off with uncertain hopes, 'you

[1] This is stated in a pamphlet entitled *A Brief View of the Conduct of Pennsylvania*, mentioned by Mr. Parkman (*Montcalm and Wolfe*, vol. i. p. 350 *n.*), and ascribed by him to William Smith, Head of the College of Pennsylvania. The passage to which I refer is at p. 58.

[2] This is stated in another pamphlet which Parkman also attributes to Smith. It was entitled *A Brief State of the Province of Pennsylvania*. London, 1755.

will see our faces under this roof no more. We must shift for our own safety and leave you to the mercy of your enemies, as an unfortunate people upon whom we can have no longer dependence.'[1]

By this time the inhabitants on the frontier were beginning to understand what really stood between them and safety, and were putting pressure on the legislature. Four hundred frontiersmen, Germans, appeared in procession, demanding vigorous measures. When another party appeared at the doors of the Assembly house, bringing in a waggon the remains of those who had fallen victims to the savages, the most hardened advocates of peace and parsimony must have been shaken.[2]

Fortunately the Proprietors taking the first step in the direction of compromise gave the Representatives a pretext for retreat. The Governor produced a letter from the Proprietors. They held fast to their claim of exemption from taxation on unoccupied lands, but they offered five thousand pounds as a voluntary contribution. The Assembly were then content to pass the bill, free from the obnoxious clause.

Franklin's share in the proceedings was characteristic. As we have already seen, he did his best to ensure the effective conduct of the war. But when the danger was over he was not going to let his fellow-colonists be condemned for resistance to authority. In 1759 he published a pamphlet full of dexterous sophistry, entitled 'A Historical Review of the Constitution and Government of Pennsylvania.'[3] The fallacy which runs through it all is the doctrine that, because the Proprietors may have disregarded

Franklin's pamphlet.

1 *Brief View*, p. 50.

2 Entick's *History of the late War*, vol. i. p. 377, referred to by Mr. Parkman.

3 It is printed in the third volume of Sparks's edition of Franklin's Works.

their obligations, therefore the Assembly were justified in doing nothing. That might have been true previous to 1755. But could any reasonable or fair-minded person contend that the legislature was justified in handing over the colony to all the horrors of an Indian massacre, that they might avoid the possibility of creating a precedent for future demands on the pockets of their constituents? The attitude was not merely cynically inhuman, it was strategically unwise. By a different attitude the Assembly would have won for themselves a sympathy and an allegiance from the whole colony which would have been an invaluable weapon in any coming struggle.

How completely Franklin had for the time sunk the patriot in the advocate is shown, when he says that 'the Assembly admit the Governor's right or power to call them together. But they insist on the proper manner of exercising it, that is to say, with a proper regard for the convenience of members at the harvest.'[1] Homesteads on the frontier are to be burnt and women and children massacred, lest the farmer on the banks of the Delaware should have his crops spoilt!

The defence put forward by the Assembly is described by Franklin as 'a noble and affecting recapitulation of the whole dispute.' The passage which he specially singles out for eulogy is the declaration that 'Those who give up essential liberty to purchase a little temporary safety deserve neither liberty nor safety.' Will anyone insult Franklin's intelligence by supposing that he was duped by this windy claptrap, or that he had any real admiration for those defenders of liberty whose own safety had never been for one moment in danger, to whom human lives were but cards in the game of politics?

The Assembly of New York was not tested as that

[1] P. 361.

of Pennsylvania was by the danger of Indian inroad and massacre. There is every reason to think from their general attitude in the past that they would have shown themselves just as obstinate as the sister colony if it had not been for a complete surrender on the part of the Crown. The demand for a fixed revenue for the Governor and other officials was withdrawn. Then, and not till then, did the Assembly vote the funds needful for billeting and clothing the troops.

The situation in New York.[1]

Indecisive successes, more or less honourable and therefore encouraging to colonial soldiers, but having little permanent effect on the issue of the war, were all that the colonists had to set off against their disasters in the west. In February Shirley, without waiting for the approval of the Home Government, proposed to the New England colonies a scheme for a joint attack on Crown Point. Massachusetts raised two thousand five hundred men, the remaining New England colonies two thousand one hundred, while New York promised eight hundred. By agreement among the Governors of the various colonies concerned the command was given to Sir William Johnson. In July he mustered his troops at Albany. He was at once met by some of the difficulties which seemed inevitable in any joint scheme of colonial operations. The New Hampshire contingent was with difficulty prevented from marching straight to Crown Point on their own account, and the Connecticut troops were delayed by a dispute about the precedence to be allowed to their commanding officer.

Operations on the New York frontier.[2]

Johnson knew enough about Indian motives and backwoods warfare to avoid one of Braddock's errors. He flattered the Indians by indulging their gluttony and imitating their usages, and he made use of Mohawk scouts to discover the situation of the defending force.

[1] Smith, vol. ii.

[2] Here I have mainly relied on Parkman.

Papers found on the field after Braddock's defeat gave the French a clue to the plans of their enemy, and warned them of the intended attack on Crown Point. Accordingly a force of rather more than three thousand five hundred men was detached to defend the position. The commander was Dieskau, a German in the French service.

On September 4 the two armies came into touch near the southern extremity of Lake Champlain. Dieskau's colonial advisers had filled him with contempt for the English militia. They were the worst troops on earth, and no doubt Braddock's defeat gave plausibility to the view. But colonial militia commanded by Braddock and commanded by Johnson were two very different things. Johnson was no great strategist. He committed an initial error, and weakened his force by sending two detachments of five hundred men to operate on the enemy's flank and rear. A sagacious old Mohawk chief pointed out his error, illustrating his view by the old apologue of the bundle of sticks. Johnson so far modified his plan as to unite the two detachments into one. But the Indian warrior was still dissatisfied; they were too few to fight and too many to be thrown away.

Battle of Lake George.[1]

The warning proved well founded. The detachment marched into an ambush and were thrown into confusion. They rallied, however, and retreated in good order, keeping up a destructive fire till they rejoined the main body.

Johnson had begun with a mistake which, but for the courage and innate good discipline of New England troops, might have been fatal. But he at least understood the elements of forest fighting, and he made good use of the axes which his men carried instead of

[1] There is a good account of the battle in the first of the *Two Letters* referred to on p. 578.

bayonets. He placed his troops behind a barricade—in *lager* as we should now say—guarded by waggons, boats turned upside down and trunks of trees, and to the best of his ability cleared the underwood immediately around. Fortunately, too, he was able to plant cannon so as to command the approach to his extemporized fort.

Before long the defeated detachment appeared and took refuge with the main body. The enemy came on, probably somewhat confused and disunited by the pursuit. Dieskau was unable to concentrate his troops for an attack on the lager. The Canadian militia and the Indian allies scattered, firing from among the trees, while the regulars were mowed down by the English artillery. Dieskau's one chance would have been first to silence the guns and then to blockade the enemy. The first would have been difficult without artillery; the second would have needed a degree of patience and a tenacity of purpose never to be looked for in the Indian.

The conflict lasted with a continuous exchange of musketry fire for about five hours. Both commanders were wounded. Johnson retired to his tent leaving Phineas Lyman, of Connecticut, in command. Dieskau was shot twice in the leg, but refused to be carried from the field. Soon after he had received his second wound, the British fire became so heavy that his troops broke and fled, leaving their commander a prisoner. His estimate of colonial troops changed, and he is said to have described the New Englanders as fighting in the morning like good boys, at mid-day like men, and later like devils.

As might have been expected, when one force fought in the open and the other behind cover, the French loss was proportionately the heavier. Out of nine hundred troops engaged they lost two hundred and eight, while the English out of about two thousand two hundred lost two hundred and sixty. Of this loss probably more than a proportionate share fell upon the detachment.

Results of the battle.

The result was eminently honourable to colonial courage and discipline, but it had no direct effect on the military situation. The enemy were allowed to withdraw and to establish themselves in safety at Ticonderoga, and no attempt was made by Johnson to press his advantage. For more than a month the British force kept its place, exposed to all the hardships of November in the latitude of Lake Champlain, and then dispersed.

Yet we may be sure the ordinary colonist, unable from lack of training to take a comprehensive view of military operations, more impressed by an isolated effort of courage in the field than by the skilful conduct of a campaign, saw in the battle of Lake George an impressive and inspiring effort of colonial soldiership, a fitting sequel to the capture of Louisburg, and even more a contrast with the defeat of Braddock.

Not yet, however, had the stars of Pitt and Wolfe broken through the clouds. Vagueness of purpose and feebleness of execution were still to cling to the conduct of the war, and the colonists had for a while to be content with witnessing and sharing in fluctuating successes and indecisive victories.

Eviction of the Acadians.

One of the best-known incidents of 1755, the eviction of those Acadians who at the bidding of their priests withheld allegiance from the British Government, has no important place in the history of the war looked at from a colonial point of view. It is true that New England troops under a New England commander, John Winslow, had a large share in the work. The real point of interest is that there is not, as far as can be ascertained, the slightest symptom anywhere that the matter presented itself to the colonists of that day as it has been presented to the world by their descendants. Winslow was manifestly a humane man, to whom the task of eviction was a distasteful one. There will always be times when the work of the soldier merges into that of the policeman, and the soldier naturally enough usually regards such work with aversion. But compassion with the victim is quite compatible with a belief in the need for severity, and so it seems to have been in Winslow's case.

The poverty of the results attained in the campaign of 1755 did nothing to abate Shirley's ardour. Early in 1756 he summoned a council of war at New York, and unfolded to them a comprehensive scheme of campaign. The French frontier was strong for purposes of attack, since it commanded the British territory on two flanks, on the north and the west. For purposes of defence it was less strong, since it might be approached at various points by forces acting in some measure from a common base. This was the condition on which Shirley's scheme of campaign was constructed. There were to be four distinct lines of invasion extending from the lower St. Lawrence to the Ohio. One force was to attack Fort Duquesne, a second Lake Ontario, a third Crown Point, and a fourth the settlements along La Chaudière, south of the St. Lawrence.

Shirley's plans for 1756.[1]

The difficulties of the scheme were obvious. The apparent advantage which the attacking force might derive from the formation of the French frontier was counterbalanced by the protection which that frontier received from the natural barrier of the forest. The progress of an attacking force must be slow. Worse still, it was uncertain, and such uncertainty was almost fatal to effective co-operation.

An even greater drawback attached to Shirley's plan. It involved complex operations to be carried on

[1] *Montcalm and Wolfe*, vol. i. p. 381.

with a heterogeneous and imperfectly organized army. It also required, as a condition of success, harmonious working between the civil authorities of the different colonies, and of that there was no hope.

The weak point in the English line was, as it always was, Pennsylvania. A nominal militia law had been Militia law in Pennsylvania. passed in the previous year, but, as Morris pointed out in his address to the Assembly, it was so defective in itself and required so much time to carry it into execution that nothing good was to be expected from it.[1] It gave no compulsory powers for exacting service or for enforcing discipline, and no man might be detained in garrison for more than three weeks or sent more than three days' march beyond the frontier. Officers were to be selected by ballot. Another hindrance to effective defence was the objection raised by masters whose indented servants were impressed.

Now as in the time of Braddock, Franklin, despite his political principles and connexions, was playing a patriotic part. What he did take in hand he might be trusted to carry through with the practical energy of a true New Englander. Thus we find him forwarding to Morris the plan which he had drawn of a fort in the deserted site of Gnädenhutten,[2] and also co-operating with the Governor in a scheme whereby foreign settlers, Swiss, German and Dutch, might serve under officers of their own nationality.[3] This had an important bearing on the campaign, since to it the British army owed the services of one of its most effective officers, Colonel Bouquet.

The very same difficulty which had been mainly at

[1] Pennsylvania Records, vol. vii. p. 121.

[2] *Ibid.* p. 16. It is stated in the *Brief View* that Gnädenhutten was destroyed. Heckenwelder says that an adjacent settlement was burnt and the inhabitants killed, and that those at Gnädenhutten fled. His information was probably the best.

[3] *Ibid.* p. 180.

the root of the difficulties in Pennsylvania was operating in Maryland. There the Assembly proposed to meet the necessary expenditure for the war by a land tax. The Governor refused to consent, because the bill taxed the Proprietors' private manor, and his instructions prohibited him from allowing any such measure.

Dinwiddie might well write, as he does in one of his despatches, 'I must say that the proprietary governments have been a great obstruction in conducting the expedition with spirit.'[1]

The Dagworthy dispute.[2]

A personal dispute which arose in the autumn of this year illustrates the difficulties engendered by the lack of organization and central control. A certain Captain Dagworthy, who had once held a commission in the regular army, but had now retired, was placed by Sharpe in command of a small troop from Maryland. On the strength of his previous commission he claimed precedence over all those who only held colonial commissions, Washington among them. Washington for all his public spirit was not the man to accept such a claim tamely. A dispute arose, which does not seem ever to have been settled decisively and satisfactorily. It cost the hard-worked Governor many hours of writing, and, what is worse, in all likelihood it contributed to create a certain coldness which unquestionably sprang up between Dinwiddie and Washington. Moreover lack of co-operation between colonies introduced constant difficulties into their dealings with the savages, and those difficulties were enhanced by dissensions and complications in the intertribal relations of the savages themselves.

The next year saw war declared between the two continental Powers. To thinking colonists it must have seemed some gain that Englishmen could no longer

[1] Dinwiddie to Halifax, Papers, vol. ii. p. 416.

[2] For this affair see the Dinwiddie Papers, vol. ii. p. 261, and elsewhere.

regard the war as a mere incident in colonial administration, that their backwoods warfare was now bound up with issues too important to be ignored by any British statesman. They were soon to learn, too, that the control over British affairs had passed into the hands of one to whose vivid imagination, at times vague and grandiose, it was at least revealed that the future greatness of Britain was closely linked with the fate of the neglected and little-known provinces beyond the Atlantic.

War declared.

Shirley's scheme for a campaign against Canada on four separate lines of invasion had to be modified for lack of troops. The New England provinces, as hitherto, showed no backwardness, whatever may have been their shortcomings in the way of organization and discipline. But neither in the Middle nor in the Southern colonies was there any show of enthusiasm. Accordingly the campaign was reduced to combined attacks on Niagara and Ticonderoga. The exterior operations, as one may call them, the invasion of the Ohio valley and the attack by way of Maine and La Chaudière, were abandoned.

That was probably not to be regretted. Another defeat on the Ohio would have been well nigh fatal to British supremacy in that quarter, and an advance through the wilderness north of Maine must necessarily be too uncertain in time to form part of a connected scheme of attack.

The remains of Braddock's force and the provincial regiments paid and officered by the Crown, and numbering about four thousand four hundred, were to be employed by Shirley against Lake Ontario. The New England troops, numbering about five thousand, were to attack Ticonderoga. It seemed as if their efficiency was to be impaired by a complicated system which placed the transport and commissariat of each colony under separate authority. A stronger instance of the inopportune introduction of the political ideas of New England into military matters could hardly be found. Fortunately however the system was soon abandoned, in compliance with the protest of the British military authorities.

Before the British forces could be in the field Shirley was superseded in favour of Lord Loudon. The new commander, however, was not expected till July. Shirley was not even allowed to retain command till Loudon arrived, but by a complicated and unintelligible arrangement, General Abercromby was to act during the interval as a *locum tenens*.

The earlier part of the campaign saw nothing but desultory operations. Of these the most noteworthy was an engagement fought between the French and a relieving force which Shirley had sent to protect and relieve Oswego, in which the New England troops showed discipline and courage. They numbered about two thousand armed boatmen, many of them trained in the use of whale-boats, and able therefore to navigate as well as to fight. In order to reach Oswego it was necessary to cross the river Onondaga in the face of an opposing force of over a thousand. The New England commander Bradstreet succeeded in carrying the supplies to Oswego, and also in defeating the French when they endeavoured to intercept him in returning.

Relief of Oswego.

If the relief of Oswego brought out the strong points of colonial soldiership, dash, and resource, the weaker side was illustrated by the later fate of that fortress. Fort Oswego was garrisoned by provincials. Patient endurance behind the walls of a fort tests to the utmost those very qualities in which half-trained troops are deficient. The civilian, taken away from his home and his business, must be com-

Fall of Oswego.

pensated by the knowledge that his sacrifices are being rewarded by visible and quickly obtained success. It is little consolation to him to know that, while seemingly passive, he is contributing to the success of a complicated machine of which he forms part. The discipline of regular troops carries with it, too, some guarantee for the observance of those rules which are needful for the maintenance of health. It is clear that the commissariat at Fort Oswego almost completely broke down, partly through waste, and that the disease which was the inevitable result was much worse by inattention to cleanliness.[1] Sick men lay on the bare ground, and even those who were not formally on the sick list were incapable of physical exertion.[2] The result was that when in August a French force, commanded by Montcalm, appeared before the fort, resistance had to be abandoned as useless, and the garrison, numbering sixteen hundred, surrendered. No blame could attach to the troops or their commander. They had only failed in a task for which their training and antecedents had done nothing to fit them. That, however, was not the English view. Defence of fortified posts under circumstances to the outward view far more trying made up some of the most brilliant chapters of British soldiership. The condemnation of colonial troops for the loss of Oswego was neither more nor less unjust than the censure of Braddock's troops for their rout by the Monongahela. But neither was the less harmful for being unjust. Each did much to destroy mutual confidence and to make joint action impossible. The immediate loss of effective co-operation was not the whole, not perhaps even the worst part, of the result.

[1] The authorities quoted by Mr. Parkman (vol. i. pp. 397–401) are all in one tale as to the plight of the garrison.

[2] Mr. Parkman quotes the report of the officer sent by Loudon to inspect.

On each side the seeds of alienation and contempt were sown, and the coming day of dissension was the season of harvest.

Precedence of regular over colonial officers.

At the very same time another influence was making in that direction. An order was issued by the Crown that officer's rank however low in the regular British army should take precedence over colonial rank however high. This created an amount of dissatisfaction which seriously embarrassed Loudon, and threatened to deprive the British army of any assistance from New England.

The question was one on which there was not a little to be said on each side. At first it might seem a grievance that as Winslow, the commander of the New England force, expressed it, the whole provincial army might be put under the command of any British officer.[1] On the other hand it must be remembered that commissions given by colonial Governors did not of necessity carry with them any guarantee for military efficiency, and, worse still, perhaps there was no security that colonial commissions would be given according to any uniform standard. Indeed it is probable that a system different from that adopted would only have substituted intercolonial jealousy for jealousy of the mother country. Already Winslow had been troubled by the necessity for settling questions of precedence between commanders from the different colonies.

Rogers and the American irregulars.

The year 1757 saw but little change in the general situation. Loudon remained, as Franklin remarked, like a mounted figure on a signboard always appearing ready to advance, but never moving. Independent, self-organized parties of rangers performed daring exploits on the frontier, unable to achieve anything decisive, yet doing something to

[1] Letter to Shirley quoted by Parkman, vol. i. p. 400.

weaken the French by a continuous strain on their watchfulness and their resources. Conspicuous among such leaders of these irregular troops was Robert Rogers. He was familiar with the French settlements, having in all likelihood carried on a contraband trade with them,[1] and had also some slight knowledge of the French language.

The natural result of such exploits as those of Rogers was worth something to the British cause. The main ultimate result was one by which the mother country was a loser. The raiders on the frontier did something to establish what one might call a military tradition: they did yet more to give the colonists training of which Great Britain at a later day was to feel the full effect. Rogers himself in the War of Independence was on the British side. But one of his subordinates was John Stark, whose skill as an irregular fighter not less than his courage was so conspicuously shown in those preliminary operations on the Mohawk which put Burgoyne at the mercy of his enemies.

There was little change in the attitude of the popular Representatives in the two recalcitrant colonies, Pennsylvania and New York. In January 1757 the Assembly of Pennsylvania voted a sum of a hundred thousand pounds, but insisted on taxing the Proprietors' lands. Denny, who had succeeded Morris as Governor, was evidently willing to make some concession. He appointed a committee of the Council to consider whether the bill could not be brought into conformity with the Governor's instructions. They reported that nothing could be done in this way, so long as the Assembly announced their intention

Disputes in Pennsylvania about a money grant.[2]

[1] This is Mr. Parkman's conjecture. He does not give his reasons.

[2] Pennsylvania Records, vol. vii. pp. 396–414.

of standing firm and not voting any money while the Proprietors' exemption was upheld.

Another subject of dispute was the embargo laid by Loudon on the exportation of provisions. This the Assembly contended would be fatal to the trade of the colony.[1] It is impossible now to judge how far this was so. But no one can doubt the soundness of one remark made by the Assembly in a statement of their case. 'There cannot be a more pregnant instance of the absurdity of giving particular instructions relative to the making of laws to legislatures which are so distant as we are from our mother country. And this will ever be the case where either misinformation or want of information must render such particular instructions improper to be observed, unsuitable to the real circumstances of the colony.'

Pennsylvania and the embargo.

Further trouble arose out of the claim of the military authorities to quarter troops on the citizens.[2] The Assembly did not formally deny that right, but they and those whom they represented did all that they could to make it nugatory. On this point we are fortunate in having a witness against whom no charge of British prejudice can be brought. It will be remembered that a force was raised among the German settlers in Pennsylvania, to be commanded by foreign officers. One battalion was under the command of Colonel Bouquet, a Swiss, who played a valiant part in the concluding scenes of the war. It might have been expected that the Assembly, which was largely under the influence of the German inhabitants, would have shown towards Bouquet's regiment a consideration which was not to be looked for in their dealings with

The billeting question.

1 Pennsylvania Records, vol. vii. p. 418.

2 For this quartering business see the Records, vol. vii. pp. 370–4.

British troops. Yet we find Bouquet loud in his complaints of the quarters provided for his men.

Men stricken with small-pox had to lie on straw in rooms unwarmed by fire. Denny did his best to force the matter on the attention of the Assembly. All the answer he got from the Assembly was, 'We likewise are determined if possible to avoid disputes with the Governor, and to do our duty to our King and country, and when it shall be made appear to us that the public-house keepers are not able to provide sufficient quartering we shall take proper measures to supply the deficiency.'[1] No one can read that and not feel that the Assembly were determined to whittle down their obligations to a minimum, and had not the least real zeal for the common cause.

Billeting in New York.

The same difficulty arose in New York, but was more easily overcome. That may have been in part due to the fact that Loudon was there in person, able to fight the battle of authority. It probably was more due to the fact that the Assembly of New York was a less united body than that of Pennsylvania, more divided by faction, and therefore less capable of organized and continuous action whether for good or evil.[2]

The fall of Fort William Henry.

The campaign of 1756 ended with a catastrophe calculated, perhaps somewhat unjustly, to discredit colonial soldiership. That of 1757 was equally unproductive of any useful result, and ended in a tragedy far more sombre, and tending to create a corresponding sense of distrust among the colonists.

As long as the combatants were at a distance, and so far as the operations of the war turned on the invasion of British territory, the French got no great advantage

[1] Records, vol. vii. p. 374.

[2] Smith and other authorities referred to by Parkman, vol. i. p. 440.

out of the formation of their frontier. They could operate from a narrower base, but that advantage was lost when a tract of wilderness was interposed between that base and the field of war. But as the British advanced the gain which the French got by their power of acting on inner lines was increased. Shirley had recognised this when he changed his plan, and discarded the intended operations in Maine and in the Ohio valley. Loudon wholly failed to perceive it when with insufficient forces he endeavoured to act simultaneously against Louisburg and Ticonderoga. The result was an attempt to hold Fort William Henry with numbers wholly inadequate.

The situation might possibly have been redeemed by a determined policy on the part of one of Loudon's subordinates, General Webb. He was posted at Fort Edward, a day's march south of Fort William Henry. It is true that by marching to the relief of that fort, he might have laid New York open to invasion. But he might have perceived that the frontier was protected by natural obstacles which more than once had of themselves stayed the tide of invasion. Moreover the Indian allies who formed a large part of Montcalm's force were as likely to be a hindrance as a help when they had to act at a distance from their own country.

Another motive, and perhaps a sounder one, may have influenced Webb. He may have felt that, even if reinforced with all the troops that he could bring, Fort William Henry would still be indefensible against the advancing French army, and his advance would only make the impending calamity more complete.

Yet if that was his view he should at least have done all in his power to induce the commander, Colonel Monro, to evacuate the fort at once.

Instead of that, Monro's urgent and repeated appeals to Webb were left unanswered, till at last, when a definite refusal came, the French troops, into whom Montcalm had now infused his own spirit of daring energy, had surrounded the fort. A large number of the garrison were prostrate with small-pox, and no course was left to Monro but to capitulate.

Terms of surrender.

The garrison were to march out with the honours of war, and to be conducted by a French escort to a place of safety. But they were to give up their artillery, munitions and stores. None of them were to serve for eighteen months, and all French prisoners captured in America during the war were to be given up. If we look back to the incidents of the two previous campaigns, that condition could not have been a very irksome one.

The massacre.

The tragedy that followed the surrender is too familiar an incident to need telling in detail. The savages broke into the English camp and then fell on the rear of the retiring force, killing some and carrying off others.

The situation of the English was not unlike that of Elphinstone's army retreating from Cabul. In each case a force which had surrendered found no security in the terms of capitulation against the attack of a barbarous enemy. But whereas in the case of Elphinstone's force the assailants were practically identical with those who had granted the terms of surrender, Monro had only to deal with the unruly allies of a civilized commander.

We may be very certain that Montcalm would have abhorred anything like complicity in such proceedings. Yet he was but reaping a harvest from seed which had been sown by generations of his predecessors. The rulers of Canada had so long acquiesced in Indian atrocities, that it must have been well nigh impossible to persuade the savages that they now created any real indignation. Montcalm and his officers seem in good faith to have made strenuous efforts to keep their allies in check, and even to have risked their own lives by throwing themselves between the savages and their intended victims. To have done even more, to have liberated these prisoners and given them the means of defence, to have at once turned their own arms against the Indians, would have been little more than what was demanded by justice and humanity. Yet it was much to ask any one man, or generation of men, to cast aside the established tradition of nearly a century. If the Indians had been thus dealt with, the alliance with them would have crumbled into dust, and with it French Canada must have perished. For in truth the very foundation on which France built her power in the New World was the readiness of her rulers to encourage the Indian in his worst passions, and to profit by his worst atrocities.

Feeling between the colonists and the British.

So far the war had done nothing to create any feeling of mutual confidence and respect between the colonists and the mother country, and not a little to hinder it. The isolated successes of irregular troops had hardly been so striking or so durable in their results as greatly to impress English generals and English statesmen. In all likelihood with them, the failure to hold Oswego counted for more than the dashing exploit of Bradstreet endeavouring to relieve it, or than the victory of Lake George.

On the other hand the unbroken and unredeemed failure which had so far followed the efforts of British regular forces might well have shattered the confidence of the colonists in the military efficiency of the mother country.

This mutual distrust was no doubt largely due to the fact that no commander had yet appeared able to see the weak points of the British military system when applied under wholly unfamiliar conditions, or to comprehend what good material there was in the provincial forces and how much might profitably be learnt from their methods. In the campaign of 1758 such an one did appear on the scene.

Lord Howe.

In the winter of 1757 Loudon was superseded in favour of General Abercromby, with Lord Howe as second in command.

The 'might-have-beens' of history make for the most part somewhat profitless material for speculation. Yet one can hardly resist considering how it might have gone with Great Britain and America if Howe had held command at an earlier stage of the war. Those who die early are always the favourites of history, and there may be a touch of exaggeration in the traditions of the hold which Howe secured on the affections of colonial civilians. But it is at least certain that he first, and one may not unfairly say alone among English generals, saw what valuable material there was in the provincial troops, and what profitable lessons might be learnt from their methods. Braddock strove to turn provincial militia into a poor imitation of British regulars. Howe sought to engraft on regular troops something of the special capacity of the American backwoodsman. English officers of the old school must have shuddered when they saw Howe's troops with Indian leggings, amputated pigtails, and tunics cut down to jackets. His reforms, too, were not based on theory, but on full personal experiences. He accompanied Rogers in his scouting expeditions, and he learnt that a soldier's mobility depends not merely on his equipment, but also on the reduction of his needs to a minimum. He learnt to wash his own linen. His troops had to carry rations for at least three weeks,[1] and officers

[1] Thirty pounds of meal. A French writer, quoted by Parkman, reckons this as a month's rations, a somewhat scanty estimate.

had to be content with no better bedding than that provided for their men.

There may have been a touch of dramatic exaggeration in his demand, that each officer should carry his own knife and fork in a sheath: a demand enforced by an invitation to a dinner where no means of eating appeared, till the guests received each a present of what was required. But, if so, it was just the kind of exaggeration calculated to appeal to the imagination and win the sympathy of the colonists.

Unhappily Howe fell not merely in his first American campaign, but in his first serious engagement.

Death of Howe.

On July 5 he advanced towards Ticonderoga with a mixed force of three thousand provincials and over six thousand regulars. The details of the expedition were apparently left by Abercromby to his subordinate. The opposing force was drawn up about Ticonderoga. The density of the forest brought with it a large element of chance. A small reconnoitring party thrown out by Montcalm in advance missed its way, and found itself in the woods. The advanced guard of the English, Rogers's rangers and two other New England regiments, passed the French, neither as it would seem knowing of the proximity of the other. Then the French suddenly found themselves face to face with the main column and opened fire. The rangers in front turned upon the enemy, and thus taken between two forces, each of superior numbers, the French were captured or slain, only fifty escaping.

They had however won a success which would have been cheaply purchased with heavier loss, since Howe

The French fort.

fell dead at the very first fire. Abercromby became not merely the titular but the actual leader, and a disaster followed which must have carried the minds of the colonists back to Braddock and the banks of the Monongahela. Montcalm had established himself on the rocky peninsula of Ticonderoga, his right flank guarded by the stream which connects Lake George and Lake Champlain, and his left by Lake George itself. With extraordinary energy and rapidity in the use of the axe, wielded alike by private soldiers and officers, a strong defence of logs and tree trunks had been thrown up, so arranged in zigzags that the assailants would be exposed not merely to a direct fire, but to a lateral one, which would take each separate party of assailants on both flanks.

Two obvious courses were open to Abercromby. He might have battered the fort with his artillery. Or he might have divided his force, leaving a part of it to check a French advance, and throwing the other part on Montcalm's communications. His superiority of numbers, fifteen thousand to five thouand, would have deprived such strategy of any show of rashness.

Aber-cromby's defeat.

Instead Abercromby committed the mistake which had so often been the bane of British generalship, and sent his troops direct against an unassailable position. An attempt to carry the position by the bayonet failed, only to be renewed, and for the greater part of a summer day assault after assault was delivered and repulsed. Among neither provincials nor regulars was there any lack of valour. Here and there some desperate combatant struggled through and over the network of trees and branches and penetrated into the French encampment, only to be bayoneted.

If a comparison suggested itself to the provincials between Abercromby and Braddock, it would have been unfair to the latter. Braddock erred in not recognising the peculiar conditions and the special difficulties of forest warfare against savages. Abercromby set at defiance the plainest principles of strategy, principles which any captain fit to hold a commission would have recognised. Braddock, too, did all that personal courage could do to redeem his errors. Abercromby showed himself as lacking in courage as Dunbar, and immediately after his defeat, fell back before a force far inferior to his own in numbers. Indeed the comparison is hardly fair to Dunbar. The rout of Braddock's force was a calamity far more calculated to weaken and dispirit both leader and troops than Abercromby's repulse.

Colonial successes.

Once more the colonists had successes, unimportant indeed in themselves, but honourable to the courage and soldiership of those who achieved them, to set off against the defeats of the regular troops. Rogers, helped by some superiority of numbers, defeated a French scouting party of between four and five hundred members. A far more important success was that of Bradstreet, who with three thousand men, mostly provincials, captured and destroyed Fort Frontenac, and carried off boats, ordnance, and stores.

Capture of Louisburg.

In spite of so inauspicious an opening, the year 1758 saw two fatal blows struck at French power in North America. Yet by a strangely perverse fate each did little to bring the colonies and the mother country together, something to confirm and extend the existing sense of estrangement.

Since its restoration to France, the defences of Louisburg had been greatly strengthened. It was also held by a commander widely different in temper from Duchambon. Unlike his predecessors in office, Pitt had already grasped the truth that till Louisburg fell there could be no security for colonial commerce, no certainty attending any operations on the St. Lawrence. Accordingly in 1758 he fitted out an expedition against Louisburg. It consisted of eleven thousand six hundred men, all, except four hundred, regulars. The transports were convoyed by twenty-three men-of-war.

Amherst, who was in command, and Wolfe, his youthful lieutenant, were the two officers who had most fully earned and best deserved Pitt's confidence.

The landing of the troops was marked by that spirit and enterprise, with even an element of recklessness, which Pitt had infused into the British service. The boats dashed through the surf to shore, and in some cases were staved in, while officers leapt into the water and scrambled over the rocks. The landing was made on June 8. By the 25th the town was invested, and for four weeks it received a heavy and continuous bombardment. The character of the coast, as it had made attack difficult, so likewise hindered relief, and rendered the case of the besieged hopeless. Nevertheless, the fort would probably have held out longer if it had not been for the distressed expostulations of the civilian inhabitants. On July 25 the garrison surrendered. The prisoners numbered five thousand six hundred, the cannon taken over two hundred and twenty.

Effect of the victory among the colonists.

The news that Louisburg had fallen was received with rapture in the Northern and Middle colonies. Even Pennsylvania, so inert in contributing to British successes, was ready to welcome this victory with fireworks and public rejoicings.

Yet for all this there must have been in New England at least an *amari aliquid*. The newly acquired strength of Louisburg and the spirit of the French commander made Amherst's victory something very different from Pepperell's, but with what fairness could the colonists be asked to remember that? To many of them the situation must have presented itself in some such fashion as this: 'This heroic and much be-praised exploit is no more than a repetition of what we did. If a British Government had not with short-sighted selfishness flung away the fruit of our labour, no second conquest would have been needed.'

Elsewhere English arms had achieved a triumph far less brilliant in execution yet hardly less valuable, a triumph not of daring but of cool and patient strategy. Pitt saw that the reduction of Fort Duquesne, and the extirpation of French influence in the valley of the Ohio, was not an isolated measure valuable only or mainly for the protection of Pennsylvania and Virginia, but an integral part of any scheme for securing the mastery of the North American continent. The command of the force designed for this purpose was given to General Forbes. His force numbered upwards of six thousand men, twelve hundred Highlanders and the rest provincials. It was composed of Virginians, Pennsylvanians, Marylanders and North Carolinians. Forbes' account of his troops at once brings home to one the wide difference which separated the Southern colonists from the New Englander. New England sent stalwart yeomen or men trained in the whale fishery, ill-disciplined it might be, according to European notions, but with no lack of corporate feeling, physically capable, and after their own fashion well equipped. According to Forbes his colonials were miserably armed with dilapidated fowling-pieces; many of them had never fired a gun, and their officers were 'an extremely bad collection of broken innkeepers, horse jockeys and Indian traders.' In short they were drawn not from the well-to-do planters, trained in field sports and animated by the spirit of a self-reliant oligarchy, but from the class of mean whites.[1]

Forbes in the west.

Contempt for the military inefficiency of his troops was not the only thing which stood between Forbes

[1] *Montcalm and Wolfe*, vol. ii. p. 135; compare 'the scum of Virginia,' p. 472.

and the colonists, and begot mutual distrust and ill-will. The same problem presented itself to Forbes which had been faced by Braddock, the question of advancing to the Ohio through Virginia or Pennsylvania.

Difficulties with Washington.

Forbes had not been brought into direct contact as his predecessor was with the factiousness, the selfishness, the disloyalty of Pennsylvania. He decided on advancing through that colony instead of using Braddock's road. Whatever arguments there had been for Braddock adopting the Pennsylvania route applied more strongly to Forbes. Forbes intended to adopt, and did adopt, the policy of a deliberate and slow progress, maintaining his communications by fortified posts. Washington's advice, given, as most of Washington's opinions were given, strenuously and without reserve, was to use Braddock's road. Forbes could not be blamed if he somewhat distrusted the disinterestedness of colonial advice in this matter, since there was little doubt that Braddock's counsellors had been swayed by commercial considerations. When a party of Indians made it a condition of their joining Forbes that he went by Braddock's road, he took it for granted that they had been suborned by the Virginians.[1] It was unfortunate that his suspicions in this matter should have fallen on one the whole tenour of whose life makes against any such view, and more unfortunate that those suspicions should find expression in such a phrase as 'Colonel Washington's behaviour about the roads was noways like a soldier.' Dinwiddie's good-will to Washington had, it is clear, not a little abated, and though another Governor was now in office it is probable that Dinwiddie's influence had, perhaps unintentionally, done something to make Forbes include Washington in his general distrust of colonial officers. To a man of

[1] *Montcalm and Wolfe*, vol. ii. p. 139.

Washington's temper the charge of unsoldierly conduct was about the most exasperating that could have been found, and it is not fanciful to suppose that Forbes's attitude, following on Washington's dissatisfaction about precedence, had an abiding influence hardly to be overrated.

The rulers of Canada, threatened as they were in other and more vital quarters, starved by folly of the King and his advisers alike in men and in supplies, could do nothing to secure the valley of the Ohio. Forbes, too, though he might despise and distrust the type of colonial soldier with which he had to deal, had none of Braddock's dull contempt for the special methods of fighting adapted to the forest. To Bouquet, who possessed a capacity for dealing with the savages which almost equalled that of Schuyler or Johnson, Forbes wrote: 'I have long been in favour of equipping numbers of our men like the savages.'[1]

Forbes and the Indians.

Forbes, too, seems to have clearly understood the temperament of the savage. He might do good service in a single engagement. His fickleness and impatience made him well nigh valueless in a long campaign. That, indeed, was one of the reasons why the English, so often worsted in the field, ultimately prevailed. They did not depend as the enemy did on the Indian alliance. The Indians responded to the inspiring appeal of Beaujeu, and the defeat of Braddock followed. But two conditions were essential if the alliance was to be permanent and stable: a spirited policy of attack, and a continuous and abundant supply of presents. The poverty of Canada in men and in resources forbade either.

The alliance or neutrality of the tribes in the Ohio valley was, in a great measure, due to the influence of one whose heroism was every whit as real as that of

[1] *Montcalm and Wolfe*, vol. ii. p. 135.

the most devoted Canadian Jesuits, while, unlike theirs, it was stained by no concession to their vices. The English had not so dealt with the Moravians as to establish any special claim on their gratitude. Yet it was to a Moravian missionary, Christian Post, that Forbes and his advisers turned to make overtures on their behalf to the tribes in the Ohio valley. It is clear from the incidents of his mission how the hold of the French over the savages was impaired. He was taken to Fort Duquesne, and forced to make his proposals to the natives under the eyes and in the hearing of the French. Barbarians as the Indians were, courage, and especially that calm courage in which there was something of fatalism, always appealed to them. It is clear that Post's stoical declaration that he did not fear them, that he only regarded the bidding of his own conscience, had its effect. In spite of French attempts to secure his person he was allowed to return, and the most important tribe, the Delawares, agreed to meet the English and to negotiate. Only, mindful, as they well might be, of past colonial disunion, they stipulated that the negotiations must be with all the colonies, and not with Pennsylvania alone.

The Moravian Christian Post.

Accordingly in October a conference met at Easton. Envoys from the Five Nations and from some of the smaller tribes in dependence on them attended. A formal treaty was made, and Post was then sent out to announce it to the more remote tribes who had not yet come in, and to invite their alliance. In this he succeeded, despite the presence of a French envoy.

There were still difficulties of transport, increased by bad weather, and the French succeeded in routing an English detachment which advanced with rash precipitation. But the way to the Ohio was cleared, and when Forbes reached Fort Duquesne he found it empty and unguarded. The real prize at stake, the valley of the Ohio, the gateway to the western lands so full of yet unexhausted possibilities, was won. It only remained so to deal with Canada that no effort for its recovery could be made with success.

Capture of Quebec.

In the crowning triumph of the war the colonists had little direct part. Nearly all the soldiers who fought under Wolfe were British. No colonial officers had the opportunity of attaining special distinction. To say that is not in any way to deny or disparage the contribution which colonial soldiers made to the total result of the war. A series of campaigns must be looked on as an organic whole. Often 'they serve who only stand and wait.' But that is not how the matter presents itself to public opinion. In the brilliant light of Wolfe's dramatic victory and death, the scattered exploits of colonial troops paled into insignificance. The defeats of the war did much to alienate the dependencies from the mother country. Its successes did little to draw them together.

And as the conduct of the war had done little to conciliate colonial opinion, so the action of the British Government in dealing with its results went perilously near to making it actually hostile. The policy which made Shirley and Pepperell's conquest of Louisburg futile was near being repeated, with far less justification or necessity. In the diplomatic negotiations which followed the war, the surrender of Canada as a means of facilitating the retention of Guadaloupe was deliberately entertained, and was perhaps only averted by the advocacy of Franklin.[1] The colonists must have long felt that there was a tendency on the part of the mother country to sacrifice their interests to those of the West India Islands, far inferior in mental and

[1] See a pamphlet, *The Interest of Great Britain in regard to her Colonies*, published in 1760.

political activity and in all the elements which enable a community to play its part in the developement of mankind.

There is little evidence in any writing or speech of that time that men on either side of the Atlantic perceived how a definite and critical stage in the history of the American colonies had been at length reached, how forces hitherto vague, uncertain, and intermittent in their action must now inevitably break out in full vitality. Our English habit of ignoring changes which lie below the surface, of only heeding those warnings which are given by some manifest outward phenomenon, has its gainful side. It is a check alike on panic and on optimism. But it has its dangers too, and they were never more fully exemplified than in the years which immediately preceded the American Revolution, in the blind reliance of English statesmen on administrative methods whose doom had been plainly foretold. We blame George Grenville and those who were associated with him. More justly should we blame those statesmen who for at least two generations had never once looked the facts of colonial administration plainly in the face.

APPENDICES.

APPENDIX I. (p. 29.)

The Population of the Colonies.

This subject has been ably dealt with in a monograph by Mr. Dexter, published in the collection of the American Historical Association.

We have no exact synchronous statement of the population in the different colonies. But inasmuch as the rate of progress in population seems to have been about equal, it is not difficult from the returns of population in the different colonies at different times to construct such an estimate. In most of the colonies the population seems to have doubled itself every twenty years. This was no doubt due to different causes. In New England it was due to habits of life which encouraged prolificity. In Pennsylvania, Delaware and New Jersey it was due to the influx of emigrants, many of them not English. In the Southern colonies it was due to the importation of slaves. In New York alone the increase appears to have been slower.

It is hardly needful to point out that an increase of a hundred per cent. in twenty years means an increase of about forty per cent. in ten years and eighteen per cent. in five.

The statistics available from official returns and reports give us the following results:

Massachusetts, including Maine, in 1731, ninety-four thousand.

In 1755 the negro population was two thousand six hundred. It is probable from the economic condition of the colony that this had but slightly increased since 1730, and that we may fairly put it at two thousand in that year.

Connecticut in 1713, about seventeen thousand. We may assume that the proportion of negroes was about the same here as in Massachusetts.

Rhode Island in 1730, seventeen thousand, of whom one-ninth were negroes.

New York in 1723, forty thousand white and black.

New Jersey in 1726, thirty-two thousand four hundred and forty-two, with about eight per cent. negroes.

This number may be taken as a clue to the negro population in New York, which was probably proportionately rather high.

Pennsylvania and Delaware in 1730, fifty thousand. Here probably the proportion of negroes to whites was smaller than in New Jersey.

Maryland in 1721, fifty-five thousand whites and twenty-five thousand blacks.

Virginia in 1717, sixty thousand white and forty thousand black.

In the case of North Carolina, and even more of South Carolina, the available statistics are confused and contradictory. This may be seen from the two appendices on the subject of population, published by Mr. McCrady, one in each volume. I only venture, therefore, to give the following as a conjectural estimate. It is to be noticed that for New Hampshire we have no trustworthy returns till 1767. Belknap gives the population as then amounting to fifty-two thousand seven hundred. The proportion of negroes was probably so small as to be negligible.

Assuming these data and reckoning an increase on the scale above mentioned, we get for the population of 1720:—

	White.	Negro.
New Hampshire (say)	11,000	—
Massachusetts	65,000	2,000
Connecticut	22,000	800
Rhode Island	12,000	1,300
New York	30,000	4,000
New Jersey	26,000	2,500
Pennsylvania and Delaware	32,000	4,000
Maryland	53,000	24,000
Virginia	65,000	45,000
North Carolina	14,000	500
South Carolina	9,000	12,000
	339,000	96,100

APPENDIX II. (p. 176.)

Here I regret to say that, as in two previous instances, I have mislaid my reference.

APPENDIX III. (p. 235.)

Whitefield and Garden.

The literature of this question is voluminous, out of all proportion to its intrinsic importance. Whitefield's side of the case is stated in his journals. Their diffuse and unmethodical character makes the process of tracing and piecing together his various statements on the subject difficult. One sermon of Garden's, preached immediately after his opponent's arrival for a second time at Charlestown, excited Whitefield's special indignation. 'Had some infernal spirit been sent to draw my picture, I think it hardly possible he could have painted me in a more horrid colour.' Considering the power of vituperation possessed and indulged in by Whitefield, and the school to which he belonged, this sensitiveness seems rather out of place.

Garden replied in a series of letters printed at New York. The first was answered by Whitefield, quite in the style of Lord Peter. 'Your letter more and more confirms me that my charge against the clergy is just and reasonable.' After that Whitefield allowed Garden to fire off without reply five more letters increasingly angry and discourteous, in which the word 'gibberish' recurs with unedifying though natural frequency.

APPENDIX IV. (p. 382.)

Sir Alexander Cuming.

There are in 'Notes and Queries' (1st series, vol. v. pp. 257, 278) various rather vague statements about Cuming. There is an extract from Lysons (vol. iv. p. 20) in which the part of the dream and the negotiations with the Cherokees are related. In Cuming's life in the 'Dictionary of National Biography' his journal is referred to. I do not know where this is to be found. One of his letters is among the Georgia Papers in the Record Office. It is a rambling document and seems to me to show signs of derangement. It refers vaguely to some great service done by Cuming's father to the King. The fact of his having brought over the Cherokee chiefs and secured a treaty with them seems to rest on incontrovertible evidence.

APPENDIX V. (p. 491.)

Attitude of the Highlanders in Georgia towards Slavery.

This declaration is noteworthy as one of the earliest denunciations of slavery, not on economical or religious grounds, but on general principles of morality, and one of the earliest prophecies of those dangers of which time has so fully shown the reality. After pointing out the danger from the proximity of the Spaniards, and also the financial risk of having capital locked up in a perishable commodity, the memorialists go on to say, 'It is shocking to human nature that any race of mankind and their posterity should be sentenced to perpetual slavery, nor in future can we think otherwise of it than that they are thrown amongst us to be a scourge one day or another for our sins; and as freedom to them must be as dear as to us, what a sense of horror must it bring about! And the longer it is unexecuted the bloody scene must be the greater.'[1]

APPENDIX VI. (p. 518.)

NUMBERS OF PROVINCIALS AND REGULARS RESPECTIVELY EMPLOYED AGAINST CANADA.

It is not easy to arrive at an exact conclusion on this point. Mr. Bury, in his History of Massachusetts, estimates the numbers as twenty-five thousand on each side. He

[1] Quoted in Jones's *History of Georgia*, vol. i.

refers to the Trumbull Papers, but I have failed to find any definite evidence in the passage to which he refers. He is, I think, fairly correct in his relative estimate, but probably overrates the whole force employed. The prominent facts may be shortly stated as follows.

In Braddock's force there were fourteen hundred regulars and four hundred and fifty provincials. In the Crown Point expedition of 1755 the force, three thousand in number, consisted wholly of provincials. In 1756 upwards of four thousand provincials were under arms, and less than a thousand regulars. In the campaign of 1757 the number under arms was small; I have failed to find any evidence of their proportion.

Of the fifteen thousand men under Abercromby just over nine thousand were colonials. In Amherst's force that took Louisburg there were more than eleven thousand regulars and only one hundred colonials. Wolfe in the Quebec campaign had eight thousand five hundred men, only seven hundred of them colonials. In Amherst's force of slightly over eleven thousand men, regulars were in a majority of seventeen hundred. Forbes's force that operated in the west was just short of six thousand, and had in it only twelve hundred British troops. There was also a detachment of about four hundred of the Royal American regiment as has been said, raised in the colonies, but in British pay, and commanded by officers appointed by the Crown.

This would seem to show a slight superiority of numbers in favour of the colonials, if we take the war as a whole. It must also be remembered that the term of service would be usually shorter with the colonials than with the regulars. It is probable, too, that the British regiments were in some measure recruited in the colonies.

INDEX.

PRINTED BY
SPOTTISWOODE AND CO. LTD., NEW-STREET SQUARE
LONDON

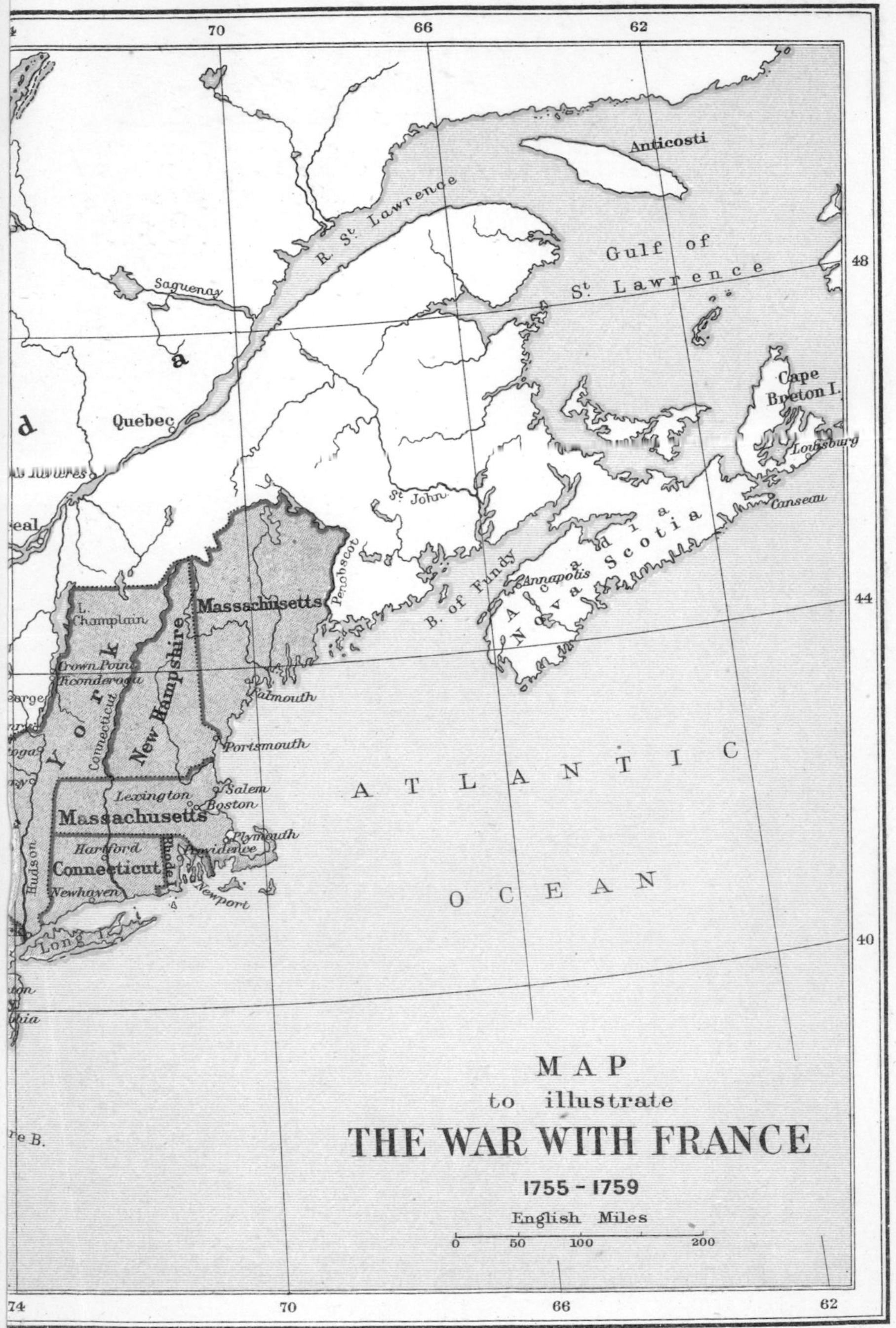

on, New York, Bombay & Calcutta.
THE LONDON GEOGRAPHICAL INSTITUTE

THE

POLITICAL HISTORY OF ENGLAND

WRITTEN BY VARIOUS AUTHORS UNDER THE DIRECTION AND EDITORSHIP OF THE

Rev. WILLIAM HUNT, D.Litt.

PRESIDENT OF THE ROYAL HISTORICAL SOCIETY, AND

REGINALD LANE POOLE, M.A., Ph.D.

EDITOR OF THE 'ENGLISH HISTORICAL REVIEW.'

In 12 Volumes, demy 8vo. Each Volume having its own Index and 2 or more Maps.

The price of each Volume is 7s. 6d. net if sold separately, but COMPLETE SETS may be subscribed for through the booksellers at the price of £4 net, payment being made at the rate of 6s. 8d. net on the delivery of each volume.

VOL. I., to 1066. By THOMAS HODGKIN, D.C.L., Litt.D., Fellow of the British Academy.

VOL. II., 1066 to 1216. By GEORGE BURTON ADAMS, M.A., Professor of History in Yale University, New Haven, Connecticut.

VOL. III., 1216 to 1377. By T. F. TOUT, M.A., Professor of Mediæval and Modern History in the University of Manchester.

VOL. IV., 1377 to 1485. By C. OMAN, M.A., Chichele Professor of Modern History in the University of Oxford.

VOL. V., 1485 to 1547. By H. A. L. FISHER, M.A., Fellow and Tutor of New College, Oxford.

VOL. VI., 1547 to 1603. By A. F. POLLARD, M.A., Professor of Constitutional History in University College, London.

VOL. VII., 1603 to 1660. By F. C. MONTAGUE, M.A., Professor of History in University College, London.

VOL. VIII., 1660 to 1702. By RICHARD LODGE, M.A., LL.D., Professor of History in the University of Edinburgh.

VOL. IX., 1702 to 1760. By I. S. LEADAM, M.A., formerly Fellow of Brasenose College, Oxford.

VOL. X., 1760 to 1801. By the Rev. WILLIAM HUNT, M.A., D.Litt., Trinity College, Oxford.

VOL. XI., 1801 to 1837. By the Hon. GEORGE C. BRODRICK, D.C.L., late Warden of Merton College, Oxford, and J. K. FOTHERINGHAM, M.A., Lecturer in Classics at King's College, London.

VOL. XII., 1837 to 1901. By SIDNEY LOW, M.A., formerly Lecturer on History at King's College, London.

LONGMANS, GREEN, & CO., 39 Paternoster Row, London, E.C.; New York, and Bombay.

2 vol
8/-